A Century of Players, Performers, and Pageants

**Wharton Field House and Browning Field
Moline, Illinois**

i

Above is a scene from Deere & Company's 100th anniversary celebration at the Moline Field House in 1937, used here courtesy of the Deere & Company archives.

The photograph on the previous pages shows Browning Field and Wharton Field House in their neighborhood context. It was taken on April 9, 2008, by Chris Carmack, who graciously permitted us to use it here.

A Century of Players Performers, and Pageants

**Wharton Field House and Browning Field
Moline, Illinois**

Curtis C. Roseman *Curtis C. Roseman*
Diann Moore *Diann Moore*

HERITAGE
DOCUMENTARIES, INC.

Moline, Illinois

Published in the United States of America
by Heritage Documentaries, Inc.
Moline, Illinois
www.heritagedocumentaries.org

First printing, 2014

Printed in the USA by Midwest Graphics Management, Inc.

ISBN 978-0-9841429-1-0

Book layout by Christine Van Lancker
Cover design by Jeff Guthrie

Heritage Documentaries, Inc. is a non-profit 501 (c) (3) organization
incorporated in the State of Illinois

Contents

Bob Moore

This book is dedicated to Bob Moore, who did so much for Moline High School. As the public address announcer, Bob was the "Voice of Wharton Field House" for 25 years and the "Voice of Browning Field" for ten years. In 1964, a year after he began teaching American History and Geography at the school, he took on the assignment of announcing the games. Bob would ask everyone to rise for the playing of both the visitor's and Moline's songs and for the singing of the national anthem. To this day Moline fans still rise for both songs, showing respect for the other school and following a tradition that Bob began. Bob loved Moline sports, having played basketball and baseball for Moline High School and Moline Community College. He continued playing basketball and baseball at Augustana College. He was the sophomore baseball coach at Moline for twenty years starting in 1964. After coaching, he umpired in Iowa and Illinois until he was seventy years old. On August 5, 2012, Bob passed away at the age of 78. He was a gentle man who never had a bad word to say about anyone and is missed by all who knew and loved him.

Foreword

Moline Mayor Scott Raes

So you think you know a lot about Moline's Wharton Field House and Browning Field? Well so did I until I read the book about these two gems by Curtis Roseman and Diann Moore. As the current Mayor and lifelong resident of Moline, I have attended hundreds of events at these facilities over my 54 years. But the details in the book about the events that took place at the Field House and Browning Field, and the famous people who appeared there, made my jaw drop.

I remember going to high school basketball games with my parents and watching stars Steve Kuberski, Scott Thompson, and Acie Earl play at Wharton to sold out crowds. I also remember the televised basketball game between Galesburg and Moline, and as a young boy being carried into Wharton on the back of "The Crusher" to watch All Star Wrestling. Among my memories of Browning Field are the undefeated 1967 Moline football team, the record setting relay team racing around the track, and even viewing fireworks from the stands. However, in reading the book I learned that this is only touching the tip of the iceberg.

Anyone who has ever lived in the Quad Cities or attended an event at one of these jewels will enjoy reading this book. It's an easy read and you will find it very informative. It will also bring back so many memories that you can't help but smile as you remember being there as the authors bring a special event or game back to life.

Get ready to be taken back into time. I'm certain that you will enjoy this book as much as I did. And thank you Curt and Diann for all of your countless hours of historical research and taking the time to put it into writing. Well done my friends!

Moline Preservation Society

The Moline Preservation Society provided a generous grant to help defray the cost of this book project in recognition of the cultural history of Wharton Field House and Browning Field and the importance of maintaining them for future generations. The Society was founded in 1986 by a group of concerned citizens who organized in an attempt to prevent the demolition of the historic 1858 Huntoon House, Moline's oldest. Although their efforts failed to save the house, the group continued and lobbied for the City of Moline to adopt a preservation ordinance and to establish a Preservation Commission (charged with advising the city council regarding Moline's historic properties). The Preservation Society has since assisted in the fight to save a number of historic buildings from demolition including the Skinner Block, the nearby buildings in the Historic Block, and the last standing Moline railroad depot. The Society annually recognizes homeowners and commercial property owners for their faithful restoration of historic properties and designates an individual as "Preservationist of the Year" for exceptional contributions to historic preservation. The Society also makes available to the public a collection of wooden miniature replicas of historic Moline buildings and walking tour booklets with photographs and descriptions of historic structures and neighborhoods.

Introduction

Moline High School annual, *M,* 1930

Above is Wharton Field House as depicted on the cover of its 1928 dedication program. The aerial photograph of Browning Field and Wharton, taken from the west, shows a crowd at a Moline High School football game on M-Men's Day in the fall of 1929.

Wharton Field House and Browning Field

For a good part of the twentieth century, and into the twenty-first, two adjacent sports and entertainment venues have played central roles in the lives of people living in Moline, Illinois, in the adjacent Quad Cities of Illinois and Iowa, and well beyond. Browning Field is more than a century old, having been willed to the City of Moline in 1910 and first used in 1912. In addition to high school football, baseball, track, and soccer, it has hosted numerous special events along with professional football and professional baseball. Among the many highlights at Browning were visits by the Chicago White Sox, Chicago Bears, Chicago Cubs, Red Grange, and Babe Ruth.

In the mid-1920s, a movement was afoot for an indoor arena in Moline to accommodate high school basketball and other sporting, community, and entertainment activities. The Maroon and White Association, an independent group headed by Theodore Finley Wharton, was created to build a field house. In the spring of 1928, the association raised a total of $175,000 through the sale of bonds. It truly was a community effort: a total of 155 volunteers, including school children, sold bonds to a total of 1,200 people.

Designed by prolific local architect William Schulzke, the Moline Field House was sited adjacent to Browning Field, dedicated in December 1928, and named after T. F. Wharton in 1941. Wharton Field House is well-known for its rich history as a basketball venue – it is still one of the largest high school basketball arenas in the United States and is the second largest in the country that dates back to the 1920s. It hosted major league professional basketball when the Tri-Cities Blackhawks, original members of the National Basketball Association, played there for five seasons.

The historical importance of Wharton Field House, however, goes well beyond basketball. Over the years it has hosted thousands of events – just about everything one can imagine. Scores of famous entertainers performed there, including Gene Autry, Jack Benny, Victor Borge, Johnny Cash, Bill Haley and the Comets, The Kingston Trio, Martin and Lewis, and the Tommy Dorsey Orchestra. Political rallies included one in 1964 for Barry Goldwater that attracted 7,000 people, and one in 1968 for George Wallace that attracted protesters. Trade shows and exhibitions included a state poultry show, boat shows, science fairs, and the 1959 Miss Illinois Pageant. Numerous musical and religious events were common, including Easter Sunrise Services for three decades. Professional wrestling was very popular at Wharton from the late 1940s to the early 1990s. A 1950 performance by Gorgeous George was one of the highlights. Among the major sports figures to appear were three famous boxers who put on exhibition matches: Max Schmeling and Jack Dempsey in 1931 and Joe Lewis in 1950.

The Book

In the following pages we tell the story of these two historic gathering places. When first envisioned, the book was to be exclusively about Wharton Field House. However, it soon became evident that the 100-plus year old Browning Field must be included in the story because of its

Kelly Farina

Moline, Illinois, is on the south bank of the Mississippi River, along a stretch of the river that flows from east to west. Immediately to the west of Moline is Rock Island, Illinois, and across the river from Rock Island is Davenport, Iowa. The three were typically referred to as the Tri-Cities in the early part of the twentieth century, but became commonly known as the Quad Cities beginning in the 1920s after East Moline had become large enough to be included the collective name of the urban area.

Browning Field and Wharton Field House are located about a mile south of downtown Moline, and about eleven blocks south of the 1914 Moline High School. Until 1936 the facilities were served by streetcars that ran from downtown southward up 15th Street hill onto 16th Street. Before moving to Browning Field, high school and professional football and baseball were played for a few years at Athletic Park, also located on a streetcar line, just east of Riverside Park. Before the Field House was built in 1928, basketball games were played at the high school gym and other facilities in downtown Moline. In 1958, the high school moved to a new facility about a mile and a half east of Wharton and Browning. Since then, the "main drag" between Wharton/Browning and the high school has been 23rd Avenue, now known as the Avenue of the Cities. In recent decades, the annual high school homecoming parade has followed that route, terminating at Wharton Field House and Browning Field.

adjacency and parallel history. Thus, two chapters focus exclusively on Browning, while some activities there are treated elsewhere in the book.

We begin the book with two chapters focusing on the history of the Field House, its origins and how it has evolved as a multi-purpose arena over the years. Chapters 3 through 7 cover the history of various types of indoor events and activities held at Wharton, along with some outdoor events at Browning. These include high school and professional sports, shows and entertainment, and meetings and exhibitions. Chapter 8 follows with the history of Browning Field and its use for high school sports and other activities. Chapter 9 covers professional sports at Browning Field. The final, capstone chapter ties together the two historic facilities by reviewing numerous special celebrations they have hosted. Among the many community events held at Wharton Field House and Browning Field over the decades, none were more significant than the gatherings that celebrated milestones in local and national affairs, including cessation of war, graduations, and anniversaries.

A Note on Sources

This book draws upon a great variety of written and online sources, all of which are listed in

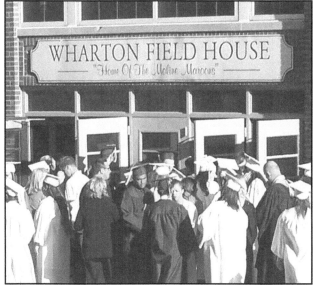

C. Roseman

Moline High School commencement ceremonies, 2013.

the bibliography. General descriptions of the evolution of Wharton and Browning are cited in key locations, but generally not repeated in the book. These general sources include the programs published for the original dedication of the Field House in 1928 and for various anniversary celebrations of the Field House and Browning, along with several newspaper articles that review the history of the facilities. Additional information about policies and expenses related to Wharton and Browning came from minutes of the Moline school board meetings and from other materials made available to us at the school district offices.

Local newspapers, most particularly the Moline *Dispatch* and Rock Island *Argus*, were invaluable sources for information about many events. We generally cite the authors of newspaper articles who we directly quote in an effort to honor those journalists who have contributed so much to this book. All quotes are given verbatim, without using "[sic]" to denote entries some may find odd or erroneous. If we do not cite a source for specific information, such as teams and scores in athletic contests or details about other events held on specific dates, the reader can assume we drew the information from a local newspaper within a few days of the event, most typically the following day. This procedure eliminates the need for repeating sources over and over, but does not prevent the reader from determining the origins of the information.

In addition to written and online sources, this book depends upon memories shared by dozens of people who grew up with Wharton Field House and Browning Field. Their general recollections, plus some of their specific stories, have added an important dimension to the book.

Acknowledgements

We are indebted to many individuals and organizations who contributed to the creation of this book. The Moline Dispatch Publishing Company gave us permission to use images from the Moline *Dispatch*, Rock Island *Argus*, and the Quad-Cities Online archives. They also gave access to their library from which we gathered a number of images and articles. The book would be much less rich in content had we not been able to use these sources. We drew materials from the Moline Public Library and the Rock Island County Historical Society; their helpful staff members significantly aided our quest for information. Other libraries and archives providing images and materials are cited in appropriate places in the book. George Van Vooren and Jack Dye helped us individually and through their 2008 book on Moline High School basketball, a key source for Chapter 3. Dennis Kelley of Kelley & Associates was kind enough to give us copies of the original Field House architectural drawings. Jerry Wallaert generously provided a number of photographs and other materials. Tom Minick, who has cared for Wharton and Browning for over 28 years, shared important insights into the recent history of the facilities.

We are also indebted to a group of Augustana College students enrolled in the 2013 winter term cartography class. They drew maps for the book under the expert guidance of geography professor Jennifer Burnham. The students are: Jake Adams, Amy Bandman, Luke Clayton, Justin Densberger, Kelly Farina, Sarah Fitzgerald, Jessica Flondro, Danna Jensen, Kevin Korus, Timothy Ludolph, Kara Noonan, Kristy Raasch, Zakarie Schmidt, Aaron Trost, and Colton Vankirk.

We thank Neil Dahlstrom and Don Hepner for their helpful reviews of a fledgling manuscript. Elizabeth Roseman spent hours reading and commenting on various drafts of the book – the final printed version benefitted substantially from her insights. Special thanks also go to Andrew Gates, a member of the Heritage Documentaries Board of Directors, who meticulously copyedited the manuscript, and to Christine Van Lancker who did a masterful job on the book layout.

We thank the Moline Preservation Society and Ben and Lois Larson McAdams for their generous donations, which helped defray book production expenses. Finally we thank the many others who helped in a great variety of ways, including providing materials and suggestions for the book. Listed in alphabetical order they are: Jeff Adams, Rick Anderson, Pat Baker, Roy Booker, John Bradley, Julie Briesch, Jayna Buckholz, Kendra Burrows, David Carlson, Chris Carmack, Shawn Christ, Susan Collins, Ken Collinson, Thelma Conrad (Cass County, Indiana, Historical Society), Dave Coopman, Karen Davis, Bud Hansen, Jack DeVilder, Debbie Faith, Bruce Firchau (Illinois Basketball Hall of Fame), Bill Fisher, John Freed, Cy Galley, Jim Green, Joan Greko, Pat Gustafson, Barbara Irish, John Jakle, Beverly Johnson, Milt Johnson, Mike Johnson, Vern Johnson, Mildred Kale, Don Kurrle, Stan Leach, Heather Lovewell, Ben McAdams, Willie McAdams, Tom MacCall, Mike McColl, Lanty McGuire, Carolyn Mesick, Janet Meyer, Bill Munn, Margaret Lievens Ostrand, Arno Panicucci, Mike Plunkett, Don Resler, Orin Rockhold, Barbara Roseman, Charles Roseman, Eric Roseman, Todd Rosenthal, Roger Ruthhart, Rick Sanchez, Gena Schantz, Steve Schwaegler, George Seaberg, Carm Senatra, Mike Shannon, Rick Simpson, Pat Shannon, Darryl Snyder, Michele Stoneking, Steve Tappa, Herb Thompson, Sylvia Valladares, David VanAcker, Martha Van Hecke. Lori Vander Vinne, Earl "Buck" Wendt, John Wetzel, Richard Wharton, Chuck White, and Laura Yeater.

Chapter 1

Moline Field House, 1928-1941

Moline High School annual, *M, 1931*

"It is with genuine pleasure that we welcome you to this new home of youth, of friendly contest and of character building." –T. F. Wharton

When the new Moline High School opened in 1915, its gymnasium became the site of Moline basketball games. By the 1920s however, "The growing popularity of basketball produced such congestion at games in the school gymnasium that only the hardiest enthusiasts could endure the discomforts of attending" (Dedication Program, 1928). A movement was born to fund and build a new facility.

Plans for the new Moline Field House were first announced to the public in 1927. Leslie Swanson of Moline, then a cub reporter for the Davenport *Daily Times,* was the youngest person who attended the initial meeting. As the last

Hanging from the Rafters. Leslie Swanson, a 1916 Moline High School graduate, saw every game played at the gym from 1919 to 1928. In a 1978 interview he recalled: "The old gym seated about 1000 fans and I remember one memorable night in about 1922 or 1923 when 1200 jammed in with many hanging from the rafters as Moline defeated a previously unbeaten Geneseo team and its famous Schultz brothers. Hundreds more stood out in the halls, unable to gain admittance to the basement gym."

surviving person of that group, he recalled in 1978:

Details of the plans for the field house had been a carefully guarded secret for months. Although I called daily for news at the offices of C. W. Holmgren, athletic manager, and Principal E. P. Nutting, I never heard a hint of what was cooking until a few days before the announcement meeting. I remember Winnie Holmgren inviting me to the meeting, saying 'they are going to announce some plans for a new field house, you better come over.' The meeting was held in the cafeteria of the old high school building on Sixteenth Street . . . As I recall Principal E. P. Nutting presided and then turned the meeting over to Wharton. There were about thirty in attendance including some civic leaders, bankers, school board members, architects and high school athletic figures. I remember T. Finley Wharton, comptroller of Deere & Co. and long a Moline High School booster, William Schulzke, prominent Moline architect, and several Moline High School "M" men from other years . . . The meeting went off very smoothly and there wasn't a single dissenting opinion the entire evening. I remember Wharton standing there with pointer in his hand beside an enlarged sketch and portable blackboard crammed with figures concerning the cost, how it would be financed, and various types of revenue which would be realized. There was revenue from tournaments, and other activities which would produce enough income to pay off the bonds.

Financing the Project

Floating a school bond issue to build the arena was deemed impossible because of state tax and bonding restrictions. During the winter of 1926-27, a committee including athletic manager C. W. Holmgren, coach George Senneff, and architect Schulzke had travelled to Indiana to examine high school arenas and methods for financing their construction and operation. That trip and other research revealed that the best method would be to create a volunteer organization to issue bonds. In his 1993 book, *Hoosier Temples,* Donald Hamilton cites numerous instances in which independent organizations were formed in the 1920s to finance and operate basketball arenas in the Hoosier state. (Two 1920s high school arenas in Indiana are discussed in Appendix A.)

In Moline, the Maroon and White Association was created in February 1928 for this purpose. Wharton became president, Dr. Perry Wessel vice president, and Holmgren secretary-treasurer. The association held its first major public meeting promoting the Field House project at the high school auditorium on February 9, 1928. Over 300 people in attendance heard enthusiastic testimony, not only from Holmgren, Senneff, and Schulzke, but also from high school principal Nutting, school superintendent L. A. Mahoney, and others. Senneff and Nutting emphasized how the facility would bring new physical education opportunities to all students in Moline.

M, 1915

The 1915 edition of the Moline High School annual, M, displayed considerable pride in describing its new school gym: "Here is shown a view of the gymnasium, one of the features of our new home, in which are held all home games of the basketball team, as well as calisthenic work, indoor track, captain ball and the like. Above is the running track – 25 laps to the mile – banked scientifically at the corners and covered with a soft cork carpet faced with felt. On either side are shower baths and dressing rooms. These are amply lighted by skylights, and facilities for both boys and girls are provided. At the far corners of the room are the instructors' offices. In one corner, a spiral staircase leads up to the auditorium, providing an easy means of communication between the two. Along the sides of the room are located collapsible bleachers, which will seat about 250. These can be easily cleared away when more floor space is wanted."

Holmgren asked the crowd for support of the new facility in view of the "crowded conditions at basketball games even at the large Augustana gymnasium" (which accommodated about 2100 for basketball games). At the meeting the following resolution was unanimously approved (Klann, 1928):

Resolved. That we approve the action of the special committee of the Maroon and White Association with reference to the new field house and that the officers and directors of the association be authorized and directed to incorporate the association under the laws of Illinois and that the president of the association appoint an executive committee of not less than seven members with full authority to proceed with the sale of $125,000 first mortgage bonds for the purchase of the necessary property and the erection of the field house.

On February 16th, the Maroon and White Association announced that Wessel would chair a subcommittee to prepare plans for a campaign to sell $125,000 worth of bonds beginning on March 1st. According to the *Dispatch* (February 17), "It is the desire of the executive committee to sell the bonds to as large a number of Moline residents as possible rather than have a few men purchase large amounts."

The following week, on February 22nd, the association was incorporated. Nine trustees, to serve in staggered terms, were elected: Wharton, Wessel, F. G. Allen, G. A. Shallberg, Beder Wood, L. R. Blackman, Lloyd E. Kennedy, H. P. Wilson, and Albert M. Crampton. During the week of February 20, 1928, Wharton penned this letter to be widely distributed:

To Moline Parents:

For many years Moline has felt the need of a building adequate to take care of large gatherings assembled for concerts, conventions, mass meetings, pageants, basketball, indoor field days, track meets, etc. The citizens have now organized to build such a structure, as you probably know. To do so requires the sale of $125,000 of First Mortgage Gold Bonds by popular subscription. The bonds will be issued in $100 amounts for adults and $50 amounts for children in the schools of Moline so that all may have a part in the enterprise, and share in the benefits from it. The bonds may be paid for in one cash payment or in installments, as desired.

These bonds will pay 5% interest per annum, and each bond will also carry the privilege of purchasing a reserved seat in a preferred section for all High School athletic contests that will become increasingly valuable as time goes on. The bonds mature in twenty years, but will be callable at any interest date, as it is expected that revenue from the

The Indiana Connection? Among those speaking at the February 9th meeting was Reverend W. A. Steinkraus, pastor of Moline's First Baptist Church. In early 1927 he had moved from Logansport, Indiana, where he helped organize the Logansport High School Gymnasium Association, which raised the money for and spearheaded the construction of a new arena there. He had helped promote the arena there and invested some of his own money toward its construction. Now, in early 1928, he was doing the same thing in Moline. (Klann, 1928)

In 1949, Klann wrote again about Steinkraus, reflecting on the pastor's stay in Moline, which lasted from 1927 to 1933. He was described as a high school sports fan who frequented Browning Field. "Steinkraus was also one of the pioneer promoters of Moline's fieldhouse, bringing the idea here from his former town of Logansport, Indiana." In spite of the central role Steinkraus likely played in the field house project in Moline, he was not appointed to the board of the Maroon and White Association, nor is his name mentioned in any of the other early publications describing the project.

games and rental of the building will provide for the retirement of the bonds. However, the reserved seat privilege will run for the full twenty-year period in any case.

We hope you can take one or more of the $100 bonds, for we want all citizens of Moline to have a share in this fine building. In case circumstances will not permit you to subscribe for the larger bonds, we urge you to buy a Junior Bond for each of your children, if possible. Many of the older students have already arranged for the purchase of bonds wholly or in part from their own savings or earnings. Payments may be made at the rate of $5.00 a month from April 1 to December 31, 1928. Many parents of younger pupils are buying bonds in their name, both because of the high rate of interest and because of the reserved seat privilege, which will be greatly appreciated by the pupil later.

This is an opportunity to promote a splendid civic project, to give your children a valuable lesson in thrift, and provide for the enjoyment of their later years in school and as graduates.

We trust that you will take advantage of it, when the subscription cards are issued next Tuesday.

The Executive Committee
T. F. Wharton, Chairman

Raising the Funds

On February 27th, the campaign to sell $125,000 in bonds was announced at a dinner meeting held at the Moline High School cafeteria. Bonds would go on sale on Tuesday, February 28th. Progress of the campaign was reported in the *Dispatch* as follows:

March 5: Almost $90,000 in bonds had been sold for the "fieldhouse and auditorium" through "largely small sales." To gain broad community support and promote sales, this and other campaign publicity described the facility not only as a "field house" but also as an "auditorium."

March 6: By this date $94,000 had been raised. The Moline school board formally agreed to pay maintenance and utilities at the "field house and municipal auditorium in consideration of the Maroon and White Association's plans to deed the structure when the bonded indebtedness has been paid." This commitment amounted to about $4,000 annually and would allow the Maroon and White Association to use most of its revenue for the payment of interest on the bonds. It was hoped that this announcement would stimulate further sales.

March 10: Wharton announced that a new campaign goal of $150,000 had been set to cover unforeseen expenses and some improvements in the original plan. "I regard this field house as the initial step in a program of civic betterment that will make our neighboring cities sit up and take notice." He also reminded readers of the reserved seat incentive for purchasing bonds.

March 16: In a letter to Moline citizens, Wharton announced that the bond drive was officially over and thanked "... all those public spirited citizens, and the students of the public schools, who gave so generously of their time and of their money, and did so much to secure the $150,000 which we felt we should have in order to complete the kind of building we want for Moline."

```
                                    Moline, Ill.
                                    March 29, 1928.

Elinor E. Johnson,


        In accordance with your subscription for
Field House Bonds the amount you have agreed to
take will be due and payable on April 2, 1928.
        Amount of bonds subscribed for $ 50.00
        Less discount at 5% per annum  $  1.25
        Balance due April 2, 1928      $ 48.75
        A check for this amount can be made out
to the Maroon & White Association and sent to the
Association at the High School Building, Moline,
Illinois, or the amount can be paid at your bank.

        MAROON & WHITE ASSOCIATION OF MOLINE.
```

Courtesy of Dorothy Johnson Roseman
Letter soliciting payment for purchased bonds sent to Moline High School junior Elinor Johnson.

The sale of $150,000 in bonds had been accomplished by 155 individuals on eleven sales teams, who sold bonds to a total of 1,200 people. Lots of publicity and special events, including two banquets at the high school cafeteria, were held to pique the interest of community members. Although much of the goal was reached through smaller sales, some companies, organizations, and individuals purchased substantial amounts, including the Field House architect William Schulzke, who bought $5,000 worth of bonds.

The site initially chosen for the new building is just west of Browning Field, on 16th Street north of 23rd Avenue, now known as Browning Park. However, legal issues stood in the way of building there, as did the nature of the ground

Nearly $50,000 was raised by Moline students in a bond sales competition among high school classes and elementary schools. Five points were awarded for each sale of a $50 bond and ten points for a $100 bond. The class of 1929 (juniors) beat the other high school classes with 565 points, having sold $5,650 in bonds. (*M*, 1929) The Garfield students won the competition among the grade schools. Both were honored by these plaques placed in the lobby of the Field House.

Courtesy of Margaret Lievens Ostrand

This house was torn down to make way for the building of Moline Field House. It was owned by Mrs. Mary Wetsell, whose husband Nels had passed away a few years earlier. Not having lived there since 1923, Mrs. Wetsell was renting the house in 1927 to Malvina DeVolder Lievens. Shown here on the back porch are Mrs. Lievens and the youngest of her four children, Margaret. Margaret, whose married name is Ostrand, was four years old at the time of the photograph. She celebrated her 90th birthday in June 2013.

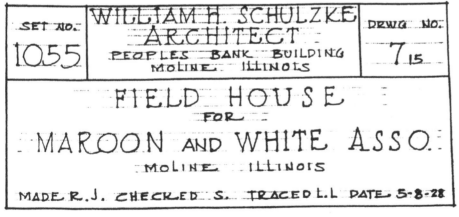

Courtesy of Dennis Kelley   *Dispatch* files

Designer of the Field House William Schulzke was one of Moline's most prolific architects, especially for large buildings. Among the other notable landmarks he designed were the 1930 Scottish Rite Cathedral and the 1931 Art Deco Fifth Avenue Building. He also designed several other downtown buildings, including the Telephone Building, Montgomery Ward, Moline National Bank (now First Midwest Bank), Sohrbecks, Carlson Brothers, Elks Club, and City Hall. Schulzke was born in Springfield, Illinois, received a B. S. Degree in architecture from the University of Illinois in 1909, and came to Moline in 1910 to work with archittect. H. W. Whitsitt. In 1914 he became a partner with Whitsitt and in 1925 purchased Whitsitt's interest in the firm.

at that site, which would have made the cost of concrete pilings prohibitive. Finally, in February 1928, an option for purchasing a property north of Browning Field was secured. Included were a lot and house fronting on 20th Avenue.

In early May 1928 plans for the building in the new location were completed and grading of the site started. However, because bids for the work totaled more than the $150,000 raised, additional funds were needed. So, a "committee of twenty-five" agreed to be responsible for the sale of an additional $25,000 in bonds. The additional bonds were sold in a week. A total of $175,000 had been raised through a community effort. A year later, the Maroon and White Association announced that delinquent payments on bond purchases totaled only $3,500, and an effort would be made to correct these transgressions. (*Dispatch*, April 20, 1929)

Field House Plans Gain Notice. As the first high school "field house" to be planned and funded in Illinois, the size of the Moline arena and the efficiency and effectiveness under which it was funded drew early attention from around the state. Howard Millard, in the Decatur *Review* (March 25, 1928), challenged his community to follow suit under the banner headline, "Decatur Talks Gymnasium While Moline Builds Field House." He wrote that "the city up along the Mississippi river not only has good athletics in its high school but it has top notch coaches and a community ready to support it in all its undertakings . . . Five thousand seats will be available in the new Field House, 3200 of which will be in permanent concrete stands with the other 1800 temporary seats to be used as needed. There will be all sorts of dressing and locker rooms, shower baths, running track and all up to date conveniences you would find not in a high school gym but a university field house."

Building the Field House

On May 26, 1928 – now having $175,000 to work with – architect Schulzke, representing the Maroon and White Association, let contracts totaling over $131,000 for the new Moline facility. A financial report filed on September 30, 1929, detailed the final costs of the project, which totaled $176,107. A deficit of $972 was covered from operating income. Expenditures exceeding $1,000 were as follows:

Stoehr and Palmgren, general contract	$ 121,311
Moline Heating & Const. Co, heating	16,000
Plambeck Plumbing and Heating, plumbing	8,474
William H. Schulzke, architect	7,500
Robins Electric Co., wiring and fixtures	6,105
Mrs. Wetsell, property for the field house site	5,786
Bleachers	2,280
Thomas Dunn & Sons, hardware	1,533
Hallberg & Co., painting	1,351

May 1928

June 1928

July 1928

Rock Island County Historical Society, Moline, Illinois

Wharton Field House site, May, June, and July 1928. This sequence of photographs shows progress in preparing the site on 20th Avenue for the Field House. The house and lot were purchased from Mrs. Mary Wetsell to make way for the new arena. Its address was 1826 - 20th Avenue. Upon completion the Field House took on the address of 1828, which was later rounded off to 1800. Visible in the background of each photograph are the canopies over the curved baseball grandstand and the third base stands at Browning Field.

Rock Island County Historical Society, Moline, Illinois

By September 1928, the steel truss arrays had been completed and the brick facade was being constructed.

Three Field House Designs

Within about a four-month period, Schulzke prepared three different designs for the arena, each shown in accompanying images. The first was for the site on 16th Street; the second and the final designs were for the 20th Avenue site. The first design not only had two main entrances on its longer (west) side but also incorporated extensions on either side of the main edifice. Both of these features were changed for the new 20th Avenue design. Now a single entrance was incorporated into the (north) end of the building and the entire structure became one single edifice.

The third and final design picks up some of the exterior features of the first two, particularly the rounded-top windows. But its roof is much higher and bulkier, to accommodate larger truss arrays to support the roof. The first two designs incorporated pillars to support the roof, common in other arenas at the time, which would have obstructed the views of some spectators. One of the distinctive features of the Moline Field House is the absence of such pillars.

MOLINE DAILY DISPATCH: SATURDAY EVENING, DECEMBER 10, 1927.

Moline's Proposed $125,000 Field House

Dispatch, December 10, 1927

This sketch is the first rendering of the Field House design, drawn by William Schulzke and published in the *Dispatch* in December 1927. This view from the southwest shows the building as it would have been located in today's Browning Park, just west of Browning Field. Two main entrances would have faced 16th Street.

Field House—Auditorium Proposed for Moline

Dispatch, February 10, 1928

This rendering shows the second design for the Field House, to be located on 20th Avenue. The front of the building, now with a single main entrance on its north side, would face the Avenue. The interior, however, would have been quite different than the chosen design. The balcony was to have been on the west side and a stage on the east side, whereas the ultimate design has a U-shaped balcony with an open end at the south, which accommodated a stage. This drawing was published in the *Dispatch* on February 10, 1928.

Dedication Program, 1928

The final design for the Field House carried very similar elements around its outside walls, but incorporated a very different roof line. According to Van Vooren and Dye (2008), the earlier designs utilized vertical support pillars on the inside that would have blocked the views of some spectators. Having seen such pillars in other arenas, Schulzke decided to eliminate them by supporting the roof with large truss arrays that are anchored near the outside walls above the balcony seats. This change resulted in a more massive-looking roof line on the outside.

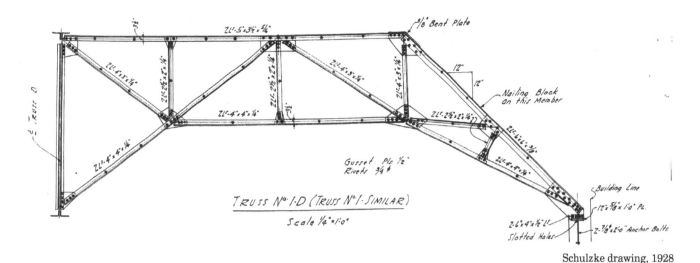

The Field House roof is supported by truss arrays

The Building

The brick Field House structure is 200 by 150 feet, with exterior walls thirty feet high to the eaves. At the initial public meeting promoting the new arena, it was described as "twice as large as the Davenport Coliseum" (Klann, 1928), a comparison to a ballroom in nearby Davenport, Iowa (now the "Col"), which has hosted a range of entertainment activities since the early twentieth century. A skylight, 30 by 70 feet, provides daytime lighting to the interior of the Field House. The interior totals 1,250,000 cubic feet of air space and is heated by Kewanee Boilers.

The original central floor was 100 by 70 feet and the basketball floor 84 by 50 feet. Although shorter than standard college-level basketball playing floors, it was larger than most high school courts of the time. Removable iron posts around the playing floor supported an eight-foot net, used during practices and games before the 1940s. A three-section, ten-ounce tan duck tarpaulin was used to protect the floor during non-basketball events. The backboards (called "banks" in 1928) were replicas of those at Huff Gym at the University of Illinois. Each was made of enameled iron and supported by an array of cantilever towers extending from a weighted base with wheels for portability.

Here is how that floor was described in the 1928 Dedication Program:

C. Roseman, 2013

A 12 by 12 inch piece of the original floor.

[The floor] is built upon a 4-inch concrete base, on which 2x2 strips are laid 3 feet apart. Across these are laid 2x4 stringers spaced 20 inches, upon which a rough diagonal floor is laid. On this is laid a floor of maple strips 1½ x 7/8 [inches], with a layer of Sisalcraft paper between the two floors.

The Class of 1928 provided an electric basketball scoreboard that hung high on the south wall. Showing scores and minutes to play, it was remotely controlled from the scorer's table at center court. A cinder track around the periphery of the interior was 1/13th of a mile in length and had a forty-yard straightaway. After the first few years, however, the cinder track was reduced to one straightaway on the east side of the building, which remained until the 1950s.

The open end of the arena floor has always been used as a practice area for the track team before moving outdoors when spring weather arrived. During the early history of the Field House, this typically required the removal of temporary bleachers used for basketball or a stage used for performance events.

All locations in the balcony provide unobstructed views of the main floor at the Field House. Here is a 2012 photograph of the seats in the northwest corner of the balcony.

C. Roseman, 2012

M, 1932

This photograph from the 1932 *M* shows an original backboard and its support as well as the net that surrounded the basketball floor.

M, 1932

This 1932 photograph shows the south end of the Field House. The track is visible beyond the basketball court.

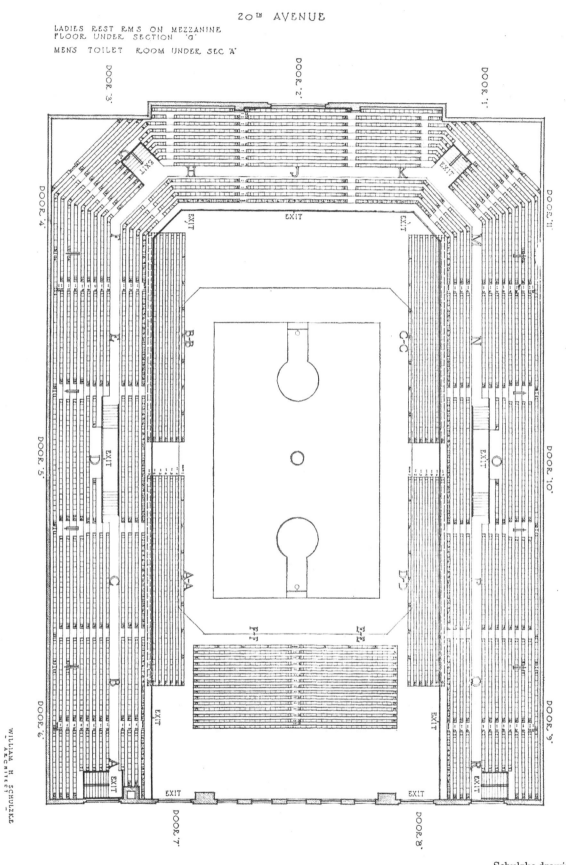

Schulzke drawing, 1928

Original Field House seating chart. The seating capacity in the balcony was listed as 3400 in the printed program for the dedication.

Samples from William Schulzke's Original 1928 Field House Drawings

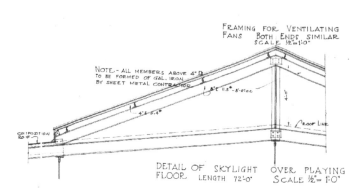

The skylight framework.

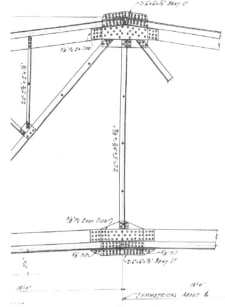

Detail of trusses supporting the roof.

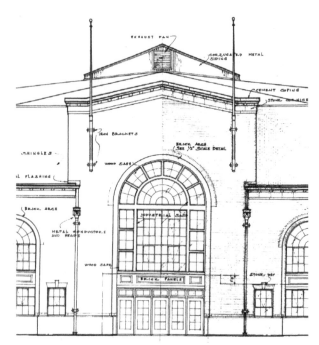

North elevation (front) of the Field House.

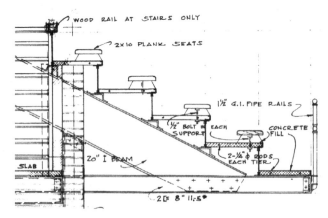

Structural and design elements of the balcony overhang.

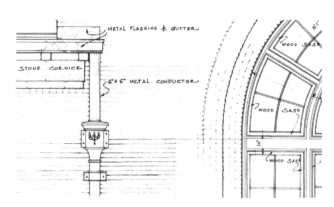

Detail from the front of the building including a drain pipe.

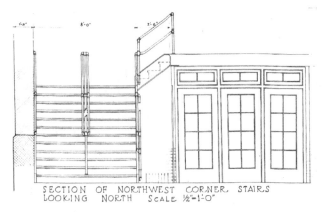

Stairway and doors at the northwest corner of the main floor.

Field House Dedication

Eager anticipation of the opening of the new arena spread beyond the boundaries of Moline. After visiting the Field House, John O'Donnell wrote in the Davenport *Democrat and Leader* (December 16, 1928):

> Moline breaks into the big time basketball circle next Friday night for it is then that the mammoth 5,200 seat field house, built at a cost of $175,000, will be thrown open to the public. For those who have not seen the structure, a pleasant surprise awaits them.
>
> Rarely has a high school in the United States had such basketball facilities to boast of as the Maroons now possess, and those in charge used vision and wisdom because the field house is good for years to come. Space, light, comfort – all the elements desirable for such a structure are found there.
>
> . . . Mr. Holmgren took the writer to a seat located the farthest distance from the floor. 'This is the worst we have,' he said. . . . The view was excellent, made the more so because of the absence of any obstructing pillars. From this 'worst seat,' every inch of the floor is visible.

The Field House was dedicated on the evening of December 21, 1928. It featured a high school basketball game between Moline and Kewanee and a college game between the University of Iowa and Marquette University. Earlier the Moline High School newspaper, *The Line O' Type* (October 29), declared the event "should bring out the largest crowd that has ever been in this vicinity (possibly with exception of the 'Lindbergh crowd')." [The 1927 visit of Charles Lindbergh attracted 10,000 to the Moline airport.] Estimates of the Field House crowd that evening vary from 3,000 to 4,000. The 3,400 balcony seats were full or nearly full, but no bleachers had yet been erected on the main floor. Whereas general admission was $1.00, people who purchased bonds to support the building of the arena were charged 50 cents.

MOLINE HIGH SCHOOL
E. P. NUTTING, PRINCIPAL

MOLINE, ILLINOIS, Dec. 7, 1928

Mr. Walter Buck,
Coal Valley, Ill.

My dear Walter:

I am enclosing two tickets for our new Field House Dedication Friday evening December twenty-first.

We are putting on a good basket ball program and expect to have five thousand people there. I hope you can use the tickets, and that you will enjoy the occasion as much as 9 enjoyed the rabbit hunt in the woods pasture last fall.

Sincerely,

E. P. Nutting

EPN-c

Courtesy of Jayna Buckholz

An invitation to the Field House dedication sent to Walter Buck, school bus driver and grounds-keeper at the high school, by Principal Nutting.

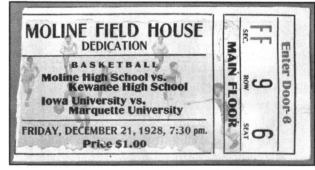

Courtesy of Dorothy Johnson Roseman

A ticket to the big event used by Elinor Johnson, a high school junior at the time. As a bond holder she would have purchased the ticket for 50 cents.

The celebration began at 7:15 with selections played by the Moline High School and Moline Community bands, followed at 7:30 with the basketball game between Moline and Kewanee (a team that probably included players whose fathers helped build the Kewanee boilers installed to heat the Field House). Moline took an early lead in the game and won 22-15.

17

C. Roseman, 2012

One of the Kewanee boilers in the basement of the Field House, 2012 photograph. They were manufactured in Kewanee, Illinois, a town located about 35 miles southeast of Moline with a 1930 population about half the size of Moline's 32,000.

Clarence "Dock" Spears, head football coach at the University of Minnesota, was a featured speaker at the Field House dedication. Huge for the time at 230 pounds, he was a two-time All-American at Dartmouth, and then went on to coach at Dartmouth and West Virginia before taking the Minnesota job in 1925. Spears recruited and developed Gopher star Bronko Nagurski, among other great players. His 1927 Gopher team shared the Big-Ten tile with Illinois. By the time he was coaching at Minnesota, Spears had managed to earn a medical degree at Rush Medical College in Chicago. After a long and distinguished coaching career at several universities he retired from athletics after World War II and opened a medical practice in Ypsilanti, Michigan. (College Football Hall of Fame, online)

After the first game, the dedication ceremony was launched by T. F. Wharton, president of the Maroon and White Association. His welcome statement was printed in the Dedication Program:

> We esteem it a great privilege to have you as our guests on this opening night of our new Field House. You boys from Kewanee High School and from the University of Iowa, and from Marquette University, have won your positions through merit. You have been selected to represent your schools because you live right, because you play the game with true sportsmanship, and because you can be victorious even in defeat. You play for the honor of your schools and for the love of the game. We who sit on the sidelines are proud of you. We believe in you. We renew our youth in watching you. It is with genuine pleasure that we welcome you to this new home of youth, of friendly contest and of character building.

Following Wharton's statement, the dedication address was delivered by invited guest Dr. C. W. Spears, head football coach at the University of Minnesota. *The Line O' Type* quoted some of Spears' comments:

> This building is dedicated to the development of the bodies and character of your youth. Nothing could be more worthwhile. Basketball games are worthwhile as are any kind of contests which train the body, the mind and the characteristics by building just such structures as this. You are indeed to be congratulated. You have a right to be proud of the achievement.

Why was Spears chosen to participate in the dedication of a basketball arena in Moline, Illinois? Two local connections likely provide the answer. Perhaps it was H. W. "Shorty" Almquist who invited Spears. Almquist had taken the job as head football coach at Augustana College in the fall of 1928 after having been a star quarterback under Spears at Minnesota. In addition, Spears was from the area. He attended high school in Kewanee, affording him the opportunity to watch Moline beat his Boilermakers in the first basketball game at the Field House.

Frank G. Allen, a local industrialist who three years later would donate his mansion, Allendale, to the Moline school board, presented Wharton with a silver loving cup in appreciation for his leadership of the Field House project. The engraving on the cup reads:

PRESENTED

TO

𝕿. 𝕱. 𝔚harton

BY HIS FRIENDS

PERRY WESSEL	LLOYD KENNEDY
BEDER WOOD	ALBERT CRAMPTON
LEE BLACKMAN	G. A. SHALLBERG
HERBERT WILSON	F. G. ALLEN

TRUSTEES OF
MAROON & WHITE
ASSOCIATION

C. Roseman, 2012

Loving cup presented to T. F. Wharton at the Field House dedication. It now resides in a Field House trophy case, having been returned to the Moline schools by Wharton's grandsons, Richard and Russell Wharton, in 1978 at the 50th anniversary Field House celebration.

The evening festivities continued with the basketball game in which the University of Iowa defeated Marquette University of Milwaukee, 38-15. The *Argus* (December 22) commented:

> Four thousand fans, preponderantly in favor of Sam Berry's Hawkeyes, found ample reason for cheering the fighting spirit of the Catholics, who battled gamely against a crushing handicap in the matter of experience and practice.

The Line O' Type, 1928

Moline native Carl Ed contributed to the dedication of the Field House by drawing this special cartoon in 1928 for the Moline High School newspaper, *The Line O' Type*. Ed (pronounced "eed" as in "Swede") was a popular cartoonist for the *Chicago Tribune*. His comic strip, Harold Teen, ran from 1919 until 1959, the year of Ed's death (Horn, 1999). Some of Ed's stock characters are shown here, including Harold, Pop Jenks, and some of the Sugar Bowl soda parlor gang. Ed was a member of the Rock Island *Argus* news staff from 1913 to 1918. Earlier his cartoons depicting action on the field of a Moline professional football team, the West Ends, drew local attention. (*Argus*, December 31, 1925)

C. Roseman, 2013

The dedication plaque mounted in the lobby of the Field House.

Early Events

Most early activities at the Moline Field House involved sports or recreation. Here is a selection of events from the first three months after the December 1928 dedication of the arena:

1928, December 23: On the Sunday after the dedication, the public was invited to inspect the new facility from 1:30 to 5:00 p.m.

1928, December 26-28: The first Big Nine high school basketball tournament was held at the Field House. Tickets for the three-day event were $2.00 for general admission and an additional 75 cents for reserved seats. In the opening game, Moline beat Princeton 31-14, in front of only 800 fans. In the second round on the next day they drew 1,800 but lost to Canton 26-10. Canton, the Illinois state champion from the previous year, went on to win the tournament, beating Galesburg in the final game 26-19.

1928, December 31: On New Year's Eve, the Moline basketball team beat Davenport 29-13. "Some 1500 fans delayed their celebration of the passing of the old year and the welcome to the new by attending the contest." The Davenport team had practiced at the Field House two days earlier to become accustomed to the large arena. (*Dispatch*, January 1, 1929)

1929, January 5: Moline beat LaSalle-Peru 26-11 in front of 2,000. At half time, a ceremony was conducted honoring Walter Holmer, a Moline High graduate who starred in football at Northwestern University. Holmer was praised for his accomplishments and given a diamond ring by Charles Deere Wiman, President of Deere & Company. The next day, Holmer returned to Evanston to resume classes. In a preliminary game, the Moline Lights (the varsity B team) beat Viola 19-12.

1929, January 17: The children of the Moline Public Schools conducted a Field House Dedication, directed by Professor Adolph Oppenheimer and Miss McElroy. It included music by White's Community Band and twelve events in which hundreds of students participated. The events and the grade levels participating as listed in the *Dispatch* were:

Sailor Drill and Dance	Free Movement	Fifth Grade – Garfield (girls and boys)
Club Swinging	Dance	Central Grammar Tumbling Nine (boys)
Spanish Dance	Push Ball	Central Grammar and High School Girls
Climbing	Marching and Pyramids	Central Grammar Boys
Swedish Dance	2B High School Girls	Advanced High School Girls
Tumbling	Central Grammar Girls	1 and 2B Against 5 and 6B Central Grammar Boys
Folk Dances	1A High School Girls	Seventh Grade
Boxing	Sixth Grade (girls and boys)	

1929, February 25-March 1: An "interstate independent" basketball tournament drew sixteen club and business teams from twelve communities to the Field House. Participating teams were:

Iowa:

Tornadoes, Burlington
Battery B, Davenport
St. Mary's Celts, Davenport
Wamsers, Davenport
Mac's Sport Shop, Iowa City
Muskies, Muscatine

Illinois:

American Legion, Cambridge
Dixon
Yellow Sleeves, East Moline
Independents, Geneseo
Star-Couriers, Kewanee
Foresters, Moline
Grays, Moline
Len's Billiards, Moline
Y Varsity, Rock Island
Savages, Sherrard

On the first night, the Kewanee team was forced to forfeit their game to the Wamsers of Davenport. They could not arrive in time for the game because their automobile was involved in a wreck near Sheffield, Illinois. The Yellow Sleeves, Grays, Wamsers, and Mac's Sport shop advanced to the final four. In the final game, Mac's of Iowa City beat the Yellow Sleeves of East Moline, 35-24, and received the $250 championship prize.

1929, March 15-16: Over the years, the Field House has been the site of many high school state basketball playoff tournaments. The first was a sectional meet in March 1929. Moline High won its first-round game over Malden in front of a crowd of 4,000, and then lost in the second round to Freeport.

The largest crowd in the brief history of the Moline field house is expected to fill the huge auditorium tonight when the Maroons open their drive for the sectional championship against the brilliant high school team from Malden. Large delegations from the other six schools in the tournament as well as thousands of quad-city residents are expected. (*Democrat and Leader,* March 14)

Beyond Sports and Recreation

Beginning on April 22nd, the first major non-sports event was held at the Field House. The first Quad Cities Pageant of Progress included five vaudeville acts and about 100 educational exhibits. One of the acts at the week-long event was the dance team of Nyland and Meridith, who presented "sensational dance routines each night. The terpsichorean artists come to Moline direct from the Terrace Gardens in Chicago and are heralded as being one of the cleverest dancing teams in the business" (*Democrat and Leader,* April 22). The first night attracted 5,483 persons. This was the first time out-of-town entertainers performed at the Field House, foreshadowing a long list of prominent entertainers to visit in coming decades.

The pageant, sponsored by the Moline American Legion, would again be held in 1930, 1931,

Rock Island County Historical Society

M, 1929

The banner over the main Field House door (left) announced the Quad Cities Pageant of Progress, which opened on April 22, 1929. Inside, the arena was festively decorated for the event.

M, 1943   *M*, 1931

C. W. Holmgren, Field House manager for 34 years. From the day the Field House opened in 1928 until 1961 its operations were managed by Charles Winfield "Winnie" Holmgren. His job not only dealt with high school athletic events, but also innumerable entertainment events, visits of celebrities, and professional sports. Holmgren was graduated from Moline High School and also from Augustana College where he was a star basketball player. In his first year at Moline High, 1920, he taught algebra and physical geography, and then taught physics for the remainder of his career. In 1922 Holmgren was the principal mover behind the creation of the M-Men's Association, which has sponsored M-Men's Days at football and basketball games since then. For decades he was an active tennis player and swimmer. Baptizing three generations of aquatics facilities, Holmgren was one of the first persons to swim in the Augustana College pool (1916), the Moline Municipal Pool (1936) and the George Senneff Pool at Moline High School (1958). (*Dispatch*, April 28, 1961 and October 19, 1966)

and 1937. Those events are covered in Chapter 7, but worthy of mention here is a significant technological improvement made at the Field House for the 1930 event. According to the *Dispatch* (April 21):

> An added feature which is expected to enhance the entertainment program this year will be the public address, or loud speaking, system which will be installed in the field house. Through electrical transmission the voice of the performer or announcer on stage will be carried with clarity to every part of the big athletic stadium.

The First Big Crowd

It took a little time – and a little encouragement – before the first truly large crowd attended a basketball game at the Field House. High school basketball during the 1928-29 season attracted crowds at the Field House never dreamed of at the old gymnasium, some well over 2,000. The largest regular-season crowd was 3,600 at the game against Rock Island, which the Rocks won 17-13. Perhaps disappointed by the attendance that first season, the nine Maroon and White board members sent a letter to the bond holders on December 5, 1929. Signed "Yours for Clean Sports," they not only asked the bond holders to purchase "as many seats as you need" for the upcoming season, but also to sell additional seats to others.

Attendance increased that second season, some games attracting about 3,000, but it was not until February 21, 1930, that a near-capacity crowd was reached. Moline beat Monmouth 26-10, on a special "ten-cent night" that brought in a crowd totaling about 5,500. The next day, Pat Patten of the *Dispatch* wrote:

> Lured to Moline's temple of sport by a special 10-cent admission rate, 5,500 fans, the largest crowd that has ever seen a basketball event in the quad-cities, watched the Moline high Maroons coast to a 26-10 victory over Monmouth last night. Every seat in the huge plant was occupied, with the exception of a very few in the remote corners of the balcony, and hundreds of

spectators stood at either end of the court. Some 6,000 tickets, in all, were sold for the game. . . . Stricken with an attack of acute stage fright as a result of being the target of 11,000 critical eyes, the warriors of both teams lapsed into the traveling habit on many, many occasions, giving Referee "Stripes" Johnson of Cambridge an opportunity to toot his whistle every minute or so. [Those 11,000 eyes may also have rattled Monmouth at the free throw line, where they missed all eleven of their shots!]

The Line O' Type (February 24) brought in the Indiana connection, which was so important to the origins of the Field House:

> Moline stole a little of Indiana's fame at the fieldhouse last Friday night when over 5,000 fans passed through the turnstiles to witness the Hoosier's favorite sport. They may become somewhat jealous when they read of this

FEB. 21

10¢ NITE, IN FIELD HOUSE . WE BEAT MONMOUTH.

"10¢ NITE," February 21, 1930, attracted the first capacity crowd at the Field House. It was part of a campaign to make the people of Moline "basketball-minded" according to the 1930 M. The campaign included a competition among students to sell adult season tickets, which were being offered for the first time. Students selling at least three tickets, which cost three dollars apiece, would receive free season tickets for themselves. The winner of the competition was Marybelle Thomson, who received a gold medal for selling fifteen. A silver medal was presented to Clark McGaughey for selling fourteen tickets, and bronze to Louis Nordine who sold thirteen.

Hoosierdome existing in Illinois and threatening to take away their renown.

The ten-cent special "fill the Field House" promotion was successful on that evening, but a basketball crowd of that size would not be seen again until the 1946-47 season. Indeed, five days after the Monmouth game only 2,300 showed up for the Rock Island game, a match-up which in later years would regularly fill the place.

Across the river the Davenport *Daily Times* (February 22, 1930) pitched in their opinion on the ten-cent Field House promotion by noting that previous crowds had been "slightly below expectations" in spite of the large investment of $175,000 in the arena. "More than half of the people of that city have never seen a basketball game it is said." Was the *Times* just a little jealous? – just four days later, Davenport High School would open its new gym less than half the size of the Field House. With 2,034 permanent seats, the new gym attracted about 2,300 spectators for its first basketball game.

Boxing Ban?

The new multi-purpose Field House in Moline would become host to a great variety of events and performances, athletic and otherwise. Controversy would not attend most of them. However, some people opposed using the arena for professional boxing. Even though it was a very popular sport at the time, boxing had been unevenly regulated and had carried something of a seamy reputation. Arguments for and against boxing at the Field House were presented to T. F. Wharton in December 1929, just a year after the arena opened.

Wharton sent a letter to the 1,150 bondholders of the Maroon and White Association asking them to vote on a request by the Elks Lodge to lease the Field House for professional boxing matches. It reads in part: "The trustees, who are elected by the bond holders and who represent them, feel that they can not properly pass upon this request without first ascertaining the sentiment of the bond holders." Attached to the letter was a postcard ballot containing "YES" and

A Fieldhouse for Rock Island? In the months before the Moline Field House was opened, Rock Island boosters were discussing a new basketball arena for that city. At the time, games were played either at the YMCA, with a seating capacity of 500, or the Augustana Gym, which seated just over 2,000. In November the high school lettermen's association was to meet with the school board to "consider ways and means of completing the stadium and fieldhouse project." School Superintendent J. J. Hagen stated that a campaign for a fieldhouse would start as quickly as possible seating over 2,000, which "could be increased to take care of three times that." (*Dispatch*, November 19, 1928) Two years later Rock Island got their football stadium, but a new gym for basketball had to wait for the completion of their new high school in 1937; a large fieldhouse would not be built there until 1958.

"NO" options and also a place where the respondent was to indicate the total value of the bonds she/he held. The proposal passed 399 to 178, with 573 not submitting a ballot. Those voting in favor held bonds at a total value of $54,750 and those voting against, $38,850. (*Dispatch*, December 30, 1929)

Two months later, on February 8, 1930, the Elks sponsored the first professional boxing card at the Field House, which attracted 3,000 fans. More would follow, including visits to Moline of some truly big names in boxing, notably Max Schmeling and Jack Dempsey in 1931, and Joe Lewis in 1949 (see Chapter 5).

The Depression Takes it Toll

The initial agreement between the Maroon and White Association, owner of the Field House, and the Moline school board allowed the schools to use the facility free of any rental charge. The board, however, had agreed to cover the costs of taxes, insurance, utilities, janitorial services, and repairs. In a September 6, 1932, memo, the board proposed to add a rental fee for its use of the facility. It reads in part:

... rental [from non-school sources] during the first three years (1928-1931) totaled over $26,000, sufficient to meet the five percent interest charges on the bonds [$8,750 per year]. The coming of the financial depression, which has forced practically all other securities into default, has also crippled the income of the Field House. Rentals the past year have fallen to a fraction of their previous total.

The board agreed to a ten-year lease that provided for an $8,000 yearly rental fee to be paid to the Maroon and White Association. The agreement also reaffirmed the right of the board to use of the property "at all times" for school education or athletic programs, and the right of the Maroon and White Association to continue to rent the facility to other organizations "whenever such rental will not in the judgment of the school authorities seriously interfere with its use by the Board of Education."

Finances continued to be a problem for the Field House owners. In a March 9, 1939, letter to the association, Wharton explained the situation and attached a 1929-38 budget summary. In spite of the rental agreement with the school board, income had declined and in the early years of the Great Depression the association was forced to borrow money to pay interest on the bonds. Then the situation improved and in 1937 they were able to pay off the loan while also paying interest on the bonds. In 1938 they earned enough to retire $4,000 worth of bonds.

Field House Becomes a "Schoolhouse"

Through the 1930s, the schools were the primary users of the Field House. The arena was rented to other organizations for a number of events, such as boxing, college basketball, and a few shows, exhibitions, and celebrations, some of which are highlighted in later chapters in this book. However, these non-school uses were few in comparison to the many and multi-faceted uses that would fill the Field House annual calendars from the mid-1940s until the early 1990s.

The original intent of the Maroon and White Association was to turn over the Field House to the Moline schools after twenty years (1948)

when the bonds would be retired. However, in 1940 a movement was afoot to transfer ownership. Petitions were circulated that called for the school board to issue bonds totaling $171,000 to pay for the Field House. It would take advantage of lower interest rates prevailing at the time. The board was already paying over $10,000 per year for use of the Field House, including rental, taxes, insurance, and repairs. If that money, plus ongoing income at the facility, were devoted to paying off the bonds, they could be retired within twenty years without a tax increase. (*Dispatch*, February 21)

A sufficient number of signatures was gathered on the petitions, and the school board went ahead with purchase plans. Because $71,000 could be drawn from cash on hand in the board's building fund, it was necessary to purchase only $100,000 in bonds, which could be paid off in ten years. The board tested the waters and found that bonds could be obtained that paid no more than 3 percent interest.

On July 25, 1940, the matter was put to the voters. Two issues were on the ballot. Before the bond issue could be addressed, it was necessary for legal reasons that the site be approved by the voters as a new "schoolhouse site." This maneuver was approved 311 to 111. Then the proposal to issue $100,000 in bonds, to be paid off in $10,000 annual installments for the next ten years, passed 347-98. Only three percent of eligible voters participated. The 497 total number was 2,023 fewer than the number voting in the April 1940 school board election. The *Dispatch* (July 26) blamed the poor turnout on the hot weather and a "lack of interest in the referendum."

The Bonds. The board accepted a bid for the bonds from the Northern Trust Company of Chicago, which reads in part: "For (all or none) the One Hundred Thousand Dollars ($100,000) par value legally issued and properly executed One and One-half Per Cent (1-½%) School Bonds of School District #40, Rock Island County, Illinois, aged September 1, 1940 and due and maturing as follows: $10,000 each July 1, 1941 to 1950 inclusive." (Moline Board of Education minutes, July 29, 1940)

A lack of interest in the Field House shown by voters would not continue. Although quite a few school and non-school events were held there during World War II, the post-war period would usher in unprecedented levels and varieties of other events and activities. The newly-acquired Moline "schoolhouse" would become a very busy multi-purpose arena.

Other Large 1920s Arenas

In early planning for the new arena, Moline sought ideas and inspirations from Indiana, where some large high school arenas were built in the 1920s and 1930s. Two of them, in Logansport and Marion, are discussed in Appendix A. However, Donald Hamilton's 1993 book reveals that only two Indiana high school arenas larger than Moline's Field House were completed in the 1920s: Vincennes Coliseum, November 11, 1926, capacity 6,206, and Muncie Fieldhouse, December 7, 1928, which held 7,600. Muncie's was the largest in the country when built. Today it seats about 6,500, making it the only 1920s high school arena in the United States that is larger than Wharton Field House.

In the 1920s basketball was becoming quite popular in the United States at the collegiate level as well as the high school level. Numerous colleges and university arenas were built in the 1920s. Many have since been replaced by newer facilities and torn down. Others, such as Huff Gymnasium at the University of Illinois (opened in 1925) and the University of Iowa Fieldhouse (1927), are still in use although no longer for intercollegiate basketball. (Both are described and pictured in Chapter 3.) A few historic arenas, however, lasted into the 21st century as basketball venues, including the following:

1925: Rose Hill Gym (seats 3,470), Fordham University (oldest NCAA Division I basketball arena still in use)

1926: Lavietes Pavilion (seats 2,195), Harvard University (second oldest still in use)

1926: McArthur Court (seats 9,087), University of Oregon (nicknamed "the Pit," it was the second oldest until the team moved to the new Matthew Knight Arena in January 2011)

1927: The Palestra (seats 8,722), University of Pennsylvania (called the "Cathedral of Basketball," it has hosted more college teams and more NCAA tournaments than any other arena).

1928: Williams Arena (seats 14,625), University of Minnesota

1928: Hinkle Fieldhouse (seats 10,000), Butler University

University of Minnesota Athletics Department

This photograph shows Williams Arena at the University of Minnesota on the night of its first basketball game, February 4, 1928. Minnesota lost to Ohio State 42-40 in a double-overtime game, which was witnessed by Dr. James Naismith, inventor of the game.

26

The two 1928 historic arenas, Williams Arena and Hinkle Fieldhouse, deserve special mention for their size, their historical importance, and the fact that they opened during the same year as the Moline Field House. Williams Arena has been home to the University of Minnesota basketball teams since hosting its first game there in late February 1928, ten months before the first game at the Moline Field House. Originally called the Minnesota Field House, its name was changed in 1950 to honor Dr. Henry Williams, who was the Gopher football coach from 1900 to 1921. Also in 1950 its original capacity of 14,100 was increased to 18,025 as part of a major renovation. Williams was the largest college basketball arena in the United States from that year until 1971, when a mammoth 22,700-seat arena was completed at Brigham Young University. More recent Williams Arena renovations reduced its seating capacity to 14,625. In this magnificent facility, affectionately known as "The Barn," the basketball student section is of course called the "barnyard." Williams has a raised basketball floor, much like Wharton did before 1997, but quite a bit higher: about two feet compared to Wharton's four inches. (Gopher Sports, online).

Hinkle Fieldhouse at Butler University in Indianapolis, Indiana, also continues in use today. The first basketball game was played there on March 7, 1928, before the building was completed (Butler defeated Notre Dame 21-13 in overtime!). The dedication of the arena came nine months later on December 21st, when Butler upset Purdue 28-27 before a crowd of 15,000. It was the same day as the dedication of the Moline Field House.

Originally called the Butler Fieldhouse, the building was renamed in 1966 for Paul "Tony" Hinkle, a long-time coach and athletic director. With an original seating capacity of 15,000, it was the largest college-level basketball venue until Williams Arena in Minneapolis was expanded in 1950. It now seats about 10,000. Scenes from Hinkle were included in the 1986 movie "Hoosiers." Like Wharton, Hinkle has a long history as a multi-purpose facility, having hosted visits by politicians, preachers, performers, and circuses, along with other athletic events including track and tennis. In the late 1940s, the Tri-Cities Blackhawks professional basketball team played several games at the Butler Fieldhouse against Indianapolis pro teams. (Hinkle Fieldhouse, online)

1930s postcard

Early postcard image of Butler Fieldhouse in Indianapolis, Indiana, before it was renamed Hinkle Fieldhouse.

Chapter 2

Wharton Field House, 1941-2013

Lake County (IL) Discovery Museum, Curt Teich Postcard Archives

"three hundred citizens . . . asked that this well deserved honor
be bestowed upon you." –E. W. Freeman

Since 1940, the field house has been the property of the Moline School District. A year after obtaining the facility, the school board made an important decision about its history and its future identity. In an effort led by the Maroon and White Association, a petition had been circulated and signed by 284 Moline residents requesting the Field House be renamed. At a July 1, 1941, meeting the petition was presented to the board, reading in part:

> Now that the Field House is the property of the Moline School system, we, the undersigned Trustees of the Maroon and White Association, M men, and other citizens of Moline respectfully recommend that the Board of Education name the structure the T. F. Wharton Field House.

Board member E. H. Beling moved that the request of the petitioners be granted, and the motion was passed unanimously. The next day, Wharton was notified of the action in this letter:

July 2, 1941

Mr. T. F. Wharton
Moline, Illinois

Dear Mr. Wharton:

It is my duty and pleasure, as Secretary of the Moline Board Board of Education, to inform you, officially, of the action taken last night at the July meeting of the Board, by which the Field House has been given your name. The action was a unanimous recognition of your invaluable services in making it possible for the schools, now, to own so fine an addition to our educational plant. The action followed the presentation of a petition signed by nearly three hundred citizens who asked that this well deserved honor be bestowed upon you.

Sincerely,
E. W. Freeman
Secretary

29

This chapter reviews the operation of the Field House since it was named for Wharton in 1941. Change came rapidly right after World War II. The popularity and success of high school basketball – already substantial – rose to new heights, the professional basketball Blackhawks arrived in late 1946, and major non-sporting activities became more commonplace. Along with these activities, numerous changes were made to the Field House itself, both inside and outside.

Lots of Parking

By the time the Field House was opened in 1928, ownership and use of the automobile had spread dramatically and most middle-class families had access to a car. The majority of people attending earlier events at the adjacent Browning Field arrived either walking or riding the streetcar. By the mid-1920s, however, automobiles were being driven to football games and parked along the south and west sides of the field. A note in the *Dispatch* (October 9, 1925) gave a warning to people who planned to do so for the game against Louisville Male High School: "Fans who expect to drive their automobiles inside the enclosure at Browning will be required to pay a fee of 25 cents in addition to the regular admission charge."

In the winter of 1929, when the Field House was new and beginning to attract crowds upwards of 1,000, even more people were driving. To initially accommodate the cars, Browning Field was used for parking, but only when the condition of the field was solid enough to accommodate vehicles. This practice was repeated numerous times in later years.

Courtesy of Richard Wharton

Theodore Finley Wharton was born in 1870 in a two-room log house on his grandfather's farm in Ohio. When he was fifteen his family moved to St. Cloud, Minnesota, where he worked for a daily newspaper after high school. Then in 1891 he moved with his family to Ashland, Wisconsin, where he first worked with his father, a lawyer, for five years then was appointed city clerk there. In 1902 he began a nine-year career with Haskins and Sells, a Chicago accounting firm. Part of that time he worked for the firm in St. Louis where he lectured on accounting at St. Louis University. Wharton became familiar with Deere & Company officials when he was in charge of auditing their books and accounts in 1910. In September 1911, he was hired by Deere as comptroller, a position he held for the rest of his life. He was active in many local affairs in his 32 years in Moline, including service on the school board from 1916 to 1934. Wharton passed away in 1943, at age 73. (*Argus*, October 13, 1943)

This November 1948 photograph shows in the foreground an L-shaped parking lot west of the Field House that accommodated 300 cars. By that year all of the properties shown directly west of the arena had been acquired by the schools. On October 12, 1948, the board approved the removal of the Yeager house, shown in the photograph, and another to its west not shown in the photograph. (A third house had been razed in 1928 to make way for the Field House.) Soon thereafter parking was expanded on the east side of the building and much of this land to its west was returned for athletic use.

Dispatch files

Soon after the schools obtained the Field House in 1940, property expansion became a partial answer to the parking problem. In February 1941, the Yeager property, a 132-by-300-foot lot west of the building, was purchased for $7,500. Then, less than a year later, three large sections of land to the east, south, and west of the building were donated to the schools by Katherine Butterworth, widow of William Butterworth, former head of Deere & Company. Initially, the newly-acquired properties to the west of the Field House were to be used primarily for parking and those to the east and southeast for athletic purposes. Over time, however, much of the latter territory was converted into the very large parking lot seen there today.

Dispatch, January 7, 1942

This 1942 photograph shows the land east of Wharton donated by Katherine Butterworth. Parts of it were first covered with crushed rock for parking in November 1948 "to ease the parking jams, which have in the past forced motorists to park sometimes a mile away from the sports arena" (*Dispatch*, November 25th). After complaints from neighbors about dust emanating from the parking lot, the school board approved $2,037.50 in July 1950 to "bald" the parking lot with oil and sand.

Dispatch files

By the time of this 1953 photograph, most of the land east of the arena had been converted to parking. Since that time it has often been filled with cars for football and basketball games and other events at Wharton and Browning. For many years spanning from the early 1970s to the early 2000s, the lot was also used as a remote parking facility for the local professional golf tournament, which was operated under a variety of names from 1971 until becoming the John Deere Classic in 1999. A proposal to build a new high school in this location was studied in 1953, but ultimately rejected in favor of the site on 23rd Avenue, where the new facility opened in 1958.

"It Was Our Play House" is how Dona Welch of Moline described Wharton. As a child she lived in the Yeager house just west of the Field House during the 1940s, before it was removed in 1948. She remembers playing in the big arena many times with her friends, sometimes placing a rock in a doorway to give them access at odd times. When stage shows were in town, they would go to the changing area and play with the clothing. She also remembers a daring act accomplished by two of them – crawling along one of the overhead beams high above the basketball floor, all the way across from one balcony to the other. She remembers it being not only scary but dirty as well – the tops of the beams were filthy!

Inside the Field House, 1940s

In 1942 rental fees for profit-making organizations were about $125 per night, for non-profit organizations about $25-30 per night. A school board meeting on September 1st of that year included a discussion on the types of activities to be permitted at the Field House. The *Dispatch* (September 2) reported:

> Erick G. Erickson proposed that use of the field house for dances and prize fights be discouraged, but other members of the board opposed his view. Ernest J. Miller and George Melin maintained that there is 'nothing wrong' with prize fights as conducted at the field

house, Mr. Miller describing them as 'wholesome sport.' Earl H. Beling, board president, asserted that the field house is more than a school building – 'it is a community center as well.'

During World War II, few major changes were made to Wharton. Among the minor changes, revealed from school board minutes, were a $1,350 remodeling of the heating system in 1942 and improvements in the running track in 1945. Also in 1945, the size of the stage at the south end was reduced to make it easier to move, and a new dressing room was prepared for use by girls in the band. The room was located under the balcony on the northeast side and similar to the boy's facility on the northwest side. Previously the girls had been dressing in the ladies' restroom.

Previous to 1947 the facility had been open to religious and patriotic programs on Sundays. An August 18th vote by the board broadened the permitted Sunday activities to include "athletic and other recreational events" sponsored by "approved organizations." Use of the facility was restricted to the 1:30 to 5:30 p.m. time period. An important stimulus to the new policy was the presence of the professional basketball Blackhawks who had begun playing at Wharton in January of that year and who would begin playing on Sunday afternoons during the following season.

Sports on the Sabbath? Arguments for the new policy that allowed sporting activities at the Field House on Sunday centered on the idea of expanding the tradition of the schools making the Field House available to the public. Opposition to the new policy was largely of a religious nature. One opponent declared that "observance of Sunday is one of the most important things in the development of character. . . . You're making a grave mistake to let in sports . . . [and] not regarding the Sabbath as it should be regarded." When asked about listening to sports broadcasts on Sunday, he replied that "Listening to the ball game is just as guilty as opening the field house." (Dispatch, August 19, 1947)

In 1948, with the prospect of many more rentals than in previous years, the school board codified a new rental policy. In a letter to the board, Superintendent Alex Jardine proposed the following:

Renters for 1-4 rentals per year pay 5 cents per admission with a minimum of $150.00 per rental. These renters will receive a rebate of half of the Board of Education's profit from concessions.

Renters for 5-9 rentals per year pay 5 cents per admission, with a minimum of $125.00 per rental. These renters will receive a rebate of half of the Board of Education's profit from concessions.

Renters for 10 events and over per year shall pay 5 cents per admission with a minimum of $100 per event. Such renters shall receive one-half of the rebate from concessions, except the Blackhawks, who are to be the concessionaires for a three year period.

Banner Years

By the late 1940s activity at Wharton had increased dramatically. As of May 6, 1949, a total of 82 events had been held there since the previous September. This included 57 basketball games (41 professional, twelve high school, and four community college), plus a range of other activities not seen in previous years. Among them were Easter Sunrise Services, a Joe Lewis boxing exhibition, and visits by entertainers including Spike Jones and Gene Autry. The attendance figures for events of that year are listed on page 33. Not included is the Miss Moline Pageant, which was held in June of 1949.

Field House manager Holmgren reported that 254,895 people attended events that year, some 30,000 more than during the previous season. And a hungry lot they were! The previous summer the school board had decided to take over operation of the concessions and hired John Stanforth to manage them. Except for the Blackhawks games, he hired boys from the Rock Island county farm home (now Arrowhead

Events and Attendance at Wharton Field House, September 1, 1948, to May 3, 1949

Sept. 8	Eddie Howard Orchestra	1,500
Sept. 13	Wayne King Orchestra	800
Oct. 30	J. C. Halloween Party	1,000
Nov. 4	Horace Heidt Orchestra	4,000
Nov. 9	Kiwanis Farm Party	5,000
Jan. 18	Joe Louis Boxing Show	4,500
Jan. 28	Senior High School Commencement	1,000
Jan. 31	Feb. 1, 7, 8 & 15 Golden Gloves	11,000
Feb. 5	Polio Dance	1,800
Feb. 18	St. Mary's vs. St. Ambrose basketball	300
Feb. 19	Coolidge vs. John Deere basketball	800
Feb. 26	Mississippi Valley Music Festival	2,000
Mar. 1	Gene Autry Show (afternoon and night)	7,000
Mar. 5	Moose – Night of Stars	4,000
Apr. 17	Churches Sunrise Service	5,500
Apr. 19-22	Moose Home and Food Show	7,000
Apr. 30	Spike Jones Orchestra	2,500
May 2	Tri-City Symphony Orchestra	2,500
	High School basketball games	54,965
	Tri-City Blackhawks games	146,430
	TOTAL	254,895

Source: Moline Board of Education files

Ranch) to sell refreshments. During the 1948-49 season, they had sold 109,448 bottles of soft drinks, 60,000 boxes of popcorn, 45,459 hot dogs (which required 44 gallons of mustard), 3200 pounds of peanuts, and 57,708 ice cream bars! Rental revenue had increased from about $5000 in 1946-47, to $6613 in 1947-48, to $11,267 in 1948-49 (Dispatch, May 6, 1949). Rental income then decreased slightly in the next year as shown below:

Wharton Field House Rental Income
July 1, 1949 – April 30, 1950

Blackhawk Sports, Inc.	$8,141.95
Rock Island County Fair	303.10
Kiwanis Farm Party	44.00
Golden Gloves	679.00
Kiwanis Home Talent Show	399.75
Grand Old Opry	150.00
Easter Services	35.00
Moline Moose Home Exhibit	600.00
Total	$10,352.80

Source: Moline Board of Education files

C. Roseman, 2013

A view from the concession stand at the southeast corner of the Field House, December 2013. The counter is made from the original Wharton basketball floor, which was replaced in 1997.

High on the Hill. On June 7, 1949, the Alton Evening Telegraph printed an AP story about the success at Wharton: "When you own the second largest downstate field house, it's big business. So the Moline board of education discovered this year as its Wharton field house brought in $11,267 in rentals, and concessions grossed $32,000. Since the beginning of school last September, an estimated 255,000 persons have flocked to the 6,000 seat area atop one of Moline's hills . . ."

All the activities and income of the late 1940s were accompanied by additional internal changes. Coincident with the presence of a professional basketball team, these collectively would give a "professional" feel to the multi-purpose arena. In 1947 the board accepted a bid of $1,680 from Ed Gordon for a new public address system, in addition to a $60 record player and a $125 remote pickup from Browning Field. Then in the summer of 1948, they approved funds for new concession and wrestling rooms, plus a new men's toilet. Costs for the major components of this project were $3,035 for electrical wiring and fixtures, and $8,798 for plumbing work. (*Dispatch*, April 20).

The summer of 1949 saw what was among the most significant additions to the arena. The school board approved the purchase of a new four-faced scoreboard, which would hang directly over the center of the basketball court. It cost $1,900 and would stand as a signature interior feature of Wharton from that fall until 1988. Manufactured by the Fair-Play Company of Des Moines, Iowa, it was one of the first to be installed in any arena. Similar scoreboards soon became commonplace in large basketball arenas all over the United States. Writing in the *Dispatch* (July 13), Jim Dix described the one at Wharton:

> It will replace the old clock and scoreboard, now on the south wall, which could not be seen from some places, and which was subject to a breakdown now and then . . . The new scoreboard will not have a clock with a hand ticking off the minutes and seconds, like the present one does. The number of minutes and seconds left to play in each period will be flashed in lighted numbers. Below these figures will be the scores for each team . . . Each face will be 6 feet across the top, 4½ feet across the bottom. The letters will be 9 inches high.

In September 1950, new single-support steel columns for backboards and baskets were purchased for $1,700, half paid by the Blackhawks. They replaced the former supports that were

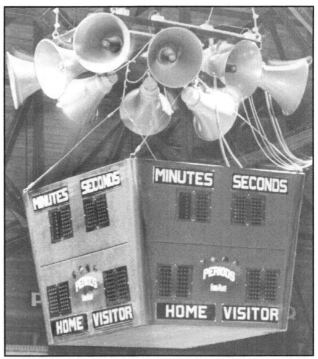

Dispatch, November 3, 1949

The Fair-Play cubical scoreboard was installed at Wharton Field House in the summer of 1949. Later that year the Augustana *Observer* (December 1) made this observation: "All concerned were plenty happy over the new scoreboard in the Wharton fieldhouse in Moline. Then Sunday afternoon [November 29] the Blackhawks registered 104 points. The management was stumped – the board only goes as high as 99." In 1978 the iconic cubical scoreboard was overhauled, including the installation of new number lights. Then in 1988 it was taken down, in favor of two scoreboards suspended from the rafters at either end of the basketball court.

M, 1974

The iconic scoreboard standing high above a high school basketball game in 1974.

composed of bulky arrays of girders, releasing more space for seating that was desired by the pro team. The new supports were used for the first time on November 9th, and according to the next day's *Dispatch* "were a howling success from both players' and fans' viewpoints . . . The seats directly in back of the backboards have suddenly become some of the best in the house." Although they had not been added for this first game, padding would later be wrapped around the tubular steel posts to protect players.

During the holiday break in December 1951, the Moline Letterman's Club participated in a floor-painting project funded by sales of programs. The out-of-bounds part of the floor was painted maroon, and a large block "M," a version of which has been there ever since, was painted in the center of the court. *The Line O' Type* (December 4) quoted Moline basketball coach Jack Foley as saying one of the main purposes was "To class Moline with the 'Big Ten.'"

M, 1974

A single-support basket can be seen behind the action at the Moline-Galesburg game in 1973-74. Note the padding encircling the base of the basket support. Moline players in the photograph include Marc Porter, Tom Doyle, and Russell Kooken.

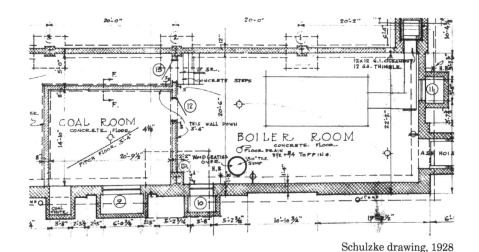

Schulzke drawing, 1928

Architect Schulzke's 1928 drawing of the coal and boiler rooms in the southwest corner of the Field House basement. In the extreme lower left corner, Schulzke labeled the coal chute through which coal (along with a couple of Augustana lads) was delivered to the coal room.

Sneaking-In. A treasured memory held by many people growing up in Moline – especially males who were teenagers in the 1930s, 40s, and 50s – was gaining unauthorized access to the Field House. Here are some of the reported methods used (names will be withheld to protect the guilty): Perhaps the most common was to slither in through a locker-room window on the west side of the building. The windows were high enough that often the thinnest boy was boosted up to the window by others; then he would open a door for his buddies. Sometimes one person would buy a ticket and let others in through a back door. Or the ticketed person might pass the ticket out through a window to another who would use it to gain entrance (a process that may have been repeated several times). Occasionally a sympathetic police officer would aid free entries. Some kids would sneak in on a Sunday and play basketball on the hallowed floor; still others would simply hide in a locker room following afternoon basketball or football practice then gain free entrance to an evening professional basketball or wrestling event.

One of the more memorable methods of sneaking-in was performed by two Moline boys who were freshmen at Augustana College. In order to attend a sold-out tournament basketball game in the late-1950s, they lifted out the large circular cover to the coal chute on the west side of the building and slid down the chute into the coal bin in the basement. Covered with coal dust, they proceeded up to the arena. Since no seats were available, they sat on the edge of the basketball floor. Looking like they had just been in a coal bin – which they had – they feared they would be thrown out of the arena. Miraculously, they were allowed to stay for the game.

Broadcasting from Wharton and Browning

Well before events at the Field House or Browning Field were broadcast over the radio, telegraph wires carried game reports long distances. For the 1925 Moline football game against undefeated Male High School of Louisville, Kentucky, a newspaper in that city had a special line extended to Browning Field by the Western Union Telegraph Company. This allowed play-by-play reports – in near-real time – to be sent back to Louisville via telegraph. The same arrangement was made by the St. Louis *Post-Dispatch* on Thanksgiving Day in 1936 when Moline completed an undefeated season, beating the St. Louis champion, Beaumont High School, 14-6. This method of reporting is reminiscent of baseball games being described by local radio announcers who received play-by-play accounts via telegraph, including Ronald Reagan who did so in 1932 on WOC in Davenport.

Only two AM radio stations were located in the Quad Cities before 1946: WOC and WHBF in Rock Island. In the 1930s WHBF broadcast high school football games, including some from Browning Field. For a few events, radio coverage of basketball games was piped into the Field House. In one such program, arranged by the Moline Association of Commerce, 1,000 people gathered to listen to Moline play Elgin in a 1945 state high school tournament game being played at Huff Gym in Champaign. WHBF in Rock Island arranged for the transmission of the game commentary from WILL in Urbana. Near the end of the game with Moline down by two points, Dwight Humphrey made two baskets to give the victory to Moline. The March 17th *Dispatch* captured the scene:

> While the huge building makes hearing difficult, Ed Gordon did manage to get the speaker toned sufficiently close enough to permit fans to follow the action. The electronic scoreboard was put in operation; all of this helped keep up with the game. When Humphrey's final basket went through, the fans cheered for five solid minutes and many in the building did not hear the finish, some not even knowing Moline had won for several minutes.

The appeal of broadcasting high school basketball on the radio led to the installation of a two-part broadcasting booth during the 1945-46 basketball season. The *Dispatch* (January 8) explained:

> At the sacrifice of 30 seats, two large broadcasting booths have been erected along the top of the west side balcony. Previously, there have been no radio facilities in the field house, but two stations can now air the Maroon games under ideal conditions.

The next season, beginning in the fall of 1946, a new Moline radio station, WQUA, began broadcasting high school, college, and professional basketball and boxing matches from Wharton, and high school football from Browning Field. For the first ten years the lead play-by-play announcer on WQUA was Roy "Bud" Dawson, who became the "Voice of the Maroons," broadcasting virtually every Moline High School basketball and football game during that time.

Courtesy of Jerry Wallaert

Bud Dawson's photograph graced the cover of a high school basketball game program three weeks after he died. The day after his WQUA play-by-play broadcast of the Moline-East Moline game on January 6, 1956, he suffered a fatal stroke. Born and raised in Texas he worked in Fort Wayne, Indiana, before joining WQUA in Moline in 1946. (*Dispatch*, January 9, 1956)

Courtesy of Rick Anderson

Ken Buel and Don Hanley of WQUA in the Wharton broadcasting booth, 1961. Buel was part of the radio team for many years. According to Dave Coopman, others who were part of the broadcasting teams after Bud Dawson's death included Bill Mason, Dale Buhl, Bob Miller, Cory Kent, Earl Spencer, Jim Albracht, Don Elliott, and Bob Allen.

M, 1960

A big crowd for a 1960 Moline High School basketball game, with the WQUA banner on the broadcasting booth atop the west balcony.

After Dawson passed away in early 1956, WQUA continued to broadcast Moline High School basketball and football games for another 22 years. Then in January 1978, the radio station announced that it would no longer cover Moline games, resulting in an outcry from many loyal fans. (Coopman, 2007) The AM radio landscape had changed. AM stations were struggling with competition from both a growing number of local FM radio stations, especially for music, and rapidly-increasing coverage of sporting events on television. At the same time WQUA, like many other local radio stations, had to compete in the larger metropolitan market and could no longer attract enough advertisers for Moline-only events. The days of a close symbiotic relationship between Moline High School sports and its "home-town" radio station were over.

On August 16, 1949, the Moline school board approved a resolution allowing WOC-TV to televise high school sporting events from Wharton and Browning. The station was planning ahead; it would not even go on the air until six weeks later. The resolution called for the station to telecast, on a trial basis and at no expense to the board, the last three home football games of the 1949 season and the first six home games of the upcoming basketball season.

WQUA Radio Announcers Move Up. Three Wharton/Browning announcers went on to quite distinguished careers in sports broadcasting. Milo Hamilton, who worked with Bud Dawson at WQUA in 1950, went on to become a renowned baseball announcer. His career took him to Chicago, Atlanta, and Pittsburgh, then to Houston in 1985 where he began a long career as the voice of the Houston Astros. Upon retirement in 2012, he had completed 59 seasons broadcasting major league games. Harry Kallas, who worked the local broadcasting booths in the late 1950s while a student at the University of Iowa, would go on to become the voice of the Philadelphia Phillies baseball team from 1971 to 2009. He also was the voice of NFL Films and received numerous awards for his work. Kallas died in 2009 soon after collapsing in the Washington (DC) Nationals' broadcasting booth. Bob Miller, who also worked at WQUA while a student at Iowa, switched to hockey and has announced for the Los Angeles Kings since 1973. He, too, has received numerous honors, along with a star on the Hollywood Walk of Fame. (Information courtesy of Dave Coopman.)

According to Dave Coopman, who published a 2010 history of WOC, the new TV station's mobile unit wasn't quite ready when the station went on the air; therefore, no football was broadcast. They were set to air the December 9th Moline-Collinsville basketball game, but instead they announced in the newspapers that, due to technical issues with the mobile unit, they would be unable to broadcast the game. "We expect to televise Moline High School basketball games on a regular schedule very soon." Finally, on December 17th, the new TV station broadcast the Moline-East Rockford basketball game, which Moline won 55-42. Russ Kiesele of the *Dispatch* (December 19) wrote "the video presentation has it all over the straight radio description. It takes less brain effort – the viewer doesn't have to transform the word-picture into a visual picture in the mind." Since only one TV station was on the air locally, the Moline-East Rockford game was the only television show on during prime time that evening. No channel surfing necessary or possible!

Perhaps the highlight of televised high school basketball at Wharton was a broadcast – for the first time in color – of the Moline-Galesburg game on February 15, 1968. The Maroons won 67-65 over the Silver Streaks, the top-ranked team in the state at the time. In an era when cameras were few and remote broadcasts presented technical difficulties, it was a major undertaking for the station. The result was probably the largest audience to ever witness any high school activity at Wharton: 6,500 viewing in person and untold numbers viewing on television.

A Wharton Field House event did not appear on national television until professional basketball returned in 1987. During their first season, the Quad City Thunder of the Continental Basketball Association hosted the Charleston Gunners in a game broadcast nationally by ESPN. A crowd of 5,137 people watched the game in person. Two years later, ESPN returned to air the 1990 CBA All-Star Game held at Wharton, attended by 4,327 fans.

M, 1968

On February 15, 1968, the high school basketball game between Moline and Galesburg was televised by WQAD, whose studios are located just ten blocks from the Field House.

M, 1968

In the 1968 televised game, Moliners celebrated their victory over the Galesburg Silver Streaks, who were ranked number 1 in Illinois at the time.

In the 21st century, only a few high school games are broadcast on the radio. However, local television stations faithfully show up for games to shoot some footage to be shown on the 10 p.m. local news. Here a photographer from KWQC television in Davenport (a successor to WOC-TV) is covering the Moline-East Moline game in February 2013.

C. Roseman, 2013

Mid-Century Momentum

The 1950s and 1960s brought to the Field House an endless parade of entertainment, sporting, and community events. Even so, boys high school basketball remained as popular as ever – and perhaps became even more popular – in the 1960s. Field House manager Ed Lemon recalled in 1998: "I remember we had 6,500 at games, maybe more with standing room . . . We had something like 5,000 season ticketholders in the '60s" (Allee, 1998).

Along with the big crowds a number of changes were made to the facility in the 1960s. In 1962 the entire Field House floor surrounding the raised basketball floor was paved. Originally, a cinder track had encircled the basketball floor, then for at least two decades a straight-away part of the track was maintained along the east side of the arena. Also up to this time, the south end of the arena still had a dirt floor.

In preparation for the 1962-63 basketball season, a new array of collapsible bleachers was installed at the south end of the Field House. They replaced portable bleachers that required significant labor and time to set up and tear down when reconfiguring the arena for different types of events. At the same time the large rectangular windows on the south wall were taken out and their spaces covered, "eliminating a glare problem for afternoon events and also removing a target for rock throwers" (*Dispatch*, November 22, 1962).

Dispatch, November 22, 1962

This large collapsible bleacher array was installed at the south end of the Field House in 1962. It was divided into four sections, each of which was extended outward or pushed back against the wall. The sections were moved by a small three-wheel motorized "mule" which was supplied with the bleachers.

Courtesy of Jerry Wallaert

Moline High basketball player Al Van Landuyt dribbles in a northward direction on the basketball floor with the south windows behind him. Those windows were removed in 1962.

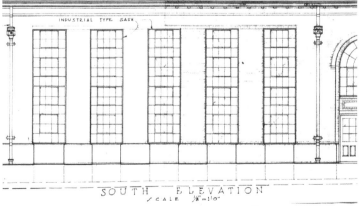

Schulzke drawing, 1928

William Schulzke's 1928 drawing of the Field House south elevation shows the rectangular windows that were taken out in 1962.

Dispatch, November 22, 1962

The new 1962 suspended broadcasting booth above the west balcony stood just a bit higher than the scoreboard above the floor. Access to the booth was provided by a stairway, just to the right of this photograph.

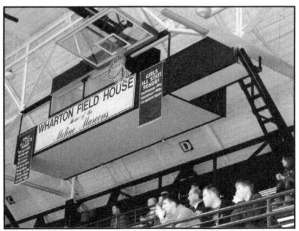

C. Roseman, 2012

The broadcasting booth as it looked in 2012.

Also in the fall of 1962, a new broadcasting booth was installed atop the west balcony. It provided more room for broadcasters and team camera operators. Unlike its predecessor in the same location, it was suspended from the ceiling, thus releasing some three dozen seats for fans. The new bleachers and the raising of the broadcast booth increased the seating capacity for basketball from 5,858 to about 6,500 (*Dispatch*, November 22).

In 1961, the year before these improvements were made, Ed Lemon took over from long-time Field House manager Winnie Holmgren, who had held the job since the facility opened in 1928. Lemon was a busy man in the 1960s and 1970s, managing a busy place. In 1971, he estimated the arena was open for about 78 public events each year. He further estimated that attendance there and at Browning Field totaled about 230,000 per year. (*Dispatch*, March 21)

In January 1971, the school board adopted a new rental policy for the Field House, which reaffirmed many of the policies that had been in place. It stated that priority would be given to school activities, Sunday events could be held only between 1:00 and 5:30 p.m., no "immoral, illegal, or subversive" organizations or activities would be permitted, and use of intoxicating liquors "of any kind or description" would be prohibited. It made special reference to two schools: Alleman High School

Dispatch files

Edward Lemon, Wharton manager for 23 years, grew up in Milan, Illinois, and attended Rock Island High School. In 1948 he was graduated from Augustana College and began teaching at John Deere Junior High School in Moline. In 1961 he moved to the high school to teach biology and take over the management of the Field House. Lemon retired from teaching in 1983, but retained the job at the Field House for another year. (*Dispatch*, October 3, 2010)

In a 1964 game against Iowa City High School, a naughty Little Hawk caused this damage to the south backboard. Field House manager Ed Lemon is shown here attending to the matter. Because of a similar experience in 1957, when Moline's Vernon Johnson was the first to break a backboard at Wharton, Lemon was prepared with a backup board and needed only a half-hour delay in the game to make the replacement.

Dispatch files

was given permission to use the Field House for basketball for the minimum rental fee, and use by Black Hawk College would be negotiated between the two schools. The standard rental rate was raised to 10 cents per admission, with a $200 minimum charge.

1980s and 1990s: New Apparatus, New Floor

During the 1987-1993 period, when the Quad City Thunder professional basketball team made Wharton home, some additional changes were made in the arena. Two changes made life easier for the Field House staff when converting the facility among different uses. One was the replacement of the four sideline basketball baskets in the late 1980s. The older ones had to be raised or lowered by manually turning a crank connected to cables. That process consumed almost an hour, whereas the new baskets can be lowered or raised with the push of a button. Similarly, a new automated bleacher array, which also can be extended or retracted with the push of a button, was installed at the south end of the arena.

Perhaps the two most striking changes, at least for basketball fans, were the removal of the cubical scoreboard and the removal and replacement of the original floor. In 1988 the iconic scoreboard, which had been suspended above the center of the court for 39 years, was replaced. Then in 1995, the Moline High School Boosters Club, which manages concessions for high school sports, paid $17,000 for two new scoreboards as part of an agreement for the exclusive sale of Pepsi products. Each of the scoreboards, which hang at either end of the basketball court, sports the Pepsi brand name and logo. (Quad-Cities Online, July 6, 1998)

Like the 1949 scoreboard, the original 1928 basketball floor at Wharton carries special memories for generations of players and fans. Raised about four inches, it had a spring-like quality. Some players have said that they could dunk a basketball at Wharton, but nowhere else. George Seaberg, who played at Moline and the University of Iowa in the 1950s, praised the floor, calling it one of the three best he ever played on, the

M, 1979

Shown in this 1979 photograph are the four sideline baskets that had to be raised or lowered by hand. Also shown are the two main baskets, each having a single support planted in the floor.

C. Roseman, 2013

This photograph shows the south bleachers in their recessed position, in this case to accommodate space for two wrestling circles. They were installed in the early 1990s to replace the 1962 bleachers.

Still No Smoking. Since the 1930s smoking had not been allowed in the Field House proper, although for many years thereafter the men's restroom in the northwest corner basement was used as a smoking room. In 1970 Ed Lemon received a request to rent Wharton for a country and western music show. In a letter dated December 16th, he turned it down: "I am sorry to inform you that the building is not available. As I understand . . . your production would be a promotional show for the Reynolds Tobacco Company. The facilities here are the property of the public school system and the Board of Education has a long standing regulation relative to the use of the Field House for advertising purposes especially in the case of the liquor and tobacco industries."

other two being in the Iowa Fieldhouse and Williams Arena at the University of Minnesota. As the floor aged it developed dead spots that may have contributed to the home court advantage for the Wharton-based high school, community college, and professional teams. In 1997 Quad-Cities Online (January 21) interviewed school officials and summarized the state of the original floor:

A new floor – one [Coach Frank] Dexter called a 'grade one and the best you can get' – is scheduled to be in place by the time the capped-and-gowned members of the Class of 1997 get their diplomas on June 6. Everyone agrees that efforts to maintain the 69-year-old floor have been exhausted. There are dead spots where a bounced ball doesn't return the way it should, nails are coming up and it cannot be sanded any further. Blemishes, most notably a scar of the CBA's 3-point line from the Quad City Thunder's days at Wharton, are still there. 'We've sanded as far as we can go and still can't get the old 3-point lines off,' [Athletic Director Mike] Owens said. Added Dexter, 'It's been sanded so many times it's almost to the point where the boards will start to break it's been worn so thin.'

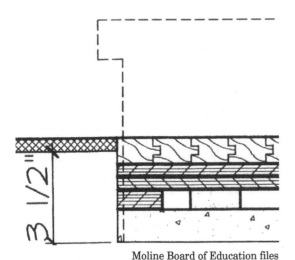

Moline Board of Education files

The old Wharton basketball floor was raised almost 4 inches above the ground floor surface. Here its profile is superimposed on a profile of the layers of the new floor, which is flush with the paved arena floor.

D. Moore

D. Moore

On the left volunteers cut the original floor into various sized pieces. The largest piece (above) included center circle containing the block-letter "M," which was saved and hung from the rafters above the east balcony

The original floor was taken up in 1997. Over a two-day period Moline High School Boosters Club members helped remove the floor and cut it into various sized pieces. Scores of Moliners purchased square-foot segments to keep as souvenirs. The center-court part of the floor, painted with the big block letter "M," now hangs over the east balcony (and is shown in Chapter 3). Parts of the floor of various sizes were purchased by individuals and made into wall hangings, table tops, or dance floors. Other pieces provide table tops in a nearby tavern, the Wunder-Y, a table in the Wharton coaches' room, and counters in the arena-floor press box.

The counter tops in the press box on the arena floor are made from sections of the old Field House floor that were removed in 1997. Other sections of various sizes and shapes can be found in homes and businesses of Moline High School fans.

The baskets at either end of the main basketball floor were also replaced in the 1990s. The original baskets and backboards were supported by an array of trusses, designed after those at Huff Gym in Champaign. Those arrays were replaced in 1950 with single-support steel poles. In the newest iteration, the baskets are suspended from the ceiling beams and can be automatically raised or lowered.

Wharton Field House in the 21st Century

Since the larger downtown Moline arena, The Mark (now the iWireless Center) opened in 1993, most of the activities at the Field House have been school-related including sports and a few other events such as dances. No longer does Wharton host large exhibitions, dog shows, political rallies, big-name entertainers, or other activities that were common in its past. Each year, however, some non-school activities are accommodated. Since 2000 they have included Red Cross disaster training, Relay for Life cancer fund raisers, Moline Schools Foundation Chili Cookoffs, and City of Moline Wellness Fairs.

Until his retirement in 1984 Ed Lemon had managed all aspects of the facility, including ticket sales. Then Eric Larson took over as manager, a position he held until the Thunder left in 1993. Since then the responsibility for management, rentals, and ticket sales have been dispersed among school district employees. The one constant in the operation of the facility has been the presence and work of Tom Minick, who was hired as custodian in 1985. Minick, a graduate of Western Illinois University, grew up in Rock Island. He taught briefly at Rock Island High School before taking the Wharton job. At first his duties were primarily at the Field House, but later he was given responsibility for Browning Field. Minick does custodial work himself and supervises part-time custodial help. He manages the change-overs necessary to move from one type of activity to another, and is present at virtually all Wharton and Browning events.

Wharton Field House is used fifty weeks a year – six days during most weeks. It is only closed for two weeks before school starts in late August. The mix of activities changes with the season, but overall Wharton and Browning have been very busy gathering places in the 21st century. During the school year, scores of varsity and sophomore games are held for football, volleyball, basketball, wrestling, and track. The facilities also have hosted numerous middle and elementary school activities, including football, basketball, track, and music productions. During the summers volleyball, basketball, and track camps have been conducted.

Quad City Thunder player Anthony Bowie posed for this photograph with Tom Minick in 1988 and autographed the back of the photo. Minick was hired as the custodian in the fall of 1985, and has been the key person handling the operation and maintenance of the arena since then.

The Seating Capacity at Wharton

The 2013 configuration of bleacher seating on the main floor plus the fixed balcony seats yields a seating capacity for basketball just over 5,500. That number has varied over time, especially owing to changing ground floor bleacher sizes and arrangements. Here is a chronological story of Wharton's seating capacity.

When opened in late 1928, the Field House capacity was listed as 5,200: 3,400 permanent seats in the balcony and 1,800 temporary main-floor seats (although some of the main floor seats were not installed until after the dedication). From opening day, the Maroon and White Association boasted of the size of the arena, not only for basketball but for the multiple purposes to which it would be put over the years.

> The building may be rented by any organization for athletic practices and contests, for concerts, conventions, lectures, musical programs, industrial parties, auto shows, etc. at fees established by the Maroon and White Association . . . For convention or concert purposes the large

stand at the [south] end of the floor may be removed, a stage erected and the main floor covered with chairs, bringing the seating capacity up to 7,000. (Dedication Program, 1928)

Perhaps earliest the large basketball seating capacity of the Field House was fashioned for a 1934 game between St. Ambrose College and the University of Iowa. Having attracted 5,000 for

C. Roseman

Throughout its history, the Field House main floor would easily accommodate hundreds of seats for stage productions and other events. This May 2013 photograph shows more than 500 chairs, with room to spare, which were set up for the Moline High School commencement ceremonies.

Former vice president and 1968 presidential candidate Richard Nixon packed the Field House for a campaign rally on the afternoon of October 10, 1968.

Years ago, a large bleacher was occasionally placed at that end of the building, so that an additional 500 customers could be accommodated.

Soon, however, additions and reconfigurations of the bleachers led to some larger basketball crowds. In early 1947, the Moline-East Moline high school basketball game attracted a record 5,400 and, during the 1947-48 season in a game between the Tri-Cities Blackhawks and the Minneapolis Lakers, the record was increased to 5,700. The *Dispatch* (June 19, 1948) noted an attendance landmark:

> Well over one million persons have seen cage games in the field house over the last 20 years thanks to the far-sightedness of T. F. Wharton and other civic leaders back in 1927 and 1928.

Led by the popularity of the Blackhawks in the 1948-49 season, seating capacity was increased to 6,000. Then, in the summer of 1949, capacity was further increased to 6,500 for basketball through an expansion of bleachers on the south end. "Some of the Blackhawk games last season proved to be such big drawing cards that customers were turned away. Those extra 500 seats are expected to avert that situation if it should arise in the coming year" (*Dispatch*, July 13).

Through the 1950s, Wharton's capacity was advertised in *Billboard* magazine and elsewhere as 6,000, increased to 6,500 with temporary seats on the main floor. Over the years, scores of activities required main floor seating at Wharton,

their game the year before, extra bleachers were built to bring the capacity to 6,000, although only 3,500 attended the game. For high school basketball, the Field House capacity was never reached in the 1930s, with only a few games attracting 3,000 or more fans. In the early 1940s, however, crowds exceeding 3,000 became common, and reached almost 5,000 in 1943. In a 1946 interview with Fil Johnson of the *Dispatch*, manager Winnie Holmgren commented on Field House seating in preparation for the February 1st, Moline-Rock Island basketball game. All reserved seats had been sold and a large crowd was anticipated. Johnson wrote on January 30th:

> The seating capacity of the field house at present is 4,600, and school officials plan to halt the ticket sale before too large a crowd of standees jam into the corners, as it isn't likely that a 5,000 total can be reached because of the impossibility of placing a large bleacher section at the south end of the court with the stage obstructing the space.

45

which sometimes expanded seating well beyond the advertized capacity, in some cases reaching 7,000.

In the fall of 1956, five years after the Blackhawks left town, Field House manager Holmgren listed the basketball seating capacity at 5,958 (*Dispatch*, November 5). A record of over 3,600 high school season tickets had been sold the previous season, and he speculated that almost 4,000 would sign up for the upcoming season. Previously only the first four rows of section F were reserved; now the entire section would be reserved. At that time adult general admission season tickets sold for $6, reserved season tickets $8.

For three decades, Wharton had been touted as having the second largest seating capacity of any basketball arena in downstate Illinois, exceeded only by Huff Gymnasium at the University of Illinois which seated about 7,000. The size and design of the Field House impressed visiting teams from towns large and small. Sharm Scheuerman, who played for Rock Island in the early 1950s and went on to play with Moline's Bill Seaberg on a championship University of Iowa team, is quoted by Taylor Bell (2004):

> When you played there you thought you had died and gone to heaven. Most high school gyms are wide open, but Wharton looked like a professional facility. When we played Moline, it was like playing for a world championship.

Wharton's basketball seating-capacity dominance ended on December 4, 1959, when the Rock Island Fieldhouse was opened with an advertised seating capacity of 6,000. Before 1937, the Rocks had played basketball at various locations, including the Augustana College gym. Then a gym constructed with their new high school provided a home court, but its size was much smaller than Wharton, having only about 1,000 permanent seats. All that changed in 1959.

Over one hundred years of athletic competition between Moline and its neighbor Rock Island has not been limited to action on the

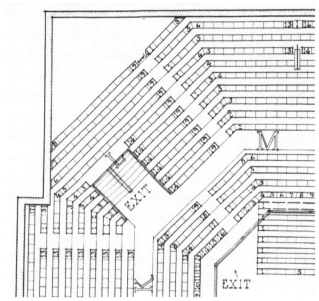

Schulzke drawing, 1928

The original design of the Field House included two flat, triangular areas at the upper northeast and northwest corners of the balcony. One of them is shown here as open space in this original Schulzke drawing. Before 1949, folding chairs were placed there to accommodate large crowds. In the summer of that year the school board approved the installation of bleachers in those areas at a cost of $2,500. Each set of bleachers has five rows that are tapered to fit the triangular space and has sixty numbered seats.

Firsts at Rock Island. The first event at the new Rock Island Fieldhouse was the high school commencement ceremony on June 1, 1959, in which 432 seniors were graduated. Five months later in the first basketball game, the Rocks beat Rockford West, 65-45 in front of more than 5,000 people. Moline played there for the first time on January 15, 1960, in front of 5,900 fans. Rock Island won that game, 68-63, with some help from a former Moliner, Brad Baraks, who led the Rocks in scoring with 23 points. Baraks had moved from Moline the previous summer.

court, mat, or field. After Rock Island opened its fieldhouse, a seating-capacity rivalry ensued. Referring to the 1962-63 basketball season, Van Vooren and Dye (2008) wrote:

> Because of its seating capacity [6,538], Rock Island's Field House is nearly named permanent site of the regional [tournament]. In response new bleachers are added at Wharton increasing its

size to 6,538. The IHSA [Illinois High School Association] then decides to continue rotating the regional. Note: If Wharton's seats were reduced to a 16" width, like those at Rocky, the place would seat 7,355 fans.

Rock Island Fieldhouse

Wharton Field House

C. Roseman, 2013

To determine if the assertion about the Moline-Rock Island seat width differential holds true in the 21st century, we measured numbered seats at both the Rock Island Fieldhouse (above) and Wharton (below). Indeed, as of January 2013, virtually every seat in the Rock Island arena is 16 inches wide. Virtually every one at Wharton is 18 inches wide, in both the permanent bench seats in the balcony and the ground floor bleachers.

Through the 1960s, 1970s, and 1980s, Wharton Field House and its Rock Island counterpart continued to attract large crowds for both regular season and tournament basketball games, not to mention scores of other activities. When the Quad City Thunder played at Wharton from 1987 to 1993, they attracted crowds averaging over 4,000 per home game in five of their six seasons at the Field House. During that period the Wharton seating capacity was 6,161, according to the 1988 Wharton 60th Anniversary Program.

Dispatch, March 19, 1963

In March 1963, a record high school basketball crowd of 6,538 attended the first round of the high school "Sweet-Sixteen" state tournament, the Moline "Super-Sectional." Ironically, Wharton's home team, Moline, was not in the game, having been eliminated earlier. Rockford Auburn defeated Aledo, 62-51. Located only about 35 miles from Moline, Aledo could have stuffed its entire population of 3,080 in the Field House that evening and still left ample room for Auburn fans.

In 2013 we calculated Wharton's basketball seating capacity based on seats that are 18 inches wide. With some space taken away for the bandstand and a camera platform, the number of balcony bench seats totaled 3,364. Adding the 120 seats in the triangular bleacher arrays in two upper corners, total balcony seating came to 3,484. Ground floor bleachers seated 2,037 with the south bleacher array fully extended. Total number of seats at Wharton Field House: 5,521.

To close this chapter, we couldn't resist yet another comparison with the Rock Island Fieldhouse. According to Rock Island High School ticket manager and former basketball coach Don Resler, the capacity there in 2013 was 5,848. That number made it 327 seats larger than Wharton. But wait, there's more! What about seat width? If Wharton's seats were as narrow as Rocky's – 16 inches – the Moline arena would seat 6,211, giving it 363 more seats than the Rock Island Fieldhouse. Let the long-standing rivalry continue!

Wharton: Number 1 in Illinois and Number 20 Nationally. For his 1993 book on Indiana high school basketball, Donald Hamilton surveyed state athletic association officials in all fifty states to determine the largest high school "gyms" in the country. His list ranks Wharton Field House as the largest in Illinois (6,200 capacity) and the Rock Island Fieldhouse (5,900) as second. These two arenas were the only ones in Illinois listed among all 36 gyms seating 5,000 or more. Nationally, the largest was the New Castle (Indiana) Fieldhouse, seating 9,314. All but one of the largest sixteen were in Indiana, the exception being an arena in Dallas, Texas, seating 7,500. Wharton ranked twentieth on the national list and Rock Island twenty-third.

Chapter 3

High School and College Sports at Wharton

"[among the] great places to watch high school hoops."
–USA Today, Februry 26, 2004

High School Basketball before the Field House

Moline began playing basketball in 1899 and first played Rock Island in 1901. Initial seasons were brief; it was not until 1908-09 that Moline played more than nine games. In the 1903-04 eight-game season Moline lost one game each to Rock Island and Augustana College, and lost two games to Davenport. Nonetheless they claimed for "the Plow City the undisputed championship of northern Illinois" by virtue of a 40-12 victory over Galesburg (Van Vooren and Dye, 2008).

Dispatch, March 14, 1951
The first Moline High School basketball team, pictured here, played during the 1899-1900 season. In the front row are Harvey McKinley, Max Taylor, and Henry "Drop-Kick" Kelting. In the rear are Bud Carlson, Axel Dunderberg, and Seth Smith. Won-loss records and other statistics were not kept, or did not survive, for seasons before 1903-04. (*Dispatch,* March 14, 1951).

A shot for the championship. Writing in 1935, Eagle et al. describe an unusual play in the 1904 game against Galesburg: "During one of the hand-to-hand scrimmages Dunderberg was knocked to the floor . . . While prone, he tossed the ball between the legs of a Galesburg guard who was standing over him and it passed through the hoop, giving Moline the lead. The shot seemed to shatter the Galesburg morale."

The Moline High School basketball team played home games in at least four different venues before the Field House opened in late 1928. All of them were cramped and awkward spaces, presenting challenges for both players and spectators. Prior to 1908 the lads played several home games in the Industrial Home Building, at 14th Street and 5th Avenue. After it was converted for use as a live theatre in 1907, the team played at least one game at the Wagner Opera House on 3rd Avenue. There Moline defeated Augustana College, the visitors complaining of an unfair home court advantage – a wet floor. After the new Manual Arts Building on 17th Street hill was completed in 1908 it became the home for Moline basketball until 1912. Van Vooren and Dye comment that there was "little room for spectators and some watch the game by looking through the windows or standing in the hall."

The next two seasons were played at the downtown YMCA on 5th Avenue and 18th Street, where the court was less than half the size of today's regulation court. It was impossible to shoot from the corners because of interference from the running track above. Finally, the Moline team got their own home court in 1915 when the new high school (today the Moline High School Loft Apartments) opened. The new gym was a big improvement for playing basketball, but was inadequate to accommodate more than a few hundred spectators who sat on bleachers on either side of the court or stood on the running track above the court.

M, 1926

Moline High School Gym, 1926. Moline beat Kewanee in this last home game of the season, 14-10.

The "Maroons." According to Van Vooren and Dye, Moline High School received permission from the University of Chicago back in 1895 to use the term "Maroons" as the nickname of their athletic teams. Early in the twentieth century, the Moline teams were referred to as the "Maroon and White." Then in the 1920s, the shorter version, "Maroons," came into use – the first mention of "Maroons" in the high school annual was in 1923. Among the other Illinois high schools whose teams are called Maroons are Belleville (West), Champaign (Central), Clinton, Elgin, and Robinson.

M, 1924

The 1920s district tournaments were held at the Augustana College gymnasium, shown here. Two basketball games could be played at one time, one on the court shown here and another on a court just out of the photograph in the foreground.

Beginning in 1916 the Augustana gym served as an all-purpose facility, hosting not only basketball and other sporting events, but college and community assemblies as well. During the month of December 1916, it was dedicated at a basketball game and also hosted a gymnastics exhibition and a performance of the "Messiah" by the Handel Oratorio Society. A diversity of events there continued until 1960 when a new auditorium, Centennial Hall, was opened on campus. Thereafter the gym primarily held athletic events until 1971 when they were moved to the new and larger Roy J. Carver Center for Physical Education and the 75-year-old gymnasium was razed. (*Argus*, February 12, 1971)

1920s postcard

Early High School Basketball at the Field House

Moline's first game in the big new arena was on the night of the Field House dedication in 1928. The Maroons took an early lead in the game and won 22-15. The *Argus* (December 22) commented:

> Kewanee was far from outclassed. In fact, after coach Ross Anderson's warriors had cast off the stage fright that hobbled them the first period or so, they were an even match for the Maroons, who seemed to be at their best amid the clamor caused by 4,000 cheering fans and the musical din of two bands.

Moline's Jim Rosborough, son of board of education president C. R. Rosborough, made the first basket at the Field House. He was a sixteen-year-old high school junior at the time. At a Field House anniversary celebration fifty years later, the younger Rosborough told Tom Bergstrand of the *Dispatch* (December 17, 1978):

> Actually, everybody else shot first. Finally it got around to me and somebody told me to shoot. And, as luck would have it, it went in. It was a two-handed set shot at the North basket from the East end of the free throw line.

For that same 50th anniversary, the coach of the 1928 Kewanee team, Ross Anderson, sent a letter of appreciation and congratulations. Among his comments:

I remember very well that visit to Wharton Field House [actually Moline Field House at the time] for the opening game there. Winnie Holmgren, then your faculty manager of athletics, met us at the door and escorted us over slat walkways to our dressing room, since there was still mud between the lobby and the dressing room area. The dressing rooms were not completely equipped and the heating of them was not completed. Never-the-less we enjoyed playing in that opening game and also later trips to your field house.

The next basketball to be played at the Field House was the Big Nine Conference tournament on December 26-28. The conference, in its first year of existence, included Moline, Rock Island, East Moline, Canton, Galesburg, Geneseo, Kewanee, Monmouth, and Princeton. Moline beat Princeton 31-14 in the first round, then lost to Canton 26-10. Canton won the tournament by beating Galesburg in the final game 26-19.

On New Year's Eve, 1928, Moline defeated Davenport at the Field House 29-13 in front of 1,500 fans. This game was the first of a thirty-year series played on New Year's Eve. All of the games in Moline were played at Wharton, and all but the first in Davenport were played at George Marshall Gymnasium, which opened in February 1930. The tradition was discontinued in the late 1950s owing to scheduling difficulties in the Mississippi Valley Conference in which both schools competed.

C. Roseman, 2012

Davenport High School's new gym was opened on February 24, 1930, with a game against Ottumwa. Ottumwa had won the Iowa state title in 1928 and placed second to Davenport in 1929. Davenport went on to win the state title a second time in a row, having been undefeated except for a loss to Moline, 29-22, on February 14 before 3,000 at the Field House. The new Davenport gym had 2,034 permanent seats in the balcony with standing room only available on the main floor. A 50 by 70 foot stage at one end, elevated three feet above the floor, served initially as the girls' basketball court. (*Argus*, February 24, 1930) The gym was named after George Edward Marshall, a principal at the school from 1907 until his death in 1932.

Davenport Schools Museum

George Marshall Gymnasium, a magnificent Art Deco structure, is situated just south of the Davenport (Central) High School building.

Having such a large home court in a large arena certainly was an advantage to Moline, especially when smaller schools with much smaller gyms came to town. But perhaps the large home court had its disadvantages too, as suggested by this January 14, 1929, note in the *Dispatch*: "Having become used to a large court, the Maroons may be handicapped by the boundary restrictions at Savanna High, whose gymnasium will be the smallest in which the Moliners will appear this year." The *Dispatch* prognostication missed the mark, however; Moline won 36-5!

In March 1929 the Moline basketball team participated in state tournament play, as they did many times over the years. Because major high school consolidations had not yet taken place, the basketball tournament landscape at the time was quite different than today. The first level of competition, the district tournament, was held at the Augustana gym and involved teams from Aledo, Coal Valley, Cordova, East Moline, Erie, Hillsdale, Joy, Keithsburg, Moline, Port Byron, Reynolds, Rock Island, Sherrard, and Viola. The two largest schools of the group, by far, played in the final game, Moline besting Rock Island 18-17 for the championship. Then tournament play moved to the sectional, which was being hosted by Moline for the first time in their new Field House. District winners from Freeport, Lanark, Malden, Macomb, Moline, Morrison, and Orion participated. Moline lost in

the second round to Freeport, which went on to win the sectional and place third at the state tournament in Champaign.

Like their football counterparts (discussed in Chapter 8), the Moline High basketball team scheduled some teams from distant places. The first such occurrence was just a year after Wharton opened; Libbey High of Toledo, Ohio, came

Eager Orion Fans. "Five automobile loads of ardent Orion fans left their city at 5 yesterday afternoon with four hours in which to drive twenty miles to see their favorites play. The third quarter was well under way before they wearily crossed the threshold of the field house. Their shoes were covered with mud. They said they had experienced a tough time. The roads between the cities were like bottomless pits" (*Dispatch*, March 16, 1929).

M, 1931

Editors of the Moline High School annual, *M*, spared no sympathy for the fans of small school teams that were forced to visit a gigantic arena and play large schools such as Moline. These two cartoons refer to the 1931 district tournament at the Field House.

on December 20, 1929. Moline won 14-11. The following day the *Argus* speculated on reasons for the victory:

> Matched with a dazzling brigade of short passers from Libbey . . . the Moline Maroons sent 2,500 fans home with joyful hearts . . . In justice to the scrappy Ohioans, it should be mentioned that they took to the floor suffering from the strain of the long train ride from the shores of Lake Erie. They were forced to spend more than seven hours in a chilly depot in Chicago because of at traffic tie-up, the result of a snowstorm.

High School Conferences

Local competition in basketball and other sports between Moline, Davenport, and Rock Island led to the establishment of the Tri-City Conference early in the twentieth century. Then it became the Quad City Conference in 1934 when East Moline joined in. It thrived until 1958 when it took a back seat to the Mississippi Valley Conference (MVC), in which the four joined Iowa teams outside of the Quad Cities. After leaving the MVC in 1969, a local conference was revived, the Quad City Metro. After 1978, however, regular season competition between Illinois and Iowa teams was minimized and the last of the local conferences, the Metro, was discontinued.

This ticket is good for One General Admission to any one of the following Basketball Games played at the Moline Field House.

Davenport H. S. vs. Moline H. S.
Friday, February 15th

Rock Island H. S. vs. Moline H. S.
Friday, February 22nd

Galesburg H. S. vs. Moline H. S.
Saturday, March 2nd

Price of ticket 50 Cents

Courtesy of Jerry Wallaert

A ticket to one of the last three regular-season Moline games during the first season of play at the Field House. The three traditional rivals did not draw as well as they would in later years. According to Van Vooren and Dye, the Davenport game drew 2,000, Rock Island 3,600, and Galesburg 1,500.

Since 1928, Moline, East Moline (United Township – UTHS – beginning in 1972), and Rock Island High Schools have played basketball in four different conferences that stretched beyond the Quad City area. Competition in the first, the Big Nine, involved only a conference tournament during the first two years. Then in the 1930-31 season, round-robin play among the teams began, a pattern that continues in conference play to the present. The Big Nine, however, lasted only until 1935. The 1936 high school annual, *M*, commented on the transition to the next:

The high school conference known as the Big Nine is no more . . . A contest for a name for the new conference was held during the summer. The winning name, "Northwest Conference," was submitted by both a Kewanee and a Moline entrant. Golf, tennis, and forensics are all included in the scoring system of the new conference, and archery is likely to take its deserved place soon. Moline had the honor of winning the first Big Nine football championship, and also the 1935 track championship, the last trophy to be given away by that organization. This season [1935] Moline captured the Northwest football championship to start the conference off on its career.

Big Nine Conference
1929 - 1935

Northwest Conference
1936-1957

Mississippi Valley Conference
1958 - 1969

Western Big Six Conference
1970 - 2013

Z. Schmidt

Moline High School sports have participated in four different conferences that stretched beyond the Quad Cities since the Field House opened in 1928. With the exception of the Mississippi Valley Conference, which included Iowa schools, the members are located in northwestern Illinois.

Eagle et al., 1935 Courtesy of Bruce Firchau

The 1934 Moline basketball team posing in the Field House. Yes, the bench seats shown in the balcony are the same ones Wharton visitors sit on today. On the right is the cover of the program for the 1934 sectional tournament, which was held at the Field House.

Dispatch, January 29, 1943

Some 4,800 people crowded the Field House in January 1943 for the game with Paris, which Moline won 37-34. It was the first defeat for Paris since they lost to Centralia in the final game of the Illinois state tournament the previous year. Unfortunately, Paris turned the tables on Moline two months later, defeating them in the state final game in Champaign, 46-37. It was a similar story the year before, when Moline beat Freeport at home but lost to them in the first round of the state tournament. And, it happened again with Quincy in 1945; a Maroon win at home and a loss in Champaign, where Moline finished fourth.

The "New Gymnasium" at the University of Illinois in Champaign was built in 1925 in the Greco-Roman style to match other campus buildings. In 1937 it was named Huff Hall in honor of George Huff, who served as athletic director from 1901 to 1935, although the building is popularly known as Huff Gym. Its original seating capacity, about 7,000, barely exceeded that of Wharton Field House. Almost every home game at Huff saw a capacity crowd for University of Illinois basketball from its opening in 1925 until 1963 when the 16,000-seat Assembly Hall was completed. Today, Huff is home to Illinois men's and women's gymnastics, volleyball, and wrestling. It now seats 4,500 for volleyball and wrestling. (Huff Gym, online)

State Tournaments

From 1925 to 1963, Huff Gym in Champaign hosted the Illinois state high school basketball tournament every March. Moline High School played in the state tournament at Huff fourteen times between 1934 and 1955. Rock Island played there in four tournaments between 1938 and 1962.

M, 1935   M, 1943

Two of Moline's visits to the state finals at Huff Gym. The photograph on the left shows the Maroons in a 1935 opening-round game in which they beat Joliet, 35-19. Number 21 is Cliff Peterson and 24 is Jim Anders, each of whom scored seven points. That year, the Maroons finished fourth. On the right is a crowd of Moliners watching the 1943 tournament where Moline lost to Paris in the championship game.

March Madness. According to the Illinois High School Association (IHSA) Website, the term "March Madness" was coined in 1939 to describe the Illinois state tournament. Henry V. Porter, assistant executive secretary of the IHSA, first used it in an Illinois Inter-scholastic magazine article. Soon it came into popular use to describe the madness at Huff Gym. In the 1970s and 1980s, the IHSA was officially using the term in various publications and today holds the copyright on "March Madness" and "America's Original March Madness." Now "March Madness" is used nationwide to characterize the high school and college basketball tournament season.

Courtesy of Jerry Wallaert

Illinois State Finals Program, 1955

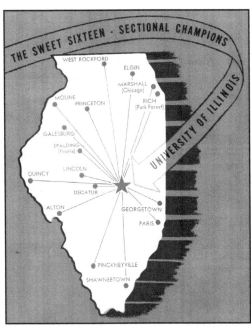

Illinois State Finals Program, 1955

Huff Gym filled for the 1954 state basketball finals, and the map showing the "Sweet Sixteen" teams for 1955, which hung on the arena wall. A light was imbedded in the map at the location of each team. When a team lost, its light would be extinguished, leaving but one illuminated light at the end of the championship game. (Bell, 2004)

C. Roseman, 2012

Banners denoting Moline's 27 appearances among the final sixteen teams in the state tournament (the "Sweet Sixteen") are proudly displayed in Wharton Field House.

Post-World War II: Great Crowds, Continued Success

After World War II Moline basketball success would continue, but now Wharton Field House would be regularly "filled to the rafters." According to the 2008 Van Vooren and Dye book, the largest attendance for regular season high school basketball games before 1945 was the 5,500 who attended the "ten cent night" game against Monmouth in 1930. During the 1930s and early 1940s, quite a few home games reached 3,000, but only six exceeded that. Three attracted at least 4,000 and the largest crowd was 4,800 at the 1943 Paris game. Then, as if a switch was turned on right after the 1945 end of World War II, attendance soared. Beginning that year, and through the 1950s, 5,000 or more fans would show up several times a year, and during the 1960s and early 1970s, the majority of games for which Van Vooren and Dye have totals attracted at least 6,000. As the 1980s were approaching, attendance gradually declined, although some games, especially against traditional rivals, would draw as many as 5,000.

Courtesy of Jerry Wallaert

Jerry Wallaert believes this is the first of the new style of Moline High School basketball programs adopted in 1949. From then onward for several decades, printed programs featured photographs of players and others on their covers, with accompanying stories about them on the inside.

Courtesy of Jerry Wallaert

Over the years numerous post-season high school basketball tournaments have been held at Wharton. Here are program covers from 1956 (above) and 1959 (right).

Shattering Experiences for Nelson and Johnson. On February 8, 1957, Rock Island defeated Moline 77-69 in front of 5,900 fans at Wharton. Rock Island junior center Don Nelson, who went on to become a professional player and coach, broke the Rocks' single-game scoring record with 39 points. Moline junior Vern Johnson also did some shattering that evening. In a pre-game drill he broke the glass backboard while attempting a slam-dunk, a shot that was outlawed during high school games at the time. The baskets and backboards were replaced at both ends of the court, resulting in a 45-minute delay in the start of the game. (Carlson, 1957) Some local fans have kept pieces of the broken glass as souvenirs.

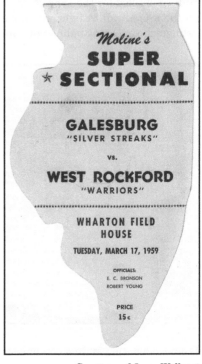

Courtesy of Jerry Wallaert

M, 1961

Jack Foley is hoisted by his players in a 1961 celebration of his 200th win over ten years as head coach of the Moline High School basketball team. Two years later Foley lost his job. In 2008 Van Vooren and Dye commented: "Roundly rebuked by his critics for failing to win a state title, his record stands for itself. More than 40 years have passed since his departure and he still boasts the highest winning percentage and largest number of All-State players developed by any Moline coach." Foley was graduated from Rock Island High School and St. Ambrose College, where he played basketball and ran track. His career at Moline began in 1945.

This 1963 Moline basketball program cover features coaches Harv Schmidt and Jack Dye. Schmidt went on to become head coach for seven seasons at the University of Illinois, where he had starred as a player in the 1950s. Jack Dye spent a career in the Moline school system as a teacher and a basketball and golf coach. In a 1998 interview he spun some memories of Wharton Field House for Bill Allee, including one about a visit by Chicago DuSable: "I remember one time I heard one of the DuSable players telling his coach that they were getting cheated, and his coach turned to him and said, 'Be quiet, this is the best place we've ever played.'"

Courtesy of Herb Thompson

Herb Thompson and his wife Ann admire a photograph of the Field House during a visit to Moline in July 1964. At the time he was basketball coach at Mason City (Iowa) High School and was being recruited for the Moline job. Thompson accepted the position and coached at Moline for the next thirteen years.

Moline Boys Basketball Coaches Who Won at Least 99 Games.

Coach	Years	Record	Winning Percentage
George Senneff	1921-40, 45	323-151	68
Frank Dexter	1995-2006	244-99	71
Jack Foley	1952-63	237-79	75
Herb Thompson	1965-77	218-112	66
Whitey Verstraete	1979-85	113-76	60
Roger Potter	1941-44, 47-48	99-56	64

Source: Van Vooren and Dye (2008)

C. Roseman, 2012

Banners hanging from the rafters on the east side of Wharton Field House honor Moline players who earned All-State honors. They are hung on either side of the large piece of the original floor from center court. As of 2013, 26 Maroons have earned the honor. Bob Van Vooren, an honoree who starred on the team that placed second in Illinois in 1951, was named one of the 100 "Legends of the IHSA Tournament" in 2007.

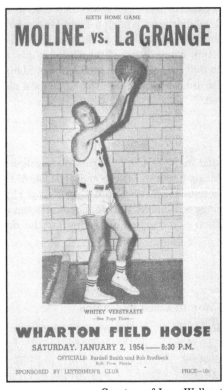

Courtesy of Jerry Wallaert

M, 1998

Two Moline boys have received All-State basketball recognition twice, Whitey Verstraete in 1954 and 1955, and Traves Wilson in 1997 and 1998. Verstraete went on to coach the Maroons from 1979 to 1985. Wilson holds the all-time career scoring record for Moline with 1,654 points.

M, 1961

Traditionally the last Moline home basketball game is Parents Night or Senior Night, when seniors on the team are honored in the presence of their parents. A big crowd showed up for this celebration in 1961.

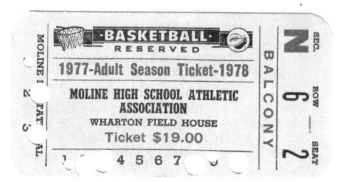

Courtesy of Jerry Wallaert

C. Roseman, 2013

The crowd was not as large, but the honors were no fewer. Senior night in Feburary 2013 at the game against United Township.

M, 1998

According to Van Vooren and Dye, the last Moline High game at Wharton to attract more than 6,000 fans was the 1998 Galesburg game, pictured here. The Maroons lost that game to the Silver Streaks, 75-59. Moline lost only three games that year, all to Galesburg, a team that went on to place second in the state tournament.

Home Court Advantage and the Oldest Rivalry

George Van Vooren compiled the Maroons' win-loss record at Wharton Field House. Through the 2012-13 season, Moline's overall record at Wharton was 777-300, a 72.1 winning percentage. Their regular season record was 674-282 (70.5 percent) and their postseason record was 103-18 (85.1 percent). Winning percentages by decade were: 1920s (53.3 percent); 1930s (77.2); 1940s (75.2); 1950s (84.5); 1960s (80.5); 1970s (61.2); 1980s (61.8); 1990s (62.8); 2000s (81.0); 2010-2013 (60.4).

In his 2004 book on Illinois high school basketball, Taylor Bell certifies that the Moline-Rock Island high school boys basketball rivalry is the oldest in the state, dating from 1901. The second oldest, between East and West Aurora, began in 1912. How has the Moline-Rock Island rivalry played out on the court? Using scores published by Van Vooren and Dye in 2008, updated through the 2012-13 season, we summed the wins by each team, shown below. The results show a remarkable balance over the 112-year period. Out of a total of 275 games Moline won just over half: 142 games or 51.4 percent. In state tournament games (district, regional, or sectional matches regardless of location), Moline fared better, winning 36 of 61 games, or 59 percent. We further parsed out the results based on the locations of the games.

In the pre-1929 era before Moline played at Wharton, Rock Island held a clear advantage both at home and away. During that period, both teams played home games at more than one location, although Moline settled into the high school gym after 1915 and Rock Island played many home games at the Augustana gym after 1916. Over the next thirty years after Wharton opened – 1929 to 1959 – Moline dominated both home and away. They won two-thirds of the games at Wharton and nearly 60 percent of the games in Rock Island, most of which were played in the Rock Island High School gym that opened in 1937 and some at Augustana.

No doubt that dominance was one of the stimuli for the Rocks to build their own large fieldhouse! In 1959 Rock Island High School

More Wharton Basketball Statistics. Van Vooren also provided these tidbits. The Maroons completed seven undefeated seasons at Wharton, including postseason play: 1938, 1943, 1955, 1962, 1965, 1972, and 2004. They also were undefeated at Wharton during the 1988 regular season but lost there in the regional tournament. The most wins at Wharton in a single year, fifteen, was accomplished in 1935, 1937, 1943, and 2004. The most games won in a row at Wharton is 21, spanning the 1942-1944 seasons, including both regular and postseason games. The record for most regular season wins in a row there is twenty, 1971-1973.

Moline-Rock Island High School Basketball Game Results, by Location, Through 2012-13

Regular Season Games Only:	Moline Wins (Percent)	Rock Island Wins (Percent)
In Moline before 1929	6 (40.0)	9 (60.0)
In Rock Island before 1929	8 (44.4)	10 (55.6)
At Wharton, 1929-1959	21 (67.7)	10 (32.3)
At Rock Island, 1929-1959	19 (59.4)	13 (40.6)
At Wharton, 1960-2013	29 (55.8)	23 (44.2)
At RI Fieldhouse, 1960-2013	21 (38.7)	33 (61.1)
All Games at Wharton	50 (60.2)	33 (39.8)
All Games at RI Fieldhouse	21 (38.7)	33 (61.1)
- - - - -		
All State Tournament Games	36 (59.0)	25 (41.0)
All Games	42 (51.4)	133 (48.2)

Source: Van Vooren and Dye, 2008

C. Roseman, 2013   C. Roseman, 2013

Although Wharton no longer is filled to the rafters for high school basketball games, some games – especially between local and long-time rivals – attract good crowds. On the left are the nearly-filled west-side stands at the Moline-Rock Island game in February 2013. On the right, the Rocks are warming up for that game.

opened a new arena of similar size to Wharton. Since then these two Illinois schools with the longest boys basketball rivalry have also had the two largest high school basketball arenas in the state. And both large arenas have provided a clear home-court advantage over the years. Overall, Moline has won 60.2 percent of its games against the Rocks at Wharton, but lost 61.1 of them at the Rock Island Fieldhouse.

Girls Basketball

A watershed in interscholastic sports was crossed at Moline High School – along with numerous other schools in the United States – during the years immediately after the landmark federal Title IX legislation for gender equality was passed in 1972. Moline girls had competed in intramural sports, including basketball, volleyball, and track at various times earlier in the twentieth century. But now they were competing against other schools – just as the boys had for decades – building new fan bases and bringing new excitement to Wharton Field House and Browning Field. Moline High began girls interscholastic competition in track in 1973, basketball in 1974, and volleyball in 1975.

Dick Matter coached the basketball team in its first five seasons, beginning in 1974-75. Two years later, in the 1976-77 season, the Illinois

Top Row — Johnson, Vernberg, Coburn, Johnson, coach, Van Wonterghem, Alsterlund, Caddy.
Bottom Row—Cowley, Long, Duncan, Thorngren.

M, 1929

During the 1910s through the 1930s, girl's teams representing each of the four classes at Moline High School competed against one another in basketball and other activities. The junior class team, shown here, won the school's basketball competition in 1929.

state girls tournament was initiated, with Sterling winning the championship. The following season, in the second state tournament, Moline placed third, losing to Mattoon by one point in the semi-finals. (IHSA, online)

From 1974 through 2013, the Moline girls compiled a 677-373 record, a winning percentage of 64.5. They won the regional tournament 24 times and placed third at state in 1978 and fourth in 1989. They lost only three games in the 1988-89 season, one of them to the previous year's state champion, the Maine West Warriors. The game brought in a crowd of 1,700 fans to Wharton on a Saturday afternoon. The win for the number-one ranked Warriors extended their winning streak to 37 games over two seasons. Again in 2009-10, the Moliners lost only three games. That season they broke the all-time single-season scoring record for the team and for girls basketball at Wharton by defeating Galesburg 97-53. Three-time All-State honoree Marquisha Harris led the individual scoring with 18 points.

M, 1975

Another first-year girls' game at the Field House.

Quad Cities Online, February 11, 2010

Three-time All-State player Marquisha Harris soars for a basket at Wharton in a game against Galesburg in 2010.

C. Roseman, 2012

The girl's team reached the Sweet Sixteen ten times through 2013.

Wharton Home Court Advantage. According to Moline High Athletic Department records from 1986 through 2013, the Moline girls had a home court winning percentage of 69.6. This compares to a 63.5 percent win rate for away games. Included in the calculation are 260 games at home and 461 away, not counting state tournament games, but including regular-season tournament games.

Girls Basketball Coaches at Moline High School

Coach	Years	Record	Winning Percentage
Dick Matter	1974-79	67-13	84
Jim Gager	1979-81	19-24	44
Paul Carther	1981-83	4-37	10
Jack DeVilder	1983-86	56-22	72
Chad Steckel	1995-96	13-16	45
Rommel Foy	1996-99	40-40	50
Steve Ford	1999-2013	305-138	69

Source: Illinois High School Association, online; Moline High School Athletic Department

The names of the Moline girls who have earned all-state honors are proudly displayed on banners astride the broadcasting booth in Wharton Field House. Ten girls have received the honor, Marquisha Harris three times.

In Support of Basketball and Other Sports

In addition to parent and community support of high school athletics, a variety of student groups have brought excitement and entertainment to basketball games and other sporting events. Before 1944, cheers were usually led by a single male, sometimes called a "yell master" or "yell leader." Beginning in 1944, female "cheerleaders" made their first Wharton appearance, at the Monmouth game in January in front of 2,000 fans. From that time forward, female cheerleaders have been an integral part of the scene at Wharton Field House.

That initial group was led by sophomore Joline Schieberl, who became widely known for her acrobatic performances. The Moline cheerleaders so impressed the fans at the 1945 state basketball tournament that Joline and her teammates Betty Randle and Frances Martens were pictured in the Champaign *News-Gazette* (March 18). The headline for the accompanying story coined a phrase that stuck: "Joline of Moline, No. 1 Tourney Cheerleader, Hales from Hollywood." Before moving to Moline, Joline had danced and played bit parts in movies, including *Hitler's Madness, Previous Freedom*, and *I Surrender.*

M, 1947

M, 1948

The team of cheerleaders on the left, pictured in the 1947 *M*, included one male member, Gene Mitchell. Surrounding him are Zee Wheeler, Joline Schieberl, and Jean Mullen. In 1948 (right) the all-female cheerleading squad was composed of Anna Mary Sheridan, Zoe Ann Wheeler, Joline Schieberl, Joy Shipley, and June Miller.

M, 1996

C. Roseman, 2013

Cheerleaders performing at Wharton Field House, 1996 and 2013.

Other student groups have contributed support as well. The pep band regularly performs from its station high in the center of the north balcony. In some years boys served as ushers or swept the basketball floor at halftime, and girls performed baton-twirling routines. And for many seasons, beginning in 1959, a girls' Pep Club cheered on the Maroons with pompons in hand, from a special section in the stands (at both basketball and football games).

M, 1961

M, 1968

On the left are Girls' Pep Club members in the north bleachers at Wharton with their white blouses and maroon and white shakers forming an "M." This photograph was taken during their second season, 1960-61, when the club was sponsored by Judy Brooks. On the right, 1968 Pep Club supervisor Bob Moore, to whom this book is dedicated, is shown with club members Betty Payden, Beth Petrovich, and Wendy Petrovich. They are unpacking new pompons for use at basketball and football games.

M, 1998

M, 2004

The Contemporaries, 1998 and 2004 at Wharton Field House.

Rivaling the cheerleaders in popularity at basketball and football games are the Contemporaires, who perform well-choreographed dance routines. According to Pat Shannon, the ensemble was founded in the 1950s by Frances Leimkuehler as a modern dance club and performed mostly at Christmas Vespers. In the early sixties, first Jan Ehlers and then Carol Youngquist coached the troupe and expanded their performances to include the half-time show of one football game and one basketball game. In 1969, Shannon initiated a physical education class for dance that met at the same time as the marching band. The name Contemporaires was coined and the group then began performing at all half-time shows for football and basketball games. Mrs. Shannon continued directing the Contemporaires until 2000.

C. Roseman, 2013

Students dressed in all manner of costumes comprised the Moline High basketball cheering section in 2013. "Super fan" Dexter Johnson is seated at the lower left.

Moline High School sports designated "super fan" is Dexter Johnson, pictured here in 2012. Dexter follows sports closely, befriends scores of students, and plays the very important role of sweeping the basketball floor between games and at half-time. A previous "super fan" was Bob "Waxy" Waxenberg, who closely followed Moline sports for most of his life, appearing not only at competitions in most sports but also showing up at most practice sessions. Waxie passed away at age 74 in October 1997 while attending a Moline football game at Ottawa.

C. Roseman, 2012

College Basketball

Numerous early college basketball games at Wharton involved local four-year institutions, St. Ambrose and Augustana colleges. The Field House offered them the opportunity to draw much larger crowds than their own gyms or other venues would accommodate. On a few occasions the Field House was chosen for games against major university squads.

When the St. Ambrose Saints played the University of Iowa team in January 1933, both the crowd and the outcome were predictable. The local lads lost to Iowa, 44-24 before 5,000 fans. It was not only the size of the college-game crowd, but its behavior that represented a significant milestone for the facility. It was the last time smoking would be permitted in the main arena of the Field House, although for decades thereafter men smoked in their basement restroom at the northwest corner of the building. Van Vooren and Dye (2008) reported on the 1933 situation:

> The crowd of 5,000 includes lots of smokers who light up in droves at half time. The resulting cloud reduces visibility and impairs the players. Beginning with the next home game, cigarettes are banned inside the building. Return passes are issued to those wanting to get outside to have a smoke.

M, 1945

In this photograph of a high school game at Wharton from the 1945 *M*, the "No Smoking" sign is visible on the balcony railing.

The prospect of another big crowd, this time cheering in smoke-free air, must have stimulated the Saints to schedule another game with the Hawkeyes a year later. Expecting a record-breaking crowd, extra bleachers were built to raise the Field House seating capacity to 6,000. Admission prices were set at the same level as those at Iowa home games: 40 cents for general admission and 75 cents for reserved seats. Telegraph wires were extended to the Field House to allow transmission of play-by-play reports to Des Moines and Chicago, and "representatives of newspapers from a vicinity of 100 miles will be in the press stands." (*Argus*, January 22 and 27, 1934) The day before the game (January 26) the *Dispatch* chimed in: "It is likely that the Hawkeyes, who already have played before 60,700 persons in eight games, will be seen by the capacity crowd of about 6,000."

But all the hype neither helped the St. Ambrose team nor the attendance. Iowa won again, 39-18, in front of a crowd of 3,500 people. Lynn Callaway of the *Dispatch* (January 29) explained: "Perfect weather conditions attended the game so the failure of the event to attract a capacity crowd must be attributed to a general feeling among cage fans that the Saints would not be able to hold the Big Ten team in check." (In the late 1930s, the St. Ambrose team nickname was changed from the Saints to the Bees, which later became the Fighting Bees.)

On December 29, 1933, the Augustana basketball team practiced at the Field House to "accustom themselves to the floor" in preparation for a game the next day with the University of Illinois (*Chicago Tribune*, December 29). But the Illini did not draw any better than the Hawkeyes. Callaway of the *Dispatch* summarized the event:

> Illinois basketball players were too powerful for Augustana in the field house Saturday night, but most of the thrills for 3,500 fans who saw the university cagers triumph, 37-27, were furnished by Mervin Horton of Moline and John Schroder of Rock Island, a brilliant pair of Vikings. Between them they scored

all of Augustana's ten field goals and half of the six free throws the Vikings managed to make out of twenty chances at the foul line [!] . . . The contest, sponsored by the Moline Junior Association of Commerce, failed to attract a crowd as large as the one which saw Iowa trim St. Ambrose about a year ago, but was a good turnout for the holiday season considering the weather. (*Dispatch*, January 1, 1934)

The following season, on February 25, 1935, Augustana met St. Ambrose at the Field House. The Vikings won "by the decisive score of 41 to 33. The game was witnessed by 3,000 frenzied fans, the largest number ever to attend a basketball contest between the two schools" (Augustana *Observer*, February 28). However, large crowds were not always present for college games. One such case was a double-header on Saturday, December 16, 1939, in which Augustana lost to Warrensburg (now Central Missouri State) 36-28 and St. Ambrose lost to Western Kentucky Teachers College 40-32. The attendance was about 1,000. Willard Anderson, sports columnist for the *Observer* (December 20) commiserated:

> Augustana College has the misfortune of being located in one of the hottest high school athletic spots of the state as evidenced by the miserable attendance of the attractive college basketball doubleheader Saturday, in the Moline field house. The night before many more faces streamed into the same place to watch Moline wallop Monmouth. While it is only natural that the townspeople of Moline, Rock Island and East Moline should be interested chiefly in their own high school teams, the situation is none too healthy financially for the athletic setup of Augustana.

Augustana drew a bit better two weeks later, when the Vikings took on the reigning national champion University of Oregon on December 27, 1939. The game was part of a double-header at the Field House, with Moline High School facing Cedar Rapids Franklin in the other game. The *Observer* (January 11, 1940) lamented the outcome:

> Before 3,000 fans in the Moline field house, Dec. 27, Augustana's listless Vikings gave way to a superior force – the University of Oregon – to the tune of 57-22. Moline High crushed Franklin of Cedar Rapids in the preliminary tilt 41-13. Only in the early minutes of the game did the Norse aggregation [Augustana] play on even terms with the Oregon juggernaut.

The Ducks, First National Champs. Exactly nine months before playing Augustana, Oregon had beaten Ohio State, 46-33, in the championship game of the first ever NCAA basketball tournament, which was held at Northwestern University in Evanston. When they played Augustana in December, the NCAA champs were on a 7,500-mile trip, meeting teams through the East and Midwest. Included was a game against Long Island University at Madison Square Garden in New York in front of 17,500 fans. The Oregon Ducks lost that game 56-55, the winning basket for LIU having been made by "Dolly" King, who later became one of the first African Americans to play in the National Basketball League. In the latter stages of the trip Oregon had lost to Purdue and DePaul, and the night before playing at Wharton, to Western State Teachers College (now Western Illinois University) 42-40 in front of a packed house in Macomb. (*Argus*, December 27, 1939)

During World War II, on January 5, 1943, the Augustana basketball team played a military team from Camp Grant (Rockford, Illinois) in a game sponsored by the Moline Junior Association of Commerce. Two weeks earlier Grant had beaten the University of Illinois "Whiz Kids," a team that was otherwise undefeated that season. One of the Whiz Kids was Gene Vance, who a few years later would play at the Field House for the Tri-Cities Blackhawks. Camp Grant's team included five players who were All-Americans in college, three of whom would play professional basketball after college! Predictably, they beat the Vikings 59-43 at Wharton before a crowd of 2,500.

Augustana probably was again disappointed in the turnout for its holiday basketball tourney, December 29, 1947, through January 1, 1948. Joining the Vikings were teams from St. Ambrose, Cornell (Iowa), Monmouth, Knox, Illinois College, Western Illinois State, and Northern Illinois State. Both Augustana and St. Ambrose lost in the first round in front of 1,500 fans. The crowd was thin partly because of tough winter weather, which only turned worse as the tourney progressed. On New Year's Eve, the semi-final games were played "before about 350 hardy customers who braved glare ice to drive, walk, or crawl to the field house." Then on January 1st, "about two hundred spectators waded through deep snow drifts" to see Western beat Northern, 60-57, for the championship (*Dispatch*, January 2).

In the late 1940s, Missouri Valley Conference teams, including St. Louis and Bradley Universities, played some games at Wharton, but never again would Big Ten basketball teams visit the Field House. Beginning in 1949, Moline Community College played home games at Wharton for many years. After becoming Black Hawk College in 1961 and moving to a new campus in the late 1960s, most of their home games were played at the gym on their Moline campus.

Finally, a Home for the Bees. Not having a large basketball facility of their own, St. Ambrose College (now University) in Davenport played home basketball games at various locations during the late 1940s and 1950s. Between 1952 and 1958, they played a number of home games at Wharton, some on Sunday afternoons. They also played at the Rock Island Armory, Davenport High School's George Marshall Gymnasium, and the small LeClaire Gym on the St. Ambrose campus. Beginning with the 1958-59 season, they began playing home games at the new Assumption High School gym, which is located near the St. Ambrose campus and seats 3,400. Then in 1983 the Bees moved home games to their new Lee Lohman Arena, which seats about 2,000.

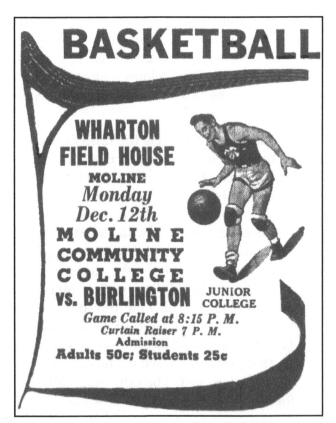

Dispatch, February 12, 1946

Among the major college basketball games played at the Field House was this match between St. Louis and Long Island Universities in February 1946.

Dispatch, December 9, 1949

The Moline Community College "Comets" played scores of home games at Wharton, beginning in 1949. During that first MCC basketball season, Moline High School graduate Joline Schieberl, "Joline of Moline," was the head cheerleader.

Sauk, 1966

Morrie Chambers goes up for a basket in a Black Hawk College game against Joliet Junior College in 1966.

Dispatch, December 9, 1949

In the fall of 1949, a new wrestling room was opened at the northeast corner of the Field House, below the dressing rooms and showers used by wrestlers on the second floor. In this photograph Coach Joe Vavrus is watching over the young grapplers.

Moline Individual State Wrestling Champions

Year	Name	Weight
1950	John Ontiveros	103 pounds
1951	John Ontiveros	112 pounds
1952	Alan Waxenberg	133 pounds
1953	Dick Duck	112 pounds
1954	Paul Hoffman	133 pounds
1969	Dwight McHenry	138 pounds
1969	Paul Carther	Heavyweight
1973	Roger Angell	138 pounds
1975 (Class 2A)	Kevin Puebla	126 pounds
1980 (2A)	Poppy Guerrero	132 pounds
1997 (2A)	Matt Lackey	145 pounds
1998 (2A)	Matt Lackey	152 pounds
2003 (2A)	A. J. Lavender	125 pounds

Source: IHSA, online

Wrestling: High School and College

During the 1946-47 school year wrestling was introduced at Moline High School. Joe Vavrus, a Moline High School teacher who had been a member of the Northwestern University team, started from scratch to build the wrestling program. Beginning in the fall of 1949, the team had a new wrestling room at the Field House and began holding some of their home meets there. When Vavrus retired in 1974, his record was 231 wins, 134 losses and 11 ties. In 1973, Vavrus was inducted into the Illinois Wrestling Coaches and Officials Association Hall of Fame.

Moline won two Illinois state team wrestling championships, one in 1969 at Champaign and the other in 1996 at Normal. In each case, one match determined the outcome: In 1969 heavyweight Paul Carther pinned his opponent to edge out North Chicago 33-32, and in 1996 112-pound Joel Catour pinned his opponent to beat Conant of Hoffman Estates 30-29.

Although some high school matches were held at Wharton in the 1960s, most were held at the high school gyms until the 1980s, when coach Todd Rosenthal moved selected matches to Wharton. Until 1997 only two circles could be accommodated there, both positioned on

C. Roseman, 2013

One of two state championship wrestling banners proudly displayed at Wharton Field House.

Courtesy of Todd Rosenthal

Four circles were used for the 4A state wrestling championships held at Wharton in 2004.

C. Roseman, 2013

A slightly different arrangement was used for this February 2013 tournament. Two circles were over the basketball court, and two nestled up against the retracted south bleachers on the left.

Moline coach Joe Vavrus (center) seems quite happy to be flanked by two 1969 Illinois state high school wrestling champions, Dwight McHenry (left) and Paul Carther. Vavrus is admiring the trophy awarded for the first state team championship won by Moline since he founded the program 23 years earlier.

M, 1969

M, 2003

The 2003 Moline wrestling team posed for this photograph in front of the Wharton Field House balcony.

the raised basketball floor. After the raised floor was eliminated, four circles could be used. The new four-circle arrangement allowed the Field House to host three state team wrestling tournaments, in 2003, 2004, and 2008. The first two were regularly scheduled meets. The 2008 meet was to have been held at Northern Illinois University in DeKalb, but was moved to Wharton at the last minute because a shooting had occurred on its campus.

Although collegiate wrestling events were few at Wharton, one stands out. The University of Illinois, ranked 17th in the nation, used Wharton Field House on February 1, 1987, to host a meet with 18th-ranked Northwestern and the nine-time defending national champion and 4th-ranked University of Iowa. The idea for the twin dual meet came from Moline High School Coach Todd Rosenthal, Kevin Puebla, and Mark Johnson. Puebla was assistant coach at the

University of Illinois, and a former state championship wrestler from Moline. He later went on to coach wrestling at Augustana College for 13 years. Mark Johnson was Iowa assistant coach, and former star wrestler at Alleman High School and the University of Michigan. Johnson went on to serve as the head wrestling coach at the University of Illinois for 17 seasons.

The Iowa Hawkeyes came into the meet with a string of 84 dual meet victories against Big Ten teams, seventy of them under head coach Dan Gable. In the Sunday afternoon event, which was witnessed by 3,500 people, Iowa defeated Northwestern and Illinois, and Northwestern defeated Illinois. Gable said that he loves meets like this; "it's like a three ring circus with something going on all the time" (*Dispatch*, February 2, 1987).

Courtesy of Todd Rosenthal

Signed program cover for the 1987 collegiate wrestling meet at Wharton Field House.

Lake County (IL) Discovery Museum, Curt Teich Postcard Archives

The birthplace of championship college wrestling at the University of Iowa, the Iowa Field House, was opened in January 1927. As it was being constructed, the Iowa City Press-Citizen (September 15, 1926) described the facility as "the largest structure of its kind in the world. With a length of 464 feet . . . and a width of 430 feet . . . the field house will contain five and one half million square feet of space." The completed structure included a basketball arena seating about 12,000 spectators, the world's largest indoor track, and 5,000 lockers. When built, its 60- by 150-foot pool was the largest competition pool in the world, and swim meets could accommodate 3,500 spectators.

The "world's largest field house" was the home of numerous Big 10 championships in wrestling, swimming, and gymnastics. Before Carver-Hawkeye Arena opened in 1983, it also was home for Iowa basketball games and hosted four NCAA regional basketball tournaments. Fifteen of the annual Iowa state high school basketball tournaments were played at the field house in Iowa City. Davenport High won the state championship there five times. In an amazing run, the Blue Devils were there every year between 1947 and 1952, winning the championship four times in that six-year stretch. The fact that Davenport was the largest high school in Iowa at the time probably did not hurt its chances!

Volleyball state banners at Wharton. The last three, 2001, 2002 and 2005, were earned while the team played home matches at the Field House.

M, 2007

M, 2011

Two views of Moline High School volleyball in the Field House. On the left, the team huddles at center court and on the right Lexie Holst prepares to hit the ball.

High School Volleyball

Interscholastic girls volleyball competition began at Moline High School in 1975 under the direction of Debby Wheeler. In that first year, they won all four games at the district tournament before being beaten by Rock Falls in the sectional. The team gained its highest ever state standing in 1985, placing fourth in the 2A class. But the team did not play home matches at Wharton Field House until 1997. Moline coach Jack Wheeler commented on the switch. "I think it will be an improved place to play and it will be an improved place to watch from and maybe that will encourage more people to come out and see volleyball" (*Dispatch*, September 5). In 2002 they took their first Western Big 6 Conference championship, beating out Quincy who had won ten straight years. Beginning that year, the Moliners won seven conference titles in a row.

This historic clock has stood forth on the south wall of the Field House for decades. Beside it is a plaque honoring Adolf "Oppie" Oppenheimer, who for 45 years was the director of physical education for the Moline schools. He was a pioneer in organized physical training for school children and was an early advocate for physical activities for girls.

C. Roseman, 2011

Physical Education Events

Over the years, a variety of other activities related to physical education have been part of the Wharton Field House scene. We close this chapter with the story of one such activity in the early twentieth century and the person who organized it. Beginning in 1895, Adolph "Oppie" Oppenheimer, supervisor of physical training for the Moline schools, organized outdoor physical education programs involving hundreds of children and thousands of spectators. Previously called "Calisthenics Days," they became "Field Days" in 1913 when they were first held at Browning Field.

The last of Oppenheimer's events was inside the Field House. It was held in the spring of 1935, a few months before he died at the age of 69 as the result of injuries from an automobile accident. The two-evening event was called a "Gym-Fest." (*Dispatch*, May 3) On the first evening, a Thursday, not only did 1,000 public school children – fifth grade through high school – perform in front of an audience of 2,500, but adults from the Moline Turner Society also put on a gymnastics demonstration. The evening was organized as a benefit for Richard "Lefty" Wendt, who had been seriously injured in a football game against Davenport High School the previous fall. Wendt received a "thundering ovation" when he was introduced to the crowd.

The second evening attracted even more fans and featured various activities by Moline school children and performances by members of the University of Iowa gymnastics team. Among the latter was a star tumbler, George Nissen of Cedar Rapids, who had been crowned the 1935 national tumbling champion at the Eastern Intercollegiate Championships in Cambridge, Massachusetts (Munn, 2012). Nissen is known as "the father of the trampoline," having invented the contraption with his gymnastics coach and having spent a career manufacturing, selling, and promoting trampolines.

Dispatch, May 1, 1935

This advertisement for the 1935 "Gym-Fest" at Wharton Field House mentions an extra charge of 15 cents for reserved seats; 140 of them were made available, all in the north balcony.

Chapter 4

Professional Basketball at Wharton

"Cars were backed up across the Bettendorf bridge . . . It was one of the saddest days of my life. We had to turn away at least 3,000 people. Kids were crying all over the place."
–promoter Mike Fitzgerald

The Field House already had been the scene of some fabulous basketball – mostly high school, some college – when the pros entered the scene in 1946. Thereafter, two local professional teams held forth there, the major league Blackhawks from 1946 to 1951 and the minor league Thunder from 1987 to 1993. Annual visits by the Harlem Globetrotters and occasional visits by non-local National Basketball Association (NBA) teams rounded out the pro scene.

The National Basketball League and the Origin of the Tri-Cities Blackhawks

In the immediate post-World War II period, professional basketball was just emerging as a major sport. It had been more than twenty years since professional football went through a similar nascent stage when the Rock Island Independents were charter members of the National Football League. Since the 1920s several pro basketball leagues had come and gone. The most robust was the National Basketball League (NBL), which was formed in 1937.

The accompanying table lists all of the teams that played in the NBL during its twelve years of existence. The league started with thirteen teams in 1937, some sponsored by companies as implied by their names and some that had origins as travelling "barnstorming" professional teams. The NBL included teams not only in big cities but also small and medium-sized markets, especially in the Midwest. Some of the teams persisted in smaller cities for a number of years before moving to bigger places in the 1950s, such

National Basketball League Teams, 1937-1949

1937-41, Akron (OH) Firestone Non-Skids
1937-42, Akron Goodyear Wingfoots
1946-49, Anderson (IN) Duffey Packers
1937-38 and fall 1946, Buffalo Bisons
1939-42, Chicago Bruins
1942-43, Chicago Studebaker Flyers
1944-47, Chicago American Gears
1937-38, Cincinnati Comellos
1943-44, Cleveland Chase Brassmen
1944-46, Cleveland Allmen Transfers
1938-39, Columbus Athletic Supply
1937-38, Dayton Metropolitans
1948-49, Denver Nuggets
1939-41, Detroit Eagles
1946-47, Detroit Gems
1948-49, Detroit Vagabond Kings/Dayton Rens
1947-48, Flint (MI) Dow A.C.'s/Midland (MI) Dow A.C.'s
1937-38, Fort Wayne (IN) General Electrics
1941-48, Fort Wayne Zollner Pistons
1938-41, Hammond (IN) Ciesar All-Americans
1948-49, Hammond Calumet Buccaneers
1937-48, Indianapolis Kautskys
1937-38, Kankakee (IL) Gallagher Trojans
1947-48, Minneapolis Lakers
1937-49, Oshkosh (WI) All-Stars
1937-39, Pittsburgh Pirates
1944-45, Pittsburgh Raiders
1945-48, Rochester (NY) Royals
1938-49, Sheboygan (WI) Red Skins
1946-49, Syracuse Nationals
1941-43, Toledo Jim White Chevrolets
1946-48, Toledo Jeeps
1946-49, Tri-Cities Blackhawks
1937-38, Warren (PA) Penns
1938-39, Warren Penns/Cleveland White Horses
1948-49, Waterloo (IA) Hawks
1937-38, Whiting (IN) Ciesar All-Americans
1945-47, Youngstown (OH) Bears

Source: Professional Basketball, online.

as the Fort Wayne Zollner Pistons, Rochester Royals, and Tri-Cities Blackhawks. Others experienced a fleeting existence of only a year or two, such as the Kankakee Gallagher Trojans, Warren Penns, and Youngstown Bears.

The league continued operating during World War II, even though it had six or fewer teams during four seasons. The league expanded in the post-war years; the 1946-47 NBL season started with twelve teams from: Oshkosh and Sheboygan (Wisconsin); Indianapolis, Anderson, and Fort Wayne (Indiana); Toledo and Youngstown (Ohio); Rochester, Syracuse, and Buffalo (New York); in addition to Chicago, and Detroit. (Basketball Historian, online)

In early December 1946, a livestock show was being held at the International Amphitheatre, home of the Gears, Chicago's National Basketball League team. As a result, their December 6th game with the Syracuse Nationals was moved to Moline. The Syracuse team had just acquired Mike Novak, "a six-foot nine-inch giant," for $5,000, the largest amount ever paid for a player in the NBL. Novak was to guard another big man, George Mikan, who was playing for the Gears in his first year as a professional after having been an All-American at DePaul University. Receiving $12,000 a year, Mikan was the highest-paid professional basketball player at the time. He went on to be the first truly outstanding big man in the pro game, and would visit the Field House on a regular basis when he

played with the Minneapolis Lakers. In the 1946 game at Wharton, Mikan out-scored Novak, 20-8, but the Nationals beat the Gears, 57-55. It was a double-header that evening with the NBL Oshkosh All-Stars playing the Chicago Negro Collegians in an exhibition game, which was won by Oshkosh, 43-20. This first-ever professional basketball event at Wharton Field House drew a crowd of 4,000. (Kiesele, 1946)

Earlier in 1946, two salesmen who had worked together at Jacobs Brothers sports concession firm, Leo Ferris and Ben Kerner, founded a new NBL team in Buffalo, the Bisons. Things were not going well early in their first season, so the pair looked elsewhere for a team location. Having known of the Quad Cities and hearing that 4,000 people showed up for the Gears-Nationals game, they made contact with Bryan Grafton of Rock Island. Grafton recruited several local businessmen to buy stock in an unnamed team to move from Buffalo. Included were Clell Harrelson and Paul Suverkrup of Moline. The decision to move the Bisons west was made in December 1946, after the team had played only thirteen games in Buffalo.

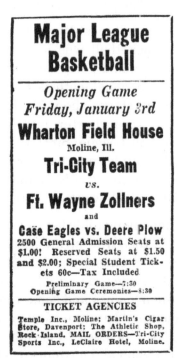

Argus, January 1, 1947

The first Blackhawks game was advertised in the *Argus* on New Year's Day 1947 before the team name had been chosen.

Flip Plays Again at Wharton. The Chicago Negro Collegians were considered the "Negro champs of the nation." Competing in their thirteenth season, the team played as amateurs for their first nine years, winning the Central AAU (Amateur Athletic Union) championship twice. Beginning in 1942 they played over three hundred games as a travelling professional team. Two players had been with the team for its entire history, Al "Big Train" Johnson and Agis "Speed" Bray. Moline High School star from the 1930s, Flip Anders "donned cage togs to help out the Collegians but weight and age showed its ravages as he was unable to contribute much to the attack." (Kiesele, 1946)

The temperature was well below zero when the Blackhawks opened on Friday evening, Jan. 3, 1947. The 3,500 attendance was almost as high as the total attendance at the thirteen Bison home games in Buffalo the previous fall. The Blackhawks lost 52-47 to the Fort Wayne Zollner Pistons, the defending champions of the NBL. Among the Blackhawks playing that evening were seven-footer Don Otten who scored nine and Wilbur "Florsheim" Schu who had joined the team an hour before the game started and did not score. Six days later the Blackhawks won their first game, 57-42, over the Detroit Gems, which attracted a smaller crowd to Wharton, about 1,700. Pop Gates led the Blackhawks in scoring with 20 points.

Argus, January 3, 1947

Coach Nat Hickey and player Nick Grunzweig watch seven-footer Don Otten dunk the ball at the Blackhawks' first practice on January 2, 1947. Hickey and Grunzweig were wearing Buffalo Bison uniforms because the Blackhawks' uniforms had not yet arrived.

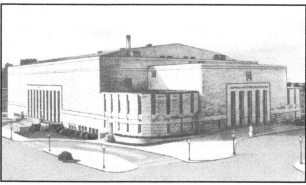

1940s Postcard

The Bisons played their thirteen basketball games in the fall of 1946 at the Buffalo Memorial Auditorium. "The Aud," as it was locally known, was built in 1940 with Depression-era federal funds and originally seated over 12,000. Given the size of the arena and the meager size of the 1946 pro basketball crowds, those games must have been played with noticeable echoing of basketballs and shoes meeting the floor, along with banter among players and coaches. Like Wharton, this all-purpose arena was home to a wide variety of entertainment, sporting, and other events over the years. To accommodate new major league professional hockey and basketball teams in 1971, its roof was raised 24 feet and an upper deck was added. This increased the Aud's capacity to 17,000 for basketball. In 1996, major sports events were moved to a new facility nearby, now called the First Niagara Center. The Aud was torn down in 2009. (Sabres Alumni, online)

National Basketball League teams who played the Blackhawks at Wharton Field House.

National Basketball League, 1946-49

1946-47

Eastern Division	Wins	Losses
Rochester Royals	31	13
Fort Wayne Zollner Pistons	25	19
Toledo Jeeps	21	23
Syracuse Nationals	21	23
Buffalo Bisons/Tri-Cities Blackhawks	**19**	**25**
Youngstown Bears	12	32

Western Division	Wins	Losses
Oshkosh All-Stars	28	16
Indianapolis Kautskys	27	17
Chicago American Gears	26	18
Sheboygan Red Skins	26	18
Anderson Duffey Packers	24	20
Detroit Gems	4	40

1947-48

Eastern Division	Wins	Losses
Rochester Royals	44	16
Anderson Duffey Packers	42	18
Fort Wayne Zollner Pistons	40	20
Syracuse Nationals	24	36
Toledo Jeeps	22	37
Flint Dow A.C.'s/Midland Dow A.C.'s	8	52

Western Division	Wins	Losses
Minneapolis Lakers	43	17
Tri-Cities Blackhawks	**30**	**30**
Oshkosh All-Stars	29	31
Indianapolis Kautskys	24	35
Sheboygan Red Skins	23	37

1948-49

Eastern Division	Wins	Losses
Anderson Duffey Packers	49	15
Syracuse Nationals	40	23
Hammond Calumet Buccaneers	21	41
Detroit Vagabond Kings/Dayton Rens	16	43

Western Division	Wins	Losses
Oshkosh All-Stars	37	27
Tri-Cities Blackhawks	**36**	**28**
Sheboygan Red Skins	35	29
Waterloo Hawks	30	32
Denver Nuggets	18	44

Source: NBL, online

The Blackhawks in the NBL

The Blackhawks played in the National Basketball League for three seasons before joining the new National Basketball Association (NBA) in 1949. Their NBL season records gradually improved, from 19-25 in their first to 36-28 in their third. First year attendance at Wharton steadily increased, with the largest crowd, 4,400, appearing for the season finale against Fort Wayne. Don Doxie observed in the Quad-City *Times* (February 4, 1996): "It came after the team was eliminated from the playoffs and it sent a message. Ferris immediately announced that the team would return for the 1947-48 season."

The first-year Blackhawks were led by player-coach Nat Hickey, who had been playing professional basketball since the early 1920s. Hickey played in eight games the first season and three games the next season at age 44 and 45. Then in early 1948, while coaching the Providence Steamrollers, he put himself in one game two days before his 46th birthday, becoming the oldest person ever to play professional basketball in the United States. (Hoopedia, online)

Among the star players for that first Blackhawks team was Don Otten from Bowling Green State in Ohio. One of the early big men in professional basketball, Otten led the team in scoring each of the three seasons the Blackhawks played in the NBL.

High Elevation? Former mayor of Moline, Stan Leach, who served as the "towel boy" for the Blackhawks, remembers that Otten was not in the best of shape. He could run up and down the court only a few times before having to visit the bench to take in oxygen, which was guarded by Leach.

Pop Gates and the Integration of Professional Basketball

William "Pop" Gates, one of the first African Americans to play professional basketball in a major league, joined the Buffalo team in the fall of 1946, then came to Moline with the team in December of that year. Some African Americans had played in the NBL for short periods in the early 1940s. Then in 1946-47 two African Americans played full seasons, Gates with Buffalo and Tri-Cities, and William "Dolly" King with the Rochester Royals. This actually predates the first African American player to join the baseball major leagues. Jackie Robinson had been signed to a contract in 1946 but did not play major league baseball for the Brooklyn Dodgers until the spring of 1947.

Gates grew up in New York City and was given the nickname "Pop" by his peers when he played stick ball with older kids. He began his basketball career in the late 1930s with the Renaissance Big Five, the "Rens," a team based in Harlem made up of all African American players. For years they barnstormed across the East, Midwest, and South. Gates played professionally into the 1950s. Reflecting on his long career, he said: "I participated in over 1,500 games . . . I averaged 14 points a game when 14 were a lot of points." (*New York Times*, December 5, 1999)

Todd Gould, in his 1998 book, *Pioneers of the Hardwood*, writes that Gates felt good about joining the NBL. Gates observed that he had been playing two games a day with the Rens, and now was making more money playing two games a week with the Blackhawks. He also felt accepted by fellow players, although ". . . there are always one or two guys out there who are going to object." Peterson (1990) quoted Gates on his Moline experience:

> As far as the team was concerned, I had no problems. But our home base was Moline, and they were used to keeping blacks out of hotels. I did stay in a hotel two days. Then came one of the team owners – Cliff Ferris or Leo Ferris – and we had a very heated discussion about pulling me out of there. I said, 'I want to stay with the team. I'm part of the team, I think I should stay with them.' However, they prevailed and I would be shunted up to a YMCA there. Later that season, a guy in Rock Island – he was reputed to be one of the mob people operating out of Chicago – said I could stay in a hotel he had. A certain number of players on the team said, 'We're going to stay with Pop over at the Rock Island hotel.' I've forgotten the name of it. There was Wilbur Schu, Don Otten and other ballplayers, maybe five of us.

On February 24, 1947, when the Blackhawks were playing at the Syracuse Nationals, Gates faced another problem. Upset at the officials for some calls against the Nationals, hundreds of fans came out of the stands after Gates, who had fouled by "Chick" Meehan. One fan pulled a knife and numerous fights broke out. (Delaney and Madigan, 2009) The *Dispatch* (February 25) added that Gates and Meehan were "engaged in fisticuffs. Meehan was forced out of the game with a cut over his eye. Gates was rushed out of the armory by police." The Blackhawks lost to the Nationals, 53-47, breaking a seven game winning streak. Meehan committed five fouls, Gates three.

Argus, December 24, 1948

Pop Gates is pictured here in December 1948 when he was player-coach for the NBL Dayton Rens. After playing 41 games for the Bisons/Blackhawks in 1946-47, he had gone back to play for the barnstorming Rens. Then in December 1948, Gates led the Dayton Rens into the NBL as a replacement for the Detroit Vagabond Kings, which folded with a 2-17 record. The all-black team finished out the season in an otherwise all-white league. Gates then joined the Harlem Globetrotters in 1949 as a player-coach. He would again visit the Field House, both with the Rens and the Globetrotters.

Although the NBL had a history of playing some African Americans, none were hired to continue in the league after the 1946-47 season, although the all-Black Dayton Rens played in the league during the 1948-49 season. The NBA, which started in 1949-50, did not accept its first African American player until the following season. Within a few years thereafter African Americans would play a transformative role in American basketball.

A Four-Man Zone in Mattoon. The Blackhawks played a few games on neutral courts, in big cities such as Chicago and New York, as well as small places including Jeffersonville, Indiana, and Sioux City and Muscatine, Iowa. One of the more memorable was on January 7, 1949, when they lost to the Dayton Rens, 51-49, in Mattoon, Illinois, located more-or-less halfway between Moline and Dayton. With over four minutes to go in the game, two of the Rens players – Pop Gates and Jim Usry – fouled out, leaving the team with only four players. The Rens were leading and held on for the win by employing a four-man zone defense. (*Argus*, January 8)

Argus, December 18, 1947

Most NBL players had competed in college basketball before joining the "World's Best" professional league.

Year Two in the NBL, 1947-48

The first Blackhawks coach, Nat Hickey, compiled a 19-25 record in 1946-47, followed by an 8-12 start during the next season. However, it was not enough to sustain his job. In late December 1947 he was replaced by another player-coach, Bobby McDermott, who had been named in 1946 as the greatest player in NBL history and was later inducted into the Basketball Hall of Fame. With McDermott at the helm, and on the floor, the team recovered to gain an even record at the end of the season, with thirty wins and thirty losses.

The Blackhawks started the 1948 NBL Western Division playoffs by defeating the Indianapolis Kautskys in a five-game series. Then they met the eventual league-champion Minneapolis Lakers in a best-of-three series for the divisional title. The Blackhawks lost two straight – the first in front of 5,569 at Wharton, 98-79; the second

Argus, November 10, 1947

The *Argus* accompanied this photograph with the caption: "IT'S JUST A GAME, FELLOWS – But there's warning in the wagging finger of Referee Frank Scanlon (left) as Umpire Max Tabacchi (center) and Coach Nat Hickey of the Blackhawks eloquently discuss a ruling taking away a basket by the Hawks in last night's 57-56 victory for the quad-city team over Oshkosh at Wharton fieldhouse. Tabacchi did not hear the horn for an Oshkosh sub to enter the game before a throw-in from the sidelines gave Whitey Von Neida the opening for the basket. Naturally, the officials won."

Dispatch, December 31, 1947

Bobby McDermott was the leading scorer in NBL history, amassing 3.582 points in 287 games. He began playing professionally in 1934, joined the NBL in 1941, and was named to the All-League team in his first six seasons in the NBL. During the season before joining the Blackhawks, he led the Chicago Gears to the NBL championship as player-coach. (NBA Hoops, online) McDermott played his first game for the Blackhawks as a player-coach on December 30, 1947. The *Dispatch* described his "sensational debut last night with 22 points against Syracuse as the Hawks won, 65-57. McDermott made eleven baskets for 22 points, the majority of them his famous 'set shots' for a distance."

at Minneapolis in front of 7,433, 84-59. Murry Nelson, in his 2009 book on the NBL, attempted to console any Blackhawk fans who might be reading:

> Besides being overmatched, the Blackhawks were hit with key injuries during the [second] game. Stan [Whitey] Von Nieda dislocated his shoulder in the first quarter and Billy Hassett fell on his back and sustained a spinal injury in the second quarter. Don Otten got 16 points, but the Lakers got 23 from Mikan.

After losing that series, the Blackhawks joined four other NBL teams in the ninth (and last) annual World Professional Tournament in Chicago. They were joined by three independent teams including the New York Rens, which had won the first tournament in 1939. (Grasso, 2011) In the first round of the tournament, on April 8, 1948, the Blackhawks eliminated Fort Wayne, which had won the tournament three times. In a semi-final game, the Blackhawks lost to the

A Sterling Event at the Field House. . "Francis 'Frannie' Curran, ex-Sterling [Illinois] Community and Notre Dame cage ace and now captain of the Toledo Jeeps, was honored by nearly 400 fans from Sterling and vicinity at Wharton field house yesterday in special Curran Day festivities . . . Curran was presented with a purse of money and then proceeded to lead the Jeeps to a 76-65 win over the Tri-Cities Blackhawks by tallying 11 points. His knee was injured in a first quarter collision with Billy Hassett of the Hawks but Curran returned to action after the halftime rest pause" (Dixon *Evening Telegraph*, Dec 15, 1947).

Rens, who were led by Nathaniel "Sweetwater" Clifton. In the final tournament games, the Anderson Packers beat the Blackhawks 66-64 for third place, and the Lakers beat the Rens 75-71 for the championship. Bobby McDermott and Whitey Von Nieda were both named to the second all-tournament team. (Nelson, 2009; Basketball Research, online)

Season Ticket Reservation
For 1948-1949

Mail To:
BLACKHAWK SPORTS, INC.
226 17th Street
Rock Island, Illinois

Please fill my reservation for _____ season tickets at price per ticket, as checked.

☐ $1.00 ☐ $1.25 ☐ $1.50 ☐ $2.00

Enclosed is $ _____ as down payment.
I prefer to sit in Section _____ in Row _____ or as near this as possible. My second choice is
Section _____, Row _____

MY NAME IS _____ (PLEASE PRINT)

ADDRESS _____

CITY _____

PHONE NUMBER _____

1. Minimum down payment of $5.00 is required on each season ticket. Further payments can be made between now and next season's opening game.
2. As soon as the National League Schedule is adopted for next season, you will be sent a statement and you can then arrange further payments at your convenience.
3. This reservation will entitle you to the same choice seats at all games.

Rock Island County Historical Society

Preparing for the Blackhawks' third season.

Argus, December 27, 1948

A group of Blackhawks players' wives watch the team beat the Dayton Rens at Wharton in December 1948. In the front row are Mary Hassett, Louise Ratkovicz, and Dorothy Von Neida; in the back are Margie Wier, Marjorie Ray, Betty Gibson, and Rosemary McDermott.

Record Crowds in the Third NBL Year

In the fall of 1948, Bobby McDermott continued coaching the Blackhawks as interest among fans was increasing. After winning 25 and losing 20, he was replaced in February 1949 by a local favorite, Roger Potter, who had coached at Moline High School where he compiled a 99-55 win-loss record. In Potter's first professional game, the Blackhawks defeated Waterloo 63-58 in front of 4508 fans. Four days later the team broke the Wharton attendance record with a crowd of 6016 and beat Syracuse 75-66 with Ward "Hoot" Gibson scoring fifteen points to lead the Blackhawks.

Argus, December 17, 1948

In the game against Oshkosh on December 16, 1948, these players were involved in "action aplenty" according to the next day's issue of the *Argus*: "As Billy Hassett (8), looks on from the left, Joe Camic has a leg hooked around Gene Berce (11), and is applying an elbow. Next toward the right is Gene Volker, and that's Gene Englund (19) with a hand on Don Otten, who has his hand on his chest while Walt Lautenbach (14), tosses a low block. The action enabled Whitey Von Neida (back to camera), to scoot around for a shot."

In the 1948-49 season the Blackhawks attracted more fans and won more games than in their first two seasons. Average attendance at Wharton was 4,594, a substantial increase. In their first season, home crowds averaged under 3,000 per game and the largest was 4,400. The average increased to 3,258 in the second season. (Doxie, 1996) The team also posted the best record of its five-season existence, 36-28. They won the first round of the playoffs by defeating the Sheboygan Red Skins in two straight games. However, in the second round the Oshkosh All-Stars turned the tables on the Blackhawks by sweeping a four game series.

The Blackhawks were again led by Don Otten in scoring, a league-leading 14 points per game. Otten, the only remaining seven-foot player in the league, was also named to the all-NBL first team, the only Blackhawk to receive that honor. None had made the all-league second team in the Blackhawks' first season. Otten and Bobby McDermott made it in 1947-48, and Whitey Von Neida and Hoot Gibson in 1948-49.

Long Shot. In a game against the Sheboygan Red Skins on January 2, 1949, fans at Wharton witnessed an amazing shot by Joe Camic of the Blackhawks, described in the Argus the next day: "The 4,300 spectators went babbling out of the arena talking about a feat that didn't even get into the scorebook – Camic's floor-length underhand hammer-toss that rattled through the hoop at the opposite end of the floor." Even though forty seconds were left in the first half, Camic put up the eighty-plus foot shot because he thought time was running out. Alas, his shot did not count because a foul had been called. The Blackhawks won, 68-54.

BLACKHAWKS
vs.
DAV. ROCKETS
and
A.I.C. GIRLS
vs.
CENTENNIAL GRILLE

All proceeds to the Ray Hampton Memorial as an educational fund for the two children of the late Ray Hampton, sports announcer.

R. I. ARMORY — MONDAY, FEB. 28

ALL SEATS RESERVED
$1.00 - $1.50 - $2.00

Tickets on sale at: Blackhawks Office, Athletic Shop, Todd's, Stop & Shop, Rock Island; Martin's, Davenport; VanDerVennetts, Moline; Agnew's, East Moline.

Argus, February 23, 1949

On several occasions the Blackhawks played exhibition games away from Wharton. This February 1949 advertisement from the *Argus* promoted a fundraiser at the Rock Island Armory for the family of Ray Hampton, sports director and broadcaster for WHBF radio who had died in December. The teams and officials donated their time for the event which raised over $2,000. The 1,800 in attendance watched two one-sided games: The Blackhawks won 58-27, and the A.I.C. (American Institute of Commerce) girls won 35-14.

Argus, February 14, 1949

In this loss to Oshkosh, 54-53, at Wharton in February 1949, Whitey Von Nieda (6) is leaping for a tip-in behind Don Otten who soared a bit prematurely. Number 20 for Oshkosh is Bob Carpenter.

C. Roseman, 2013

This large photograph of the Blackhawks, about eight feet wide, hung for many years in downtown Moline taverns. Today it is displayed at the Wunder Y Tap, on 16th Street just four blocks from Wharton Field House. On the left is Billy Hassett, and on the right, Whitey Von Nieda. In the front row of the team picture are Hassett, Von Nieda, Bobby McDermott, Marko Todorovich, and Dee Gibson. In the back are Wally Osterkorn, Joe Camic, Don Otten, Don Ray, an unidentified player, and general manager Ben Kerner. The date of the photograph is unknown.

Creation of the National Basketball Association

Back in 1946 a new professional league, the Basketball Association of America (BAA), had been inaugurated with eleven teams located primarily in larger cities, most of them in the East. Some consider its establishment as the beginning of the NBA, although the NBA officially did not exist until the BAA merged with the NBL in 1949. The BAA league champions in its first two seasons were the Philadelphia Warriors and the Baltimore Bullets. The transition to the BAA's third and final year of existence is summarized on the NBA History Website:

> The BAA clearly had the best arenas in the bigger cities, but the National Basketball League, which featured teams in smaller Midwest cities, claimed the best players. However, this changed prior to the 1948 season, when the NBL's four best teams – Fort Wayne, Rochester, Indianapolis and Minneapolis – jumped to the BAA. Overnight, the best players and the biggest arenas, in the largest

Home Court Advantage? In the days of the NBL and the early NBA, the arenas and playing courts varied considerably, providing most teams a real home-court advantage. The Quad-City Times (February 5, 1996) quoted Murray Wier as saying: "Most of them were not good places. The place in Anderson, Indiana, reminded me of a bullpit. God, it was horrible . . . Sheboygan and Oshkosh played in high school gyms. They were bad. Even some of the large city arenas were problematic. Some that also hosted hockey teams were cold or subject to puddling on the basketball court because of the lack of insulation from the ice. The Minneapolis arena had an odd-sized court which was long and narrow."

media centers, were brought together for the first time.

The championship of the twelve-team 1948-49 BAA was won by the Minneapolis Lakers. This began a period of dominance by the Lakers, who won the NBA title during four of the league's first five years in existence led by their superb big man, George Mikan.

After losing four teams to the BAA in 1948, including the Lakers, only nine teams comprised the NBL in 1948-49, its final season. Then in 1949, six of them joined with BAA teams to form the NBA: Anderson, Denver, Sheboygan, Syracuse, Tri-Cities, and Waterloo. Another team, the Indianapolis Olympians was added, creating a seventeen-team league with three divisions.

1949-50 NBA Standings

Western Division	Wins	Losses
Indianapolis Olympians	39	25
Anderson Packers	37	27
Tri-Cities Blackhawks	29	35
Sheboygan Red Skins	22	40
Waterloo Hawks	19	43
Denver Nuggets	11	51
Central Division	**Wins**	**Losses**
Minneapolis Lakers	51	17
Rochester Royals	51	17
Fort Wayne Pistons	40	28
Chicago Stags	40	28
St. Louis Bombers	26	42
Eastern Division	**Wins**	**Losses**
Syracuse Nationals	51	13
New York Knicks	40	28
Washington Capitols	32	36
Philadelphia Warriors	26	42
Baltimore Bullets	25	43
Boston Celtics	22	46

Source: NBA Universe, online

Red Auerbach, shown here at the Field House, coached the Blackhawks during the 1949-50 season, then went on to a legendary career as coach of the Boston Celtics. Fourteen years later, in 1963, when the Celtics were at Wharton playing the Baltimore Bullets, the *Dispatch* (September 27) looked back on the coach's experience with the Blackhawks: "A fiery competitor, Auerbach leaped and bounded around the bench during that 1949-50 season. His antics helped the Black Hawks enjoy one of their best years in Moline."

Dispatch files

First Year in the NBA: New Coach, Record Scores, Record Crowds, and Many Fouls

The Blackhawks began their two-year stint in the NBA in the fall of 1949 with Roger Potter continuing as coach. They opened the season at Wharton by beating the Denver Nuggets, 93-85, but then lost four in a row. Potter was fired. To replace him, Kerner hired Red Auerbach, who later became a renowned coach of the Boston Celtics, winning nine NBA championships in that role and another seven as president and general manager of the team. He was named coach of the Blackhawks on November 9th, and his first game was three days later. In subsequent weeks both scores and excitement increased. Here are some highlights:

Saturday, November 12: "Breaking a Wharton fieldhouse scoring record just a point shy of 100, the Quad-City Blackhawks Saturday night successfully installed Arnold 'Red' Auerbach as their new head coach. They did it while decisioning Waterloo's Hawks, 99-89, before 4,300 spectators who saw the quad-city club snap a 4-game losing streak in National Basketball Association play" (*Argus*, November 14). In that game, Hassett scored 15 and Von Nieda 14. In a preliminary game the East Moline Legion beat

Farmall, 43-32. Often, industrial league matches would precede Blackhawk games at Wharton.

Sunday, November 27: On Monday Russ Kiesele, sports editor of the *Dispatch*, noted a large crowd at Wharton: "Though a number of fans were left outside beating on the doors for entrance, a new field house record was set as 6156 jammed through the portals." The Blackhawks beat the Indianapolis Olympians 104-88, setting a new scoring record for the team.

Monday, December 26: The Blackhawks' 78-76 loss to the Lakers was described by Bill Kinney of the *Argus* (December 27): "There was a hole in the bottom of the Blackhawks' Christmas stocking. They reached down the full length but couldn't come up with a decision over the Minneapolis Lakers before 6,270 spectators – the greatest crowd ever to watch the quad-city pros in Wharton fieldhouse." No doubt one reason for the large crowd was the presence of the Lakers' big All-Star center George Mikan who scored 22. John O'Donnell of the Davenport *Democrat and Leader* (December 28) observed:

> The official attendance may never be known because of the fire laws.

Sardines in a can had swimming room compared to the room the individual fan had at the fieldhouse for the Lakers' game. And twice the Blackhawks' management asked the Moline cops to stick around to handle the crowd – which couldn't get tickets.

January 7, 1950: During the Auerbach season, the Blackhawks had a strong tie to the University of Illinois. Three members of the 1946-47 Illini team were on the roster. In a game against the Sheboygan Red Skins, which the Blackhawks won 98-86, the Illini led the scoring: Dike Eddleman with 24, Gene Vance 14, and Walt Kirk 9.

January 22, 1950: At half-time the Blackhawks celebrated three years of basketball at Wharton Field House with a birthday cake. The team added icing to the celebration by posting a record score for the Field House in a 111-97 crushing of the Denver Nuggets.

BLACKHAWKS FOURTH ANNIVERSARY

Tomorrow — 4th Anniversary
3 P. M. DENVER VS. BLACKHAWKS
Square Dance Jamboree, 1 p.m.
Under the Direction of Ray Olson
15 Sets of Contestants—Trophies for the Winners
Representatives from Henry, Mercer Counties, Clinton
Quad-Cities
GUEST OF HONOR
MR. MAURICE PODOLOFF
(President of N.B.A.)
HONORS FOR DON OTTEN
(Original Member of the Squad)
ANNIVERSARY CAKE
GALA EVENTS—PLAN TO ATTEND
BLACKHAWKS FOURTH ANNIVERSARY

Argus, January 21, 1950

Argus, January 23, 1950

The Blackhawks celebrated their fourth season on January 22, 1950. On the left is an *Argus* ad for the party, and on the right is NBA president Podoloff lighting candles atop the cake, with Mike Fitzgerald of the Blackhawks describing the action over the public address system.

"Greatest Athlete." Dwight "Dike" Eddleman played for the Blackhawks during their two years in the NBA. The University of Illinois considers him the "greatest athlete ever to have competed for the Fighting Illini." He starred in three sports at Centralia High School, leading the Orphans to a state championship in basketball and winning the state high jump championship three times. At Illinois he earned eleven varsity letters in football, basketball, and track. He played in the 1947 Rose Bowl victory over UCLA, was named All-American in basketball in 1948, was the 1948 NCAA high jump champion, and won a silver medal in the high jump at the 1948 London Olympic Games. He chose to play professional basketball with the Blackhawks, even though he was drafted by the professional football Chicago Bears. He was twice named an NBA All-Star, once for the Blackhawks and once with the Milwaukee Hawks, and finished his NBA career in 1953 with the Fort Wayne Pistons. (Eddleman Obituary, online)

"DAVID AND GOLIATH"

Courtesy of Pat Gustafson

Murray "The Wizard" Wier looks up to Don Otten standing near the main entrance to Wharton Field House. The photograph and heading appeared in the 1949 *National Pro Basketball League Magazine*.

Entering the rarified air of the NBA, local interest in the Blackhawks continued to be quite high. In 1948-49, their last season with the NBL, the Blackhawks had attracted 147,012 fans to 32 games at Wharton, a 4,594 per-game average. The next year, their first in the NBA, the total went up to 155,622 for 35 home games, although the average dipped slightly to 4,447 per game. (*Argus*, November 9, 1986)

In its first NBA season, two records set by the Blackhawks became permanently etched into the NBA record book. Their first record will never be broken – Don Otten holds the record for the most personal fouls in a game, eight! Against Sheboygan on November 24, 1949, six Blackhawks fouled-out, including Otten, each having committed six transgressions. This left the team with only four players. Under these circumstances, the rules at the time allowed a coach to re-insert a player who had fouled-out with the stipulation that each additional foul committed by that player would give the opposing team an extra free throw. Otten re-entered the game in overtime and committed two more fouls. Soon thereafter, the NBA changed that rule. (NBA History, online)

The second Blackhawk NBA record might someday be broken, although it is highly unlikely. The team committed the highest average number of personal fouls per game, 32.1, in that same season. To reach that average, they commited 2,057 fouls in 64 games. Even though

The Wizard Back Home in Muscatine. On March 1, 1950, the Blackhawks honored Murray Wier by playing a game against the Denver Nuggets at the Muscatine (Iowa) High School gym. Often called "The Wizard," Wier had been a star at Muscatine High School and then at the University of Iowa. That evening, the Blackhawks prevailed, 97-80, and The Wizard tied Marko Todorovich for scoring honors: "the home town folks were treated to some of Murray's fancy shooting as the little ex-Iowa flash knocked in 17 points" (*Dispatch*, March 2). Seventeen was well above Wier's season average of 7.7 points per game; it truly was "Murray Wier Night" in Muscatine.

the Blackhawks hold the season record for fouls, they did not reach the record for the greatest number in a single game. That honor goes to the Anderson Packers whose players committed 66 fouls in a game at Syracuse on the same day as Don Otten's eight-foul performance in November 1949. That game also holds the record for the most fouls by both teams, 122! (NBA History, online)

In 1949-50 Marko Todorovich had the highest scoring average for the Blackhawks, 13.6, followed by Dike Eddleman's 12.9. Don Otten, who had led the Blackhawks in scoring the three previous seasons, was third with a 12.1 average. Even though Auerbach posted a mediocre 28-29 record with the Blackhawks, it was good enough to get the team into the playoffs. However, they were eliminated in the first round by the Anderson Packers. The Blackhawks won one home game in that series, but lost two at Anderson. During that season, Auerbach found himself in a power struggle with Ben Kerner, who made several attempts to micro-manage the team. Don Doxie (October 30, 2006) wrote: "If not for Kerner's incessant meddling, Auerbach said he would have stayed in the Tri-Cities for a long time. He might have built the Blackhawks into something special."

Argus, February 2, 1950

In a game won by the Blackhawks, 91-83, Walt Kirk makes a basket in spite of a hand in his face supplied by George Ratkovicz (6) of the Syracuse Nationals. Also in the photograph are Don Otten (15) and referee Jim Biersdorfer.

NBA teams playing against the Blackhawks at Wharton Field House during the league's first two seasons.

1950-51 NBA Standings

Western Division	Wins	Losses
Minneapolis Lakers	44	24
Rochester Royals	41	27
Fort Wayne Pistons	32	36
Indianapolis Olympians	31	37
Tri-Cities Blackhawks	**25**	**43**

Eastern Division	Wins	Losses
Philadelphia Warriors	40	26
Boston Celtics	39	30
New York Knicks	36	30
Syracuse Nationals	32	34
Baltimore Bullets	24	42
Washington Capitols	10	25

Source: NBA Universe, online

1950-51: A Smaller NBA and the Blackhawks' Final Season

After its initial season, 1949-50, the NBA lost six teams and reorganized into two divisions. Three of the small-market teams, from Anderson, Sheboygan, and Waterloo, left the NBA to join a new league, the National Professional Basketball League (NPBL). Joining them were teams from Denver, Grand Rapids, Kansas City, Louisville, and St. Paul. All the NPBL teams, however, disbanded during or after the regular season and no playoffs were held. Initial NBA

HANK DEZONIE

No. 11—Hailing from Clark University, in Atlanta, Georgia, is the Ren's tallest man, six and one-half feet. He is a good floorman, and great things are expected of him in the future. He has been called a second Willie Smith at the center position. He is not as tall as most of the N.B.L. centers, but his fancy shooting amazes the fans. He travels up and down the court with a slow skip that serves as sort of a change of pace. When he shoots, he stretches every bit of his 6'6" toward the basket.

Courtesy of Pat Gustafson

The First Black NBA Players. African American players were not welcome in the three-year history of the BAA, nor in the NBA during its first year (1949-50). That unwritten policy changed during the 1950-51 season. "The door to integrating the NBA wasn't burst open by a flood of black players. Instead it was nudged open, inch by inch, by a trickle of players" (Thomas, 2002). The first, Earl Lloyd, played his first game for the Washington Capitals on October 31, 1950; the second, Chuck Cooper, played his first game for the Boston Celtics the next evening. Nate "Sweetwater" Clifton, a former star for the Globetrotters and the New York Rens, was the third. He debuted in the NBA with the New York Knickerbockers on November 4 in a game against the Blackhawks at Wharton Field House. The Blackhawks won, 87-76; Clifton scored sixteen for the Knicks.

The fourth African American NBA player had a short and unhappy career with the Blackhawks. Hank DeZonie, another former player for the Rens and Globetrotters, first played in a game at Wharton on December 3 against the New York Knicks. He scored six points. DeZonie played only five games and was released on December 14. Thirty-five years later, Thomas (2002) reported that DeZonie was dejected and had quit. "DeZonie said that because he couldn't reside with his teammates, Kerner arranged for him to live with an old woman who chewed tobacco and had a house devoid of radio and television." He had "cut his NBA career short because he had burned out on basketball and couldn't tolerate his segregated living conditions in the Tri-Cities."

Before his brief stint playing for the Blackhawks in the NBA, Hank DeZonie played in the NBL for the Dayton Rens during the 1948-49 season. This photograph and description was featured in the 1949 *National Pro Basketball League Magazine*.

91

teams from Denver, Chicago, and St. Louis folded, leaving a 1950-51 NBA with eleven teams.

Reasons for teams folding during that era were varied and included lack of fan interest, financial issues, and ownership squabbles. Teams moved for a variety of reasons, too, probably the most fundamental of them being market size. Grasso (2011) claims that "the NBA established a minimum arena seating capacity requirement that effectively eliminated several of the former NBL teams." Nonetheless, four teams in relatively small markets, including the Blackhawks, were retained for the second NBA season.

In the fall of 1950, at the beginning of the Blackhawks' second and final year playing in the NBA, Ben Kerner was in charge. His former partner Leo Ferris had moved on to Syracuse, and Kerner was the major stockholder and executive Director of Blackhawks Sports, Inc. A November 24 article in the Argus praised Kerner for paying $30,000 to obtain some top-notch players and predicted that the Blackhawks "look like a probable winner in this season's league campaign." The same article also reminded readers of the small market size in which the team "was competing alongside representatives from the nation's largest metropolitan areas . . . taking a tip from Green Bay, Wis., which has established itself as a pro football power."

The Blackhawks' first regular-season game of the 1950-51 season was at Wharton Field House against their old coach Red Auerbach and the Boston Celtics. The home team won 79-65 in front of 4,200 fans on Thursday evening, November 2. The next day, the Dispatch could not resist comment on Auerbach's demeanor during the game:

Coach Red Auerbach, former Blackhawk mentor now with the Beantown Irish, was in top form with windmilling arms, slapping foot, and flapping jaws. And Red even drew a technical foul for ungentlemanly language with tooter Max Tabacchi.

Hillsboro Here We Come. In early October, 1950, the Blackhawks held a two-week training camp at the Hillsboro (Illinois) Community High School gym. The camp's location had been announced eight months earlier: "They'll desert Wharton fieldhouse for Hillsboro in order to give the players 'a quieter training atmosphere'" (Dixon *Evening Telegraph*, January 11). According to Mike Plunkett, editor of the Hillsboro *Journal-News*, the team stayed at the Red Rooster Inn, a 1902 hotel on Courthouse Square that is still in operation. The quiet of a small central Illinois town may explain the two easy victories in the Blackhawks' first preseason games: on October 15, they defeated Fort Wayne, 74-60, at the Hillsboro gym; two days later they travelled to nearby Taylorville where they beat the Toledo Mercurys, 78-56. The Blackhawks paid for use of the Hillsboro gym by giving their school half the gate receipts for the game against Fort Wayne.

Another former Blackhawk who came with the Celtics was Bob Cousy, who went on to be an NBA star and member of the NBA Hall of Fame. Not only was he a prolific scorer, but he also led the NBA in assists for eight straight seasons from 1952 to 1960 and became known as "The Houdini of the Hardwood" (Basketball Reference, online). Cousy had been drafted on April 25, 1950, by the Blackhawks after starring at Holy Cross College where he averaged 19.4 points per game in his senior season. Alas, the Blackhawks traded Cousy to the Chicago Stags before he ever played a game for Tri-Cities. Then on October 5 he was picked up by the Celtics in a dispersal draft after the Stags folded. So, Cousy's first appearance at Wharton was in a Celtic uniform. He scored ten points.

On the court, the Blackhawks' fortunes faded in their final season in Moline. Their 25-43 season record was the worst in their five-year history. A revolving door for coaches probably did not help. Dave McMillan coached the first 23 games, lost fourteen of them, and was fired. Thirty-year-old Johnny Logan, who was also a player, took over in December of 1950, but coached only three games because he had to report for duty with the Army Reserve. The season was completed by another player-coach, Marko Todorovich.

Argus, January 29, 1951

In this January 1951 NBA game at Wharton, won by the Philadelphia Warriors, 96-86, Blackhawk player-coach Marko Todorovich is fouled in the act of shooting by Paul Arizin. Looking on are Dike Eddleman (18) of the Blackhawks and Andy Phillip (7) of the Warriors.

Blackhawks' Coaches, 1947-51, and their Won-Loss Records

1946-47: Nat Hickey (19-25)
1947-48: Nat Hickey (8-12); Bobby McDermott (22-18)
1948-49: Bobby McDermott (25-20); Roger Potter (11-8)
1949-50: Roger Potter (1-6);
 Arnold "Red" Auerbach (28-29)
1950-51: Dave McMillan (9-14); John Logan (2-1);
 Marko Todorovich (14-28)

Frank Brian led the Blackhawks in scoring in 1950-51 with a 16.6 points-per-game average; Dike Eddleman was second with a 15.3 average. (For perspective, note that George Mikan averaged 28.4 points for the Lakers that season!) Brian, who previously had been a star with the Anderson Packers, was selected to the All-NBA team that year, the only Blackhawk to ever receive that honor. Both Brian and Eddleman played for the Western Division in the first NBA All-Star Game on March 2, 1951, at the Boston Garden. In front of a crowd of 10,094, Brian scored 14 and Eddleman 7 in a game won by the Eastern Division 111-94.

Argus, September 30, 1950

Dispatch, November 21, 1950

Before preseason practice began in Hillsboro, Illinois, on October 2, 1950, radio station WQUA interviewed Blackhawk personnel. Then in November a *Dispatch* advertisement promised radio coverage of all the Blackhawk games during the 1950-51 season. It also celebrated the rarified air of big eastern cities whose teams competed with the local small-market team. The next three games to be broadcast were against the Baltimore Bullets (in New York's Madison Square Garden), the Washington Capitols, and the Boston Celtics.

Blackhawks' Highest Individual Season Scoring Averages, 1947-51

Name	Season	League	Average	Comments
Frank Brian	1950-51	NBA	16.8	Seventh in the NBA
Dike Eddleman	1950-51	NBA	15.3	
Don Otten	1948-49	NBL	14.0	First in the NBL
Don Otten	1947-48	NBL	13.7	
Marko Todorovich	1949-50	NBA	13.6	
Dike Eddleman	1949-50	NBA	12.9	
Don Otten	1946-47	NBL	12.9	
Whitey Von Nieda	1947-48	NBL	12.1	
Don Otten	1949-50	NBA	12.1	
Bobby McDermott	1947-48	NBL	12.1	
Billy Hassett	1947-48	NBL	10.7	
Whitey Von Nieda	1948-49	NBL	10.0	

Sources for this table and other Blackhawks' statistics: NBA History, online; and Basketball Reference, online.

Blackhawks' NBA Individual Game Scoring Records at Wharton Field House

Most points, individual: 41 by Frank Brian vs. Minneapolis	Jan. 11, 1951
Most field goals, individual: 13 by Frank Brian	Jan. 11, 1951
Most foul shots made, individual: 15 by Frank Brian	Jan. 11, 1951
Most points, team: 116 by Blackhawks vs. Waterloo	Feb. 18, 1950
Most field goals, team: 40 by Blackhawks vs. Denver	Jan. 22, 1950
Most foul shots made, team: 39	
Blackhawks vs. Philadelphia	Feb. 8, 1950
Blackhawks vs. Anderson	Mar. 23, 1950
Most points, both teams: 222 (Minneapolis 113; Blackhawks, 109)	Jan. 11, 1951

Source: Allee, 2005

The End

During mid-season, keeping the team in the Quad Cities became a major concern. On January 20, 1951, Bill Kinney of the *Argus* noted:

> The Blackhawks have been hit at the box office. Last year, the team, despite many inferior attractions, drew a total of 155,633 for an average of 4,447 [for 35 home games] and made in excess of $10,000. This year the gate is down to an average of 3,384 on a total of 71,070 for 21 games.

Beginning in January numerous attempts were made to increase attendance. In one early campaign, letters were mailed to 1,300 season ticket holders, asking them to bring "friends and fill the fieldhouse" for the January 28th game against Philadelphia (*Argus*, January 23). In subsequent games, the *Dispatch* and Eagle Super Markets sponsored a giveaway of sets of four Libbey-Owens tumblers with photographs and signatures of four Blackhawk players.

Then on February 22nd the *Dispatch* announced a special Booster Night for the February 28th game against Baltimore "to give the Quad-City pros a shot-in-the-arm in the attendance column and help convince prospective local purchasers of the franchise to retain the National Basketball Association team here." The paper wrote that the local stock owners had the option to purchase controlling interest in the team from Ben Kerner, but at this point – near the end of the 1950-51 season – they had become concerned about attendance. The *Dispatch* reported that Bryan Grafton said "his group wouldn't be interested unless attendance showed an upswing in the latter part of the season." For Booster Night the paper offered two tickets for the price of one, to see the Blackhawks defeat Baltimore, 100-85.

Attendance did not increase substantially for the last few games and the Blackhawks were defeated in their last two. The first was a tough overtime loss, 92-91, to the Minneapolis Lakers on Saturday night, April 17, 1951, in front of

These two advertisements from the *Argus* promoted attempts to boost attendance in the winter of 1951. The ad on the left announces a gift of a set of glass tumblers, signed by players, to the first 1,100 women to attend the February 1st game against Fort Wayne. The ad on the right promotes a continuation of the tumbler giveaway and sweetens the pot by offering two-for-one tickets. Neither game drew more than 2,500, crowds far short of many previous home games at Wharton. The tumblers became – for hundreds of fans – souvenirs of the Blackhawks' last season at Wharton Field House.

2,700 fans at Wharton. Leading scorers for the Blackhawks were Marko Todorovich with 21, Frank Brian 15, and Dike Eddleman 14. Leaving little doubt that by this time George Mikan had been established as the premiere big man in basketball, he put up 38 points for the Lakers. (Six weeks earlier he had set the Wharton Field House NBA individual scoring record of 46 points.) The next day the Zollner Pistons beat the Blackhawks, 95-82, in front of 3,600 fans in Fort Wayne.

After losing those two games, the Quad Cities lost the team. Friction had developed between Kerner and the local team owners. One reason was Kerner's spending habits. Jim Meenan (1986) quoted Russ Kiesele, who was *Dispatch* sports editor when the Blackhawks were in town.

After games he would take eight to 10 to 12 people out to the Plantation. Free drinks, free dinner. After the game we'd come down to the paper, write our stories, then go out to the Plantation, have

a couple drinks and steak dinner with Benny. Kerner was that way all the time.

Meenan noted that the Blackhawks were also facing the reality of being a team from a place out in the hinterlands with an unrecognizable name, the "Tri-Cities," which could not draw big crowds in New York, Boston, or Philadelphia. Eddie Gottlieb of Philadelphia and Ned Irish of New York, in particular, were opposed to the continuance of the Blackhawks, probably for this reason.

In a September 8, 2005, article in the Quad-City *Times*, Don Doxie summarized the demise of the Tri-Cities Blackhawks. By the end of the 1950-51 season, the 31 stock holders, led by Bryan Grafton, were at loggerheads with Kerner. The stockholders refinanced to cover a $30,000 loss that season, but Kerner retained a 51 percent majority ownership. On August 2nd, the board released Kerner as executive director. On September 5th, Grafton and the team's secretary, Wayne G. Cook, met with NBA officials in

New York in an attempt to wrestle ownership from Kerner and retain the team in Moline. Apparently, most of the NBA owners could not accept this arrangement. Grafton said "they simply didn't want us in the league anymore." Almost immediately, the NBA bought out the stockholders and, at a meeting at the Fort Armstrong Hotel in Rock Island on September 10th, the stockholders accepted the offer. The Blackhawks were no more.

Moving Out and Up

The lure of a much larger market won out. Kerner successfully negotiated with Milwaukee interests to move the team there. Apparently the NBA had wanted a team in Milwaukee the previous season but a new arena was under construction there and not ready. Now, in 1951, the 11,000-seat Milwaukee Arena was available, providing additional incentive for the move. The Blackhawks became the Milwaukee Hawks.

One by one the teams in the smaller metropolitan areas left or folded in the 1950s. The last team leaving a smaller market, the Syracuse Nationals, hung on

1950s Postcard

In 1951 the newly-completed Milwaukee Arena became the home of the Milwaukee Hawks. It was constructed next to the 1909 Milwaukee Auditorium. In 1974, the two facilities were merged into a convention and entertainment complex called the MECCA, which in 2000 was renamed the U. S. Cellular Arena. (U. S. Cellular Arena, online)

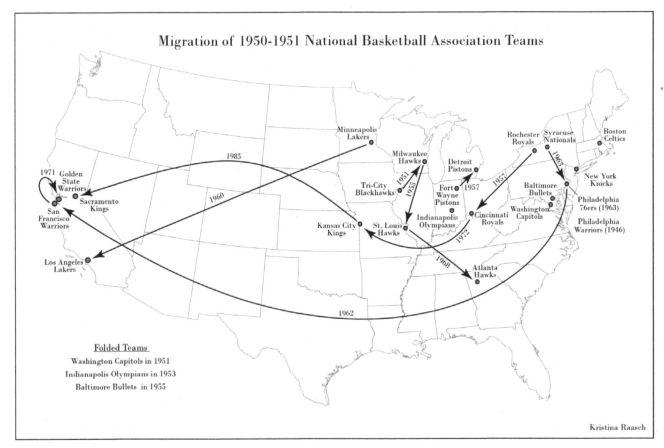

What happened to the 1950-51 NBA teams?

1950 Metropolitan Area Populations, 1950-51 NBA Cities

Metro Area	Population	NBA Team
New York	12,912,000	
Philadelphia	3,671,000	moved to San Francisco in 1962
Boston	2,370,000	
Washington	1,464,000	folded in January 1951
Baltimore	1,337,000	folded during the 1954-55 season
Minneapolis/St. Paul	1,089,000	moved to Los Angeles in 1960
Indianapolis	552,000	folded in 1953
Rochester	487,000	moved to Cincinnati in 1957
Syracuse	342,000	moved to Philadelphia in 1963
Tri-Cities	234,000	moved to Milwaukee in 1951
Fort Wayne	184,000	moved to Detroit in 1957

Source: 1950 U. S. Census of Population

until 1963 when they moved to Philadelphia. After the shuffle, each of the nine NBA metropolitan areas in the mid-1960s had well over a million people, Cincinnati being the smallest with about 1.3 million. Later the league would expand significantly – to thirty teams in 2013 – but never again would a market with fewer than a million people have a major league professional basketball team.

The Hawks in Milwaukee, St. Louis, and Atlanta

The Hawks lasted in Milwaukee only four seasons, primarily owing to rather poor performance on the court. They compiled four losing season records and finished fourth twice and fifth twice in the NBA Western Division. In 1955, Kerner took the team to St. Louis where they lasted until 1968. Between 1957 and 1961 they won five straight Western Division titles, and in 1958 they defeated the Boston Celtics for the NBA championship, the only NBA title in Blackhawks/Hawks franchise history. Their primary home in St. Louis was the 10,000-seat Kiel

The Piston Story. The Zollner Pistons stayed in Fort Wayne, Indiana, the smallest of the 1950-51 NBA metropolitan areas, until moving to Detroit in 1957. Fred Zollner, owner of the team and head of the Zollner Corporation, was able to keep the team in Fort Wayne because of his dedication to the town and his deep pockets. As a millionaire industrialist, he loaned money to the NBA and in 1951 he was the first owner to provide a private plane for his team. (Nelson, 1995) When the end finally came, Zollner was quoted in the *Dispatch* (February 15, 1957): "We had about 3,000 loyal fans in Fort Wayne. If we had 5,000 we'd have been in business. It's a red-hot basketball town, but just too small for us. As long as we stayed there, we couldn't keep pace with the growth of the rest of the league."

Auditorium and they played some games at the larger St. Louis Arena. Because the former was too small and the latter poorly maintained, Kerner wanted a new arena in St. Louis. When it did not materialize he sold the team in 1968 to Tom Cousins and Carl Sanders, who moved it to Atlanta. (NBA History, online)

Arenas used by the Blackhawks and Hawks and their Seating Capacities

1946-51	Wharton Field House	Moline, IL	6,000
1951-55	Milwaukee Arena	Milwaukee, WI	11,000
1955-68	Kiel Auditorium	St. Louis, MO	10,000
1968-72	Alexander Memorial Coliseum	Atlanta, GA	7,166
1972-97	Omni Coliseum	Atlanta, GA	16,378
1997-99	Georgia Dome	Atlanta, GA	21,570
	Alexander Memorial Coliseum	Atlanta, GA	9,300
1999-	Philips Arena	Atlanta, GA	20,000

Source: NBA Hoops, online

NBA in the Quad Cities after the Blackhawks

During their first season in Milwaukee, the Hawks scheduled eight games at Wharton. These games represented an attempt by local promoters to revive professional basketball in the Quad Cities. However, they played only seven of them, winning three and losing four. The other game was to have been played against the New York Knicks on December 18, 1951. At game time, 8:30 p.m., the visiting Knicks were at Wharton ready to play. The "home team" Hawks were late, arriving on the train from Chicago at about 8:40 p.m. Confusion reigned. Players were told at the station that the game was cancelled, but the crowd of about 500 waited until 9:12 p.m. before being informed of the cancellation. The Knicks were declared winner by forfeit and a 2-0 score. This and other Milwaukee Hawks games did not draw well at Wharton during the 1951-52 season, and no regular season NBA games would be played there again until 1962.

In the 1960s, some NBA games were played at Wharton, including the Chicago Packers against the Knicks on January 23, 1962, and the Boston Celtics versus the Baltimore Bullets on October 3, 1963. Then in 1966, the Celtics came to town again for a pre-season game with the Cincinnati Royals. But for the first time in Quad City history a local NBA game was played at a location other than Wharton. Because Don Nelson, a Rock Island native, was on the Celtic team, the game was held at the Rock Island Fieldhouse. A capacity crowd of 6,304 bought tickets for $2 and $3 and saw the Celtics prevail 101-89. Tom Sanders led the Celtics with 22 points; Oscar Robinson led the Royals with 21. Star player Bill Russell was coaching the Celtics for the first time, having taken over from long-time successful coach Red Auerbach, who had coached the Blackhawks in their first NBA season, 1949-50.

Dispatch, December 14, 1951

This *Dispatch* advertisement promoted one of the games the Milwaukee Hawks had scheduled at the Field House during the 1951-52 season. The other seven were played, but this one was cancelled. Because the Hawks were late arriving they were forced to forfeit the game. Only 500 fans, however, were disappointed.

Harlem Globetrotters

Beginning in 1950, the celebrated African American team visited Wharton annually, displaying spectacular moves, shots, and passes, and further entertaining audiences with creative stunts. In that first year they played two consecutive nights, March 30th and 31st, against the Toledo Mercurys. Not surprisingly the 'Trotters won both games, in front of 5,400 fans the first night and 6,000 the second, for a total attendance of 11,400. They returned most years thereafter, but typically played only one game per visit. After The Mark of the Quad Cities, now the iWireless Center, opened in 1993, the Globetrotters continued the tradition there.

In some years owner and coach Abe Saperstein would bring along other entertainment to complement the basketball performance of the Globetrotters. On Saturday evening, October 29, 1960, in a game against the Washington Generals, two sets of entertainers would appear. The evening opened with a forty-minute performance by Olsen & Johnson's "Hellzapoppin" stage review. Unfortunately, Ole Olsen was not able to appear because he was recovering from injuries he suffered in an automobile accident near Cedar Rapids three days earlier. At half-time, four table tennis players demonstrated their skills as part of a nationwide championship tour. The 2,100 attendance that evening was atypically low for a Globetrotters appearance at Wharton.

The 1971 visit of the Globetrotters to Wharton Field House generated widespread excitement, along with considerable disappointment. A new Saturday-morning Globetrotters cartoon show had increased the team's popularity among young people. In a contest sponsored by the Bob Eriksen Chevrolet dealership, boys and girls were asked to respond, in 25 words or fewer, to the statement "I like basketball because . . ." The first prize winner would become the team mascot for the Sunday game. Second through fiftieth prizes were autographed basketballs, and 51st through 100th prizes pairs of tickets to Sunday's game. Thousands entered. (*Argus*, February 19)

Before the Sunday game, the box office was opened at 10 a.m. Murray Hurt in his *Argus* column (March 8) quoted promoter Mike Fitzgerald: "Cars were backed up across the Bettendorf bridge . . . It was one of the saddest days of my life. We had to turn away at least 3,000 people. Kids were crying all over the place."

Courtesy of Jerry Wallaert

In 1966, forty Slovakian Folkloric Dancers came with the Globetrotters.

The Wizard Versus the Globetrotters. The 4,400 fans who came out on December 22, 1951, were thrilled to see not only the Globetrotter stars, including Goose Tatum and Marques Haynes, but also a former Blackhawk player, Murray Wier. "The Wizard" came from Waterloo where he was coaching to help out the Toledo Mercurys, the team to be sacrificed to the Trotters that day. The *Argus* (Nov 23) commented: "The little redhead still shoots 'em out of his back pocket, but last night he could count on only 10 points." As usual, the Globetrotters beat their opposition; this time 83-58.

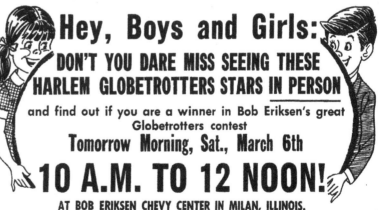

Dispatch, March 5, 1971

In 1971, a local automobile dealer sponsored a writing contest for boys and girls. This *Dispatch* advertisement urged contest entrants to visit the Field House on Saturday, the day before the Globetrotters' March 7th game, meet some of the players, and see if they were winners. Players Paul "Pablo" Robertson and Hubert "Geese" Ausbie appeared there on that day.

Courtesy of Jerry Wallaert

The Globetrotters' popularity never waned at Wharton. Here is a poster for their 1983 appearance.

Dispatch, November 22, 1962

Former Globetrotter Goose Tatum created a spin-off group of "All-Stars," which visited the Field House on Thanksgiving in 1962. The opponent was the New York Rens coached by legendary baseball pitcher Satchel Paige. Musical entertainment was provided by the Ink Spots.

The Sound of Thunder

In 1986 rumblings were heard about the possibility of professional basketball returning to the Quad Cities. The minor-league Continental Basketball Association (CBA) was seeking a new team to begin play in 1987. CBA leaders told the *Dispatch* (December 28, 1986) that three requirements had to be met for any new franchise: having an arena seating at least 5,000; a guarantee of at least 1,500 season tickets sold the first year; and local investor(s) willing to purchase at least ten percent of the franchise. The first

requirement was easy to meet: Wharton Field House was the only choice locally.

On February 25, 1987, the Quad Cities Basketball Club, Inc. officially obtained the franchise for a team to be called the Thunder, even though an agreement on the use of the Field House had not yet been finalized. Soon a group of local potential purchasers met; out of the meeting came one owner, Anne DeLong. She bought 100 percent of the team from Robert E. Ligums who had courted over a dozen communities to bid for the franchise. Ligums originally

100

became familiar with the area on a visit to the Bix Beiderbecke Jazz Festival in Davenport the previous July. The Quad Cities did not receive an expansion franchise; Ligums was selling an inactive CBA club, the Maine Windjammers, which had gone bankrupt in 1983. (DeVrieze, 1987)

In July 1987 a final hurdle was crossed when an agreement was made between the Moline school board and the CBA, allowing the new team – already named the Thunder – to use the Field House. The board agreed to rent the facility on a non-profit basis. Board president, Jim Scott, declared: "The bottom line is that we want to get people back into Wharton any way we can." (Pearson, 1987) That goal was certainly accomplished – the Thunder attracted 126,663 spectators during their first season, only the second franchise in the history of the CBA to surpass 100,000.

Thunder general manager Rich McArdle said the agreement would allow the team to make some changes to the Field House, including improvements to the concession area and seating renovations. He also mentioned that a new scoreboard was needed to replace the four-sided cube with two-digit score indicators, and that it should be suspended higher above the floor. In 1988 two new scoreboards, mounted at either end of the court, were installed to replace the historic cube. The size of the court also was a point of contention. It would remain 84 feet in length, ten feet shorter than standard CBA professional courts, and probably contributed to a home court advantage for the Thunder. In granting the franchise to the Quad Cities, the CBA had reluctantly permitted the Thunder to play on the short court.

The first season, 1987-88, was a financial success. During the last week of the season, Rick McArdle reported that the Thunder would come close to breaking even, in spite of the fact that "No team in this league has made money" (Burlington Hawk Eye, March 13, 1988).

Dispatch files

Anne Potter DeLong, pictured here in 1989 at the Field House, owned the Thunder until 1996. She was named CBA Executive of the Year in 1988-89. DeLong was the daughter of long-time owner of the Rock Island *Argus* Ben Potter and his wife Margaret Potter.

The wide geographical distribution of CBA teams meant extensive travel for the Thunder. One of their more arduous trips occurred during their first winter at Wharton. At the end of a two-week road trip, the team found themselves in a snowstorm in Wyoming. They took a two-plus hour bus trip to Denver but were not able to continue to Moline on a commercial flight. Instead they chartered two Lear jets, costing about $12,000, and arrived in Moline more than an hour after scheduled game time. General manager Rich McArdle said that a mid-afternoon decision to charter the flights was made because afternoon sales were "going hot" and "a decision to cancel at that late hour would have been unfair to the fans." Indeed, 5,088 fans waited for the 9 p.m. start of the game with the Mississippi Jets, which the jet-lagged Thunder lost 151-146. (DeVrieze, January 19, 1988)

Thunder at Wharton

The first game played by the Thunder was a home game at Wharton on November 20, 1987. For that game they attracted 6,047 fans but lost

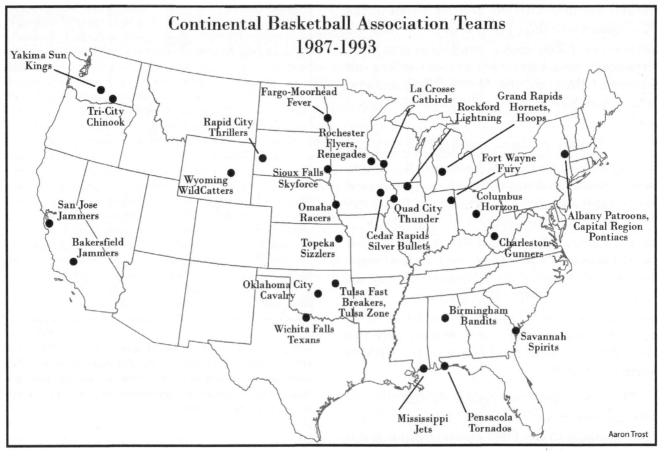

Continental Basketball Association Teams
1987-1993

Yakima Sun Kings

Tri-City Chinook

Fargo-Moorhead Fever

La Crosse Catbirds

Grand Rapids Hornets, Hoops

Rockford Lightning

Rapid City Thrillers

Rochester Flyers, Renegades

Fort Wayne Fury

Wyoming WildCatters

Sioux Falls Skyforce

Columbus Horizon

San Jose Jammers

Omaha Racers

Quad City Thunder

Albany Patroons, Capital Region Pontiacs

Bakersfield Jammers

Cedar Rapids Silver Bullets

Topeka Sizzlers

Charleston Gunners

Oklahoma City Cavalry

Tulsa Fast Breakers, Tulsa Zone

Birmingham Bandits

Savannah Spirits

Wichita Falls Texans

Mississippi Jets

Pensacola Tornados

Aaron Trost

Shown here are the teams that played the Thunder at Wharton Field House. Thirteen teams comprised the league when the Thunder joined the CBA in 1987. It expanded to sixteen teams in 1989 and included at least that many through 1993 when the Thunder left the Field House for The Mark. The number declined to nine in 1997. During the entire history of the league from 1978 to 2001, teams from 74 cities played in the league, some for only one year. (CBA History, online)

to the La Crosse Catbirds 123-104. The new team then proceeded to lose five more games before winning its first, against Rochester on December 2nd. In spite of those six straight losses, the team ended the season with a 30-24 record in its initial season. (QCThunder, online)

The Thunder played six seasons at Wharton, before moving to the new downtown Moline arena, The Mark of the Quad Cities, which seated almost 10,000 people for basketball. Their first coach, Mauro Panaggio, who led the Thunder at Wharton from 1987 to 1991, compiled a regular season record of 132 wins and 88 losses. He was succeeded by his son Don, who carried on until 2000 at both Wharton and The Mark with an overall record of 313 and 191.

Tip-off at the first Thunder game at Wharton Field House, November 20, 1987. Note the Thunder logo placed over the M in the center court circle. A crowd of 6,047 watched the La Crosse Catbirds defeat the Thunder, 123-104.

Dispatch files

Quad City Thunder Season Records During the Wharton Era

Season	Record	Place/Division	Playoffs
1987-88	30-24	3rd /Western	Lost to Rockford, 4-3, in first round
1988-89	36-18	2nd /Western	Lost to Rockford, 4-3, in first round
1989-90	34-22	2nd /Central	Lost to La Crosse 3-0, in first round
1990-91	32-24	1st /Central	Lost to Wichita Falls, 4-3, in CBA final
1991-92	42-14	1st /Midwest	Lost to La Crosse, 3-2 in second round
1992-93	38-18	2nd /Midwest	Lost to Grand Rapids, 3-2, in first round

Source: CBA History, online

Dispatch files   *Dispatch* files

Two photographs showing Thunder action in Wharton Field House.

Leading Scorers for the Thunder at Wharton Field House

Season	Player	Per Game Average
1987-88	Mitchell Wiggins	27.2
1988-89	Kevin Gamble	27.8
1989-90	Bill Jones	25.2
1990-91	David Henderson	26.1
1991-92	Anthony Bowie	20.7
1992-93	Derek Strong	20.0

Source: QCThunder, online

Coach Mauro Panaggio, with one net around his neck, clipped the net at the other end of the Wharton Field House floor after the Thunder clinched the CBA American Division championship in April 1991 by defeating Omaha four games to one. Panaggio went on to coach seven more Thunder games in the CBA finals against Wichita Falls, before handing the coaching duties over to his son.

Dispatch, April 8, 1991

During their six years at Wharton, the Thunder fell below second place in their division only once, and each year they earned a spot in the playoffs. In 1990-91 they reached the CBA championship finals, but lost to the Wichita Falls Texans, 102-90, in the final game of a seven-game series. The game in Wichita Falls' D. L. Ligon Coliseum attracted a crowd of 5,045.

The Thunder regularly racked up well over 100 points per game, as was the norm in minor league basketball of the time. In their second season, 1988-89, they averaged 118.3 points per game, the highest in team history. That year, Kevin Gamble, a local favorite from the University of Iowa, led the team in scoring average, 27.8, although he played only eighteen games before being called up to the NBA, the first Thunder player to receive this honor. He had the highest individual scoring average through the entire history of the Thunder.

CBA All-Star Game in "a pit"? In spite of opposition from some CBA team owners to having the league All-Star Game at a small, ancient arena, general manager Rich McArdle and owner Anne Potter DeLong managed to land the All-Star Game for 1990. One factor that swayed owners was the fact that the Thunder led the CBA in attendance in 1989-90. Some owners opposed the idea because using Wharton would damage the upscale image the CBA was trying to project. Cedar Rapids Silver Bullets general manager Kevin Krause, speaking from his fancy digs in the relatively new Five Seasons Center, called Wharton "a pit." (DeVrieze, 1989)

The Ice Man Cometh. On December 18, 1989, the *Los Angeles Times* told this story: "[In 1979] George (Iceman) Gervin held the basketball world in his large, finely boned hands. He was 27 and living a millionaire's life in San Antonio, Tex., flying across the country in chartered jets while purposefully carving a path toward the second of his four NBA scoring titles and the third of nine consecutive All-Star appearances. Sunday [December 17, 1989], headed home to the Quad Cities and seeming as handsome and polite and graceful as he ever was, George Gervin set out on day 10 of his campaign to retain a grip on the larger world and reclaim some small corner of his sport. He is 37 now, a recovering cocaine addict with only some of his magic left, flying puddle-jumpers to Continental Basketball Assn. stops like Grand Rapids, Mich.; Sioux Falls, Iowa [sic]; Rapid City, S.D., and Wichita Falls, Tex., searching out the fastest route back to the big time."

A highlight for the Thunder came on the night of December 13, 1989, when the team set a record by scoring 172 points against the Santa Barbara Islanders at Wharton in front of 3,100 fans. Leading scorers on both teams were named Gervin. Former NBA All-Star George Gervin, who was attempting a comeback at age 37, scored 43 for the Thunder. His younger brother Derrick scored 37 for the Islanders, which managed to score a mere 122 points as a team.

The 1990 CBA All-Star Game was held at Wharton Field House on January 21st. The National Conference beat the American Conference 107-105, in a new format for the contest. In the previous seven CBA All-Star Games, the host team played an assemblage of CBA All-Stars, the latter winning five of them. Two Thunder players, Bill Jones and Jose Slaughter, started on the American Conference team. The game was attended by 4,327 fans and broadcast on ESPN. It was the second Thunder game to have been televised nationally, the first being a game against the Charleston Gunners in January 1988.

Sizing Up Wharton

From the beginning the size and particular character of Wharton Field House was an issue. Back on February 14, 1988, nearing the end of the first season, Craig DeVrieze wrote in the *Dispatch:*

> League-wide, the CBA has made a push to place its clubs in modern civic facilities, and a Quad-Cities franchise was welcomed to the league last February with an understanding that its club wouldn't play indefinitely in Moline's aged Wharton Field House.

DeVrieze quoted Thunder owner DeLong: "We must have an arena by the 1989-90 season. I don't know how I can ask the league to wait much longer." DeLong had followed with interest some local proposals for new facilities and even engaged in preliminary discussions about her financing a new arena on Davenport's riverfront. Already, two nearby smaller metropolitan areas with CBA teams had new civic centers. In 1979 Cedar Rapids opened the Five Seasons Center (later the U. S. Cellular Center), seating 6,900 for basketball. The 10,000-seat Metro Center (later BMO Harris Bank Center) had been opened in Rockford in 1981. In addition, the 11,000-seat Peoria Civic Center Carver Arena had been opened in 1982. In spite of DeLong's concerns and actions, a new facility would not be available until five years later when The Mark opened in downtown Moline. During that five-year period, however, the Thunder and its ample fan base thrived at Wharton.

Not unlike the Blackhawks of forty years earlier, the Thunder organization promoted its product by creating a carnival atmosphere at games and conducting imaginative promotions. In its first year, halftime entertainment included an acrobatic show by the Bud Light Daredevils, Jackson Five imitators, the Famous Chicken, and the Mad Chainsaw Juggler. They instituted the traditional promotion of awarding prize money to fans who could make a basket from half-court (which would be a bit easier at Wharton because half-court is five feet closer to the basket than at other professional arenas!). Former NBA stars, including Walt Frazier, Oscar Robinson, Bob Cousy, and Rick Barry, were suited-up as guest players. They also hired "Crazy George" Schauer who used juggling and

"In Wharton There is no Beer." Of all the marks against the Thunder playing at Wharton – "aging" facility; short court, etc. – none is mentioned more often than the lack of beer sales. Rich McArdle noted that Wharton was the only professional basketball arena that did not serve beer. Of course, from the beginning the Thunder knew that the school board would not allow the sale of beer or any kind of alcoholic beverage. After an extensive discussion among school officials and the public, the Thunder's final request to the school board was turned down on May 10, 1988, following the completion of their first season. After the decision, McArdle said: "Now we just have to become more creative in how we package our product the second year." (Pearson, 1988) Indeed, the Thunder nicely compensated for the lack of this amenity, creating a family atmosphere by reaching out to young people and providing some non-basketball entertainment at Wharton. They succeeded. Attendance at Wharton averaged over 4,000 during the first five seasons there and nearly 3,500 in their last.

D. Moore

The Famous Chicken, along with some chicks, entertained the crowd at a Thunder game at Wharton Field House on December 30, 1989.

105

trick ball-handling routines at games and promoted the Thunder at school assemblies in and around the Quad Cities.

Perhaps the short court, old raised wooden floor, bench seats, cramped seating, and no beer worked as an advantage for the Thunder. John Marx (1993), in writing something of an obituary for the Wharton Thunder, calculated that the team won 129 games and lost 35 in six seasons at the Field House, a 79 percent winning rate. Marx quoted Casey Kahler, Thunder radio announcer:

> No other team in the past six CBA seasons had a better percentage on its home floor than the Quad City Thunder. That's an amazing statistic in itself. It tells you about the kind of advantage the building gives our team and the confidence we play with in there.

The Thunder left Wharton Field House as winners. In the last regular-season game, on Friday March 26, 1993, they played in front of 6,288, a record crowd for the team at Wharton. In that game they defeated the Capital Region Pontiacs, 113-108, to complete a 38-17 regular-season record. The following Wednesday and Friday they launched a best-of-five game playoff series against the Grand Rapids Hoops with two home victories. They won the first, 120-89, in front of a rather thin crowd of 1,512. Perhaps buoyed by the 1-0 series lead, 4,138 fans showed up two nights later to watch the Thunder win again, 99-88. The series continued in Grand Rapids, where the Hoops won three straight games to take the series 3-2 and move on to the next playoff level. Those three Hoops' home victories at Welsh Arena in Grand Rapids drew meager crowds of 1,116, 1,621, and 2,018.

The Phone Booth. With good basketball and a variety of gimmicks, Thunder games were usually entertaining. A special addition to the entertainment was provided by Rockford Lightning coach Charley Rosen. Having the privilege of playing home games in a newer and larger arena, Rosen showed disdain for Wharton Field House. On a trip to Moline during the Thunder's first season, Rosen called the Field House a "phone booth." The next time he was in town, someone brought in a cardboard phone booth and set it up in mid-court before the game. During that and subsequent Rosen appearances, a telephone ring was blasted over the public address system and fans chanted, "Charley, Charley, it's for you" (QCThunder, online).

To The Mark

The Thunder's success on the court continued after they left Wharton Field House in 1993. They won their division four times while playing at The Mark, and twice won the CBA championship. In the 1993-94 championship series they defeated the Omaha Racers four games to one. For their second title, in 1997-98, they beat the Sioux Falls Skyforce in the final series, four games to three. (CBA History, online)

For the first few years at The Mark, total season attendance was near or above 100,000, although they never reached the 126,000 level attained by the Thunder in their first two years at Wharton. Beginning in 1995, attendance at The Mark began to taper off, in part because of competition from a new minor league hockey team, the Mallards, which began sharing The Mark with the Thunder that year. Soon after their arrival, the Mallards were outdrawing the Thunder. By 2000, interest in the Thunder had waned significantly, and in early 2001 – in mid-season – they and the entire CBA folded.

Attendance at Thunder Home Games, by Season, 1987-2001

Season	Total	Average	High	Low
At Wharton:				
1987-88	126,663	4,690	6,237	1,801
1988-89	126,267	4,677	6,137	2,267
1989-90	116,904	4,175	6,287	2,218
1990-91	113,460	4,052	6,194	2,168
1991-92	114,691	4,096	6,146	1,827
1992-93	97,804	3,493	6,288	1,802
At The Mark:				
1993-94	108,922	3,890	8,601	2,196
1994-95	121,260	4,331	9,879	2,650
1995-96	101,769	3,635	9,742	2,103
1996-97	106,324	3,797	7,557	1,977
1997-98	97,076	3,467	9,007	1,866
1998-99	90,671	3,238	9,236	1,632
1999-2000	79,404	2,835	9,308	1,368
2000-01	7,475	934	1,150	611

Source: Wendland, 2001

Dispatch files

A good crowd at The Mark for a Thunder game in 1995.

Chapter 5

In the Ring

C. Roseman

"Let the boys in." –Joe Lewis

As multi-purpose venues, the seating and performance spaces at both Wharton Field House and Browning Field were often modified to accommodate special events. In the case of boxing or wrestling, a ring would be set up in the center of the basketball floor at Wharton or in the baseball infield at Browning, and temporary chairs set up to provide "ring-side" seating. Two other types of special events at Wharton, circuses and roller derby, also required special "ring" arrangements. These four activities are reviewed in this chapter.

Throughout the first half of the twentieth century, boxing was a very popular sport in the United States. At the professional level, boxing and baseball were by far the most prominent national sports, before football, basketball, and hockey emerged as big-time sports in the 1950s. Boxing was equally important locally, with the Field House being one of the important sites for matches.

Over the years, Davenport held more boxing events than either Moline or Rock Island. They were held at the Coliseum (now the Col), the Masonic Temple (now Lyceum Hall of the Palmer School of Chiropractic), Turner Hall, and other indoor venues. In warmer weather some were held at Municipal Stadium (later John O'-Donnell Stadium and now Modern Woodmen Park). If a major name was coming to town, providing the potential for a very large crowd, the stadium in Davenport and the Field House in Moline were the primary choices, and the latter a better choice in the winter.

Boxing Before Wharton

For more than two decades before the Field House was opened in late 1928, some professional boxing programs had been held in Moline, most at the downtown Turner Hall and a few outdoors. Beginning in 1919, the Moline

This undated aerial photograph shows the stadium in Davenport with the Centennial Bridge in the foreground and the Mississippi River on the right. Called Modern Woodman Park since 2007, it has been the home of minor league professional baseball since 3,000 fans appeared for opening day, May 16, 1931. For many years it also hosted entertainers and festivals, as well as other sporting events including boxing, professional wrestling, and football. This view shows how the football field was articulated with the baseball diamond. First called Municipal Stadium, the facility was built by the City of Davenport through the issuance of $150,000 in bonds. Today it is one of the oldest professional baseball parks in the United States. In 1953 it was turned over to the Davenport Park Board and in 1971 was renamed John O'Donnell Stadium in honor of the long-time Davenport *Times-Democrat* sports reporter and editor. (Svendsen, n.d.)

[baseball] Fans' Association sponsored outdoor matches to raise money in support of the local minor league baseball team, the Plow Boys. The first of these was at Athletic Park, located just east of Riverside Park, on August 14, 1919. Close to 2,000 people showed up to see the main event in which Frankie Mason of Fort Wayne, Indiana, fought to a draw with Earl Puryear of Tulsa, Oklahoma. The Fans' Association subsequently sponsored boxing events at Browning Field, two of which were held on Independence Day in 1923 and 1924. Heading both cards was a local favorite, Lawrence "Sailor" Larson, a 137-pound featherweight who was a junior at Moline High School in 1923.

In the feature fight on July 4, 1923, Larson defeated Johnny Harris of Des Moines in ten rounds (although Harris, lying prone on the canvas in the seventh round, was saved by the bell at the count of seven). About 1,000 fans were in attendance. Harris received his guarantee of $200 plus expenses; Larson, who had not asked for a guarantee, got $300; and the baseball cause received $450.

Exactly one year later four bouts at Browning were highlighted by Larson defeating Babe Asher from St. Louis. By this time Larson's home-town-favorite status had been elevated to the point that the Dispatch (July 3) beamed:

Lawrence Larson, "Sailor"

Yell Master

Sailor stepped into the cheer leader's rubbers with the experience of the platform and athletic training behind him. His was a task requiring real ability and the record of his accomplishments is pleasing. His jolly temperament and his stock phrases, "Well, we got another speaker" and "He's going to tell you all about the game," never failed to bring a laugh and pep the student body up for a roaring yell.

"SAILOR"

M, 1924

At Moline High School "Sailor" Larson was not only a Yell Master but also a champion extemporaneous speaker and president of the student body. He began a six-year professional boxing career while still in high school.

With the weather the only doubtful feature, preparations are being made to entertain the greatest crowd of fistic followers in the history of Moline and perhaps of the Tri-Cities at Browning field tomorrow afternoon when Sailor Larson, Moline's foremost exponent of the glove-wielding profession will meet the most accomplished foe of his career in Babe Asher, now a 123 pounder, who formerly was bantamweight champion of the American expeditionary forces. The show is being sponsored by the Moline Fans Association. While the Larson Asher scrap, of course, will be the main magnet for the hundreds of bugs expected to sit in, a supporting card worthy of the caliber of the principals in the main go will whet the fans' appetite for the climax.

However, a record crowd did not appear. Just like the year before, about 1,000 fans were there. Overall, Sailor Larson won 27 bouts, lost nineteen, and had seven draws in a professional career that extended from 1923 to 1929. Through 1926, most of his fights were in Illinois or Iowa, and most of them victories. Locally he fought in Davenport at the Coliseum and the Palmer School Arena, and in Rock Island at the Legion Hall. Beginning in 1927 he travelled widely across the East and the South, where he won only seven of 23 bouts before retiring. (BoxRec, online)

After the Field House was opened in 1928, outdoor boxing in Moline was rare. On August 8, 1940, the Moline Fans' Association sponsored an amateur boxing show at Browning to raise money in support of the struggling Plow Boys baseball team. Fighters from the Quad Cities and other towns in Iowa and Illinois participated. Fourteen boxers fought in front of 1,500 fans. Two local Golden Gloves champions both won their matches, Bobby Hallgren of Moline and Tommy Campbell who had recently moved from Kansas City. Lynn Callaway of the *Dispatch* injected a bit of boosterism in his preview of the event:

> While the primary purpose of tomorrow's boxing show was to help raise funds for a losing ball club, [the Association] wanted to give boxing fans a summer treat and, at the same time, discover how much interest an all-star fight show could create in the city which always has been red hot for Golden gloves in the winter months.

In 1946 another amateur program was held at Browning as part of a Sports Day in conjunction with the 98th anniversary celebration of the City of Moline. In the feature fight in front of 5,000 fans, heavyweight Bill Stohl of Geneseo defeated Scottie Dowell of Galesburg who failed to come out for the third round. Perhaps the beginning of the end was when, in the first round, the Geneseo lad "tore into Dowell with a flurry of rights and lefts which sent Dowell through the ropes into the ring-side crowd in less than 20 seconds of the round" (*Dispatch*, August 7).

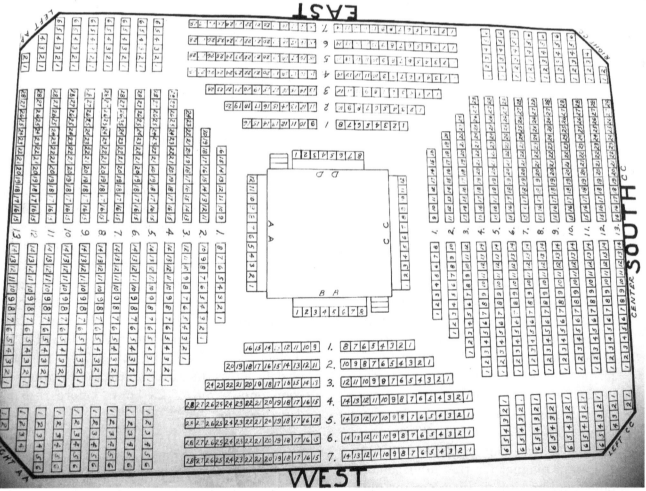

Chairs were configured in this way for at least some boxing and wrestling matches at Wharton Field House. Shown are the ring in the middle and the locations of 1,260 chairs on the raised basketball floor. With this many seats on the main floor, the arena could accommodate crowds approaching 7,000.

Professional Boxing at Wharton

In February 1930 the Moline Elks Club sponsored the first professional boxing card at the Field House. According to the *Dispatch* (February 3), these matches were the first in Moline to be "within the law." The Illinois Boxing Commission had been organized in 1926 and began sanctioning and regulating a controversial sport that previously had been banned in many places. The new rules allowed Chicago to host the famous 1927 fight in which Gene Tunney defeated Jack Dempsey for the World Heavyweight Championship. Often referred to as the "long-count" fight, it attracted over 100,000 fans to Soldier Field.

Having been cleared by the Maroon and White Association, that first boxing program at the Field House featured a bout between Al Isoz of Rockford and Battling Burner of Chicago and attracted 3,000 people. Both pugilists – with their managers, trainers, and seconds – arrived in Moline several days before the February 7th

Schmeling Ready to Demonstrate To Moline How He Lays 'Em Cold

MAX SCHMELING.

Dispatch, April 8, 1931

match and trained in the basement of the Elks Club, albeit at separate times. An innovative ring was brought to Moline for the event.

> The Hessenauer brothers, matchmakers for the Elks . . . have arranged with Lew Barnes of Chicago, ringmaster for the elite of the resin realm, to deliver at the field house not later than Thursday [February 6] an all-steel ring, enclosed in velour-covered ropes. The layout, speaking in round numbers, is valued at $700 and may be set up or taken down in two-thirds of an hour. (*Dispatch*, February 3, 1930)

Lew Barnes was also known for having invented an elevator-style ring in use at Madison Square Garden in New York. The ten-round match between Isoz and Burner resulted in a draw. Dispatch writer Pat Patten reflected on the event (February 8, 1930): "If the cheers of 3,000 customers can decide the future of boxing in Moline, the city's first entertainment, conducted in the field house last night under the rigid regulations of the Illinois Athletic Commission, will not be its last."

Patten's prognostication was correct. The Elks sponsored another card on March 3rd in which 2,000 fans saw Young Camp of Kewanee beat Jacquette Elverrillo of Panama. Subsequent boxing events were arranged and now, with the large seating capacity of the Field House, it was possible to attract some big names to the Quad Cities. Two world-famous boxers visited in 1931, Max Schmeling and Jack Dempsey.

The appearance of Schmeling, Heavyweight Champion of the World at the time, prompted this story lead by Lynn Callaway in the *Dispatch* (April 9):

> Herr Max Schmeling of Germany didn't exactly take the fight fans of the quad-cities by storm in the field house last night, but he did put on a boxing show with two sparring partners that pleased the rather slim gathering for three rounds. [He] stepped off three fast sessions with Pedro Lopez and Tony

Marullo in which he proved an ability to hit straight, hard jabs with both hands and demonstrated a skillful bit of footwork that is surprising for a man of his size. Maxie apparently satisfied the 2,500 to 3,000 fans who watched his workout . . . If the showing is any indication, he is an unrelenting puncher of the type that will cause Willie "Young" Stribling lots of trouble when they meet for the world title this summer.

Three months later Schmeling retained his title by knocking out Stribling in the 15th round of a match in Cleveland on July 3rd. Like the champ's appearance in Moline, this fight was held in a relatively new arena, Cleveland's Municipal Stadium, which was completed just two days before the fight. And like the Field House event, only half the seats were filled there. Whereas the huge stadium could seat 78,000, only about 35,000 attended. Municipal Stadium was torn down in 1996 after having been the home of the Cleveland major league professional baseball and football teams, the Indians and Browns, for several decades.

In contrast to the Schmeling appearance in Moline, Dempsey's exhibition in November 1931 drew a capacity crowd, estimated between 6,000 and 7,000. He had performed at the Coliseum in Davenport two years earlier, filling it with a "record crowd," (*Dispatch*, October 5, 1929), which was less than half the size of the Field House crowd. In attendance at the Moline event were a number of out-of-town state and national boxing officials, along with several Chicago sports writers including Arch Ward, who served as sports editor of the *Tribune* from 1930 to 1955.

The "Manassa Mauler," as Dempsey had become known, faced two different opponents, two rounds each. He "labored through four rounds of rough mixing with George Neron of Greece and Pete Wistort of Chicago, a couple of slow heavyweights who managed to stay the limit with the former champion of champions" (*Dispatch*, November 14, 1931). Dempsey had been world champion from 1919 to 1926. In one

of the other fights on the card, Kid Leonard of East Moline defeated Pep Justo of Chicago.

After the Dempsey appearance, Callaway of the *Dispatch* (November 14) wrote: "It was thrilling to see so many persons packed into the field house. It was something worth talking about to know that hundreds of fans came in to Moline from cities for miles on either side in Illinois and Iowa. Moline was on the map plenty last night."

Arch Ward put a rather different spin on the evening:

> Neither exhibition was soul stirring, scarcely heart thrilling. They lacked the elemental savageness you expect in a Dempsey fight . . . The crowd of 6,000, the largest boxing turnout in Moline's history . . . were booing as Jack left the ring. These are the type of people who would delight in seeing Nero toss Christians to the lions. Nobody gets a thrill out of watching Babe Ruth bunt or Pug Rentner [All-American at Northwestern] pick up a yard or two off tackle. It's that way with Dempsey. If he is to regain his old popularity, he must win with one of those 'clear the track, here comes Casey Jones' finishes. Nobody cares to see him win on points. (*Chicago Tribune*, November 14, 1931)

More Local Favorites

Kid Leonard of East Moline was a local favorite who fought at the Field House four times in the early 1930s. The Kid, a middleweight whose real name was Leonard Van Der Walle, won 53 of 75 matches in a professional career that extended from 1928 to 1937. About half of his matches were in the Quad Cities, mostly in Davenport; his first at the Coliseum and some at the stadium in that city. Other fights were all over the Midwest, including several in Chicago. His only foray outside of the region was for a June 1934 fight at the Civic Auditorium in San Francisco, where he was defeated by Sammy Slaughter. (BoxRec, online)

Dispatch files

Tommy Campbell, who grew up in Kansas City, Kansas, and lived in Muscatine for a while in 1940 before moving to Rock Island, won the national Golden Gloves championship in Chicago in 1941. After serving in World War II, he began a five-year career as a professional boxer. During the summer before the 1946 Field House bout, he fought four times at Municipal Stadium in Davenport. Known as the "Chocolate Ice Cube," he won 64 bouts, lost 12, and drew 6 as a professional. After a few fights in the Midwest, he moved to Los Angeles in 1947 and travelled widely for matches. Among his prominent fights was a 1948 loss to Enrique Bolanos, "lightweight pride of Mexico," in a bout in front of 10,400 at the Olympic Auditorium in Los Angeles (*Argus*, December 1). In 1950 Campbell was involved in a scandal in which a Los Angeles promoter, Babe McCoy, was accused of fixing fights. For his last fight, on September 11, 1951, Campbell came back to the Quad Cities. In front of 2,200 fans at the Davenport stadium he beat Wallace Bud Smith of Cincinnati in a ten-round decision. (*Dispatch*, June 16, 1969 and BoxRec, online)

No professional boxing was held at the Field House in the late 1930s or during World War II. After the war, fights resumed at Wharton for a few years and then were not held again until 1980. The first major event, on November 11, 1946, featured Tommy Campbell, who prevailed over Danny Robinson of Chicago in a ten-round decision in front of 1,800 fans. Five years earlier Campbell had won a Golden Gloves championship at Wharton and went on to win the lightweight crown in the 1941 Chicago Golden Gloves Tournament of Champions.

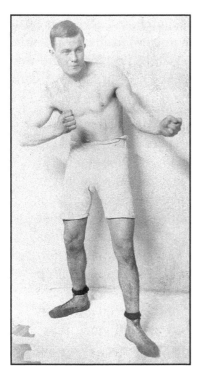

Courtesy of Judy Belan

Leonard Van Der Walle of East Moline boxed under the name "Kid Leonard." In a nine-year professional career, he appeared four times at Wharton Field House.

More Big Names

In the post-war period some big names in boxing again were featured at the Field House. The first of these was Joe Lewis who appeared on January 18, 1949, for an exhibition match sponsored by the Moline Optimist Club. Lewis, weighing 221 pounds, had been World Heavyweight Champion since 1937 and defended his title

"Big Boy" Indeed. In a 1950 fight at the Field House sponsored by the Moline Optimist Club, light heavyweight champion Joey Maxim won a ten-round decision over Al "Big Boy" Brown. The *Chicago Tribune* (November 22) revealed: "The match was billed as a heavy-weight contest. Maxim weighed 184 and Brown, 263. Some 1,000 customers attended."

THE PERFECT
CHRISTMAS GIFT!

TICKETS

To See

Joe Louis

AND

4—All Star Bouts—4

Wharton Field House

TUESDAY EVENING **JANUARY 18**

Sponsored by the Optimist Club of Moline

Tickets NOW on Sale!
Moline Optical Co. and Temples
—Moline.
Todd's—Rock Island.
Agnew Drug Store—E. Moline.
Martin's—Davenport.

Mail Orders—Include Postage
DEAN HADDICK
1305 Fifth Avenue   Moline, Ill.

— PRICES —
$1.30; $2.60; $3.90; $5.20
Including Tax

Argus, December 22, 1948

Probably the biggest name in boxing at the time, Joe Lewis, appeared at Wharton Field House in January 1949.

25 times. At Wharton he headed a card of five bouts. The day after the match, *Argus* sports writer Howard W. Hargrave wrote:

> Heavy-weight Champion Joe Louis needed only occasional recourse to the tools of a fistic king last night to handle Dick Hagen of Chicago in their exhibition bout at Wharton fieldhouse, but the legendary Brown Bomber's gate appeal worked overtime to attract a crowd of 5,600 quad-city residents to the arena through stormy weather.

The "stormy weather" had piled up the deepest snow of the season in the area. Nonetheless, the big crowd forked over enough to make the *Dispatch* (January 19) proclaim: "The gate was $16,650, the largest in modern local sports history."

Two years later, on February 15, 1951, big-time boxing returned to Wharton, but this time on small screens. The Tri-Cities Blackhawks arranged for an early start of their basketball game against the Indianapolis Olympians. Fans were offered cookies and ice cream and invited to stay to view the television broadcast of the

fight between Sugar Ray Robinson and Jake LaMotta. For that purpose ten nineteen-inch television sets were placed on the main floor (and in those days, TV sets of that size were considered quite large!). Of the 2,350 fans who showed up to Wharton for basketball (and ice cream and cookies), about 1,000 stayed for the boxing show. (Kiesele, 1951) Robinson won in a thirteenth round TKO in front of 14,802 fans at the Chicago Stadium. The fight became known as Chicago's second "Saint Valentine's Day Massacre." Back at Wharton, before the big fight began, the Blackhawks had won the basketball game 98-91.

In June 1954, the next big event, a championship bout between heavyweights Rocky Marciano and Ezzard Charles, attracted a much larger crowd, over 47,000! That number, of course, was the live attendance at Yankee Stadium. But a big crowd showed up at Wharton to watch the match on a large screen via closed-circuit television. Not shown on live television, the broadcast was piped to dozens of venues in over forty cities across the United States. Weather affected this match, too, as it was postponed because of rain in New York. Skies cleared for the June 17, 1954, fight and Marciano won in a fifteen-round decision. The *Muscatine Journal and News Tribune* described the event:

> For the first time in the history of the Quad-City area, sport fans will get an opportunity to view a closed circuit presentation – just as fans in larger cities have been able to see such attractions in movie houses. A 16 by 20 foot screen will be erected and preparations are being made . . . to seat more than 6,500 for the world's championship battle. There will be no reserved seats . . . since the size of the screen and location of chairs on the fieldhouse floor, plus balcony seats, will assure everyone attending a fine, unobstructed view of the proceedings.

Then in January 1971, plans were being made for two more big names in boxing to appear on the screen at Wharton. Mohammad Ali would

"Let the boys in." Milt Johnson of Moline and three of his teenage buddies had become accustomed to sneaking into the Field House for amateur boxing matches, especially the Golden Gloves events. They would simply knock on the window of a locker room on the west side of the building, and someone inside would open the window and let them slip in through the narrow opening. So, naturally, the lads showed up on the night of the Joe Lewis fight and knocked on the window. A gruff-sounding gent said "What do you want?" They replied that they wanted to come in to watch boxing, to which the gent said "go around to the front and buy a ticket." After mentioning that they had no money, Milt heard a voice coming from the other side of the locker room: "Let the boys in." It was the Brown Bomber himself, having his hands wrapped in his dressing room. After slipping into the room, Milt looked at Lewis and thought "he was the biggest man I ever saw in my life." Sounds like he was not only big in stature, but also in heart.

meet Joe Frazier on March 8th in what was called the "fight of the century" at Madison Square Garden in New York. An estimated 300 million people in fifty countries around the globe watched the match on closed-circuit television.

The fight drew widespread attention not only because Ali and Frazier were the two best heavyweights at the time, but also because of the saga of Ali's personal life and his public pronouncements. He had converted to the Muslim faith, opposed the Vietnam War, and refused induction into the armed forces. As such he was a polarizing figure, supported by civil rights and anti-war activists, and opposed by others. He polarized the Moline school board as well when promoters proposed to show the fight at Wharton. On January 13th, eight weeks before the fight, Dave Stickle wrote in the *Dispatch*:

> Boxer Muhammad Ali and the Moline District 40 Board of Education went two rounds in voting last night on the question of whether or not a closed-circuit telecast of a March 8th world heavyweight championship prizefight would be allowed in the school's Wharton Field House. In the final vote of the second round, Ali won. The Board allowed the rental of the field house to a Davenport promoter to show the fight between Ali and Joe Frazier.

In the first round of voting, permission was denied by a 4-3 vote, with board President Robert G. Seeds breaking a 3-3 tie and voting no. This was followed by a frank discussion among board members, who expressed their opinions for and against. In a second round of voting, six board members stayed with their previous votes, but Seeds changed his vote, allowing the event to be held at Wharton. The result of the debate in Moline, however, was for naught – the fight was shown at the RKO Orpheum in Davenport. Frazier won the fifteen-round match by unanimous decision.

Pro boxing had not appeared live at the Field House for many years when a series of six events were arranged for the 1980-81 winter season by

Dispatch, March 6, 1971

The 1971 Frazier-Ali fight closed-circuit television showing was moved to the RKO Orpheum [now the Adler] Theatre in Davenport, which seated about 2,700 at the time. Attendance figures reported in local newspapers ranged from 1,172 to 2,500!

PROFESSIONAL BOXING

"THE BUNNY PIERCE BOXING SPECTACULAR"
Wednesday, November 19, 1980

MAIN EVENT - 10 ROUNDS		
PEDRO ACOSTA - Panama		AVERISTO RODRIGUEZO - Chicago
South American Light	vs.	U.S World Class Light
Welter Weight Champion		Welter Weight

SEMI-MAIN EVENT - 8 ROUNDS		
CARL CROWLEY		JEFFREY MADISON
Muscatine, Iowa	vs.	St. Louis, Missouri
– Two Very Exciting Middle Weights –		

Also . . .
2 6-Round Preliminary Matches   2 4-Round Warm Up Matches

- - TICKETS ON SALE AT THE FOLLOWING LOCATIONS - -

MOLINE	ROCK ISLAND	DAVENPORT
Joe's Gym and Fitness Center	The Athletic Shop	Kunkel's Sporting Goods
3158 - 23rd Avenue	1825 3rd Avenue	730 E. Kimberly Road
Temple's Sporting Goods	Parkridge Furn TV Appliances	Craton's Sporting Goods
1524 - 6th Avenue	3708 - 11th Street	222 Harrison Street
EAST MOLINE	GENESEO	MUSCATINE	BETTENDORF
Percy's Tire Spot	Cherry's Sporting Goods	C & K Sports Shope	Waterbed Creations
1347 - 18th Avenue	Geneseo, Illinois	1500 Park Avenue	411 - 14th Street

Ringside - $8.00   Gen. Admission - $5.00
Show Starts at 8:00 p.m. — Doors Open at 7:00 p.m.

WHARTON FIELD HOUSE
1800 - 20th Avenue   Moline, Illinois

Courtesy of Jerry Wallaert

This poster promoted the first professional boxing card at the Field House in the 1980-81 season. For the main event Averisto Rodrigueo was replaced by Carlos Gonzales of Durango, Mexico, who lost to Pedro Acosta in three rounds. This was the first of six events, held on November 19 and December 10, 1980; and January 7, February 18, March 15, and April 24, 1981. (BoxRec, online)

promoter Terry Snyder of International Professional Sports Promotions. The programs included some fighters from around the Midwest who were national-level contenders as well as some locals. One card was held each month from November 1980 through April 1981. After the first of these, which attracted 1,500 fans, Snyder said that receipts were adequate to continue professional boxing at Wharton and "We didn't expect to get rich, we just wanted to let people know we're here." (Marose, 1980)

Won and Lost. On the November card, nineteen-year-old Carl Crowley of Tipton, Iowa, won his match at Wharton, defeating Jeffery Madison of St. Louis in a ten-round decision, but lost his clothes! After the match Crowley found that his clothes and passport had been taken from the locker room, "forcing him to roam the field house in his trunks and robe until other garments arrived." Aside from winning the fight, it was not a good week for Crowley; he had been robbed in Chicago the night before. (Marose, 1980)

The event in December attracted about 1,400, and the numbers for January and February were probably no higher. In March the event was scheduled for the first time on a Sunday afternoon. Promoter Snyder had obtained a court order to gain permission for a boxing card on Sunday, in violation of a state law that prohibited boxing on Sunday. (Marose, 1981) But his efforts were not rewarded; the Sunday crowd was small owing to nice weather and competition from other events, including racing at Quad City Downs and a televised basketball game between the University of Iowa and Wichita State.

Recognizing that the Sunday scheduling was a mistake, Snyder scheduled the April event on a Friday evening. One of the locals on the seven-bout card was Rocky Molina of Moline who lost to Willie Alexander of Chicago. Molina was urged on by fans chanting "Rocky, Rocky, Rocky." Another local was middleweight Carl Crowley, who had fought in two previous events at Wharton that season. He knocked out Frank Anast of Milwaukee. Paul Marose of the *Dispatch* (April 25)

relayed the bad news for Anast: "Besides losing the bout, Anast also forfeited some permanent bridgework according to referee Ed Stage, who also was decorated with Anast's blood." It was bad news for professional boxing fans too. The crowd was again "sparse" and this was the last professional boxing event to be held at Wharton Field House.

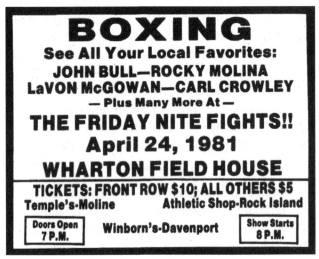

Dispatch, April 23, 1981

Several local fighters were featured in this 1981 boxing card at Wharton.

Amateur Boxing at Wharton

Alongside the professional version, amateur boxing was very popular in the United States from the 1930s into the 1950s. One of the more prominent early events at the Field House was the three-day Mississippi Valley sectional boxing tournament in April 1936. Sponsored by the Amateur Athletic Union, the event attracted seventy boxers from teams representing Burlington (Iowa), Danville, Joliet, Peoria, Quincy, Rockford, and Springfield (Illinois), in addition to the Quad Cities. Winners went on to the national AAU tournament in Cleveland. (*Argus*, March 30).

Beginning in 1930, Golden Gloves tournaments were held nearly every year at the Field House for over two decades. In the 1930s they were sponsored by the Davenport *Daily Times* and in the 1940s and early 1950s by the Moline *Dispatch*. Winners advanced to the Golden Gloves finals in Chicago each year.

Argus, April 4, 1936

Winners of the 1936 AAU boxing tournament who advanced to the national tournament, shown here in the ring at the Field House. In the front row are Gilbert Longtin of Danville, Johnny Fairchild of Rockford, Johnny Balmer of Peoria, and Les Morris of Davenport. In the back row are Elwood McReynolds and Frank Nelson of Davenport, Robert Ray of Danville, and Oliver Odom of East Moline.

The events grew dramatically at Wharton during the 1930s. In 1934, 106 boxers participated, a number that increased to 147 in 1935. Over 3,000 attended the 1935 preliminaries on February 7th, almost twice the crowd ever achieved for an opening program. In 1937, 250 boxers participated, including 21 former champions. Over thirty bouts were held each of the first two nights of the five-night tournament. (*Chicago Tribune*, January 27, 1937)

In February 1941, ten months before the United States entered World War II, the finals of the twelfth annual local Golden Gloves tournament attracted 6,000 fans to Wharton Field House. The eight champions hailed from Rock Island, Aledo, Silvis, Kewanee, and Muscatine. Each would fight the following two weeks at the finals held at the Chicago Stadium. (*Dispatch*, February 19)

Howard Barry's words in the *Chicago Tribune* (March 8, 1941) about the Chicago finals symbolize the importance of the 1941 tournament and of Golden Gloves in general during that era:

The 1941 Golden Gloves tournament came to a traditionally spectacular climax last night as eight boys emerged finally victorious from a struggle in which 23,000 [boxers] had been engaged through many weeks of campaigning, The crowd of 21,650 packed all available space in the [Chicago] Stadium to watch the concluding program of the annual show run off under the sponsorship of Chicago Tribune Charities, Inc.

Two champions from the Quad City tournament reached final matches in Chicago. Tommy Campbell won the 135-pound championship by beating Richard Scholl of Peoria. Eddie Hudson lost in the 126-pound final match to Jack Haley of Kansas City. The *Tribune* identified both Campbell and Hudson as from "Moline," probably because they had emerged from the Field House tournament in Moline. Both grew up in Kansas City.

Hudson Praised. Barry highlighted one particular match in his *Tribune* story: "In the course of the 13 years of Golden Gloves history there have been great bouts but last night's crowd saw one in particular that was worthy of taking its place with the magnificent battles of the past. It was the engagement in which [Jack] Haley, a good looking red-headed Irish youngster from Kansas, beat Eddie Hudson of Moline, one of the most rugged and courageous colored boys who ever stepped in to a Golden Gloves encounter."

Dispatch, February 10, 1948

Golden Gloves competition was at its peak of popularity in the late 1940s. On the left is the cover of the 1948 printed program and above a notice of matches being broadcast on the radio, also from 1948.

In announcing the 1949 Golden Gloves finals, which attracted 5,100 fans, the Davenport *Democrat and Leader* (February 15) touted the continued interest in local boxing:

> Despite the snow and ice, a huge crowd of fans is expected to turn out for this classic. Each year the Golden Gloves finals have ranked along with the traditional sport meetings between the local high schools as 'musts' on the calendar for thrills and action. The doors will open at 7, and there'll be plenty of good seats available at the gate. The parking lot will be in condition for all the autos with the added feature of a tow truck on hand to aid anyone whose auto fails to start or becomes stuck.

Golden Gloves tournaments continued into the early 1950s at Wharton. Then, after almost two decades of no amateur boxing at the Field House, the sport returned on February 7, 1971. The program was sponsored by the All-Time Glove Association of the Quad Cities, along with local firefighter groups and the county Muscular Dystrophy Agency. In addition to several local boxers, a few came from elsewhere in Iowa and Illinois. The feature bout pitted two who had won state championships, Bill Robinson of Oskaloosa, Iowa, and Pat Sullivan of Peoria, Illinois. Sullivan won a unanimous decision in front of about 2,000 fans.

A 1982 amateur program at the Field House provided some drama if not good boxing. The West Side Boxing Club of Moline invited the Muhammad Ali Boxing School of Louisville, Kentucky, to bring fighters to compete with a group of Golden Gloves champions from Northern Illinois and Eastern Iowa. The results were disappointing to the "600 or so fans who rattled around the field house" (Shane, 1982). Mario Terronez of the Moline club was exasperated:

> I'm not happy about it at all. We had good fighters ready for this and expected the same from them (the Louisville club). Some of those guys didn't belong in the ring with our guys at all.

Nonetheless, the event may have been worth the admission price had the Louisville club's namesake made an appearance. Earlier in the week promoter Terry Snyder said that Muhammad Ali was "supposed to be in Chicago then drive here." When he did not show up, Bob Cunningham, coordinator of the Louisville club, revealed that Ali "was not even in the area. Actually his connection with the club is not very

strong anymore." (Shane, 1982) Alas, this was the last – or one of the last – amateur boxing shows at the Field House. According to Tom Minick, who has cared for the Field House since 1985, no boxing programs, amateur or professional, have been staged there since that year.

Professional Wrestling

Whereas the popularity of boxing as a sport was waning in the 1950s, another "sport" conducted on a mat surrounded by ropes was rapidly gaining popularity in that decade. Professional wrestling came to television sets and local arenas across the country, including Wharton Field House. For at least three decades before television, however, pro wrestling was promoted locally and held at numerous smaller venues,

Argus, February 1, 1950

"The Quad-Cities' Greatest Sports Event" was held at Wharton Field House in February 1950.

Courtesy of Jerry Wallaert

Perhaps the last amateur boxing program to be held at the Field House was this one in 1982.

121

including the Labor Temple and Centennial Club in Rock Island, the Coliseum Ballroom and other locations in Davenport, and the Moose Hall in Moline.

Just like those of the Wharton and television era, earlier wrestlers were showmen who displayed distinctive personas and put on performances that many fans thought were "real" athletic contests. One of the more interesting wrestlers was Maurice Tillet, the "French Angel," who appeared in the Quad Cities numerous times in the 1940s. About 550 fans appeared at the Swedish Olive Hall in downtown Moline on April 27, 1944, to watch the Angel battle Don Koch of Platteville, Wisconsin. Early in the match Koch administered a headlock on the Frenchman, then a body slam. Tillet fell on his head, was unable to continue, and was out cold for thirty minutes. The *Dispatch* (April 28) noted that he magically recovered in the locker room and "There was considerable argument among fans here as to whether the injury to the Angel was serious or might have been part of the show." Apparently he quickly exited the locker room, consumed a steak dinner, and left for Chicago.

An early, and perhaps all-time, highlight of professional wrestling at Wharton was the January 1950 appearance of Gorgeous George. By that year, the "Gorgeous One" had become nationally famous as a wrestler and performer, having appeared on national radio shows with such stars as Jack Benny, Bing Crosby, and Bob Hope. Although he was often described as a tough and competent athlete, his flamboyant presence was the appeal. The *Dispatch* (January 10) described George:

> G.G., whose real name is George Wagner, won fame through a number of spectacular devices, including his butler, who sprays with perfume and disinfectant any area to be occupied by the Gorgeous One. George also flaunts a mop of glamorous blond hair, tastefully arranged by a skilled hairdresser and held in place by his famed 'Georgie Pins.'

HE'S GORGEOUS — What the well-dressed male should wear is exhibited by Gorgeous George who will meet George Temple tonight in the feature bout of the wrestling show at Wharton fieldhouse.

Argus, January 20, 1950

The *Argus* promoted the first visit of Gorgeous George to the Field House in 1950.

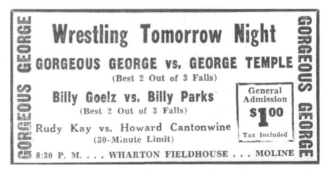

Argus, January 19, 1950

The match, sponsored by the Tri-Cities Black-hawks, pitted the Gorgeous One with George Temple from Hollywood, brother of film star Shirley Temple. The event, from its unfolding to its painful end, is best described by Jim Dix, the *Dispatch* drama critic. Dix was recruited by the sports department because the sports writers felt "inadequate to deal with the thespian elegancies of the Gorgeous George show." The commentary by Dix, below, was published on January 21, 1950.

One thing may be said in praise of the drama at Wharton Fieldhouse last night. The timing was perfect. It started out on a dramaturgically correct minor key, setting the mood for the coming of the star, and then, at exactly the right moment, the star appeared, like a disdainful Caesar, come to intimidate the Roman senate.

First appeared the straight man, an earnest, brown-haired young fellow named George Temple. Unaccompanied, he went on stage – that is to say, the ring in the center of the basketball floor – walked to his corner like little Jack Horner and stood there mum – a well-executed piece of business but a relatively easy one in that it didn't require any memorizing of lines.

Second to show was a little man with a bald head and mustache, dressed in morning coat and trousers, black tie and green vest. He was bottle-bearer to the star. After laying out a yellow towel and blue mat, he, with spray gun in hand, proceeded to wet down the surroundings with cologne – a sensible precaution. It turned out, in view of the slightly different olfactory nature of what was to transpire, and a service to the public regrettably lacking at certain theatrical presentations, Channel Cat No. 5, I believe it was.

Finally, at precisely 9:38 p.m. while the atmosphere swelled with organ music and smelled like clover and some other cash grain crop, in came The Presence. Gorgeous George had made his entry. Entry? Ah, no, his manifestation. Most of the 3,600 citizens present stood up to see him come down the northwest passageway, bowing his marcelled locks (a Moline-produced coiffure) to the balcony and sashaying saucily to the ring like a prize bull that has just eaten the farmer. Inside the ropes, he bowed again, from the hips, whereupon his batboy ministered to his toilet.

At this point, it was time for that scantily clad girl to walk across the stage, followed by that lecherous-eyed old man. But somebody, possibly the Quad City Blackhawks management, who produced the show, had neglectfully overlooked this bit. So next the three principal performers, Mr. Temple, whose sister Shirley also acts; Gorgeous, and a master of ceremonies, one Ed Whalen of Chicago, displaying remarkable artistic discipline in keeping straight faces, met at the center of the ring. This as to allow Mr. Whalen to search the other two for concealed gats [guns], or something.

Whatever the purpose, G.G., clutching his black, gold-spangled, yellow-lined toga about him, would not let the emcee lay a hand on him. His line, exquisitely delivered and, as all good lines are, surely audible in the back row, was: 'Keep your filthy hands off me.' The fertile creator of the snappy dialog remains modestly unidentified in the program.

Pretty soon, Straight Man George and Gorgeous George went into their song and dance, and during the next half hour, at quiet moments, you could hear Farmer Burns turning in the grave. (That would be a sensational gimmick to work into the act, come to think of it.)

From 9:55 to 10:10, Gorgeous and Not Gorgeous were doing the samba (perhaps it was the maxixe – I'm a little hazy on the dance) or were on the mat executing what appeared to be a horizontal terpsichorean interpretation of les crappes. For these episodes the M.C. got down there with them, calling out numbers from time to time, symbolizing, probably, the tragic fate of man, crapping out every time with a two or a three.

At 10:10, time enough for Gorgeous' retainer to have changed costume, they stopped a while to rest, G.G. having pinned his partner with a toe hold in 15 minutes, 10 seconds. Enter valet, in green sweater, and with smell salts. Exit valet.

In the second scene, I am saddened to relate, Gorgeous let his role get away from him. He ran the gamut (good word; like to work it into my critiques wherever I can) from tortured pain, to stormy anger, to injured innocence, and, in a burst to histrionic heights, screamed 'No! No! No!' while Mr. Temple broke his leg. All of these bits had possibilities, but they were slightly over-done. Gorgeous should remember Hamlet's dictum to The Players: 'Oh, it offends me to the soul to hear a robustious periwig-pated fellow tear a passion to tatters, to very rags . . .' All high-class drama, and all high-class reviews, should bear due reference to Shakespeare.

After 3 minutes, 18 seconds, Mr. Temple leaps into the air, kicks up his heels, and almost boots Gorgeous in the mouth. Gorgeous staggers, Gorgeous falls to his knees, Gorgeous collapses on the canvas – a direct steal from the demise of Don Jose in the last act of Carmen, only this one was accomplished by a kangaroo kick and body twist, an angle Bizet never thought of. That makes a horse

on Gorgeous. Tied up. Enter caddie with mirror. Examining teeth to see if any are missing. Exit caddie.

Final scene: Gorgeous George has a fresh approach. As he dispatches the other George practically to death's door with mighty body slams, excruciating wrist locks and mortifying double-action, dyna-flow half gainers with a left-hand thread and two dips of ice cream, he barks just like a dog. He goes: 'Grrf. Grrf.' And George Temple now gets some dialog. He bleats like a sheep while Big Bo Beep fractures the knuckles of his left hand, one by one. Gorgeous George holds George Temple still with a body press, at 9 minutes 35 seconds.

Gorgeous George becomes world champion of Wharton Fieldhouse. Make that the middle of the basketball floor at Wharton Fieldhouse. Curtain.

EDITOR'S NOTE – Our critic was seen going home at 1:55:18 a.m. with a hammer lock on himself, and hasn't been seen at the office all day.

Argus, January 21, 1950

Gorgeous George in the ring at Wharton Field House. The caption for this *Argus* photograph reads in part: "Although he visited a hairdresser yesterday afternoon, Gorgeous George didn't derive any extended benefit from the treatment . . . Gorgeous, his golden locks in wild disarray, flips George Temple over as they maul each other on the floor."

A caricature of Jim Dix, who wrote eloquently in the *Dispatch* about Gorgeous George at Wharton Field House in January 1950.

Dispatch, January 21, 1950

From 1950 onward, the Field House hosted pro wrestling during most years until 1975, then again from 1987 until 1992, after which The Mark of the Quad Cities became the preferred site for this "sport." Typically the Field House matches would be held during fall, winter, and spring, with the stadium in Davenport hosting summer matches. For some events at Wharton, fans were offered rides on special buses from downtown Davenport. In the 1950s, the busiest year was 1955, during which at least ten programs were held at the Field House. (Wrestling Data, online)

Gorgeous George, of course, was a harbinger of what was to come, an activity that was personality-driven and full of outrageous gimmicks. Gradually it turned farther and farther away from legitimate amateur wrestling. But large crowds flocked to the Field House to cheer for those who played the "good guys" ("face wrestlers") and boo those who projected evil in their performances ("heels").

Most wrestlers in the 1950s and 1960s went by their real names: Among those appearing in Moline were: Verne Gagne, Benito Gardini, Rene Goulet, Larry Henning, Art Neilson, Leo Nomellini, Pat O'Connor, Hans Schmidt, and Lou Thesz. Some, however – like the Gorgeous One – modified their names, a practice more commonly used by heels. So, the Field House greeted such creatures as Reggie "Crusher" Lisowski (or simply "The Crusher"), Larry "The Ax" Henning, Killer Kowalski, The Mighty Atlas, Moose Cholak, Mr. Moto, Mad Dog Vachon, Yukon Eric, and Dr. X. Some midget wrestlers also appeared with interesting names, including Lord Clayton Littlebrook and Pee Wee James.

Local newspaper coverage of professional wrestling was minimal. Typically the results would not be reported or would be given only a

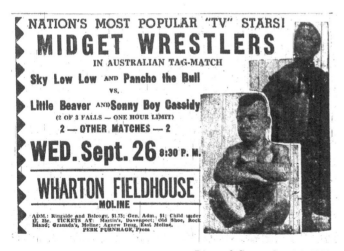

Dispatch, September 24, 1951

Argus, January 6, 1956

Professional wrestling of the time was not limited to large muscular or beefy males. Midget wrestlers were featured at the Field House in September 1951, including Sky Low Low and Little Beaver, and females in 1956, including Belle Star.

short paragraph on the sports page. Longer stories and big headlines were reserved for high school and college sports, along with legitimate professional sports, especially baseball. Even in those short pieces on pro wrestling, however, sports writers seemed to relish the opportunity to inject sarcasm into their coverage, following the lead of Jim Dix in his piece on the 1950 Gorgeous George performance. Below is a sampling from the write-ups in the Rock Island *Argus* during the very busy local wrestling year, 1955:

February 28: "Saturday night's pro wrestling show at the fieldhouse nearly ended in a free-for-all as massive Yukon Eric was disqualified for unruly tactics in his match with Don Leo Jonathan. After the first 10 minutes of the main event between the two behemoths, the ring couldn't stand the tremendous pressure and gave way at one spot. This prompted Eric to get exceedingly rough, and after a chair-hitting incident the powerful lumberjack was sent to the showers and Jonathan emerged the victor."

March 21: "The world's tag team title changed hands at Wharton fieldhouse Saturday night, when Pat O'Connor and Roy McClarity won two out of three falls over unruly Art Neilson and Reggie Lisowski [the "Crusher"] in a bout that had nearly 3,000 fans standing on their chairs."

March 31: Leo Nomellini, an All-American football player at the University of Minnesota and professional star for the San Francisco 49ers, was to meet Lou Thesz in an upcoming match. "Thesz is no gent to be taken lightly . . . He has been heavyweight champion since 1948, the year Ed (Strangler) Lewis took him under his wing and made him a top draw." The *Argus* quoted Nomellini as declaring: "If I beat Thesz and win the title, I'll quit football and concentrate on wrestling." Indeed, the gridder won

two out of three falls from the champ, one of them by disqualification. But the National Wrestling Alliance hastily invented a policy in which a title could not be lost by a disqualification. So, Thesz kept the title and Nomellini continued with the 49ers for another eight years. The grid star also continued wrestling in the off-season under the name Leo "The Lion" Nomellini.

October 10: In the previous week, Mr. Moto had beaten Bob Orton at the Field House to earn the right to face "the unruly" Hans Schmidt, a heel to be sure. "Terrible Hans Schmidt, long the scourge of professional wrestling, will clash with Japan's Mr. Moto in the main event of this Saturday's mat card at Moline's Wharton Fieldhouse." Schmidt won in two of three falls.

ALL STAR WRESTLING

Wharton Fieldhouse, Moline, Ill.

Wed. April 27

8:30 p. m.

PRIMO CARNERA vs.
LEO NOMELLINI

RAS SAMARA vs.
(Negro Champion)
HARDY KRUSKAMP
New York

Leo Nomellini

Primo Carnera

—SPECIAL EVENT—

Benito Gardini vs. Pedro Escobak
(New York)   (Spain)

OPENING MATCH
ORVILLE BROWN JR. vs. DON CORTEZ

MAIL ORDERS
PAYABLE:
ZAL SPORTS
P.O. Box 56
Moline, Illinois
Tickets: $2.00-
$1.50-$1.00

TICKETS: MARTIN'S Dav., OLD SHOE, R.I.
AGNEW'S DRUG & CAMERA, E. Moline
GRANADA TAP, Moline

Last Indoor Show Of The Season
CHILDREN UNDER 14 FREE WITH PARENTS
Box Office Opens 4:30
On Sale 3000 Gen. Adm. Seats 1.00
Plus Good Reserved Seats

Argus, April 29, 1955

The "last indoor show of the season" at Wharton Field House was in late April 1955. Summer wrestling shows were held at Municipal Stadium in Davenport.

WRESTLING FANS!
ED "Strangler" LEWIS
WILL BE AT THE
OLD SHOE
3RD AVE. AT 17TH STS.   ROCK ISLAND
TONIGHT - 7 to 9 P.M.
FOR THE PURPOSE OF
SIGNING AUTOGRAPHS

GET YOUR TICKETS NOW FOR THE
T H E S Z — N E I L S O N
CHAMPIONSHIP WRESTLING MATCH
To Be Held At
WHARTON FIELD HOUSE - SAT., JAN. 29

Argus, January 27, 1955

The "Strangler" visited downtown Rock Island in January 1955.

PROFESSIONAL WRESTLING
WHARTON FIELDHOUSE
Moline, Illinois
RINGSIDE

Established Price $1.65	
Federal Tax .... .16	**$2.00**
Illinois State Tax .... .16	**TOTAL**
City Tax .... .03	

SEC. D ROW 1 SEAT 13

SAT'DAY, NOV. 19, 1955
In case of postponement because of bad weather, this ticket to be exchanged for ticket to next wrestling show or money will be refunded. — ZAL SPORTS, INC., Promoter.

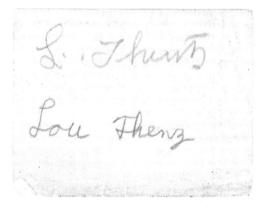

Courtesy of John Wetzel

Two tickets from 1955 professional wrestling matches at the Field House. At the top is the front of a $2.00 ringside seat for a November match. Below it is the reverse side of a January 29 ticket, signed by Lou Thesz. His signature is on top and his name was written below by the holder of the ticket. Thesz beat Art Neilson in a heavyweight championship match.

ALL STAR WRESTLING
Wharton Fieldhouse, Sat., Oct. 15, 8:30 P.M.

MAIN EVENT
2 out of 3 Falls-1 hr.
MATCH OF THE YEAR
Plus
3 other matches

Mr. Moto   Hans Schmidt

TICKETS $2 $1.50 $1   50c

Martin's, Dav., Old Shoe, Rock Island. Granada Tap, Moline, Agnew Drug, East Moline
MAIL ORDER TO ZAL SPORTS, P. O. Box 56, Moline, Ill.
Bus Leaves 3rd and Brady at 7:30 p.m.

PROFESSIONAL
BASKETBALL
Sunday, Oct. 30th 3 P.M.
Wharton Fields, Moline
SYRACUSE NATIONALS
(World's Professional Champions)
VS
FORT WAYNE PISTONS
(Runner-Up World's Champions)
SEE THESE ALL AMERICANS IN ACTION
★ Larry Faust   ★ Max Zalofsky ★ Red Rocha
★ Ed Yardley   ★ Dolph Shayes ★ Sonny Wilson
★ Mel Hutchins   ★ Paul Seymour ★ Earl Lloyd
POPULAR PRICES $2.00 $1.50 $1.00   50c
TICKETS ON SALE:
Martin's, Dav. .. Todd's, Rock Island ..
Vander Vennets, Moline .. Agnew Drug, East Moline
MAIL ORDER: Promotions Unlimited Box 293, Moline Illinois

Argus, October 14, 1955

Although the professional basketball Blackhawks had left for Milwaukee in 1951, some NBA games were held at Wharton in later years, including this 1955 exhibition game between Syracuse and Fort Wayne. These two advertisements appeared next to each other in the *Argus* on October 14, 1955, reminding us of the professional basketball past and the prevailing popularity of professional wrestling.

Mad Dog Food? As a little girl Pat Gustafson attended many events at the Field House with her dad, who frequently served as an usher. She remembers vividly an interesting scene at a wrestling match featuring Vachon. At least two men seated near ringside had brought large bags of dog food into the arena. When Mad Dog stepped into the ring they threw handfuls of the food at the wrestler while he was prancing around the ring flexing his muscles.

127

After a hiatus of two years, professional wrestling returned to Wharton on December 17, 1960. The event was a memorable experience for the 1,500 fans in attendance. The *Dispatch* (December 19) likened it to the Cold War missile crisis of the time:

> The Quad-Cities' first wrestling show in two years ended in a riot Saturday night. With all four wrestlers from the feature tag-team match going at it with the customers in the aisles at Wharton Field House, the Illinois State Athletic Commission disqualified everybody in sight and declared the match no contest. The melee started during the tag-team match in which Boris and Nicoli Volkoff [faced] Don Curtis and Mark Lewin. One of the Russians, apparently caught up in the current missile craze, tried to put Lewin into orbit. The first stage fired okay but the second stage failed to ignite and Lewin plummeted to earth right in the middle of the fourth row.
>
> A group of pacifists in the crowd decided to punish the Russians for inhuman treatment after that, but when a man went after one of the Russians with a chair, the gendarmes stepped in. The chair-wielder was run off the premises and various other agitators were quieted but the fight was declared no contest.

Vern Gagne, among the most popular pro wrestlers to regularly appear in Moline, was the ultimate face wrestler who played the crowd to adore him. He first appeared in the ring at Wharton in December 1951 in a match against the Mighty Atlas, and last appeared in November 1967. Gagne's "sleeper hold," which he regularly used to finish-off heels, was a big hit with the fans. Gagne also got into the wrestling promotion business while continuing to star on the mat. For over thirty years, beginning in 1960, he ran the American Wrestling Association, which promoted matches and their broadcasts on television, mostly in the Midwest and Great Plains. Joining Moline on the AWA regular circuit were such places as Denver, Omaha, Sioux City, Fargo, St. Paul, Minneapolis, Winnipeg, and of course Davenport during the summers.

The AWA was the major promoter in the Quad Cities, and made Wharton a busy place between 1963 and 1975. During those years the AWA organized 164 wrestling programs at Wharton, an average of more than a dozen per year, in addition to 73 programs at the Davenport stadium during the summers. Then for about a dozen years, Wharton was spared the grunts, groans, and chair-flinging, during which time the AWA held about fifty matches at Palmer Auditorium in Davenport.

VERN GAGNE

★ ★ ★ ★

Dispatch files

Courtesy of Ben McAdams

On the left, Verne Gagne is pictured in the *Dispatch* before his March 8, 1958, heavyweight match with Angelo Poffo at the Field House. In the photograph on the right, Gagne (left) is pictured with Ben McAdams of Moline at the 1996 NCAA wrestling meet at Williams Arena in Minneapolis.

Toll Takers Grapple with Crowds. In 1972, Field House manager Ed Lemon highlighted the popularity of wrestling over the preceding two decades: "Before they eliminated tolls [in 1970] on the Iowa-Illinois Memorial Bridge [now the I-74 bridge], we got calls on nights of pro wrestling shows asking what time the programs would end. The tolltakers changed shifts at 11 p.m. and cut down to one man in the booth, but they would hold the second man if the wrestling card was running late." (*Dispatch*, March 21, 1972)

Personal Tragedies

In spite of their posturing and acting, wrestlers are human beings. Two of those who had visited Wharton experienced personal issues with tragic consequences. One was Larry Cheney who wrestled there the evening of October 1, 1964, before driving his car toward home in Detroit that night. He was killed early the next morning when his car left Interstate-80 north of Ottawa, Illinois, and flipped over. Found in his car was a speeding ticket for going 92 miles per hour, issued a few hours earlier near Atkinson, Illinois. Cheney had experienced car trouble on the way to the match and then lost to Larry

Henning at Wharton. He was forty years old, married, and the father of six. His real name was Arthur L. Bauchene. A face wrestler, he was sometimes called "Leaping Larry," and his favorite finishing move was the flying head-scissors. According to the *Argus* (October 2, 1964), he also had been billed as the "Detroit Speedster!"

Verne Gagne faced another kind of tragedy many years later. Gagne had played football and wrestled at the University of Minnesota. He won NCAA collegiate wrestling championships in 1948 and 1949 in the heavyweight category, and was a member of the 1948 United States

Olympic team. Like many other pros in the 1950s and 1960s, he had a solid legitimate wrestling background. In a career on the mat that lasted thirty years, he won numerous pro wrestling "world" titles.

As a wrestler and a promoter, Gagne reached legendary status. He was well-respected by many, with the possible exception of a handful of heels. However, he was involved in an unfortunate incident in 2009 when he was 83 years old. Gagne had been diagnosed with Alzheimer's disease and was living in a care facility in Bloomington, Minnesota. In an altercation, Gagne pushed or threw 97-year old fellow resident Helmut Gutman to the floor, in a move that may or may not have been drawn from Gagne's deep kitbag of wrestling moves. Gutman broke his hip and died eighteen days later. Neither Gutman nor Gagne was able to remember the incident. Although the death was officially ruled a homicide, Gagne was not charged owing to his mental condition. (Pro Wrestling America, online)

From Wrestling to Rasslin'

By the 1980s, the professional wrestling landscape had changed. Little by little over the previous decades, any similarity between actual wrestling, as practiced at the amateur level, and the professional version had been cast aside. A new style had emerged in which performance was everything, in clothing choices, in television interviews, and in the ring. The World Wrestling Federation, WWF, came to dominate in the promotion of pro wrestling with spectacular programs and nationwide television audiences. (In 2002 the WWF was forced to change its name to WWE – World Wrestling Entertainment – as the result of a lawsuit brought by the World Wildlife Fund.) Hulk Hogan and Andre the Giant were among the products promoted by the WWF.

During the five years immediately before wrestling was moved to The Mark in 1993, the action was revived at the Field House in twelve WWF-sponsored programs. At least half of them drew over 3,000 fans. A November 22, 1989, program drew 6,500, but perhaps the pinnacle of the

WWF experience at Wharton was on January 12, 1990, when a sell-out crowd of 6,876 paid to watch the WWF "Intercontinental Title" match in which Ultimate Warrior defeated Dino Bravo. Others on the card that evening included Earthquake, Tugboat, Hercules, Sapphire, and Brutus Beefcake. Another highlight was on March 8, 1990, when Big Boss Man defeated Rick Rude in a steel cage match in front of 5,500 loyalists. The last WWF extravaganza at Wharton, on March 1, 1992, drew 4,000 to a card highlighted again by a cage match. (Wrestling Data, online)

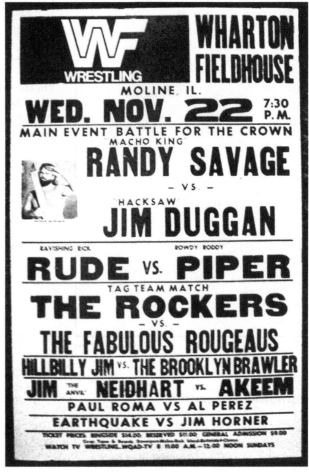

Courtesy of Jerry Wallaert

Rasslin' at Wharton, 1989

An Elephant in the Back Yard. Dona Welch, who lived in the Yeager house just west of the Field House during the 1940s as a child, remembers being thrilled to see an elephant tied to a walnut tree in her back yard. Nearby, clowns were prancing on a balance beam and juggling balls in this mini-circus outside of Wharton.

Argus, September 16, 1946

Dispatch, February 24, 1947

The advertisement on the left promoted the October 1946 Zal Grotto-sponsored circus. Above is an ad for the March 1947 circus sponsored by the Fraternal Order of Eagles. The fine print in the Eagles' ad promises "Positively the greatest array of circus stars ever assembled." In addition to "Hi-wire trapeze acrobats – Monks – Chimps and clowns galore," Prof. Kellers was to bring his jungle that included "Killers – Lions – Tigers – Panthers – Pumas – Elephants – Hyenas." (Over the years, the Moline Maroons also hosted Lions, Tigers, and Panthers at Wharton, but perhaps not Elephants, Hyenas, or Killers.)

Circuses

Only small circuses could appear at Wharton. The larger shows, such as the Ringling Bros. and Barnum & Bailey Circus, travelled by train and required venues near railroad tracks. In the late 1940s at least three circuses visited Wharton, two in 1946 and one in 1947.

The Clyde Brothers circus played the Field House for four days in October 1946 in front of a total of 6,200 people. It was sponsored by Zal

131

Grotto, an organization affiliated with the Moline Masonic Lodge, to benefit its cancer research fund. Three matinee and four evening performances featured a variety of acts. Among them were Art and Marie Henry, "wizards of the silver strand;" the Snyders, "premier aerial artists;" Gus Kanerva, "the up-side-down athletic marvel;" Carl R. Clark and his "amazing trained animals;" and "clowns galore."

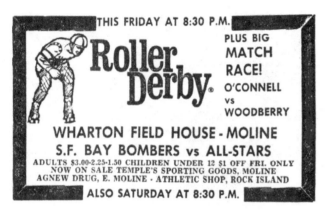

Argus, March 13, 1968

Roller Derby

One of the numerous television crazes of the 1950s and 1960s was roller derby, a performance "sport" in which skaters wearing helmets and knee pads race around a short banked track attempting to nudge each other out of the way or – better yet – off the track. Roller derby came to the Field House several times in the 1960s. In 1967 and 1968, perhaps the most popular of the teams, the Bay Area Bombers, appeared there. One of their stars was Joan Weston, who played on male as well as female teams and was one of the highest paid female athletes of the time.

Dispatch, May 4, 1964

A 1964 Roller Derby visit to the Field House featured the Midwest Pioneers, whose star roller was Joe Kosmal. The *Dispatch* (May 4) described Kosmal as "one of the world's top speed skaters" and "a one-time record holder for a measured half-mile track."

Chapter 6

On the Stage

Do you want to see the show?
–one of the Fontaine Sisters

In the mid-twentieth century the Moline Field House played a major role in the Quad Cities as a venue for visiting entertainers. Before the arena was named for T. F. Wharton in 1941, few entertainers were hosted there, and then a small number were booked during World War II. Thereafter, for three decades beginning in the mid-1940s, Wharton was a busy place for visiting stars.

Some of the Entertainers who Performed at Wharton Field House

Jan Garber Orchestra	1936	February 10
WLS on Parade	1941	November 11
Lawrence Welk	1943	April 28
Tiny Hill Orchestra	1943	May 7
Hollywood Ice Revels of 1944	1944	March 7
Eddie Howard Orchestra	1944	May 22
Harry James Orchestra	1944	October 27
Don McNeill's Breakfast Club	1945	October 13
Gene Krupa	1945	October 30
Water Follies	1946	May 8
Clyde Brothers Circus	1946	September 23
Eagles Circus	1947	March 24
Tommy Dorsey Orchestra/Moline Centennial	1948	June 24
Chicago Theatre of the Air/Moline Centennial	1948	June 26
Horace Heidt Talent Show	1948	November 3
Gene Autry Show	1949	March 1
Skating Berries/Night with the Stars	1949	March 5
Spike Jones	1949	April 30
Jack Benny	1950	May 20
Hank Williams/Grand Ole Opry	1950	April 13
Boys Town Choir	1950	October 13
Frankie Laine, Patti Page	1952	May 5
Skating Vanities/Olsen & Johnson	1952	October 8
Dean Martin and Jerry Lewis	1954	May 17
Water Follies	1954	June 11
Bill Haley and the Comets	1956	March 8
Victor Borge	1956	March 17
Carabinieri Band of Rome	1956	November 6
Grand Ole Opry: Ray Price, Jim Reeves and others	1957	February 9
Marty Robbins	1957	March 23
Pat Boone, Four Lads, Fontaine Sisters	1957	May 18
Black Watch Regimental Band	1957	October 26
Captain Kangaroo, Grandpa Happy, Tri-City Symphony	1959	April 18
WQUA Shower of Stars	1959	April 22
International Ice Review	1959	June 5, 6
Johnny Cash, Dion and the Belmonts	1959	October 17

Johnny Cash, Johnny Horton, Red Sovine	1960	May 20
Brenda Lee	1961	January 1
USSR Gymnastics	1961	February 19
Jimmy Dean, Patsy Cline, Leroy Van Dyke	1961	November 17
Kingston Trio	1963	March 9
Johnny Cash, Skeeter Davis, June Carter	1963	April 19
Grand Ole Opry	1964	May 16
Harry Belafonte	1966	October 22
Steppenwolf, The Chosen Few	1969	December 26
Jeannie C. Riley	1971	December 17
The Byrds. The Ides of March,1984 Love Machine	1972	April 3
Wishbone Ash, Speed-O-Meter	1972	November 1
Ozark Opry	1977	November 12
DJ Jazzy Jeff and the Fresh Prince	1990	March 13

NOTE: This is not a complete list, but it does illustrate the variety of visiting entertainers who performed at the Field House before The Mark (now the iWireless Center) was opened in 1993.

Early in its history, the large new arena drew the attention of people from a broad hinterland around Moline, much like the iWireless Center does today. This is illustrated by a January 20, 1936, announcement in the Thomson [Illinois] *Review*. Thomson is located about forty miles north of the Quad Cities:

One of America's greatest dance bands will bring its smooth rhythm to the dance lovers of this territory on Monday evening February 10th, when the Quad City Theatre Managers Association holds its second annual Movie Ball at the Moline Field House in Moline, Illinois. The band, Jan Garber and his famous orchestra will come to Moline especially for this event direct from the Aragon Ballroom in Chicago . . . His appearance at the Moline Ball is expected to attract a record-breaking throng of dancers. Already many reservations for tickets have been requested from cities and towns as far distant as 145 miles from Moline. Because of the fact that this will be Jan Garber's only appearance in this territory during 1936, it is especially important that his admirers plan to attend this event . . . In spite of the almost unlimited room for dancing in the Moline Field House, only three thousand tickets will be sold for dancing. Because of the fact that the Movie Ball is almost as much a stage show

Argus, February 8, 1936

This 1936 *Dispatch* advertisement ballyhoos one of the first visits to the Field House of big-name entertainers. The thirty-piece band played "Exactly as they play for dancing in the Aragon and Trianon in Chicago" [two widely-known dance ballrooms]. Dancing continued until 2 a.m.! A note at the bottom of the ad also reveals the range of transportation options for patrons: streetcar, bus, taxi, and automobile. (Just eight months later streetcar service was discontinued in the Quad Cities, except for the bridge line between Rock Island and Davenport, which lasted another four years. Buses replaced the trolleys.)

as a dance, four thousand additional tickets will be sold at reduced rates for those who wish only to watch the show and dancing from the balcony.

Although the big band era was in full swing when the Field House was built in 1928, few of the bands performed at the Field House. Over the years many appeared elsewhere in the Quad Cities, especially at the Coliseum Ballroom and the Masonic Auditorium in Davenport. Nonetheless, some were booked into Wharton in the 1940s.

In April 1943 Lawrence Welk brought his bubbly sound to Wharton. By this time, Welk was nationally-known and had regular broadcasts over the Mutual Radio Network carried by station WGN in Chicago. Among his featured acts was singer Jane Walton, the "Champagne Lady," who sang several songs in Spanish including "Maria Elena," a tune she made famous. Also featured were baritone Bill Kaylor, comedy singer Holly Swanson, and of course the maestro himself wielding the accordion. The program was arranged to provide continuous music from 9 p.m. to 1 a.m., with a forty-minute stage show sandwiched in at some point. Regular prices were charged for people who wanted to dance and half-price tickets were provided for people who merely wanted to watch from the balcony.

Singer Eddy Howard and his orchestra appeared on May 22, 1944. Howard had become famous with the Dick Jurgens Band and, like

Dispatch, May 13, 1944

According to this May 3rd *Dispatch* advertisement, dancing with Eddie Howard lasted only until 1 a.m.!

More Bands? A crowd of 2,700 appeared for the 1943 Lawrence Welk show, which was arranged by the former Davenport Orpheum Theatre manager Jack Neary. The afternoon after Welk's April 28th appearance, the *Dispatch* reported that Neary "thanked those present for their splendid cooperation in making the affair such a success, and promised that many more fine dance bands would be brought to the field house, the first on Friday, May 7th, when Tiny Hill and his orchestra will play for dancing. Other orchestras booked are Fletcher Henderson, Sammy Kaye and Blue Barron." However, we found no evidence that any of these orchestras actually appeared at the Field House.

"He did it for Eddie": Local promoter G. Laverne Flambo told Dorothy Buresh (1971) a tragedy-turned-opportunity story from Eddie Howard's later visit to the Quad Cities. "One time [1953] I brought in Eddie Howard to the Rock Island Armory for an auto show. After a night of entertainment he fell off the stage – a heart attack" Flambo recalled. Dejected at being left without a name attraction, Flambo was driving through downtown Rock Island when he noticed that Harry Cool was playing at one of the nightclubs. He made Cool a proposition to take over the band, but to make it look good he flew Cool to Chicago and then back to the Quad-City Airport where he was met by all the press. Cool wouldn't even take money for the engagement, Flambo remembered, "He just did it for Eddie." (Cool and Howard had known each other; both had been vocalists with the Dick Jurgens Band.)

Jan Garber, had been featured at Chicago's Trianon and Aragon Ballrooms. Compared to other attractions here, however, this one did not hit the jackpot. "About 500 persons attended, largely couples dancing, with a few sitting in the bleachers" (*Dispatch*, May 23, 1944).

Later in 1944, Harry James brought his thirty-piece orchestra to the Field House for a show and dancing on a Friday night. Reporter Dorothy Green, who had visited James at the LeClaire Hotel Friday afternoon, filed this report in the *Dispatch* on Saturday (October 28):

[The hotel] lobby was filled with 'bobby socks' fans storming the place to get a glimpse of their favorite musician . . . James, who sent 'em to the rooftops last night in the Moline field house with his sweet and jivey tunes, was cordial to the reporters assigned to finding out what makes a celebrity click. He regretted that his wife, Betty Grable, who had made part of the tour, had returned to Hollywood where she is making another picture.

The trumpeter hails from Beaumont, Texas, and played with Benny Goodman before organizing his own outfit of thirty members, including six discharged servicemen. 'The boys enjoyed making Private Buckaroo' [a movie] James said, 'but after your first movie it becomes work like anything else.' After a two day stay in Chicago the band will return to Hollywood to make another picture for M. G. M.

The James band played to 800 wounded veterans at Mayo Army Hospital in Galesburg yesterday [Friday] afternoon. Some of the men stood in line for two hours to get a front row seat for the performance . . . James said it is the policy of the band to play at as many hospitals as possible.

Dispatch, October 17, 1944

More dancing 9 p.m. until 1 a.m., when Harry James appeared in October 1944.

A major venue for dance bands and other entertainment since 1914 is the Coliseum ("Col") Ballroom in Davenport, shown here. Bands appeared there virtually every week for a century – and several bands during many weeks. Other events there, ranging from professional wrestling to rock star visits, were commonplace. It hosted a long list of nationally-famous entertainers, including Glenn Miller, Tommy Dorsey, Frank Sinatra, Louis Armstrong, Moody Blues, Jimi Hendrix, B. B. King, and Stevie Ray Vaughan. The roots of the Coliseum date to 1896 when German Americans built a 5,000-seat wooden arena, the Saengerfest Halle, for a large festival that drew 100,000 people to Davenport. After serving as a warehouse, it was expanded in 1906 and named the Coliseum. After the wooden building was destroyed by fire in 1913, it was replaced by a brick building across the street, which remains today. Its name was changed to the Col in 1956, and in 1995 it was purchased by the Quad Cities Mexican American Organization. One of the oldest operating ballrooms in Iowa, it was inducted into the Iowa Rock and Roll Music Association Hall of Fame in 1999. (Col Ballroom, online)

Argus, June 15, 1954

These ads appeared side-by-side in the *Argus* on June 15, 1954. Through the twentieth century, dance bands and other entertainment appeared at the Coliseum much more often than at the Field House.

Sounds of the 1940s

Don McNeill: In the 1930s and 1940s, radio was the dominant provider of home entertainment in the United States. Several performers who visited the Field House during that era and into the 1950s had become stars on the radio. One mainstay on national network radio, Don McNeill's Breakfast Club, originated in Chicago every weekday morning and was broadcast locally on Davenport's WOC. It started in 1933 and continued until 1968, making it the longest running radio entertainment show of all time.

In October 1945, McNeill brought a travelling version of his show to the Field House for a two-hour Saturday-evening show, sponsored by the Moline Optimist Club and the Moline Junior Association of Commerce. Among McNeill's cast were songstress Marion Mann, "Chief Heckler" Sam Cowling, and Fran Allison who played "Aunt Fannie" and later became widely admired for her part in the early television puppet show, Kukla, Fran, and Ollie. Also with the troupe was an orchestra conducted by Eddie Ballantine.

Rock Island County Historical Society

Cover of a sixteen-page booklet containing introductions of the Breakfast Club performers along with local advertisements.

138

WLS On Parade: In that era Quad City area people listened not only to local stations (WOC and Rock Island's WHBF, plus WQUA in Moline after September 1946), but also to powerful stations broadcasting from many other places including Cedar Rapids, St. Louis, and Chicago. One of them was WLS in Chicago, the "Prairie Farmer Station," which had a rural theme and played country music before becoming a rock-and-roll giant in 1960.

On Armistice Day (now called Veteran's Day), November 11, 1941, a group of WLS stars visited Moline. Sponsored by the Willard L. Velie Jr. Post No. 5123 Veterans of Foreign Wars, the WLS on Parade show was performed at the Field House once in the afternoon and twice in the evening, with proceeds going to the VFW emergency fund. The show was hosted by a popular comedian, Jimmy James, and included individual and group singers, harmonica and xylophone players, and a juggler. The Dispatch (November 12) reported: "The show, headlined by Lulu Belle and Skyland Scotty, stars of the WLS national barn dance program, featured rural rhythm and rustic humor."

March of Dimes Show and Dance: Numerous events at the Field House were held as fundraisers for various causes, including the campaign to eradicate polio, which was rampant in the United States from the 1940s to the 1960s. Two versions of the March of Dimes Show and Dance, one in 1949 and one in 1951, were held at Wharton. All services and entertainment for the first, on February 6, 1949, were donated, leaving substantial profits for the Rock Island chapter of the National Foundation for Infantile Paralysis (Polio). Entertainers included baritone Norman Clayton; the Czupka family orchestra with members ranging from age 6 to 18; the Viking Quartet, which had performed at Wharton for Prince Bertil of Sweden in 1948; and a variety of other acts. Bob Lofgren's orchestra played for the dance scheduled for 9:30 to midnight. Admission was $1; children under twelve were free with parent.

Boys Town Choir: A fifty-voice choir from Boys Town in Nebraska stopped in Moline in October 1950 on their fourth annual tour. Directed by the Reverend Francis Schmitt, and sponsored by Leo Council, Knights of Columbus of Moline and East Moline, the group performed in front of about 800 people. The review of the performance in the *Dispatch* (October 14) was sanguine: "the choir lived up to expectations. The harmony and sweetness of the voices, from boy soprano to young bass, tinted the selections with new sincerity and richer meaning. The program, while beautiful, was a little passive for such exuberant and robust youngsters."

Ice, Skates, and Water

The first ice-skating show at Wharton was presented by the Ice Revels of 1944. Sponsored by Zal Grotto, the skaters performed Thursday (March 2) through Saturday evenings and on Saturday at noon. The entourage, which

---

MARCH of DIMES
VARIETY SHOW & DANCE

Friday, March 2d
WHARTON FIELD HOUSE

Featuring:

AL GUSTAFSON, EMCEE
JOLINE'S STUDIO OF MOLINE
BURCH STUDIO OF DAVENPORT
THE SERENADERS FROM KSTT
SWANSON & LYNN HORACE HEIDT WINNERS
THE TEENSTERS
BE-BOPING TEENERS
ALSO TAPS AND SONGS BY VICTIMS OF POLIO

Tickets: $1.00 each
Children Under 12 Free
Accompanied by Parents

Tickets on Sale at the following stores:
Band Box Music Store, Moline; Agnew's Drug Store,
East Moline; Todd's, Rock Island

Dance to Music of Jack Manthey's Orchestra
Sponsored by Relatives and Friends of Polio Victims

Dispatch, March 1, 1951

The 1951 version of the March of Dimes show was sponsored by Relatives and Friends of Polio Victims.

---

included 72 ice skaters and a twelve-piece orchestra, had come from a three-day stand in Peoria and would go on to Cedar Rapids for their next shows. The *Dispatch* (March 2) deftly described the arrangements needed to put on the show:

> The skaters will perform intricate dances and stunts on a refrigerated ice rink, which was installed this morning at the field house. It takes eight hours for the rink to be installed and ready for use. It is the only one of its kind in the country. A protective covering for the floor is laid, a layer of cork insulation, then the cooling unit is attached and layers of ice cover, a layer of calcium carbonate, which provides the skating layer. Snow is banked around the rink. The rink, which cost $30,000, was built and designed for this special purpose by the York Ice Machinery Company of Chicago.

Skating Berries: Skating returned to the Field House in 1949, this time of the roller variety. As part of a Moose Club-sponsored variety show, A Night With the Stars, the Skating Berries appeared. This family – a mother, father, and three young children – opened the show in front of a crowd of 3,800. "Their routines included just about everything in the roller skater's repertoire." (*Dispatch*, March 7, 1949)

Ice Review: A newly-organized show, the International Ice Review, was held at Wharton beginning on June 5, 1959. It arrived amid considerable local interest, but departed abruptly before completing its three-day run. The previous week *Billboard* magazine (June 1) previewed the travelling show:

> New ice show, the International Ice Review, produced by Tom Parker, has 23 performers, the star being Audrey McColl, a Scottish figure skating champion. The show . . . is framed to play places that don't get principal Icers. It is small, tho – as with the new-trend

139

cars – it is probably more descriptive to say 'compact,' because it is significantly larger than most units that have played fairs and hotels . . . Parker's current tour is for six weeks, which will take it into Illinois, Wisconsin, Minnesota and Michigan. Early stands have the show in such typical buildings as the Dixon Armory, Urbana Armory, Jacksonville High School Gym, Quincy College Gym, Knox College Gym at Galesburg, and Wharton Fieldhouse in Moline, all Illinois, and the Cedar Rapids (Ia.) Municipal Auditorium.

The show was brought to Moline by the Black Hawk Shrine Club, in support of their youth work including sponsorship of the Quad City Soapbox Derby. The featured skater, Audrey McColl, was sixteen years old and had won several national championships in Scotland before moving to Davenport with her parents five months earlier. She performed several routines, including one to the tune of "Highland Fling." Other members of the troupe combined skating with such activities as baton twirling, trick roping, and comedy. Ticket prices were $1.55 for adults and $1.00 for children.

About 4,450 people attended the first five shows, two on Friday (June 5) and three on Saturday including a special performance for children in the morning. An estimated 1,800 were on hand for the final performance on Sunday

Dispatch, October 7, 1952

Ice skating returned to the Field House when the Skating Vanities performed in October 1952. This time Olsen and Johnson, the "Kings of Komedy," performed. Their five-day gig included nightly performances plus Saturday and Sunday matinees.

Dispatch, June 4, 1959

Shown here is the top part of a very large advertisement for the Ice Review that appeared in the *Dispatch*. Below this part of the ad the text reads, "Starring Scotland's Queen of the Ice Audrey McColl, Scottish figure skating champion in her first American appearance." McColl was living in Davenport at the time.

140

afternoon. However, they were disappointed when the skaters refused to perform because they claimed the owner-producer Tom Parker owed them back wages. President of the Black Hawk Club, Carl Wessel, tried to convince the cast to perform the final show, but to no avail. They refused his offer of giving them Sunday's box office receipts, contending that it would be hardly enough to get them out of town. Apparently the show had experienced financial difficulties since it opened a month earlier in Hammond, Indiana. Wessel took on the difficult task of informing the 1,800 people in the Field House that the show would not go on. However, their money would be refunded. (*Dispatch*, June 9, 1959)

The 1959 International Ice Review was the last ice show to be held at Wharton. Indeed, through the years, skating shows were rare at the Field House, perhaps because of the difficulty of installing ice over the basketball floor. However, such shows played elsewhere in the Quad Cities. The Skating Vanities came to the Quad Cities several other times, usually performing at the Rock Island Armory. And the more famous and elaborate Holiday on Ice was an annual visitor to the Armory for many years.

Water Follies: On May 8, 9, and 10, 1946, the Moline Optimist Club brought in the Water Follies of 1946, to raise money for their youth program. This, too, involved the installation of special equipment:

> The show will be presented in two portable swimming pools which will fill the field house stage and which hold 80,000 gallons of water. To add to the effectiveness, the backdrop

Lake County (IL) Discovery Museum, Curt Teich Postcard Archives

Argus, April 23, 1949

The Rock Island Armory, opened in 1937, was the only other large indoor arena in the Illinois Quad Cities until The Mark was opened in 1993. For decades it hosted auto shows, sports shows, boxing, basketball games, political and community events, and numerous ice shows, including annual visits by Holiday on Ice from the 1950s through 1992. In addition some big-name entertainers performed there, including Johnny Cash, Ella Fitzgerald, and Fats Domino, some under the auspices of G. Laverne Flambo. Perhaps the most popular event there was the nine-day Autorama in 1955, which attracted a total of 44,907 attendees (*Argus*, February 7). The feature attraction was the McGuire Sisters, who played several performances over the last four days of the show. Their February 3 audience totaled over 6,500, perhaps the largest crowd ever packed into the Armory. Before the show a line several blocks long formed and the balcony seats were filled a full hour before the show began. Shown in this photograph is a scene from the 1949 Mississippi Valley Sports and Travel Show, with an inset of Sam Howard diving from a lofty springboard into a small pool on the arena floor. (*Argus*, April 23)

will include palm trees, tropical flowers and green grass, giving the setting a Hawaiian atmosphere (*Dispatch*, April 12).

The cast of 85 included swimming and diving stars and "a bevy of shapely mermaids." The star of the Water Follies was movie star Buster Crabb whose aquatic acrobatics were well known. Crabb grew up in Hawaii, was a star swimmer for the University of Southern California, and participated in the Olympic Games twice, winning a gold medal in swimming in Los Angeles in 1932. People in attendance at the Field House remember him diving into the $50,000 pool from a platform near the Field House ceiling. Crabb also addressed students at John Deere Junior High School at their Lyceum, the school assembly.

Largest Pool: In 1954, another water show appeared when Sam Snyder's Water Follies played from June 11 through June 16. An advertisement in the Galesburg *Register-Mail* (May 27) proclaimed:

> World's greatest water and stage show. Presented here in the world's largest portable pools and stage. 2½ hours of exciting entertainment. World Champion Divers. Famous stage acts. 13 water scenes. 10 stage numbers. Funny diving clowns. Stage and water ballet.

A promotional advertisement in *Billboard* magazine (November 28, 1953), which was seeking bookings nationwide, boasted that this travelling water and stage musical review was "the pioneer of this type of entertainment!" The Follies, sponsored by the Moline Lions Club, attracted about 3,000 spectators for its first night's performance.

Argus, May 1, 1954

Lots of water was needed in Wharton Field House for the 1954 Water Follies.

Argus, June 11, 1954

Workers assembling the stage and two pools that flank it on the Field House floor in preparation for the Water Follies show. The entire array was composed of 1,700 pieces and was so large it occupied much of the Field House floor space. Together, the pools held 80,000 gallons of water.

Dispatch files

G. Laverne Flambo was a promoter who brought entertainment to the Quad Cities from 1945 to 1969. He was also owner/general manager of Moline radio station WQUA during the 1950s, and continued to work at that station until his death in 1977. As a promoter, his first major booking was for Janette McDonald at the Masonic Temple in Davenport on October 19, 1945, and his second was drummer Gene Krupa at the Field House on October 30th. He went on to bring in dozens of other entertainers, some to the Field House, others to the Davenport Masonic Temple, the RKO Orpheum Theatre (now the Adler), the Rock Island Armory, and (after 1960) Centennial Hall at Augustana College. After a brief retirement from the booking business in 1961, he partnered with Milt Troehler to create GMT Productions, which continued for another eight years to bring big-name entertainment to the Quad Cities. (Much more on Flambo can be gleaned from Dave Coopman's 2007 book on WQUA.)

Flambo and the Golden Era

From the late 1940s to the early 1990s, Wharton Field House hosted scores of entertainment events. Beginning in 1945, promoter G. Laverne Flambo was a major force in bringing big-time entertainers to the Field House and other Quad City venues.

Flambo's first two promotions in the Quad Cities, both in October 1945, couldn't have contrasted more. Writing in the *Dispatch* (August 21, 1971), Dorothy Buresh described that contrast:

He first brought Jeanette McDonald [to Davenport]. On this venture he cleared $3,500 which he promptly lost the next week when he brought Gene Krupa, the famed drummer, to Wharton Field House. (At the time Krupa was under indictment on a drug charge.) Flambo said of the 94 paid admissions, 24 of them were revenue agents.

Argus, October 30, 1945

This 1945 advertisement in the *Argus* announced the first Field House promotion taken on by G. Laverne Flambo. Gene Krupa became famous as a drummer in the 1930s while playing for the Benny Goodman Band, and then formed his own orchestra in 1938. Apparently Krupa's visit to the Field House was a flop, as very few people appeared that evening.

After a rocky start at the Field House in which almost nobody showed up to see Gene Krupa, Flambo rarely presided over flops. Numerous of his later productions were quite successful at Wharton. Jack Benny, Spike Jones, and Martin and Lewis were big money-makers for him there. But Flambo did not always do it for the money. He brought in Horace Heidt for a 1948 event that raised $2,800 to support the Moline Boys Choir (Buresh, 1961 and 1971).

Argus, February 23, 1949

Gene Autry and his horse Champion appeared on March 1, 1949, under the sponsorship of the Moline Junior Chamber of Commerce.

Dispatch, April 30, 1949

What large entertainment venue, in the 1940s or 1950s, would be satisfied without a performance by the wacky musicians directed by Spike Jones? The *Dispatch* (April 23) previewed this 1949 Jones visit by noting that his real name was Lindley Armstrong Jones and his sidekick for this performance, Doodles Weaver, was a "string bean blonde" who had graduated from Stanford University.

Dispatch, May 13, 1950

Advertisement for the 1950 Jack Benny show in the May 13th *Dispatch*. By this time, a week before the performance, the expensive seats ($4.80!) had been sold out. Other ads specified that "positively only one performance" would be held and "only capacity will be sold."

Broad Reach. Many of the big-name shows at the Field House were advertised at some distance from the Quad Cities. Their ads appeared regularly in newspapers in Muscatine and Clinton (Iowa), and Galesburg and Sterling (Illinois). Some went farther afield – the Jack Benny show, for example, was advertised in Cedar Rapids, Burlington, and Mount Pleasant, Iowa, which at the time were between an hour-and-a-half and two hours away by automobile.

The 1950 Jack Benny show brought in $27,000, the largest gross up to that time. Benny, perhaps the most popular comedian of the time, visited the Field House on Saturday, May 20th. The "39-year-old" Benny had become nationally famous for his radio show which was broadcast on national networks from 1932 to 1955. His visit to Moline predated by five months the debut of his national television show, which ran from late October 1950 until 1965. He brought with him his sidekick Rochester (Eddie Anderson), Phil Harris and his band, and a cast of forty.

Benny's Field House show was advertised in local papers as "The Greatest Stage Revue in the History of Show Business." His visit to the Quad Cities was such a big deal that various businesses incorporated the comedian into their ads during the week before his appearance. The pinnacle of this advertising strategy was a very large two-page ad for the New York Store, located in downtown Moline, which ran in the *Dispatch* the Monday after Benny's show (May 22). It shows a picture of the comedian – who was famous for closely guarding his money – at the store and includes the following text:

. . . more proof that the New York Store
is the Quad Cities leader for <u>THRIFT</u>!

JACK BENNY SHOPS HERE!

Famous radio personality . . .
He has the largest of
All radio audiences!
Famous for THRIFT . . .
He naturally shops at the
New York Store when in
The Quad Cities

On May 17, 1954, Dean Martin and Jerry Lewis drew 6,000 fans to Wharton. "It was reported that this show was not only the largest attended one-time event held there, but it also netted Flambo the biggest profit of any show he booked to this point" (Coopman, 2007). Seats

Argus, April 24, 1952

The "Biggest Show of '52" featured singers Frankie Laine and "The Singing Rage" Patti Page.

ranged from $2.50 to $5, including tax, and advertisements for the show boasted of "40 great stars." Harvey Hoffman, writing for the Davenport *Daily Times* (May 18) opined that Martin and Lewis "were funnier in person than on the screen, radio or TV." He raved about Dean's singing, and liked Jerry's antics. "Lewis evoked screams from the audience with his high, squeaky voice, and his comical antics. He yelled, took falls on the floor, imitated a seal and did about anything that came to his mind."

Argus, April 23, 1954

For the first time at Wharton Field House, the price for a visiting entertainment act reached as high as $5 when Martin and Lewis performed in 1954.

A Comedian is Born. When he was thirteen years old, Don Hepner walked from Springbrook Courts on 41st Street in Moline to the Field House to watch the Martin and Lewis show. As a child he came to love the style of comedy Jerry Lewis was famous for. Hepner's seat was in the very top row, in a position that allowed him to view frenetic activities behind the stage, which fascinated him almost as much as the comedy being delivered front stage. Observing thousands of people laughing, Hepner decided that he, too, wanted to make people laugh. He went on to develop comedy routines and participate in plays while in junior high and high school in Rock Island; then followed a long career as a comedian, actor, producer and director of plays, and drama teacher. Today, he is back living in Moline, not far from Wharton, and regularly performs stand-up comedy.

Dispatch, March 8, 1961

Promoter G. Laverne Flambo with Eddy Arnold, who appeared at the Field House in January 1956. The promoter is trying his hand with the singer's guitar.

By 1956, many big name entertainers had visited the Field House, with more to come. Two appeared in March 1956. One was Victor Borge, who performed musical tricks on the piano based primarily on classical music and invented interesting contortions of the English language. He was a sensation by that time having worked in radio and television and on stage, and continued to be very popular for many years thereafter. At the time of his visit, he had just completed the longest-running one-man show on Broadway, "Comedy in Music," an accomplishment for which he is honored by the Guinness Book of World Records. An interesting feature of his act at the Field House was the revolving stage that was set up in the center of the floor. This arrangement facilitated the clever interactions with the audience for which Borge was widely known.

March 1956 also marked the beginning of rock and roll music at the Field House when Bill Haley and the Comets presented their "Rock and Roll Jamboree." Probably most famous for their early rock hit, "Rock Around the Clock," which they recorded two years before this performance, the band was clearly on the forefront of a new genre of music that would attract young audiences for years.

Argus, March 1, 1956

Two very prominent, but rather contrasting, visitors to the Field House in 1956 are featured in these side-by-side ads in the March 1st issue of the Rock Island *Argus.*

Dispatch, October 30, 1956

Two more mid-1950s performances added to the diversity of big-name entertainment presented at Wharton Field House. The Carabinieri was an Italian military band; and Pat Boone, the Four Lads, and The Fontaine Sisters were American popular music stars.

Dispatch, May 19, 1957

How could he say no? On a spring day in 1958, Jim Wallaert finished high school baseball practice at Browning Field, then showered and dressed in Wharton. Because a show was to be held that evening – featuring the Fontaine Sisters – he and his teammates were chased out of the Field House before the performance. Jim's curiosity led him to peek back into the Field House through the door at the southeast corner of the building. Seeing Jim's face pushed up against the glass, one of the Fontaine sisters opened the door and said "Do you want to see the show?" The answer, of course, was yes, and she let him in.

The Carabinieri Band of Rome, which was billed as "A Magnificent Spectacle of Colorful Music & Brilliant Pageantry," used the "entire floor" of the Field House for its 1956 performance. A September 30th wire service story introduced the band:

> NEW YORK (UP) – The famous Carabinieri Band of Rome, a 102-piece military group, will make its first visit to the United States this fall. The band will arrive Oct. 3 and begin a tour the following night in New Haven, Conn. A tour of 38 cities in seven weeks has been arranged. The band is famous for its parade and pageant abilities as well as its music. There will be two appearances in New York – the first in Carnegie Hall Oct. 13 will be purely instrumental; the second, in Madison Square Garden Oct. 16, will include all of the colorful exhibition work.

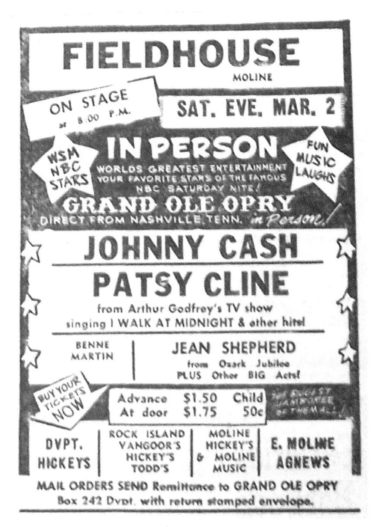

Dispatch, February 9, 1957   *Argus*, February 22, 1957

These two Grand Ole Opry shows, which appeared at the Field House in early 1957, featured some big names. For decades regular Saturday-night Grand Ole Opry shows in Nashville have been broadcast over AM radio station WSM, whose after-sunset signal covers most of the eastern half of the United States.

No: 2353

ADMIT ONE
ADULT TICKET
$1.00

Since this ticket is for a Benefit Show, Purchase Price is not refundable and ticket can not be exchanged.

Colona Community Volunteer Fire Department
PROUDLY PRESENTS
1st Annual
Country Music Stage Show
ON STAGE — IN PERSON
The Nation's Greatest Country Music Jamboree
Direct From Nashville, Tenn.
25 — GREAT ARTISTS — 25

**WHARTON
FIELD HOUSE
TUESDAY
OCTOBER 18, 1960
7:30 P.M.
Moline, Illinois**

Courtesy of Jerry Wallaert

Over the years a variety of organizations used the Field House for fundraising events. Here is a ticket from a 1960 country music show sponsored by the Colona, Illinois, Community Volunteer Fire Department. Comedienne Minnie Pearl was featured among the 25 performers. This was a cheap ticket; others went for $2.50 and $1.50.

While rock music was just emerging in the mid-1950s, country music had already become a big business, both on the radio and on stage. Several country music shows – with their singing and picking stars – appeared at Wharton over the years. Among the first were Gene Autry in 1949 and Hank Williams in 1950; among the last were Jimmy Dean in 1965, and Lee Mace and his Ozark Opry in 1977.

WQUA Gets Into the Act

During the time Flambo owned WQUA in the late 1950s, the Moline radio station sponsored several events at the Field House. Flambo had created a "Crocodile Club" for teenagers, which sponsored regular dances called "Croc Hops." The club was directed by new announcer Don Nelson. The first Croc Hop, which was held on April 12, 1957, at the American Legion Hall, packed the place with 2,300 teens. Another 1,500 were turned away. So, the Field House was booked for a May 8th Hop. "Don Nelson spun records, the Hal Wiese Orchestra was on hand for dancing, and the Diamonds, a popular national recording group, sang their hit songs to more than 3,200 crocodiles." (Coopman, 2007)

Johnny Cash. The Man in Black appeared in the Quad Cities several times, including at least three times at Wharton, in each case through the promotion of G. Laverne Flambo. Dave Coopman (2007) described two of the Cash visits to the Moline arena. In a 1960 appearance when Cash was late coming on stage, host and WQUA announcer Jack Tieken entertained the audience by interviewing the Fendermen, Cash's sidemen. Johnny suddenly appeared in an obviously inebriated state, but nonetheless performed flawlessly. Coopman went on: "Evidently Cash let Flambo down only once. During another booking at Wharton Fieldhouse, Cash failed to show up. Flambo found him passed out in his room at the LeClaire Hotel. Flambo refunded the audience's admission, but didn't sour on booking Cash again and again."

Dispatch, April 17, 1963

Courtesy of Don Nelson

WQUA radio announcer and "Croc Hop" host Don Nelson pictured here with Pat Boone who appeared at Wharton on May 18, 1957.

Dispatch, April 21, 1959

A star-studded advertisement for the 1959 WQUA Shower of Stars. The show was headlined by Frankie Avalon, who had recently recorded a number-one song, "Venus." The troupe performed in the afternoon and evening in a benefit for Cerebral Palsy.

Travelling Troupes. Entertainers visiting Wharton, or any of the other entertainment venues in the Quad Cities, often were on extended tours. Local promoters scheduled visits to fit in with other Midwest performances. In town in October 1959 to perform in the Johnny Cash show, Dion and the Belmonts were travelling around the Midwest, giving nightly performances and typically enduring over-night road trips. *Billboard* (October 12, 1959), listed part of their itinerary:

October 13: Arkota Ballroom, Sioux Falls, South Dakota
October 14: Surf Ballroom, Clear Lake, Iowa
October 15: Auditorium, Omaha, Nebraska
October 16: Danceland Ballroom, Cedar Rapids, Iowa
October 17: Wharton Field House, Moline, Illinois
October 18: Riverside Ballroom, Green Bay, Wisconsin

More Variety Entering the 1960s

The Captain: On Saturday April 18, 1959, the Junior Board of the Tri-City Symphony Orchestra Association sponsored a unique combination of storytelling by childrens' television personality Captain Kangaroo and music by the orchestra. A total of more than 8,000 attended afternoon and evening performances. The Captain made his opening entrance accompanied by the tune "Pop Goes the Weasel." Then after several orchestra selections, including "Parade of the Wooden Soldier" and "Johnny Comes Marching Home," the marsupial told the story of "Peter and the Wolf."

This Argus photograph shows three-year-old Molly Mallette of Burlington, Iowa, in the foreground with her mother at one of the 1959 Captain Kangaroo/Tri-City Symphony concerts. The caption quoted Mrs. Mallette: "this appearance of the beloved Captain was the only thing Molly talked about for weeks."

Argus, April 20, 1959

Argus, March 6, 1963

Reviewing the Kingston Trio show for the *Argus*, Sanders (1963) gushed: "The Kingstons are kings with tons of fascinating folk music, spiced with between-song humor, as some 5,000 persons discovered when the trio paid its first visit to the Quad-Cities Saturday night." The trio, whose visit was sponsored by radio station KSTT, performed many of their favorites, including their latest hit "Greenback Dollar," for an audience "composed of mostly teens and just-post-teens."

Harry and the Acoustics: Locals remember Harry Belafonte complaining about the acoustics during his 1966 visit to the Field House. This concern was not new. The year before, Bill McElwain (1965), writing in the *Dispatch*, had asked promoter Fred Epstein of Midwest Concert Productions why he did not book Lawrence Welk for a performance in the Quad Cities. Epstein replied that he "wouldn't touch Welk." McElwain explained:

> Very simply, he would have to guarantee between $15,000 and $17,500 to hear Welk say uh-one, uh-two. And the maestro of the bubbly music refuses to do more than one show a day. To make money on a deal like that, you'd have to put Welk in a place the size of Wharton Field House and charge top prices. And anyone who has ever been in Wharton Field House knows that the acoustics

Argus, October 20, 1966

These combined advertisements in the *Argus* featured two 1966 events promoted by Flambo's GMT productions, one at the Field House and one at the RKO Orpheum Theatre in Davenport. Belafonte and his entourage performed at the Field House on October 22nd and pianist Roger Williams a week later at the RKO. Prices for the Belafonte show were as high as $7.50 for a seat on the basketball floor surrounding the stage, which had been set up in the center of the floor.

> are hideous and the seating mighty uncomfortable. Promoters steer away from it. So, that eliminates Welk from the local scene unless you put him in Davenport Muny Stadium or at the fairgrounds. And then you have the weather to worry about. Remember when Arthur Godfrey and his horses were scheduled into Muny Stadium a couple of years ago? The rains came and Godfrey (and the horses) was hastily

moved to Masonic Auditorium, where he was seen by a much smaller crowd than the 10,000 that had been hoped for at the stadium.

McElwain went on to note that the other major local promoter of the time, G. Laverne Flambo, then with GMT Productions, had been pushing for someone to build a larger theatre in the Quad Cities, a place seating about 5,000 people for stage attractions, meetings, conventions, etc. Of course, eventually this would come to pass – in a much larger venue than Flambo envisioned – with the 1993 opening of The Mark of The Quad Cities in Moline.

Courtesy of John Flambo

The only venue in the Quad Cities that could accommodate crowds larger than the Field House was Municipal ("Muny") Stadium in Davenport. This photograph shows the 10,000 people gathered there for the Don McNeill show on August 25, 1955.

Argus, December 26, 1969

Davenport Public Library

The Masonic Auditorium in Davenport hosted a great variety of events through much of the twentieth century. Opened in 1923, as many as 2,750 people could be packed into the auditorium for entertainment shows, political rallies, and boxing and wrestling. The building was sold in 1996 to Palmer College to become its Museum of Chiropractic History.

Rounding out a busy decade of the 1960s at the Field House, promoter Fred Epstein brought in Steppenwolf and The Chosen Few in late 1969.

153

The Golden Era Fades Away

After Flambo retired from promoting in 1969, relatively few big-name entertainers visited the Field House. The Moline arena had lost some of its attractiveness for such events – audiences were less inclined to enjoy bench seating in a large barn-like arena. Even though they were smaller venues, entertainers continued to perform at the RKO Orpheum and the Masonic Temple in Davenport, each of which seated about 2,750, and the relatively new Centennial Hall on the Augustana College campus in Rock Island, which was opened in 1960 and seats 1,600.

However, a few more concerts were booked at Wharton, including popular rock bands of the time. Among them were Steppenwolf and The Chosen Few appearing in 1969, and The Byrds appearing on April 3, 1972, with The Ides of March and 1984 Love Machine.

Another popular rock group, Wishbone Ash appeared on November 1, 1972, with Speed-O-Meter, a New York band warming up the crowd. The next day Dawn Easterlund (1972) reviewed their performance for the *Dispatch*:

> After rising to the top of the rock scene in Britain in three years, Wishbone Ash is on their fourth tour of the United States in hopes the wave will carry them to the top here. The four-man group [received] a thunderous reception with the music from their three albums . . . Although still struggling for recognition on this month-long tour of the United States, which is half over, many people knew their music and responded to it enthusiastically. Wishbone Ash is getting recognition for perfecting a system of using two guitarists [Andy Powell and Ted Turner] without either one dominating.

From Vaudeville to Hip Hop

In April 1929 the first entertainers from outside the area performed at the Field House for the Quad Cities Pageant of Progress. One of the last appearances of outside entertainers came 61 years later, on March 13, 1990, with the performance of DJ Jazzy Jeff and the Fresh Prince, a prominent Hip Hop group. In 1929 the entertainment was provided by eleven vaudeville acts; in 1990 the entertainment was Hip Hop music. Tastes and styles of music and entertainment had changed dramatically through the twentieth century. These two contrasting events represent bookends to the six-decade history of big-name entertainment at the Field House, which in the interim included big band, rock and roll, and country music, as well as performances by singers, comedians, and other individual stars.

DJ Jazzy Jeff and the Fresh Prince featured Will Smith who went on to become a television and movie start. They had won their first Grammy Award the year before their 1990 visit to Moline and had become very popular, especially with a youthful, radio-listening audience. However, coming to a conservative place like Moline the promoter, Victor Westbrook, was obliged to assure locals the act was "positive entertainment," free of profanity and vulgarity (Lewis, 1990). Indeed, the Field House management was hesitant at first, but agreed to the booking after researching the group. Interestingly, no advertisements or post-show reviews appeared in either the *Argus* or the *Dispatch*, perhaps because the show was primarily promoted via the radio.

The show, which utilized 200 lights and a huge backdrop, was opened by a band called Technotronics, whose hit song was "Pump Up the Jam." Moline resident Neil Dahlstrom attended the performance as a thirteen-year-old lad with his older brother Jeremy. They sat on the ground floor – on the west side near the stage – and remember waiting a long time for the show to start because of problems with the lights.

The Mark

From 1993 onward, the primary venue for large-crowd entertainment in the Quad Cities has been The Mark – since 2005 known as the iWireless Center – in downtown Moline. The

$33.4 million multi-purpose arena was funded by Illinois state funds derived from racetrack revenues. Civic centers in Rockford, Peoria, and Springfield had previously drawn on the same funds for their construction. Dee Ann Rexroat (1993) of the Cedar Rapids *Gazette* placed The Mark into a regional context:

> When the 12,000-seat Mark of the Quad Cities holds its first concert tonight, it will open not only its doors but a whole new market for concert-goers. The Quad Cities, with a population base of 400,000, has been starved for an arena. For years its residents had to travel to Cedar Rapids, Iowa City or Peoria for major arena tours.

In its first calendar year of operation, from late April through December 1993, the new arena hosted at least nine major concerts, including performances by: Neil Diamond, Bon Jovi, Def Leppard, The Moody Blues, the Beach Boys, REO Speedwagon, Kenny G., and Barry Manilow. Over the twenty years of its existence, The Mark/iWireless has hosted an average of over a dozen big-name entertainers per year. (Classic Rock Concerts, online)

In addition to big time shows, the new arena took the Quad City Thunder professional basketball team away from the Field House and has hosted other sporting events, including professional hockey, arena football, college basketball, and professional wrestling shows. It also is the site of circuses, religious and political rallies, various community events, college commencement ceremonies, and a great variety of other activities.

In short, The Mark took over a role that the Field House played for several previous decades as the large local multi-purpose arena. Today it attracts crowds from a wide hinterland surrounding the Quad Cities, just as Wharton Field House did in the past.

A Dual Performance at The Mark and at Wharton?
On the evening of January 22, 2005, country music star Toby Keith performed at The Mark. Earlier that day he also made an appearance at Wharton – playing basketball for two hours with his band mates. Court time was arranged by Moline athletic director Todd Rosenthal, who was also roped into playing with the troupe. Rosenthal, a championship wrestler and coach, said: "I had jeans and a T-shirt, and I told them I was a wrestler. That didn't bother them – they just wanted to play, and I was a body." Rosenthal said Superintendent Calvin Lee approved the plan to use the Field House, "but we had to keep it a secret because he (Keith) has had some threats made on him with his (pro-war) stance on Iraq. It was like holding the world's biggest secret." (John Marx, QCOnline, January 24, 2005)

C. Roseman

This 2013 photograph shows the main entrance of the iWireless Center, formerly The Mark of the Quad Cities.

Chapter 7

Showplace and Meeting Place

"an ideal setting for everything from sports events and dog shows to musical events"
–Moline *Dispatch*

The first major exhibition at the Field House was the week-long Quad Cities Pageant of Progress, held in April 1929, four months after the Field House opened. In addition to vaudeville acts it included about 100 educational exhibits. In the decades to follow an incredible variety of meetings, shows, and exhibitions utilized the Field House. They ranged from poultry, sporting, and home shows to religious and school-related gatherings. Many were sponsored by service clubs and other local organizations, which used the big arena to raise money for the various causes they embraced. Three of the early events featured automobiles, dogs, and gardens.

Automobiles: In March 1930, about 2,500 attended the four-day Moline Auto Show where seventy cars, three boats, a truck, and some outboard motors were on display. Automobiles included: Hudson, Olds, Essex, Desoto, Hupmobile, Marquette, Roosevelt, Lincoln, Oakland, Graham, Chevrolet, Whippet, Studebaker, Erskine, Viking, Dodge, Buick, Chrysler, Marmon, Ford, Nash, Pontiac, Willys, and Durant. At the time each of the Tri-Cities held its own auto show. In future years collective Quad Cities shows would be held, many of them at the Rock Island Armory.

A generous dose of boosterism is apparent in this advertisement for the Auto Show held on March 13-16, 1930, sponsored by Moline automobile dealers.

Canines: In the 1930s, Wharton Field House hosted at least two dog shows. On April 5 and 6, 1932, the Tri-City Kennel Club's annual show attracted about 2,000 spectators and 500 dogs. The "best dog in show" went to a brown and white pointer named Nancolleth Beryl, exhibited by Giralda farms of Madison, New Jersey, and owned by Mrs. Madeline Rockefeller Dodge. In March 1937, the Emma J. Kough Circle of King's Daughters sponsored another two-day all-breed dog show, the seventh annual Tri-City Kennel Club event. About forty breeds were judged. According to the show's program, class winners were awarded ribbons and cash ranging upwards from $1, depending on the number of dogs entered in the class. The best in show was a German boxer, Lustig von Dom of Tulgey Wood,

The
Automobile Show

It is a boost for Moline . . . . It brings people to Moline. Let's boost the Automobile Show

It Opens at the Field House Tomorrow

▼

Peoples Savings Bank & Trust Co.

"Solid As A Rock Since 1857"

Dispatch, March 2, 1930

Tri-Cities' Biggest
Dog Show
Now Open to Public

Moline Field House

1800 Block, 20th Ave., Moline

500 — Aristocrats of Dogdom — 500

Including many of the finest dogs in America. Don't miss seeing 'em Tuesday, Wednesday, April 5-6. Doors open 10 a. m. to 10 p. m. Judging afternoon and night.

Popular Prices, Adults 50c, Children 25c

Follow the Crowd to the Big Dog Show

Argus, April 5, 1932

Argus advertisement for the Tri-City Kennel Club's 1932 Dog Show.

157

handled by Jimmie Sullivan of Chicago. Apparently this show attracted more people than the 1932 version. The *New York Times* (April 1, 1937) reported: "The crowd that saw the final judging was the largest ever to attend a dog show in the Tri-Cities and the Moline Field House was packed to the doors."

Gardens: On June 8-10, 1934, the Tri-City Garden Club sponsored a garden and flower show. The June 8th *Dispatch* attempted to whet the appetites of potential attendees for both the show and the five-year-old Moline Field House:

> Even though your horticultural knowledge may not extend beyond the point of knowing the difference between a rose and a pansy, you shouldn't miss the flower show at the field house. It is without a doubt one of the most outstanding attractions the Tri-Cities has had for many a day and brings Moline further praise for its field house, which has proved itself an ideal setting for everything from sports events and dog shows to musical events.

Pageant of Progress, 1930, 1931 and 1937

Building on the success of their first Pageant of Progress held in the spring of 1929 (see Chapter 1), the American Legion sponsored three more. Each week-long event featured scores of educational and commercial exhibits provided by local businesses and nonprofit organizations including the YMCA, YWCA, 4-H clubs, Boy Scouts, and the public library. In addition, each of the pageants brought in outside entertainment as promised by the *Dispatch* (April 21) for the 1930 show:

> Aside from the many exhibits, which constitute a show in themselves, there will be an elaborate program of professional entertainment. Vaudeville and circus performers from Chicago and New York are being imported to stage what is heralded as being one of the most comprehensive programs of entertainment ever staged in connection

with an event of this nature. Singers, dancers, musicians, acrobats, comedians, tight wire walkers, radio stars are all included on the variety program which will be given every night this week.

Perhaps the most unusual features were public weddings held on the opening nights of these three pageants. The three couples and the number of people attending their weddings were:

1930, April 21: Beulah Veeder and Clarence Peterson of Moline; 6,500

1931, April 21: Clarice Wenberg and Ivan Murtey of Moline; 3,500-4,000

1937, April 26: Blanch Larson of Silvis and John Cole of Moline; 3,500

Moline Field House

AUSPICES MOLINE POST No. 246
AMERICAN LEGION

Admission
Adults . . 35¢
Children . 15¢

Doors
Open From
7 until 11

EXTRA! TONIGHT ONLY!

MISS CLARICE WENBERG   IVAN MURTEY
PUBLIC WEDDING
of Clarice Wenberg and Ivan Murtey

Dispatch, April 20, 1931

The 1931 wedding of Clarice Wenberg and Ivan Murtey was prominently advertised.

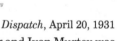

PUBLICITY PASS

ADMIT ONE

QUAD-CITY PAGEANT OF PROGRESS
MOLINE FIELD HOUSE   APRIL 20-25

This Pass is issued in return for courtesies extended the Moline Post, No. 246, American Legion, in its promotion of the Quad-City Pageant of Progress.

GOOD ANY NIGHT   ONE NIGHT ONLY

Courtesy of Jerry Wallaert

A pass for one night of the 1931 event.

Dispatch, April 22, 1930

Pictured here is the wedding party for the first of three weddings at the Field House performed in conjunction with the Pageant of Progress in 1930, 1931, and 1937. In the center are bridegroom Clarence Peterson and bride Beulah Veeder. In front of the groom is the youngest sister of the bride, Martha Veeder (now Martha Van Hecke), who served as a flower girl. Peeking between the bride and the groom is Reverend W. A. Steinkraus, who performed the ceremony. Steinkraus had played an instrumental role in the planning of the new Field House which opened two years earlier. A total of 6,522 people were on hand to witness the wedding.

The 1937 Legion Pageant of Progress (April 26 - May 1) featured 100 displays by merchants, manufacturers, and some other organizations including the Moline Schools. They covered the main floor and were squeezed under the east and west-side balconies. The arena was decorated with flags and bunting and a large stage was constructed at the open end of the U-shaped balcony for the entertainment. Among the featured entertainers was the Maple City Four, stars of the Barn Dance program on Chicago radio station WLS.

Dispatch, April 17, 1937   *Dispatch*, April 19, 1937

Two advertisements for the 1937 pageant show its diversity of offerings. In addition to exhibits, entertainment was provided by orchestras, fashion reviews, ten "Vodvil" acts, and of course a wedding on the first evening.

Displays at the
1937 Pageant of Progress

Photographs from the
Rock Island County Historical Society

A prominent display at the 1937 pageant was provided by Deere & Company and positioned right in front of the main entrance to the Field House.

Even though about 11,000 attended the first five days of the 1937 event, the afternoon *Dispatch* on the last day, May 1st, lamented that the total "may miss by several thousand that of the 1929 and 1930 pageants." In 1929 and 1930, 15,000 and 18,000 people attended. As far as we know, 1937 was the last year this event was held.

Deere & Company archives

Coming to Town: Rural and Farm-Related Events

Kiwanis Farm-City: One of the most popular and long-lasting recurring events at the Field House began in 1929 and continued for 28 years. The Moline Kiwanis Club hosted an annual series of dinners and programs especially for local farmers. Their website (Kiwanis Moline, online) describes the series:

In 1926, a series of farm-city dinners was started by the Club's Agricultural Committee. Rural churches were invited to sponsor chicken dinners in the fall which Kiwanis members and guests would support. At the end of the season the club entertained their hosts and hostesses at a banquet at the LeClaire Hotel. By 1929 the program had

Courtesy of Bud Everett and the Moline Kiwanis Club

The Field House was all set up for the Kiwanis chicken dinner on November 18, 1930, which was attended by farmers and local merchants.

expanded to the point that more farmers were invited and the season finale had to be moved to Wharton Field House where 1,400 people were served and merchants contributed $2,200 to the cost. Eventually the crowds were such that the dinner was discontinued and the Field House was filled with people coming to the program. The president's report for 1947 stated that 7,000 packed the Field House and even into the early '50's full houses were reported. It was not until 1956 that interest in the program had finally fallen victim to television and disinterest in chicken dinners and the last program took place in 1956.

Courtesy of Bud Everett and the Moline Kiwanis Club

The 1930 Kiwanis dinner included entertainment provided by a band performing from a stage at the south end of the Field House. In later years, the annual event would discard the dinners and focus on entertainment.

On November 3, 1941, the fifteenth annual Kiwanis farm-city event attracted 3,000 to the Field House. It featured the Moline High School band, a vaudeville act, and a visit by Chicago radio personality Bob Elson of WGN. Now without the chicken dinners, attendance over 5,000 was reached every year until the mid-1950s. The high school band performed again in 1946, along with eight vaudeville acts and the Roy Knutz orchestra. In 1947, vaudeville acts included Francisco & Delores; an acrobatic team; Vic Hyde, a one-man band; and comedian and magician Jack Herbert.

Rock Island County Historical Society

IT'S THE BIG NIGHT!
Thursday, Nov. 8th
31st ANNUAL
MOLINE KIWANIS
Farm Party Carnival
"Where Town and Country Folks Meet"

Show Starts Promptly at 8 P.M. — Doors Open at 6 O'clock

WHARTON FIELD HOUSE
20th Avenue and 18th Street, Moline

5 BIG VAUDEVILLE ACTS

PETER & GEORGE BAUER — Hand Balancing. Thrilling Action!
BEN BERI — Outstanding Juggler!
AL HOFFMAN — In A Slide For Life. Unusual, Original!
SHIRLEY & DALE — Personality in Puppetry!
JOHN SHIRLEY — Balloon Creations!
THE FOUR MUSICAL WADES AND JACKIE BURTELL — In A Jet-Styled Revue!

Dispatch, November 7, 1956

The 31st annual, and last, Kiwanis Farm Party was in 1956. As in previous years a variety of acts were featured, as listed in part of a November 7th *Dispatch* advertisement shown here. Perhaps the most interesting vaudeville act was a foot-juggling routine delivered by George and Peter Bauer: "the son does a full twist summersault and lands on the soles of his father's feet, from which he started." (*Dispatch*, November 2)

Courtesy of Jerry Wallaert

The Moline Kiwanis Club also sponsored, in 1950, a minstrel show called "Now and Then" utilizing local talent. Dozens of performers danced and sang using costumes and special scenery supplied by the John B. Rogers Producing Company, Fostoria, Ohio. Two female lead performers played the roles of "Miss Now" and "Miss Then." Miss Moline of 1949, Joline Schieberl, was Miss Now, and Miss Rock Island of 1949, Nancy Lepoidevin, was cast in the role of Miss Then. The Dispatch (March 16) described the first evening's show, which attracted 2200 people, as "Old-time vaudeville, with a few added gestures of cheesecake and cob-fresh corn." Shown here is the cover for the program. Inside the program, president of the club John S. Perry explained that the purpose of the event was to raise money for "aid to under-privileged children, promotion of worthwhile activities for boys and girls, support of churches, promoting interest in public affairs and getting behind projects for the betterment of our community."

Poultry Show: On December 4-7, 1929, almost a year after the Field House was opened, more than 10,000 people attended the four-day Illinois State Poultry Show, sponsored by the Moline Association of Commerce and the state and county poultry associations. The December 3 Dispatch noted the need for a local show by pointing out that a University of Illinois survey "indicated a surprising deficiency in poultry products in Rock Island County [which] imports more than 300,000 dozen eggs annually." The show would provide "the largest and most interesting exhibit of poultry, pigeons and rabbits in the history of the annual event."

Saving Labor: On February 26, 1945, Wharton hosted a farm show and exhibition of labor saving devices, sponsored by the Illinois Farm and Home Bureau. The Moline event attracted more people than any others in a series of over 25 of these shows across Illinois. Prizes were awarded for the best homemade inventions. The first prize, a $25 War Bond, went to Lloyd Walther of Port Byron for his "wagon that unloads itself." Second went to S. S. Stenson of Bowling Township for his phosphate spreader, and third to Mrs. Elmer Nelson of Cordova for her collection of clothes-processing gadgets.

County Fair: For two years, in August 1948 and 1949, the Rock Island County Fair was held inside and outside of the Field House. The fair traces its origins to the nineteenth century but did not find a permanent home until 1955 when it acquired the East Moline fairgrounds for the event. Before World War II it was held sporadically, under a variety of names and sponsorships, at various locations around the county. After being held in 1941 at Douglas Park in Rock Island, it took a five-year hiatus. After the war, the Rock Island County Fair Association was organized and began to transform the event into a more urban-oriented affair with carnival rides and entertainment in addition to the traditional farm products orientation (*Dispatch*, July 28, 1967).

The fair was revived in 1947 at Indian Bluff Forest Preserve (called Blackhawk Forest Preserve at the time) south of the Quad City

Airport. Then it moved to the Field House in 1948. The *Dispatch* (July 29) called for volunteers to "help set up tents, build fences, drive posts and otherwise prepare for opening of [the fair] in the Wharton field house area." The paper went on to quote county farm advisor George H. Reid:

> We will need 50 to 75 men and boys and 25 women . . . The six large tents will be here Monday, August 2. Workers will need to bring hammers, pliers, bailing wire and a truck or two could be used. We also will need a few iron post drivers and a post hole digger or two.

The fair site was most commonly advertised as "Wharton Field House and grounds," implying that Browning Field was not used. Indeed, a decision may have been made to avoid Browning for fear of damaging the football field about a month before the autumn gridiron season was to begin. The main activities of the fair were held on the grounds east of the Field House, which today is occupied by a large parking lot. That land had been donated to the schools by Katherine Butterworth in 1941.

For the 1949 fair, bleachers for 3,000 spectators were set up outside the Field House for the western stock horse show on the first night of

"Wild West Show Added Feature At County Fair"
Under this headline, the *Dispatch* (August 4, 1948) described a fair side-show: "Housewives, motorists and children along a 14-block path northwest from Wharton . . . had ringside seats for an unexpected wild west show this morning." It seems that a steer owned by teen-ager Paul Price of Buffalo Prairie bolted and dragged the lad along the ground. After suffering skinning and burning the boy finally let go of the rope tied to the bull and "the candidate for a purple ribbon in tomorrow's baby beef show took off at a fast pace in the general direction of the Price Farm (which is 25 miles or more from Moline)."

Along the route, a woman was bringing clean laundry outside to hang on the clothesline, then saw the running bull, dropped her laundry basket and ran back into the house. Mrs. Swan Johnson who lived about fourteen blocks from Wharton, was also surprised to see from her kitchen window a large bovine bounding through her back yard. Several people helped Price finally corral the bull and bring it back to the Field House "but only for a brief stay. As soon as Paul could get his truck backed up the steer was started on the trip back to the farm."

the fair, which included horse races. To accommodate the Ray Pearl orchestra visit on the the last evening, the "entire south half of Wharton field house will be reserved for dancing." (*Dispatch*, August 9) About 3,000 people turned out for the dance.

Argus, August 4, 1948

Siblings Carol and Orville Hutchinson of Milan, Illinois, brought their steers to the 1948 county fair on the Wharton Field House grounds in preparation for the 4-H livestock show and judging.

After two years at the Field House, the fair was held in 1950 at the Quad City Speedway (west of the Quad City Airport), then for four years at Illiniwek Forest Preserve in Hampton. In 1955 it settled down at the new fairgrounds in East Moline, where the event has been held annually.

Argus, August 23, 1949

The 1949 county fair was bigger and better than the one at Wharton a year earlier. This ad from the *Argus* (August 23), ballyhoos the entertainment side of the fair, but gives short shrift to the farm-related activities such as livestock judging, homemaking exhibits, and farm machinery displays. In a sign of the times, the ad includes a "For Your Protection" notice, indicating that the entire grounds, including grandstand and food tents, "has been sprayed with DDT for protection against POLIO."

World War II Patriotic Events

On September 1, 1942, nine months after the United States entered World War II, Moline School Superintendent C. R. Crakes informed the school board that "numerous calls had been received from organizations seeking use of the field house for patriotic events, and that an increasing number may be expected during the course of the war." (*Dispatch*, September 2) On that evening the school board decreed that:

All groups seeking use of Wharton field house free or at cost for patriotic events, such as affairs to raise money for war relief societies or the purchase of war bonds, must first obtain certification from the Moline Association of Commerce and the Rock Island county defense council.

Indeed, several war-related events had already been held at the Field House and others would follow. Below is a summary of some of them.

"Flying Kernels" Send-off: On February 22, 1942, the Field House hosted a ceremony for a new U. S. Navy air squadron from eastern Iowa and western Illinois, which was poised to begin training at Glenview, Illinois. A mile-long parade snaking through Davenport, Rock Island, and Moline preceded the ceremony, which was attended by political, military, and educational leaders from the region. About 1,000 people attended the Field House ceremony where some forty state, city, military, and college officials were seated on the stage. The audience was addressed by Governor George Wilson of Iowa and Lieutenant Governor Hugh Cross of Illinois, among others, while 25 "Flying Kernels" were inducted into the Navy.

Kick-off to War Bond Campaign: On a Sunday afternoon, May 10, 1942, 4,500 people gathered at the Field House for a variety show sponsored by Rock Island radio station WHBF. The event was a precursor to a massive three-day door-to-door campaign conducted by hundreds of local volunteer "minute men and women." They solicited pledges from residents to purchase war bonds on the following Monday, Tuesday, and Wednesday.

The Field House event, which was broadcast live on WHBF, included performances by the Augustana College choir, a WHBF-based band, the Oklahoma Outlaws, and a duet, Marilyn Barclay and Florentina Palos, who had appeared on the Mutual Radio Network. Also appearing was Jack Manthey's dance orchestra, featuring Louis Bellson, a senior at Moline High School who had won national solo drum competitions as a teenager. After the show, the crowd was able to inspect a collection of tanks, jeeps, and other war-related equipment outside of the building, and then participate in parades in downtown Rock Island and Davenport.

Marilyn Barclay, who sang at the 1942 War Bond variety show, was born in Rock Island and grew up in Moline. Among her prominent appearances, she performed with Lawrence Welk in 1942 in an act, "The Two Young Ladies of Song." In June 1949, Barclay played a lead role in the first Quad City Music Guild production, "Sweethearts." (Oldefest Obituary, online)

Courtesy of Don Hepner

The Oklahoma Outlaws performed at the 1942 war bond campaign at Wharton. This photograph shows them posing in 1937 with Gene Autry who is wearing a white shirt and a bandana. The band performed with Autry in the 1937 movie Rootin' Tootin' Rhythm. At the time they were based at radio station WHO in Des Moines. During the 1930s the Outlaws moved among several radio stations in the Midwest, then in the early 1940s they were based at WHBF in Rock Island. During that time period the band originated a show over 242 Mutual Radio Network stations. In 1942, they settled in Tulsa, Oklahoma—where their name finally matched their location. The head of the band, Al Clauser (seated immediately in front of Autry) launched the singing career of Patti Page and was the first to use the term "Western Swing" as a description of the style of music played by his band and many others. (Clauser Bio, online) Autry's sidekick, Smiley Burnette, is standing in the rear of the photograph. The band member in the foreground is Al "Slim" Phillips. Other band members, left to right, are Larry Brandt, Don Austin, Clauser, and Harry Edward "Tex" Hoepner. [OKOutlawsHoepnerGeneAutry]

Let Freedom Ring: A patriotic song pageant, presented on May 15, 1942, by over 1,000 Moline elementary, junior high, and high school students, was attended by some 3,000 spectators. Two 500-member choruses performed, in addition to other musical acts and specialty dances and pantomimes. "Patriotism ran high at the conclusion of the program, as lights were turned out, a spotlight was thrown on the American flag, and choruses and audience rose to sing the Star Spangled Banner" (*Dispatch*, May 16).

Civilian Defense Show: In September 1942, the Moline Safety Council sponsored a Saturday and Sunday evening event that featured demonstrations and exhibits by local civil defense units and a speech by U. S. Senator from Illinois, C. Wayland Brooks. On Sunday evening 500 attendees witnessed arm bands and certificates being presented to Moline air raid wardens and a patriotic speech by Senator Brooks who warned: "It is a fight to the finish to determine whether free men or despots shall determine the future course of civilization" (*Dispatch*, September 21).

Labor for Victory Rally: On October 27, 1942, a joint committee representing the AFL and the CIO (two labor unions that merged in 1955) sponsored a rally that included talks by labor leaders, vaudeville acts, and a competition in which local people matched wits with three network radio prodigies, the "Quiz Kids" aged eight, ten, and twelve. Featured speakers included former Augustana College faculty member Wendell Lund who was director of the labor production division of the War Production Board, and Eugene Casey, special executive assistant to President Roosevelt. Estimated attendance at this free event was between 700 and 1,000.

Radio Personality: On November 6, 1942, a prominent newscaster, Fulton Lewis Jr., was invited by the Moline Junior Association of Commerce to speak at the Field House on "What's Happening in Washington." Lewis' radio broadcasts were carried five days a week at 6 p.m. on Rock Island radio station, WHBF. The

Moline High School band played before the presentation in front of 700-800 attendees.

Deere Exhibit: People flocked to the Field House on June 20, 1943, to view a variety of war materials produced at the eight Deere & Company manufacturing plants in Moline and East Moline. Materials on display included military tractors, mobile laundry units, aircraft parts, and ammunition. The Rock Island Arsenal loaned Deere a medium tank with a transmission made by the company. It was displayed outside, just south of the Field House. Inside the arena, music was supplied by the Jack Manthey Orchestra throughout the afternoon and evening.

Scenes from the 1943 John Deere War Equipment Exhibit at Wharton Field House

Photographs from Deere & Company archives

Scenes from the 1943 John Deere War Equipment Exhibit
at Wharton Field House

Photographs from Deere & Company archives

Award Postponed. The Deere war materials exhibit at the Field House went on as scheduled, but an accompanying award ceremony at Browning Field was postponed. Deere & Company and its 7,000 local employees were to have been presented an "E" award from the United States Army and Navy for excellence in the production of war equipment. A full page ad in the *Dispatch* on June 18, 1943, suggested that the award was postponed because of a strike at one of Deere's plants. It cited one of the requirements for recipients of the award was "avoidance of work stoppages." The strike, which started a week earlier, was in protest of a wide differential in wages between some employees working on government contracts and some building farm equipment.

Circus Basketball: To conclude a 1944 war bond sales drive, the fourth to have been held in the Illinois Quad Cities, the Field House was host to "the most unusual basketball show ever offered . . . a Lincoln Day circus basketball carnival" (*Dispatch*, February 12). The main basketball feature of the evening was a game with four ten-minute quarters, each quarter pairing different high school teams: Rock Island vs. East Moline in the first; Moline vs. St. Joseph's Catholic (of Rock Island) in the second; East Moline vs. St. Joseph's in the third; then Rock Island vs. Moline in the fourth. A cumulative combined score would determine the winner, Rock Island schools versus the others. Using a similar format, a preliminary game was played with combined ninth-grade teams from Rock Island opposing those from Moline and East Moline. The Rock Island Schools won the varsity competition, 41-35, but Moline/East Moline beat the Rocks and the Shamrocks in the freshman competition.

The event promoted the purchase of U. S. government war stamps and war bonds, which provided support for the war effort. At the time the smallest denomination war bonds sold for $18.75 and yielded $25 after ten years. Stamps came in denominations as small as ten cents and were to be saved toward the purchase of bonds. Admission to the event was $1 in stamps for adults and 25 cents in stamps for students. Two reserved seats came with the purchase of a war bond, either in advance or at the Field House.

No doubt the highlight of the evening – at least for some people – was the auction of six captured German helmets at halftime of the featured contest. Three World War II helmets captured in North Africa attracted the highest bids: Rock Island County Superintendent of Schools Floyd Shetter bought one for $500 and Otto Schweinberger bought two, for $575 and $500. A First World War helmet attracted a bid of $300 from Herbert Liljegren. Owing to the length of the auction and the amount of basketball being played, the event lasted until well after 11 p.m.

Argus, February 14, 1944

This *Argus* photograph shows the four high school teams lined up on the Field House floor for the national anthem and the beginning of an evening of "circus basketball." On the right end of the court are the Moline and East Moline teams, and on the left are two teams from Rock Island schools, St. Joseph's and Rock Island High.

They'd Like This for Trophy Case

Argus, February 12, 1944

One of the German war helmets to be auctioned off at the circus basketball war bond event is being held by high school basketball centers Jerry Russ of Rock Island High and Nick Kupresin of East Moline. The helmet was captured in North Africa.

War Affects High School Graduation: The Moline annual spring graduation ceremony held in 1944 featured an address by Samuel Orathwell, who was affiliated with the Universities of Kansas and Minnesota and spoke on the subject, "There is nothing to fear but fear." Not only was his choice of topics influenced by the war; so too was the attendance. The *Dispatch* (June 10) explains that the commencement address by Orathwell:

> was heard by one of the smallest graduating classes in years, with relatives and friends, resultantly, not filling Wharton field house to capacity as has often been the case. Of the 148 students in the June division, eleven had already left for the armed service

War Movies: On Saturday, August 26, 1944, the civilian advisory council on military activities, with the assistance of the Moline Senior and Junior Associations of Commerce, presented a showing of "restricted" war films. They included: *Earth Movers* showing military Seabees

and engineers at work; *Film Communiqué No. 8* showing war action from various locations; and *The Case of the Tremendous Trifle*, which tells the story of the Schweinfurt raid, an air raid in Germany that resulted in severe losses for the U. S. Army Air Force.

Gobs of Fun: On February 13-14, 1945, Navy trainees from St. Ambrose College presented a musical comedy, "Gobs of Fun." Originally to be performed at the Scottish Rite Cathedral, brisk advance ticket sales moved the sponsors, Zal Grotto, to switch the performance to the Field House to accommodate larger crowds. Indeed, several thousand people attended the two shows.

Earlier that month the show had been staged at the Davenport Masonic Temple. Proceeds from all the shows were used to support a dance for the 200 new Navy men and their dates. On the Saturday following the Field House shows, the dance was held at the Sky-Hi Ballroom atop the LeClaire Hotel in Moline.

"Door" prize. Milt Johnson of Moline remembers the awarding of a door prize as part of the Gobs of Fun program. A woman from the audience who was selected to receive the prize went up onto the stage to retrieve it. Out came the prize: a full-sized door!

Aircraft Physics for Teachers: On June 1 and 2, 1945, at the Field House, personnel from the Army Air Force training command conducted demonstrations for teachers on the application of the laws of physics to aviation. The event, open to educators and the public, included displays of aircraft instrument, hydraulic, and electrical systems and aircraft engines.

Wounded Soldiers Visit Music Fest: Less than a month before the Japanese surrendered to end World War II in 1945, the fourth annual Moline Youth Music Festival embraced soldiers from Schick and Mayo hospitals (located in Clinton, Iowa, and Galesburg, Illinois, respectively). Several bus loads arrived to be fed at the local

USO, then occupied a special reserved-seat section of the Field House for the Sunday evening concert on July 22nd. Captain George W. Campbell, "one of the most entertaining community song leaders in the country," led the audience in favorite songs and vocal stunts (*Dispatch*, July 18). The event was sponsored by the Associated Council of Dad's Clubs.

Fashion and Beauty

Century of Fashion: On June 25, 1948, as part of the Moline centennial celebration, forty local women modeled the latest fashions, along with fashions from a hundred years earlier, at the Century of Fashion show. In a highlight of the show modern and Victorian wedding parties were contrasted. The program, which was held both in the afternoon and evening, also included song and dance.

1848 *1948*

A Century of Fashion

A hundred years of the smartest styles

Friday, June 25, 1948—Wharton Field House, Moline

Matinee — 2:00   Admission — One Dollar   Evening — 8.00

Sponsored by Retail Division, Moline Association of Commerce

Dispatch files

Miss Moline Pageant: The first Miss Moline beauty contest, held on June 18, 1949, attracted about 600 to Wharton. Eighteen-year-old Joline Schieberl, who previously had been dubbed "Joline of Moline" for her high school cheerleading talent, won the crown over ten other contestants. She won a $250 scholarship, a trip to the Miss Illinois contest in Quincy, a large "Oscar," and fifty hours of dancing lessons. On June 20th, the *Dispatch* commented: "A successful business woman at 18, who jumped into a career fresh from high school in the spring of last year, won't need the dancing instruction. She has her own studio in Moline and lists 128 pupils in dance instruction." After the crowning ceremony at the Field House, the Viking Quartet provided music for dancing.

Miss Illinois Pageant: The Moline Chamber of Commerce hosted the Miss Illinois pageant at Wharton Field House on May 29 and 30, 1959. The first evening, a Friday, attracted a sparse crowd of 300. The Saturday edition of the *Dispatch* noted: "A Jaycee representative attributes the dearth in attendance to a rash of graduation exercises in the Quad Cities last night. He added that advance ticket sales indicate close to a full house for the performance tonight." Indeed, some

Modern Bridal Party Is Climax of Style Show

The 1948 Century of Fashion show at the Field House concluded with a bridal party theme.

Dispatch files

A panel of judges, seated in the right foreground, review thirteen Miss Illinois candidates in swimsuits at Wharton Field House on the first evening of the 1959 pageant in front of a small crowd. The other thirteen candidates posed in evening gowns that evening. Then the two groups switched modes of dress to be judged as part of the finale the following evening.

3,000 showed up for the final judging and crowning of Miss Illinois.

Saturday evening, twenty-year-old Suzanne Johnson, Miss Moline, was crowned Miss Illinois by the reigning Miss America Mary Ann Mobley of Mississippi. The first Miss Moline to win the Miss Illinois title, Johnson would a few days later be graduated from Augustana College summa cum laude, where she majored in music. Possessing the state crown, she headed for the September Miss America contest in Atlantic City, where she was a top ten finalist.

Miss Moline, Fred Waring, Dwight Eisenhower, and Nikita Khrushchev. Band leader Waring had heard Johnson sing at the Illinois State Fair and offered her a job with his band, The Pennsylvanians, if she did not win the Miss America crown. Not having won, she headed for New York to join Waring immediately after the Miss American pageant. Waring's next performance was at the White House with the leaders of the United States and the USSR. Johnson sang with the chorus, having had one day to learn the songs they performed for the luminaries assembled, including President Eisenhower and Soviet Premier Khrushchev. (*Dispatch*, September 23, 1959)

Religious Gatherings

Biggest Crowd?: Dr. E. Stanley Jones, a missionary and evangelist, made the rounds of the Quad Cities for several days in 1944, appearing at the Field House on the first day of his visit, February 27. His preaching was coupled with choral music in a Sunday afternoon "mass meeting" sponsored by the Rock Island County Council of Churches. The event was chaired by A. W. Wood, principal of John Deere Junior High School in Moline. Reverend W. T. Coleman, pastor of the St. Paul African Methodist Episcopal Church in Moline gave the benediction, and Augustana College President Dr. Conrad Bergendoff introduced Jones. Music was provided by the Augustana orchestra and the Bach Chorus of the Augustana Oratorio Society. The following day, the *Dispatch* declared:

> The biggest crowd ever to hear a speech in Moline and probably the biggest crowd ever to gather at Moline field house or any event packed the large building yesterday afternoon to hear E. Stanley Jones . . . Every seat in the

galleries was taken and the main floor was jammed with at least 1,300 persons.

Youth For Christ Rally: A eight-day event in Moline, celebrating the first anniversary of the Youth For Christ organization, was culminated with a program at Wharton on November 10, 1945. Rallies were held at the Scottish Rite Cathedral on each of the preceding seven days. The Saturday-evening Field House rally featured a sermon by Dr. Martin R. DeHaan, a teacher of a radio bible class broadcast weekly on the Mutual Radio Network. About 3,500 people attended the three-and-a-half hour program, which included short speeches, hymn singing, and other music. Patriotic songs were played by a combined band composed of students from Moline and East Moline High Schools under the direction of Earl Youngdahl, and choral music was provided by a 500-voice choir composed of youth from area churches.

Ordination: On June 13, 1948, ordination for 23 graduates of the Augustana Theological Seminary was held at Wharton, with about 4,000 in attendance including Swedish dignitaries. The Most Reverend Erling Eldem, archbishop of Uppsala in Sweden, presented greetings to the assembled at the ordination. It was the culmination of a week-long centennial celebration for the Augustana Lutheran Church Synod.

Argus, June 14, 1948

Augustana Luthern Church Ordination ceremony, June 13, 1948.

Final Concert

Festival of Sacred Music

NORMAN CLAYTON   ROSA PAGE WELCH   DR. CHARLES HIRT

See and hear these famous personalities this Sunday. Norman Clayton will sing a group of solos and will join the combined chorus in the singing of Gonud's Sanctus. The chorus, composed of choirs from 34 Protestant churches in Rock Island county, will be directed by Dr. Charles Hirt. Rosa Page Welch will lead the chorus and audience in congregational singing.

WHARTON FIELDHOUSE
Sunday, April 29th, 3 p. m.

Argus, April 24, 1951

This ad trumpeted the appearance of guest performers on the final day of a twelve-week festival of sacred music in 1951.

Sacred Music: In 1951, a series of twelve Sunday afternoon sacred concerts was held by the Rock Island County Council of Churches, all broadcast over radio station WHBF. The first eleven featured individual church choirs. The finale, on April 29th, attracted 3,500 and featured the combined voices of choirs from 34 Protestant churches in the county, along with visiting artists. Dr. Charles Hirt, minister of music at the First Presbyterian Church of Hollywood and professor of music at the University of Southern California, directed the chorus. Former Moline resident and prize-winning baritone soloist Norman Clayton came from New York, where he was studying at the Juilliard School of Music. Chicagoan Rose Page Welch, known as the "Marion Anderson of the Disciples of Christ," came from Chicago to perform solos. (*Dispatch*, April 28 and 30)

Rise and Shine: Among the most memorable and lasting offerings at Wharton Field House were the Easter Sunrise Services, held each year from 1948 through 1973. Depending on what date Easter fell upon, the services would start at 5:45 or 6:00 a.m. The first one attracted 5,800 worshipers and in later years upwards of 6,000 attended each year.

Beginning in 1974, sunrise services were held at Centennial Hall on the Augustana College campus. No longer would worshipers experience the first sun rays of dawn streaming through the skylight at the center of the Wharton Field House roof.

In a typical year, daylight would be breaking as the Wharton Easter Sunrise Service was beginning. In the absence of cloud cover, the sun would soon splash light into the Field House interior through the 30 by 70 foot skylight, pictured here in April 2012.

C. Roseman, 2012

Argus, April 6, 1953

Early morning rays of sunshine through the Field House south windows and the overhead skylight for the 1953 Easter Sunrise Service. More than 6,000 were in attendance to hear Reverend Charles B. Templeton from the National Council of Churches of Christ in America deliver the sermon.

174

Easter Services

On the AIR

WHBF

WHBF

DIAL
1270

WHBF-FM
on the Air
12:30 to
10:15 p. m.
Channel 255
Dial 98.9 mc.

6:00 a. m. SUNRISE SERVICE from Wharton Fieldhouse, Moline

7:00 a. m. EASTER SERVICE from Soldiers Memorial, St. Louis

7:30 a. m. HOLLYWOOD BOWL broadcast of Easter Service

9:00 a. m. Free Church Hour

10:00 a. m. Message of Israel

10:30 a. m. Hour of Faith

11:30 a. m. Rev. Axel Pearson

12:30 p. m. National Vespers

5:30 p. m. THE GREATEST STORY EVER TOLD: 'The Resurrection'

10:15 p. m. Old Fashioned Revival

American Broadcasting Company

Dispatch, March 27, 1948

Sunrise services were regularly broadcast over the radio, WHBF in Rock Island carrying them for a number of years beginning in 1948. This advertisement for the 1948 services lists their religious programs on Easter Sunday. The Wharton services at 6 a.m. were followed by Easter services from the Soldiers Memorial in St. Louis, then from the Hollywood Bowl in California.

Rise and Shine! In the late 1940s and early 1950s, special early-morning bus runs leading to the Field House were arranged by the Tri-City Lines. Generally they followed regular bus routes and could be boarded anywhere along those routes. For the 1949 service, the *Argus* (April 16) published the schedule. Buses left at 5:15 a.m. from two locations in Rock Island, a bus from Watertown through Silvis and East Moline also started at 5:15, and two Moline routes started at 5:25 and 5:35.

Crusade: Evangelist Merv Rosell appeared at the Field House for three weeks in 1954, from Sunday, April 25th, through Sunday, May 16th. Evening programs were presented Monday through Saturday, afternoon sessions on Sundays. Various vocalists, musicians, and speakers joined him for the programs, which were broadcast over Moline radio station WQUA. One evening featured an appearance by Mrs. Billy Sunday and another featured Dr. Clarence Jones of the internationally famous shortwave radio station, HCJB in Quito, Ecuador, "The Voice of the Andes." The event was sponsored by the Ministers Association of Rock Island, Moline, and East Moline.

Youth and Music

Early School Music Festivals: We asked numerous people who grew up in Moline to recall their earliest memory of Wharton Field House. The most common answers related to basketball: regular season Moline High games; high school regional/sectional games, not necessarily involving Moline; Tri-Cities Blackhawks' professional games (1947-51); and the Harlem Globetrotters' performances. Some other events mentioned include professional wrestling, the visit of a particular band, performer, or politician, sports shows, and Easter Sunrise Services. Two people recalled going to the arena to be vaccinated for polio while in elementary school. However, next to basketball, the most common earliest memory was one of the many music festivals in which Moline school students participated.

WHARTON FIELDHOUSE, MOLINE
TIME: 5:45 A.M.

SPEAKER . . . Rev. Dr. Thorwald W. Bender, Professor, Eastern Baptist Theological Seminary, Philadelphia.

TRUMPET TRIO . . . United Township High School, East Moline: Director, Malley Williams

MUSIC . . . A Cappella Choir, Davenport West High School: Director, Robert Stevens.

ORGANIST . . . Robert Stevens, Director of A Capella Choir, Davenport West High School.

SPONSOR . . . Council of Churches, Scott and Rock Island Counties

Argus, April 3, 1969

Advertisement in the Argus for the 1969 Sunrise Service.

Dispatch, July 19, 1943

Youthful singers performing in July 1943 on a stage set up on the Browning Field baseball diamond.

During the summers of 1942 and 1943, Youth Music Festivals were held outdoors at Browning Field. Both were sponsored by the Associated Dad's Clubs of Moline. The 2,000 who attended the 1942 event were entertained by the Moline Youth Chorus and the East Moline High School band. In 1943, more than 300 youth, from grade school to high school ages, performed in bands and choruses in front of 1,500 spectators. Earl Youngdahl directed the bands and Frederick Swanson the choruses. (*Dispatch*, July 27, 1942, and July 17, 1943)

Indoor music festivals were more common. In May 1942, the first Moline Public Schools spring concert was held at the Field House, attracting 3,200. The May 12, 1944, edition featured 1,500 students on the floor and 3,500 people watching in the stands. Then in July 22, 1945, the fourth annual Moline Youth Music Festival involved 140 instruments and 200 singers.

In 1948 and 1949 the "Orchestra-Chorus Festival" brought to the Field House hundreds of children to show their musical talents. The 1949 version, on Saturday evening, February 26th, involved 190 orchestra members and 200 choir members who started rehearsing at 2 p.m. "Before Saturday they had never rehearsed together and by evening the long grind had made them very weary. The audience asked for

Dispatch, July 23, 1945

Some of the 140 instrumentalists and 200 singers at the 1945 Youth Music Festival in Wharton Field House.

encores, but the young musicians only bowed. They were too tired" (*Dispatch*, February 28). Frederick Swanson, director of music for the Moline schools who organized the festival, directed the Quad City Boys Choir in its first and only year of existence. The following fall it would be reorganized by Swanson as the Moline Boys Choir.

Music festivals at Wharton continued through the 1950s. One of them, held on July 23, 1954, was of special significance for some of the participants. About 1,500 spectators viewed performances of 500 youths in bands, string ensembles, and choruses. Proceeds from the event supported two trips to out-of-town events. The senior band went to South Milwaukee the following week to participate in the Wisconsin Spectacle of Music, and the senior chorus participated in the Chicagoland Music Festival at Soldier Field on August 21st.

On May 3, 1964, a special band concert was held at Wharton in honor of Earl Youngdahl, band director for the Moline schools for over thirty years who had passed away in February. Three junior high bands plus the high school concert band performed. Proceeds from ticket sales and donations were used to establish an Earl Youngdahl Memorial Scholarship fund.

Second Annual Mississippi Valley District
ORCHESTRA - CHORUS FESTIVAL
CHILDREN'S ORCHESTRA OF 300   BOYS' CHOIR OF 300
FREDRICK SWANSON   KARL AHRENDT
Directors
Wharton Field House
Saturday, February 26—7:00 P. M.
Adults, 50c Incl. Tax—Children, 14c

Dispatch, February 25, 1949
About 1,200 people attended this 1949 event, which included orchestras from Freeport, Galesburg, Geneseo, Kewanee, Monmouth, Davenport and Moline.

Young People's Symphony Concerts: During the 1940s and 1950s, the Tri-City Symphony Orchestra (since 1985 known as the Quad City Symphony) presented annual spring youth concerts at the Field House and at venues in Rock Island and Davenport. Beginning in 1944, about 2,500 Moline school children would be dismissed from school on a Monday morning each year to listen to the orchestra, which would give the performance on the same day in Rock Island and Davenport.

The April 12, 1953, symphony concert held two sessions, for junior high students at 8:30 a.m. and elementary students at 10. In the earlier session, Symphony Conductor Harry John Brown selected two John Deere Junior High

School students, Scott Wood and Marilyn Strosahl, to conduct "The Bartered Bride" by Tchaikovsky.

The Moline performances of Tri-City Symphony young people's concerts continued at the Field House through 1958. Then the concerts were moved to the auditorium at the new Moline High School, which had opened in the fall of 1958. The 1959 Moline performance was on Monday morning, October 19th, followed by an afternoon performance in Bettendorf, and then performances in Rock Island and Davenport the next day.

Sixth Grade Music Festivals: For over thirty years beginning in 1970, sixth graders from all Moline elementary schools gathered at the Field House to participate in a songfest coordinated by high school music teachers, first Frederick Swanson, then Kermit Wells. A theme and related songs were distributed to sixth grade teachers, who rehearsed with their students for several weeks. Then on the day before the public festival, all the six-graders came together to rehearse in the big arena. The festivals, held in the evening, attracted large numbers of parents and others. Originally they included some art displays and physical education activities, but later they focused exclusively on music.

More Bands: At least two school band concerts were held at Wharton during the 1990s. On October 5, 1992, a "Band-A-Rama" featured three Moline High School ensembles: the "Marching Maroons," the Concert Band, and the Flag Corps and Twirlers. The printed program

177

for the event indicates that the evening started with the National Anthem, followed by "Moliners" (the high school fight song). Then came a variety of band arrangements sandwiched around a "standing commands demonstration." Playing to school loyalty, the program ended with another rendition of "Moliners."

On the evening of April 19, 1994, about 560 Moline school students from fifth through twelfth grades participated in the biannual All-City Band Festival held at the Field House. The combined fifth grade band led off the festival. They were followed by performances by the sixth, seventh, and eighth grade all-city bands, then the high school concert and symphonic bands. The evening was culminated in a combined performance of John Phillip Sousa's "Stars and Stripes Forever."

Dispatch, April 20, 1994

Here Wilson Middle School band director, James Kelly, directs the combined fifth grade band at the 1994 All-City Band Festival. At the close of the evening, all the assembled bands played together a rousing rendition of "Stars and Stripes Forever." Barbara Roseman described the scene as "spectacular," with 560 instruments wielded by 560 young people filling every corner of the arena with music.

High School Activities

Over the years, Moline High School has utilized Wharton Field House for a great variety of non-sports activities. They include dances, festivals, and other gatherings.

M, 1926

A scene from a dance held at the high school gym in 1926. Since the Field House opened in 1928, dances have been held at there off-and-on until the present.

M, 1963

The Polio scare prompted schools to vaccinate students on a regular basis in the 1950s and 1960s. Here high school students are receiving the Sabin oral vaccine at Wharton from Moline High nurse Mrs. Geneva Henss in 1963. The students are Karen Corder, Bill Rives, and John Boyer.

M, 1971   M, 1972

For several years Moline High School students organized large festivals at Wharton where they would sign up for organizations and activities. On the left is a photograph from the 1971 version. On the right is a scene from the 1972 festival, which was dubbed "Whartonstock," a not-so-subtle reference to a rather infamous concert held three years earlier. In other years the event was a "hoedown," at which students in western dress danced among bales of hay.

M, 1971

Courtesy of Allison Condit

Anyone who harbors doubts about Wharton Field House being an "all-purpose" arena should ponder this photograph of a "donkey basketball game" held there in 1971. Sponsored by the high school student council, it was a real basketball game between faculty and students. Special shoes on the donkeys protected the uncovered basketball floor.

Field House all decked-out for the 2013 Moline High School Sadie Hawkins Dance on Saturday, February 28th. The theme for the evening was "Sadie's for the 80s."

Political Events

Willkie Rally: Just three days before being defeated by Franklin D. Roosevelt in the 1940 presidential election, Wendell Willkie appeared at the Field House on the evening of November 2nd. The rally started at 6:30 with a "torchlight" parade through downtown Rock Island, Moline, East Moline, and Silvis, in which "Passengers in the automobiles will hold lighted flares out the windows as the procession moves through the four cities" (*Dispatch*, November 2).

The Field House doors opened at 7:30. Entertainment was provided there for those who arrived before the parade. Included were an orchestra, the Moline Turner's Glee Club, the Moline Moose Lodge drill team, and recordings of speeches by Senator Robert A. Taft. Wilkie and other politicians appeared on the stage beginning at 9:00, after which dancing and refreshments were offered.

Dispatch, April 26, 1948
Presidential candidate Henry Wallace walks toward the stage in Wharton Field House in April 1948.

Henry Wallace Rally: The former vice president and third-party candidate for president spoke at the Field House on April 25, 1948. It was the first stop in the Quad Cities by a presidential candidate since Wendell Willkie appeared eight years earlier. Wallace's address followed an hour-and-a-half of preliminary speeches. The Wallace committee had predicted

that 6,000 people would attend the rally; however reports of the crowd size that evening were much lower, ranging from 2,800 to 3,650. The former number was an estimate "by a Moline man experienced in estimating field house crowds." The latter was determined by a local Wallace supporter who counted ticket stubs collected at the door. (*Dispatch*, April 26)

Wallace's "Americanism is Questionable"? Apparently some people in Moline felt that Wallace's Progressive Party was too left-wing and wanted to do something about it. The day before the Wallace rally, the *Dispatch* reported that postcards protesting his visit were being distributed in Moline. Written on the cards:

> As a citizen of the city of Moline, I want to protest the action of the Moline school board in permitting use of Wharton field house by Henry Wallace or any other group whose Americanism is questionable.

Although the postcards were made available at both the American Legion and Veterans of Foreign Wars posts, the leaders of both organizations claimed they "had no part in it." However, an unidentified witness said the idea originated at a meeting of veterans groups. He went on to say that their opposition was not as much against Wallace as against "Communist groups" that associated with Wallace's party. The Baltimore *Sun* (April 28) reported that Harley Moorhusen, president of the Board of Education, had received hundreds of these cards. Moorhusen was quoted as saying "The field house is a public building, paid for by the taxpayers, and it would not be right to deny Wallace's backers the use of it. If we discriminate against a political party, we are going to lose our freedom." The show went on as scheduled.

Goldwater, 1964: On Saturday afternoon, October 3, 1964, 7,000 people packed the Field House to hear Senator Barry Goldwater, who was running for president against Lyndon Johnson. Hundreds more stood outside the arena listening to the proceedings over a public address system. Occupying prime seating locations on the main floor of the arena were members of the Moline Boys Choir, about fifty local and state Republican leaders, 100 news reporters and photographers, and 500 Goldwater volunteers.

As many as 1,000 supporters were on hand at a downtown depot to greet Goldwater's train, which had backed-in from Barstow.

Douglas Campaign: On October 28, 1966, 74-year-old Paul Douglas arrived to campaign for his fourth term as United States Senator from Illinois. Ten days later he would lose the election to Charles Percy. Douglas was accompanied by Senator Edward Kennedy, the popular younger brother of President John F. Kennedy who had been assassinated three years earlier. The *Chicago Tribune* (October 29) commented on the crowd that attended the rally at Wharton:

> The Kennedy name and hard grass roots work served up the largest downstate crowd today that Sen. Douglas has seen outside of Cook County. Sen. Edward M. Kennedy stole the show as he drew a total of more than 5,000 persons, including many teen-agers. Hordes of squealing teen-age girls greeted Kennedy and Douglas when they arrived at the Moline airport. They were among a crowd of 500.

Argus, October 3, 1964
Senator Barry Goldwater (arrow) amongst the massive crowd at the Field House in October 1964.

Argus, October 25, 1966
One of several advertisements promoting the 1966 campaign visit of Paul Douglas and Ted Kennedy. The *Chicago Tribune* gave attendance figures for seven Illinois rallies in which Douglas had Kennedy in tow: Moline, 5,000; Ottawa, 4,500; East St. Louis, 3,000; Joliet, 3,000; Peoria, 2,000; Elmhurst, 1,400; Aurora, 1,200.

Gold Water? At the 1964 Goldwater rally, Rock Islanders Margaret and Roald Tweet purchased a six-pack of "Gold Water" and gave it to Margaret's dad, who apparently was a Barry Goldwater fan. The orange-flavored drink was promoted as "the right drink for the conservative taste." When Goldwater was offered a taste he took a sip, spit it out, and declared: "This tastes like piss! I wouldn't drink it with gin!"

According to the Davenport *Times-Democrat* (October 29), Democratic Party officials estimated the crowd to total 8,000, which probably was a bit high unless it included people who were not able to gain entrance to the Field House. The 34-year-old Kennedy was visiting six years to the day after his brother, John F. Kennedy, campaigned in the Quad Cities on his successful bid to become president.

1968 Nixon Visit: Not to be outdone by his Republican colleague, Barry Goldwater, who four years earlier packed the Field House, Richard Nixon did the same in his 1968 presidential campaign. On the chilly evening of October 9th the former vice president was greeted at the Quad City Airport by 4,500 cheering fans. Then the next afternoon 6,500 packed the Field House to hear and see the future president. Some 4,000 others were turned away.

The Illinois 19th Congressional District Nixon for President Committee
cordially invites
you, your family and your friends
to hear an address
by the
HONORABLE RICHARD M. NIXON
at the
Wharton Field House
Moline, Illinois
Thursday, October tenth
program begins at twelve noon

Free Admission

Courtesy of Barbara Sandberg

Dispatch files

George Wallace and Protesters: The 1968 visit of Alabama Governor George Wallace, who was running for president with the American Independent Party, created considerable controversy at Wharton. A staunch segregationist, Wallace attracted some 6,500 people to Wharton on October 21st. Among them were some 200 vocal protesters, mostly students from Augustana and Black Hawk Colleges, who opposed Wallace's racist views. Wallace could not complete his prepared speech on farm policy because of the frequent interruptions. Scuffles between some of the protesters and Wallace supporters started inside the building and continued on the outside. Some fifteen people were hospitalized, mostly for minor injuries inflicted by flying objects, and the building incurred about $1,600 in damages.

Sauk, 1969

Protesters inside the Field House at the 1968 George Wallace rally.

Robert P. Hey, a Christian Science Monitor reporter was on the scene (October 30, 1968). Hey confirmed the protests inside the Field House and elaborated on the protests outside: "But the hottest action was outside. Five hundred to a thousand Wallace opponents were locked outside the building, whose 6,500 seating capacity was virtually reached. Almost all were youthful." Hey went on to describe the scuffles outside, which resulted in some minor injuries and a few broken windows. He also praised the police for displaying restraint in handling the protest.

Midwest Sports Show

From 1957 onward, the Moline Conservation Club annual sports shows at the Field House attracted large crowds. Their first was called the "Moline Sports Show." In subsequent years "Midwest" was substituted for "Moline." The 1957 show, a Friday through Sunday affair, displayed about a dozen boats on the Field House floor and another, too big to fit through the eight-foot door, in the east parking lot.

Dick Karstens, president of the Conservation Club, was angling for paid admissions totaling 15,000 people. His hope was buoyed by the fact that a two-day show in Dubuque attracted 27,000 and a ten-day Kansas City show nearly 300,000. However, the Moline show attracted fewer than 11,000.

The night before the 1958 sports show opened, Dick Impens of Moline demonstrated an escape act for press, radio, and television media representatives. Outfitted with a straightjacket and hung by his ankles from the Field House rafters, Impens managed to escape in about sixty seconds, and repeated this and other acts during the three days of the show.

Courtesy of Michele Stoneking

A popular attraction at the sports shows were demonstrations by Porky and Ponce, two men who produced a popular local television show "Along the Outdoor Trails," which focused on fishing, hunting, and other outdoor activities. In this scene at Wharton, Orville "Porky" Meyers is holding the microphone and behind him wearing a hat is Harry "Ponce" DeLeon.

Dispatch, April 2, 1959

The third annual Wharton sports show drew a record crowd of over 11,000 in 1959. A variety of attractions complemented the forty-plus exhibits.

The show grew steadily in the early 1960s. The 1962 event included fifty exhibits – the most ever – displaying hundreds of items of sports equipment. Although each year sports displays and activities dominated the proceedings, a stage show would typically be included. In 1962, a balancing act complete with dogs and monkeys, was put on by a mother, father, and three children

comprising the Johnny Laddie Act (*Dispatch*, March 30). The 1963 show featured Countess Maritella, performing a "sensational aerial trapeze act" with a "blood-chilling 'roly-poly' climax." Joining her at Wharton was banjo artist Larry Tobler presenting a "humorous and novel treatment of music, highlighted by a unique imitation of two banjos playing at the same time and a realistic portrayal in sound of the modern streamliner." (*Dispatch*, March 25) Local country music artist and disc jockey Jack Barlow was a featured entertainer at several of the annual shows. For a number of years the three-day show continued to attract 10,000 to 12,000 people.

Dispatch, March 21, 1966

By the time of this 1966 photograph, Jack Barlow was travelling widely presenting country music shows and recording in Nashville. Previously he worked as a disc jockey, first in his home town of Muscatine, Iowa, then at Moline radio station WQUA. For years he performed regularly at local night clubs in addition to the annual sports show at Wharton Field House.

Dispatch, April 3, 1970
Advertisement for the 1970 sports show.

Athletic Prowess on Display

Over the years, a substantial number of events at the Field House have involved team athletic competition, most especially basketball. In addition, a variety of athletic exhibitions appeared, including gymnastics, basketball, and tennis. Some of them were local in origin, whereas others featured major sports stars. Here are some examples.

"Babe" Visits Wharton: The first non-boxing professional sporting event held at the Field House was on December 1, 1933. Appropriately it was basketball, but with an interesting twist. Mildred "Babe" Didrikson, one of the greatest female athletes of all-time, played with the All-Americans, a men's team that was touring the Midwest. The *Dispatch* (December 1) promised:

[she] will perform tricks with the leather-covered sphere [and] expects to demonstrate her wizardry and stamina in a man's game on the spacious Moline floor…she may be expected to bring out a large crowd of fans. Various estimates place the probable turnout at well over 2,000.

Alas, only 500 turned out to see Babe's team lose to the local all-stars, 36-30. The locals were led by a former University of Iowa player Gueldner Krumbholz of Davenport who scored eleven points. Didrikson played only parts of the first and third quarters, and made two of three free throws, but failed to make a field goal. Nonetheless: "Once she cut loose with an amazing display of speed and ball handling which indicated that she was not a stranger on the hardwoods" (*Dispatch*, December 2).

Nashville versus Davenport: Meant to educate locals on the value and rules of "girls' basketball," two women's teams played an exhibition game at the Field House on February 24, 1942. The American Institute of Commerce (AIC) Stenos of Davenport faced the Nashville Business School team of Tennessee in what the *Dispatch* (February 25) called the "first big-time girls' game to be played in Moline." In addition to a few minor rules differences from the boy's game, the girls played six on a side. To enhance the educational experience, "fans are assured that [the rules] will be fully explained before and during the game by competent experts on girls' rules." (*Dispatch*, February 21) The Stenos beat the Tennessee sextet, 28-25 in front of a "small

The Champion Stenos. AIC sponsored the Stenos from the late 1930s until the 1950s. The height of their success came just after appearing at Wharton, as reported at Hoopedia, online: "The Stenos reached the apex of its success in 1942 and 1943 when it won consecutive national AAU titles. In 1942, AIC smashed the Hazel Walker-led Little Rock Motor Coaches in the title game, 42-25, with long-range shooting by Ruth Campbell and Margaret Macomber. This was the youngest AAU women's team to ever win a championship. Most of the team was still in high school or just out of high school, and averaged 17½ years of age. Three AIC players made the All-American team – Campbell, Macomber, and Viola Meyer. The 1943 tournament final was an all-Iowa affair, with AIC beating AIB, 41-31. [The AIB team, called the "Secretaries," was sponsored by the American Institute of Business, a sister institution to AIC located in Des Moines.] AIC garnered two All-Americans that year—Helen Joura, who was also chosen as the Most Valuable Player, and Francis Stansberry."

but enthusiastic crowd of about 750." Free throws may have been the deciding factor; the Stenos made thirteen of seventeen, whereas their opponents made only five of eighteen.

"Miss Basketball:" The all-female All-American Redheads appeared at Wharton to deliver some basketball comedy antics and play men's rules against a local team on December 5, 1947. The Redheads were led by Hazel Walker, who at the time was considered "Miss Basketball" on a parallel with Bobby McDermott who was often referred to as "Mr. Basketball." At the time McDermott was playing for Sheboygan; then just a few weeks later he joined the Tri-Cities Blackhawks as player/coach. Walker was famous for challenging any male in the house to a free-throw contest at halftime, frequently making 49 out of fifty shots.

The local opponent at the Field House was the McKay Plumbers team. The *Dispatch* (December 5) prognosticated: "In addition to providing some hot cage competition, the Redheads will toss in plenty of comedy tricks and devilment to confuse the Plumbers' array of talent." The Redheads lost the game 39-31 in front of 2,000 fans. However, they came out winners in the comedy department and Walker defeated plumber Mel Montz at the freethrow line. She sank fifteen consecutive shots and added five more in a row on her knees. Montz hit only 13 of 15. The event was sponsored by the Moline American Legion Drum and Bugle Corps.

Tennis Anyone? Probably the first tennis event at the Field House was on May 1, 1934, when touring players put on an exhibition that featured a singles match between Bill Tilden and Elsworth Vines. Tilden had been a star player for two decades and, according to the May 1st *Dispatch*, "He occupies a place in the net sport similar to that of Bobby Jones in golf." The basketball court was increased in size to create a tennis court of 70 by 120 feet and a big crowd was hoped for. "There will be 4,000 seats available and because there are no pillars or posts in the field house every seat will be a good one." Previous stops on the tour had drawn between 2,000 and 28,000 spectators. In Moline both Tilden and the Field House lost: he was beaten by Vines in front of fewer than 1,000 spectators.

In spite of bad weather, considerably more fans showed up in 1941 – about 2,600 – when Tilden appeared for another exhibition, accompanied by tennis stars Don Budge, Alice Marble, and Mary Hardwick. Sponsors of the event, the Moline City Tennis Committee and the Moline High School Athletic Association, decorated the arena with flags along the balcony railings and decked out the ushers and ball boys in maroon and white outfits. The night before the April 3rd exhibition, Tilden conducted a tennis clinic sponsored by the Junior Chamber of Commerce. It was held in the ballroom on the top floor of the LeClaire Hotel, which could accommodate up to 500 persons.

> **Tilden Flies In.** "The famous tennis troupe is arriving in Moline in three automobiles and a truck, and therein reposes a tale in itself. First to arrive is always Bill Tilden. He'll be alone, not because he dislikes to have company on his travels, but simply because he has yet to find a colleague interested in 'flying' with him in his high-powered automobile. Big Bill had a crackup going to St. Louis this winter, but long before that the other members of the quartet had decided that it wasn't safe to ride with him" (*Dispatch*, April 2).

> **Barnstorming.** Before appearing at the Field House the Redheads had barnstormed around the country for eight years, taking on men's teams and winning a majority of their games. They had played in front of over two million fans, including service personnel on a USO tour of the Philippines. The Redheads played at arenas and towns large and small, on this trip arriving in Moline after one-night appearances in Fort Wayne, Indiana, and Streator and Belvidere, Illinois.

At the Field House, Marble beat Hardwick and Budge had no problem handling the 48-year-old Tilden, 6-1, 6-1, while Tilden paired with Marble to win the mixed-doubles match. The crowd was entertained not only by the tennis but also by the attitudes displayed by two of the visitors. The *Dispatch* (April 4) commented:

> Mr. Tilden, and Miss Marble to a lesser degree, furnished the expected temperament by indicating dissatisfaction with the ball boys and the linemen, who after all were doing the best they could, and for nothing too. If the 48-year-old Tilden played a match any time anywhere without being dissatisfied with the officiating and showing it, it would be news.

In 1947, Don Budge again played the Field House. The feature match was between Budge and Fred Perry, who had been playing each other since the mid-1930s when they both were in Davis Cup matches. Sponsors, the Junior Chamber of Commerce, provided 2,500 tickets for Quad City school children. For others reserved tickets were $1.50, and general admission, $1.00. Because a large crowd attended the April 25th exhibition, the troupe agreed to perform again the next evening. Apparently their decision to do so was influenced by the facilities. Tour manager Martin Buxby "stated that Wharton was the finest court and had the best general tennis facilities that had been encountered on the tour to date" (*Dispatch*, April 26).

Clever Stroke. Chuck White of Moline attended the 1947 tennis exposition and was impressed with a trick performed by Don Budge. The tennis pro demonstrated an amazing ability to hit the ball, rather accurately, with the edge of the racket.

In spite of the fine facilities, few tennis programs would again visit Wharton. Perhaps the last two were in 1977. A May 15th exhibition scheduled a women's match between Wendy Overton and Valerie Ziegenfuss and a men's match between Dick Stockton and Wojtek Fibak. Unfortunately Stockton could not appear because he advanced to the final match in the World Championship Tennis tournament against Jimmy Connors to be held on the same day. Also,

Fibak was unexpectedly called home to Poland. So, a substitute men's match was arranged at the last minute with Dennis Ralston and Charles Pasarell, who flew to Moline from Los Angeles on the day of the match. A benefit for the Quint Cities Tennis Foundation and local parks' tennis programs, the event drew a smaller crowd than expected, about 1,700.

Then on October 12, 1977, Arthur Ashe and other tennis champions were featured in a fundraiser sponsored by the Moline Public Hospital Auxiliary. Reserved seats were $10 and patron tickets $25. Patrons were invited to an instructional clinic before the event and a reception at Deere & Company headquarters afterwards. The mixed doubles match that followed was described by Bill Allee in the October 13th *Dispatch*:

> Although Cuypers and Ashe are both good doubles players, they couldn't match the wizardry of Okker and Stove out on the court . . . Okker and Stove volleyed their way to an 8-4 victory as Okker, on a few occasions, blocked back hard returns from Ashe between his legs.

Gymkana: Through the 1940s a variety of gymnastics activities and demonstrations, along with some entertainment, were packaged into annual Gymkana programs. After 2,500 attended the first one at the Field House in 1939, some 3,500 attended in 1940. Both of them featured a visit by the University of Illinois Gymkana troupe, which included both Big Ten and national gymnastics champions. (*Dispatch*, April 17, 1940) Added to the mix in 1940 were dances, singing, drills, and comedy skits. These events were sponsored by various Moline High School clubs and organizations.

Beginning in 1941, the Moline Turner Society, an organization of German-American origin focused on education, music, and gymnastics, was organizing the event and providing many of the performers. By then the Gymkana had become a variety show, with newspaper descriptions occasionally using the term "follies" or "vaudeville" to describe the offerings. The diversity of activities at the 1942 event was detailed in the *Dispatch* on May 6th:

Overture, Follies of 1942	Hal Sears and his orchestra
U.S.A. America the Beautiful	Kindergarten
Draftees, Remember Pearl Harbor	Boys I
Captivating Capers, South of North Carolina	Girls I
Tumbling Tramps, Popular	Boys II
Rhythmics, Valse [waltz] Blue	Actives
Whirlwind Taps, He's in the Army	Girls II
Melodies, Anniversary Waltz, My Little Banjo	Women's chorus
Doin' the Derby, You and I	Women's class
Side Horse Vaulting, Popular	Junior boys
Bell Hops, Dark Town Strutter's Ball	Women's class
Harmonies, Something About a Soldier, Riff Song	Glee club
Horizontal Bar, Popular	Actives
Evolution of the Dance, Medley	Junior Girls
Rythmettes, Valse Bluette	Women's class
Daddy and Daughter, Popular	Herbert and Sharon Ellstrom
Valse Brilliante, Valse Brilliante	Women's class
Quartet, Skinny Gal, You're a Grand Old Flag	Carl Anderson, Les Benck
	Thor Anderson, Glen Moore
Side Horse and Parallels, Popular	Actives and women
Remember When, The Old Mill Stream	Seniors
Rhumba, Yours	Actives and women
Finale, national anthem	Ensemble

The 1947 Gymkana at Wharton was organized jointly by Turner Societies from Moline and Clinton (Iowa) along with three from Davenport. About 1000 performers from the five clubs participated and 2500 others attended the event on May 23, the second of a two-evening show. The performers then took their show to Washington Junior High gym in Clinton for two more evenings of Gymkana. Funds raised by the performances were to be used to send representatives of the societies to St. Louis in June 1948 for a celebration of the 100th anniversary of the Turners' organization. For several additional years, beginning in 1949, a more modest version of Gymkana was held at the John Deere Junior High School auditorium.

German Gymnasts: On January 30, 1958, the Moline Turners sponsored a visit by West German gymnastics teams, which featured eight men and six women. Included were several gymnasts who participated in the 1956 Olympics in Melbourne. The group had been in the United States for three weeks and appeared at a number of Midwest locations including the Universities of Illinois and Iowa. About 1,600 attended the two-hour show at Wharton.

Not-So-Cold War: In 1961, the *Dispatch* (January 18) called the visit of the USSR gymnastics troupe: "One of the most outstanding sports events ever staged in Moline's Wharton Field House." The group of six men and six women, which included several Olympic champions, was on a two-week tour of the United States. Capacity crowds showed up to see them in such places as West Point, Pennsylvania State University, Coe College, and the Universities of Iowa and Illinois. After performing in Moline, they stayed overnight at the LeClaire Hotel and then flew to New York to conclude their tour three days later with a performance at Madison Square Garden, where they would appear before a capacity crowd of 20,000.

The day after the Moline performance, Dispatch writer Jim Llewellyn praised both visitors and hosts:

A champion Russian Olympic gymnastics team and a crowd of some 2,500 in

Wharton Field House did their own parts last night toward breaking down cultural and communication barriers that exist between the two countries. One spoke through the grace, strength and continuity of motion of a fine performance, and the other responded with good will and applause. After the exhibition, the Soviet gymnasts proved capable on the dance floor at a party for them at Marando's Nightclub. The gymnasts and other members of the delegation drank, ate and danced with enthusiasm despite their weariness from their heavy schedule of exhibitions.

Argus, January 18, 1961

The Russian Olympic champion women's gymnastics team appeared with their male counterparts at Wharton Field House in 1961.

Girls Gymnastics: Whereas gymnastics meets have been rare at Wharton over the last few decades, two were held in 2008. In the first, over 600 girls, age six through twelve, participated in a three-day Illinois Junior Olympics Girls Level 5 State Championship meet on April 11th - 13th. Sanctioned by USA Gymnastics, it was sponsored by the Quad City Gymnastics Academy and organized by its coach David Van Acker. The only state champion among the fourteen girls from the local club was Ellie Cheline, who won the vault competition in the children's age group. Then on December 13th and 14th, the Academy organized "Rollin on the River" an

invitational drawing eleven teams from across Illinois. Twenty-seven girls from the Quad City Academy participated.

Everything, Including the Kitchen Sink

A substantial number and variety of Field House events have been described in this and other chapters of the book. The variety is further illustrated by the sampling of events described below.

Merchants, Manufacturers, Automobile, and Better Homes Show: The Moline Moose Lodge gets the prize for the longest title of any event ever held at the Field House. They sponsored the first version of this ambitious offering in 1948 and held them annually for at least three more years.

The 1949 show, which ran Tuesday through Saturday evenings, April 19-23, was free to the public and sported "Exhibits of everything from automobiles and home appliances to soda pop and scout handicraft" (*Dispatch*, April 20). Scouts, 4-H clubs, the Red Cross, and other nonprofit organizations set up displays, as did numerous businesses attempting to promote their products. A scale model home was on display, as were a full-sized kitchen and full-sized living room, each containing various interior home products. A focal point of the show was a ten-foot square scale model of Mooseheart, a "city" north of Aurora, Illinois, operated by the Moose for orphaned children. The model was designed and built by Hector Noel Polyer, a former Mooseheart student, and had already been exhibited in seventeen states. President Harry Truman and Vice President Alben Barkley, both members of the Moose organization, had also viewed it. Like most of the major shows at Wharton, entertainment was not ignored. Singer Lois Ann Stillian and organist Dale R. Madden, who brought along his $4,000 Hammond organ, performed hourly. The Moose band, winners of national competitions in 1947 and 1948, also played periodically. The first night attendance was 500.

Argus, May 1, 1951

By 1951, the name of the Moose event had been shortened to Better Homes Exhibit and admission was no longer free.

More Dancing: Dances and other activities were often held in support of various causes. One polio benefit dance and show in support of the Rock Island County March of Dimes was held on March 4, 1950. All facilities and talent were donated for the event. A variety show included several acts, one of which was the appearance of the "green Swede from Minnesota," played by humorist J. Edward Ekstadt of Moline. The Buddies of the Airlanes, a musical combo who had regular radio and television shows on WHBF in Rock Island, appeared at 8:30 p.m. Their performance was broadcast live on the radio. Following the acts, the Jack Manthey orchestra provided music for dancing.

Deere Films: On four days in December 1956, Deere & Company employees and their families were invited to attend two-hour sessions to preview new company films. Six films had been produced to show John Deere products in action on farms, including products having been

Courtesy of Jerry Wallaert

A dance held in 1956 by the Youth Guidance Committee of the Order of the Eastern Star.

Courtesy of Karen Davis

Over the years numerous gatherings at the Field House involved Boy Scouts and Girl Scouts. Pictured here are Hazel Weber (rear center) and her Troup 12 from Willard School in Moline participating in a Girl Scout activity in 1948.

produced in the Quad Cities. The films would subsequently be shown by dealers, clubs, and civic organizations in farm communities throughout the United States and Canada, to a total audience estimated to be over a million people. (*Dispatch*, November 23)

Science Fair: In 1959, 328 entrants from 26 area high schools and junior highs entered the third annual Quint City Science Fair. Free admission was offered the public to view the exhibits on Friday evening and all day Saturday, April 10 and 11. About 1,200 people were in attendance for the awards ceremony. In the high school division, two grand winners took their exhibits in May to the National Science Fair in

Hartford, Connecticut, and the grand junior high winner received a set of science books. Other science fairs held at Wharton included the ninth annual, on April 9 and 10, 1965, which featured 243 exhibits and attracted 6,500 visitors.

Argus, April 11, 1959

Winners at the 1959 Quint City Science Fair. In the foreground is Joseph Roos of Bettendorf High School demonstrating his exhibit, "A New System of Stereo Transmission." Standing behind him are Walter Wise of Edison Junior High School in Rock Island, Darrell Goar, physics teacher at Moline High, and Stewart Pack of Davenport High. For winning the junior high competition Wise received a ten-volume set of the Book of Popular Science. Grand prize winners, Roos and Pack, went on to the national competition in Hartford, Connecticut, accompanied by Goar.

Musicians and Mule Skinners: On May 2, 1964, the Montana Centennial Train stopped in Moline as part of its tour from Montana to New York and back. Inside some of the cars were displays celebrating Montana history including western art, big game trophies, and a million dollars' worth of gold nuggets and dust. Riding on the train were over 300 Montana residents, "including cowboys, cowgirls, Indians, musicians, mule skinners, and state officials." To accompany them the train carried "75 horses, a chuck wagon, a Conestoga wagon, and other vehicles of ancient vintage." (Muscatine *Journal*, April 29) After the tour, seven of the cars were returned to New York to become permanent displays at the World's Fair held in 1964 and 1965.

With the train parked in downtown Moline, the entourage paraded around the Tri-Cities, performed a street dance near the train, and showed movies at the LeClaire Hotel. The

192

capstone event of the day was an evening gathering at the Field House where Montanans entertained the assembled Midwesterners.

Argus, May 1, 1964

A Colorful Sight was described by the *Dispatch* on May 2nd. "The train pulled into the Moline station carrying 300 enthusiastic boosters from the state of Montana, a colorful sight to behold it was. There were 75 finely-conditioned parade horses in part of the 25-car train . . . The station platform was a fascinating place this morning with western ranchers in 10-gallon hats, high-heeled boots and string ties mixing with rodeo queens in fringed jackets and Indian dancers togged out in brightly-hued, feathered regalia."

Antiques: Several antique shows, which included sales, were held in the 1970s and early 1980s at Wharton. Typically they were three-day affairs, open from noon to 10 p.m. on Friday and Saturday and from noon to 5 p.m. on Sunday. Admission fees were nominal but had risen to $1.50 in 1979 (May 11-13) and $2.00 in 1980 (October 17-19). The 1974 show (October 1-6) included an antique car display.

Home Show: On Saturday and Sunday, May 14 and 15, 1988, the Great American Home Fling was held at the Field House, under the sponsorship of the Rock Island County Board of Realtors and the *Dispatch* and *Argus* newspapers. Sixteen realtors promoted the sale of 265 homes, and local financial companies conducted seminars on home financing.

Literature: Since 1978 the Children's Literature Festival has been held annually in the Quad Cities. From 1980 through 2002 it was held at Wharton Field House, attracting hundreds of participants. Elementary students, teachers, authors, and illustrators gathered to engage in discussions and other activities related to writing and books. Among the largest crowds of students and teachers at the Field House were 440 in 1987 (April 20) and 800 in 1996 (April 26). None was held in 1997; then the nineteenth Festival, held on April 29, 1998, attracted 500 to Wharton. That year the event was named after David R. Collins, a Moline teacher and author of children's books, who co-founded the festival with Rochelle Murray.

Chili Challenge: For several years in the 21st century, the Moline Public Schools Foundation sponsored fundraisers at the Field House focusing on food. The Foundation used proceeds from these events to support school district projects, such as a professional development center at the high school, as well as teachers' instructional needs. At first the annual event was a "Chili Challenge," then later the "Taste of the Quad Cities." Anthony Watt (2006) described the 2006 chili affair:

> Hundreds of people, from children to adults, milled about, many lining up at one of the 15 booths where Moline School District schools or teams of schools were offering up their particular version of the spicy concoction. The sign for John Deere Middle School read: 'Wild Bill's Not For The Faint of Heart, Eat at Your Own Risk, You're a Daisy if You Don't, Amazingly Smokin' Hot Chili All Others R.I.P.'

Courtesy of Children's Literature Festival

Dispatch, April 26, 1996

At the eighteenth annual Children's Literature Festival in 1996, students were seated on a Wharton Field House stairway to listen to Virginia VanHook, an author from Virginia. Each year, in addition to stairway locations, discussion groups would be scattered throughout the arena, some seated in various balcony locations and some on the arena-floor.

Courtesy of Children's Literature Festival

A discussion group in the southeast corner of the Field House at one of the Children's Literature Festivals.

Chapter 8

Browning Field
High School Sports and More

"Unbridle your fancy a moment. Picture, if you can, a beautiful green field,
around which there is a splendid quarter mile oval track." –Rock Island Magazine

As a community partner to Wharton Field House, Browning Field has been the scene of many – some quite memorable – sporting and other events since it opened in 1912. In this chapter we begin by interweaving the stories of the origins and development of the facility with the evolution of Moline High School football through its one hundred-plus year history. We then review other high school sports played there, and cover a variety of non-sports events that have been sprinkled throughout Browning's history. Professional baseball and football, which were major draws to Browning Field during the first half of the twentieth century, are covered in Chapter 9.

Browning's Bequest

John T. Browning was born in New York on June 11, 1828, attended law school in Rochester, New York, and came to Moline in 1858 to set up his law practice. He served as the first city attorney under Mayor Daniel Wheelock, was elected as Moline's first Library Board president, and served two terms in the Illinois legislature beginning in 1874. Through his bountiful career, Browning managed to acquire quite a bit of land in Moline.

About two months before his death in 1910, Browning gave some of that land for today's Browning Field to the City of Moline. The gift was specified in a codicil to his will written by Doctor A. M. Beal. The *Dispatch* of August 23 describes the occasion:

Dr. Beal, who looked on Mr. Browning almost as a father, and who administered his business affairs during Mr. Browning's long illness [about two years], suggested the bequest during a business talk in early June. 'What do you think of it?' was Dr. Beal's question, after he had outlined the plan. 'I hadn't thought of it,' was the characteristically frank reply. There was a moment of silence, then Mr. Browning said: 'I'd like to do it. Take care of the matter for me.'

The article goes on to describe the Browning Field bequest:

Eight-acre tract one-half block east of Fifteenth street [today's 16th Street], and extending between Twentieth and Twenty-third avenues, to be forever held in trust by the city of Moline for a public playground and an athletic field,

Browning's will provided cash and land for various causes and for his family. He made public bequests of $1,000 each to the YMCA, Moline City Hospital, and the Moline Salvation Army. He gave his law library to the Moline Public Library and a large tract of land just west of Prospect Park to the Tri-City Sanitarium. To his surviving relatives he gave numerous additional tracts of land throughout Moline, including his 240-acre farm south of town in the Rock River Valley, where he was at the time of his death.

and to be known as the John T. Browning Memorial Playground and Athletic Field.

Through this bequest, the City of Moline became the owner of Browning Field in 1910. In 1928 the City purchased land for a playground between Browning Field and 16th Street, popularly known as Browning Park. Then in 1947, the school district and the City entered an agreement that transferred ownership the athletic field to the schools for the price of one dollar. The agreement specified that land must continue to be used as originally intended by Browning in his will. (Browning Agreement, 1947) Since that time the school district has conformed to that agreement.

The Browning Field site had been used for sports well before it was officially deeded to the City in 1910. Beginning in the 1890s, the Stewartville Tigers (later the Thornbloom Tigers) played semi-professional baseball where the football field is located today – in what was essentially a pasture. The Tigers played several local teams as well as teams from Davenport, Muscatine, and Peoria, and maintained their headquarters at the Crippen pool room two blocks away.

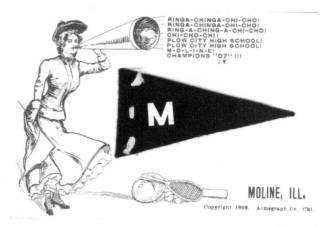

1907 Postcard

Moline High School athletic endeavors got a boost from this 1907 postcard.

High School Football before Browning

Before 1910, Moline High School football teams played their games at a field on 4th Avenue in what is now the northwest corner of Riverside Park, just west of the lagoon. It was conveniently located near the streetcar line that served Riverside Cemetery, allowing easy access for fans coming from all over the city. After a fire station was built there in 1910, the team played two seasons at a nearby park before moving to Browning Field in 1912.

The pre-Browning high school teams were very successful and the scores they racked up astonishing. Between 1900 and 1911 they were undefeated in three seasons and in four others they lost only one game. In the undefeated season of 1904 they outscored their opponents 304-0 and won the unofficial state championship by defeating Chicago Englewood, 24-0, on Thanksgiving Day before a crowd of 3,000 in Moline. In 1905, the Moliners outscored opponents 135-6, while losing to Rock Island 4-0. In 1907 they lost only to Monmouth College, which scored 14 of the 19 points racked up against Moline during the entire season. Again that year they won the state title by beating Rockford in a post-season game, 23-0. (M-Men's Day program, 1937)

Field of Dreams? "[Before 1910] the field was not as large as now, a slough running across the west end [where Browning Park is now]. There were no bleachers or grandstand, and spectators stood on the sidelines and rooted for the favorites and not infrequently a flying bat or hard-hit ball was stopped unwillingly by some spectator . . . Browning's pasture was by far the best diamond of the four [Moline baseball fields]. It was rough but was covered with sod and was accessible to street cars and more centrally located than any of the others. In addition, the Stewartville team was the strongest in the city and drew larger crowds of rooters, and members finally solicited merchants and others interested and secured enough funds to erect a small section of seats. The need of a public athletic field was greatly felt at that time. Nearly all athletic events were held in Browning's pasture and it came to be the best known athletic field in the city" (Moorhusen, 1931).

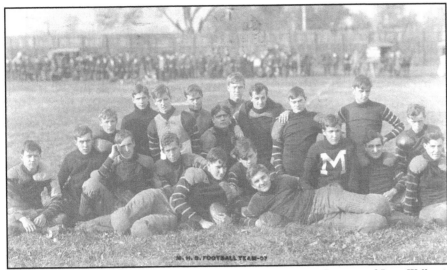

Courtesy of Jerry Wallaert

The 1907 Moline team lounging on the Riverside Park field. An old fire station now stands on the site.

World Record! One early highlight was a high school world record for scoring in 1902, when Moline beat Galva 172-0. Another record in that game was provided by Henry Keiting, who kicked 27 "field goals" (conversions after touchdowns in today's parlance) out of 29 tries, fourteen of them in succession. (*Dispatch*, July 31, 1928)

The 1911 "Riot"

The football rivalry between Moline and Rock Island, dating back to 1899, was interrupted in 1912 and 1913. Up to 1911, the year before Moline started playing at Browning Field, the Maroon and White had five wins to Rock Island's four, and they tied four times. On the afternoon of November 18, 1911, Rock Island won a tight game, 14 to 11 at their home field. After the game, a group of Rock Island lads, including a few dozen fans and some team members, held a mock funeral for the Moline team on the Mississippi River levee in downtown Rock Island. Incorporated into the ceremony was a wooden coffin they had crafted for the occasion. After parading around Rock Island, they boarded a streetcar, coffin and all, for a ride to Moline to conduct a similar ceremony in the Plow City. Dozens of Moliners caught wind of the visit and gathered in wait.

After the Islanders poured out of the streetcar at 5th Avenue and 15th Street in downtown Moline, the Moline lads saw to it that the coffin was smashed to bits. A major scuffle ensued. Weapons included not only fists but also pieces of coffin wood, pieces of coal picked up from a nearby coal yard, and some eggs. The *Argus* (November 20) described one scuffle: "One of the Moline braves attacked an Islander. He had been smoking a cigar, but it, in company with a couple of his molars, journeyed down into his throat as the result of a well directed blow."

Most of the windows of the trolley car were broken, and at some point the arm extending from the roof of the car was disengaged from its overhead power wire. In hopes of escaping the melee, the trolley conductor climbed on top of the car and reengaged the arm allowing the car to move again. In the process he managed to avoid multiple missiles aimed at him. Soon the Rock Island boys were back on the streetcar headed west.

On Monday, November 20th, newspapers from opposing towns both called it a "riot." But, as we might expect, they put differing spins on the event. According to the Rock Island *Argus* the Rock Island boys "intended to have only a peaceable little chat with the defeated neighbors.

They had intended to refrain from talking of the game, but of course their faces showed too much of the spirit of happiness for the self control of the Plow City mob. Had the easterners won, they would have done the same thing for they had a nice little box all fitted for such a trip." The Moline *Dispatch* concluded: "The visitors came, they saw, but they failed to conquer."

Following this incident, the games were cancelled for the 1912 and 1913 seasons. Had the games not been cancelled, Rock Island would have played at Browning during its first season of high school football. Instead, the Rocks did not play at Browning until two years after it was opened.

High School Football at Browning

In 1912, Moline football teams, both high school and professional, began play at Browning Field. In preparation, an area large enough for the new football and baseball fields was leveled. This entailed cutting the land down on the south side, which created an embankment that is still there. The dirt removed was used to fill ravines on the west and east sides of the field, and the first bleachers were constructed.

The Maroon and White began practicing on the new field on September 18, 1912, and played their first game there on Saturday afternoon, September 28th. They defeated the Moline Alumni 6-0. A week later they played their first game against another school, beating Maquoketa, 34-0. In reporting on both games, the Dispatch commented that the Moliners won despite being "greatly outweighed." Moline players ranged in weight from 120 to 165 pounds and averaged 145!

> **First-Class Facility.** Just before the Maquoketa game the *Dispatch* (October 4, 1912) assessed the situation at the new facility: "Browning park is the best football field Moline ever had. The grounds have been put in first-class condition, the new feature being the wire fence to keep people off the gridiron. The grandstand is near the sideline, and from it every play of the game can be comfortably witnessed."

That first football season at Browning was a clear success. The high school lads won five games there before losing to Davenport in the last game. Moline professional teams also played there, most prominently the Illini who won three, lost one, and tied one at Browning that season. (The history of the Illini and other professional teams playing at Browning is included in Chapter 9.)

1912, The First Football Season at Browning Field. Below is a timeline of events involving the Moline High and Illini teams. Quoted passages come from an article written by high school football coach W. G. Burroughs for the 1913 High School annual, *M*:

September: "When school opened in September, 1912, the prospects for a winning team were rather poor. Of the fifteen men who won "M's" the year before, only five were in school . . . Because of hot weather, no practice was attempted during the first two weeks of September."

September 18: Practice began. "In spite of rain, the squad worked with a very willing spirit."

September 28: The high school team lost to the Alumni, 6-0. "The team was out-weighed about fifteen pounds to a man . . . Still the Alumni were forced to play all the football they knew to score one touchdown."

October 5: In the first regular-season high school game at Browning, Moline faced Maquoketa on a Saturday afternoon. The visitor's "defense proved weak and they were defeated 34-0."

October 6: The next day, in the first professional game at Browning, 1,000 watched the Moline Illini tie another Moline team, the Olympics, 0-0.

October 12: Moline defeated Aledo, 39-7.

October 13: The Illini lost 6-0 to the Rock Island Independents, 2,000 in attendance.

October 19: Moline hosted East Aurora, the 1911 state champions; "it proved a walk-over for Moline with a score of 34-0."

October 27: The Illini defeated the Kewanee Regulars 12-0, in front of 800 fans.

November 2: Moline beat Monmouth, 34-0.

November 3: 2,000 fans watched the Illini beat the Olympics 13-0.

November 16: Moline hosted Danville. "The night before the game a very successful mass meeting was held on the high school terrace. Speeches were made by all the players, and the large crowd attending showed great enthusiasm, which contributed to a large extent, to the 38 to 6 victory for Moline the next day."

November 23: "The Moline [High School] team, as guests of the Moline Athletic Association, witnessed the Iowa-Wisconsin game at Iowa City."

November 24: The Illini defeated the Moline West Ends, 12-7.

November 28: "On Thanksgiving day a crowd of nearly 5,000 assembled at Browning Field where a hard, close game with Davenport took place." Early in the game "Moline scored a touch-down, completely outplaying their opponents. Then several penalties aided Davenport and a blocked kick, resulting in a touch-down, put them ahead 7 to 6. A twenty-five yard penalty gave them the ball on Moline's fifteen yard line where a series of line plunges carried it over for a second touch-down. Neither side scored in the second half, though Moline made a desperate effort in the last five minutes, attempting several forward passes and fake plays. So the game closed with a 13 to 6 victory for Davenport where there should have been a tie."

For a November 1914 game at Browning, about 2,000 fans crowded into bleachers on the north side of the field. Two years later, a large wooden grandstand was built on the south side of the field, which remained in place until 1995.

Dispatch, June 19, 1948

A construction crew at work on Browning Field, June 1915. Two seasons of football were interrupted by work on the field itself along with the construction of new grandstands. In the front of this photograph, wearing a white shirt, is job contractor John L. Littig.

The Maroon and White played through the 1914 season at Browning, and then played two seasons at the Moline Athletic Park, located on 4th Avenue near 37th Street. A new cinder track was installed at Browning, the football field was improved, and new wooden stands were erected on the south side of the field. The high school track team started using the new track in the spring of 1917 and the football team returned that fall. (*M*, 1918)

M, 1916

Moline High School football team playing at Athletic Park, just west of Riverside Park, in 1915.

Alumni Games: In most years between 1901 and 1920 the Moline High School football team led off the season with a game against the Moline Alumni. In a majority of those years the school boys had little difficulty defeating the alums. However, a dramatic turn-around occurred in 1920 when the older lads clobbered the youngins 60-7! After that year no more alumni games were scheduled!

Courtesy of Jerry Wallaert

This undated photograph shows the Moline football team practicing in the alley just south of the high school building that was opened in 1915. Playing on that hard or gravelly surface must have toughened them up!

More Wins in the 1920s

The team's winning ways continued through the 1910s. Moline did not have a losing season until 1920, when it won four and lost five. This was followed by three spectacular seasons: In 1921 they lost only to Davenport (6-0) and in 1922 only to Champaign (28-0). In the latter season, not counting the Champaign game, Moline outscored their opponents 488-14. That year the local boys were particularly hard on some smaller schools out in the hinterland. They beat Princeton 92-0 and Kewanee 93-0! Several of the 1922 players, coached by George Senneff, went on to play college ball: one at the University of Iowa, Marvin Schmidt, and two at Northwestern, Walt Holmer and Mickey Erickson. Holmer was captain of the Northwestern squad in 1928 and played in the 1929 college East-West All-Star game in San Francisco. In 1923, the Moliners got

revenge by beating Champaign 33-3, and again lost only one game, 34-0 to Scott High School in Toledo, Ohio. (Eagle et al., 1935)

Despite Moline's success against other Illinois schools, the Maroon and White regularly had difficulty defeating a team from across the Mississippi River, Davenport High School. They beat the Iowa school only seven times before 1922, the year when a five-year hiatus in the rivalry was initiated. According to Van Vooren and Dye (2008), Moline suspended play with Davenport in all sports after a fight following their 1923 basketball game in Davenport. Football games between the two rivals began again in 1927.

1922 Moline High School Football team. Note on the far left is the canopy over the crescent baseball grandstand. A similar canopy over the third base stands had not yet been added.

The Line O' Type, December 6, 1922

M, 1924

This aerial view of Browning Field was taken on November 10, 1923, during a football game in which Moline defeated Champaign High, 33-3. It was a sweet victory because a year earlier Champaign had won the match, 28-0, and spoiled an otherwise undefeated season for Moline. The photograph was taken from the southwest, with 23rd Avenue (now Avenue of the Cities) visible on the right. Cars lined that street and also were parked on the west and north sides of the football field. In the upper part of the photograph, at the far eastern end of the football field, is the baseball diamond and grandstand constructed in 1920. In the lower left of the photograph is the land that later became Browning Park, which was originally proposed as the site for Wharton Field House. As plans evolved, however, a location in the upper left corner of this photograph was chosen for the indoor arena.

SOUVENIR PROGRAM

FOOT BALL

MOLINE
HIGH
SCHOOL

VS.
ROCK ISLAND
HIGH
SCHOOL

THANKSGIVING DAY NOV. 29, 1923
BROWNING FIELD · · MOLINE

FOOTBALL
ROCK ISLAND HIGH SCHOOL
VS.
MOLINE HIGH SCHOOL
THANKSGIVING DAY
November 29, 1928, at 2.30 P. M.
DOUGLAS PARK
RESERVED SEAT $1.25
GLOBE TICKET COMPANY, PHILADELPHIA

GRANDSTAND
SOUTH SIDE
Sec. B
Row 3
Seat 30

Courtesy of Jerry Wallaert · · · · · · · · · · · · · · · · · · Courtesy of Jerry Wallaert

This program cover and ticket stub are from the Moline-Rock Island Thanksgiving Day football games in 1923 and 1928. For many years that traditional rivalry game was played on Thanksgiving.

The Lament of the Jinx

"My subjects have canned me,—
alas and alack!

They have told me quite plainly to
never come back.

So I've packed up my duds,—I'm
going, in short,

There's just one place for me, and
that's *Davenport.*"

M, 1923

In 1922, Moline beat Davenport, 34-0, to break a five-year "jinx" against the Iowa team. The Moline High School annual, *M*, celebrated by publishing this caricature and poem. The scores in Davenport's victories over the previous five years, 1917-1921, were: 41-6; 52-0; 33-0; 32-2; and 6-0.

Since 1926 Davenport High School (now Davenport Central) has played their football games at Brady Street Stadium, which has large concrete grandstands on both sides of the football field. Shown here are the east stands in the 1950s. The stadium opened after the construction of the first sections of similarly-designed stands on the west side of the field. Later a press box was placed atop them, and then in 1937 lights were added to the stadium. In the early 1950s, the west stands were replaced with new ones housing new locker rooms. Since the opening of Brady Street Stadium, Davenport High School, along with other public high schools in the city (after 1960), have been playing football there. By the 1990s, St. Ambrose University and Assumption High School joined them, making it a very busy place in the fall. In 1993 alone, 83 football games were played there (Quad-City *Times*, October 2, 1994).

Davenport continued for three more decades to be the Maroons' nemesis, even during many of Moline's best seasons. They played each other every year from 1927 through 1986, except for 1936 and 1951. The overall football records between the two schools, stretching from 1900 to 1986: Davenport 49 wins; Moline 26 wins; and six ties. The adjacent table shows the Maroons' records against the teams they played at least 25 times. Davenport's dominance is clear. The only other team to have a winning record against the Moline is Rock Island, but their all-time margin is much narrower than Davenport's.

Davenport Public Schools Museum

202

Football Teams Most Frequently Played by Moline High, 1899-2012

	Games	Moline Wins	Oponent Wins	Ties
Rock Island	117	52	58	7
Galesburg	90	62	24	4
East Moline/UTHS	85	62	21	2
Davenport/Central	72	26	49	6
Alleman	59	31	26	2
Quincy	44	34	10	
Kewanee	40	30	5	5
Monmouth	25	23	2	

Source: Dye, 2012

M, 1925

Before 1944, when teams of females first led cheers for both football and basketball, cheering for Moline High School sports was directed by just one or two male students, sometimes called "yell leaders." Pictured here is Ted Smith, the lone yell leader for the 1924 football season. The school annual *M* described Smith: "'Teeda,' Diminutive and peppy cheer leader, displayed real ability for his task and the volume of sound he elicited from his band of tooters in the bleachers was a tribute to his efforts."

Travelling by Train

During the 1920s, high school teams commonly travelled to distant games by train. Some of Moline's games were not only distant, but a state or two away. On October 20, 1923, the Maroons travelled to Toledo, Ohio, where they lost to Scott High School 34-0. A year later, October 13, 1924, they visited Muskegon, Michigan. A clearly unbiased source, the Moline High School *M* described the outcome there: "Incompetent work on the part of the officials, later acknowledged in a letter from them, gave the game to Muskegon 11-6, but unbiased spectators conceded the game to Moline."

Later that fall, on November 6th, Coaches Senneff and Holmgren, plus seventeen players and trainer Yeager, boarded a 4:36 p.m. train for Chicago. That evening they transferred to a train with sleeping cars for a 9:16 departure for Louisville, Kentucky. Arriving there at 7:30 a.m. they would spend a day in Louisville before playing a powerhouse team from Male High School on Saturday afternoon. The Male High team had played five games that season, including two in Indianapolis and one in Cincinnati. They had scored 218 points, while allowing only one touchdown to be scored against them. Male High coach Tom King, who would go on to coach at the University of Louisville between 1925 and 1930, was quoted as describing the Moline game "as the supreme test of the year." *Dispatch* (November 6) commentary prior to the game was enthusiastic:

> Most Moliners feel fairly confident that the team will win despite the impressive record made this year by the Kentuckians . . . The southerners regard Moline as one of the greatest prep elevens in the country as the result of its fine showing in 1923."

Perhaps the *Dispatch* should have been more guarded in its optimism. Male beat Moline, 72-0! It was the worst defeat ever for the Maroons, the previous worst defeat having been witnessed by 6,000 fans at Browning on Thanksgiving Day in 1914 when Davenport won 68-0. The Moline crew arrived back in the Plow City at 2 p.m. Sunday afternoon. The Davenport *Democrat and Leader* (November 9, 1924) commented:

The Male high boys appeared as a regular college team and did not make a play which did not net a gain. The Moline team, which is one of the best in the central United States, was completely swept off its feet and Captain Carlson was the only visitor who could penetrate the Male high defense for even a slight gain.

The 1925 *M* summarized the Louisville experience: "Here they met with overwhelming defeat at the hands of the Dixie titleholders. A croaking jink dogged the footsteps of the Maroons throughout the entire game."

The following year, on Friday, November 13, 1925, a group of thirty from Male High School, including players, coaches, and trainers, arrived at the railroad depot in Moline and took up residence in the LeClaire Hotel. The "Male High machine" was in Moline for a rematch at Browning Field. Like the previous season, they were undefeated and had allowed only one touchdown to be scored against them. According to Pat Patten of the *Dispatch* (November 13) they stayed at the hotel because:

> they have so much respect for the Maroons they are desirous of obtaining a night's rest from the fatigue of their long journey before engaging in a contest which may mar their substantial claim to national title consideration.

Monday's *Dispatch* headline let the hometown fans down gently: "Fighting Moline High Eleven Holds Louisville Stars to Low Score." The Male High Colonels had remained undefeated, winning 10-0 in front of 3,500 spectators. The 1926 *M* called it the "greatest game ever at Browning Field."

SOLDIERS FIELD AND FIELD MUSEUM AT THE LAKE FRONT, CHICAGO

Lake County (IL) Discovery Museum, Curt Teich Postcard Archives

The year before Moline had ventured to Kentucky to play Male High, Austin High School of Chicago played there and lost by the identical score of 72-0. Male High's return engagement in Chicago, on October 4, 1924, produced a result similar to the Male return engagement in Moline; the Colonels won 26-0. The 1924 Austin-Male match was the first football game played at the new Soldier Field in Chicago, shown here in a historic postcard view.

Soldier Field served for decades as a multi-purpose arena. It regularly attracted crowds of over 100,000 people and was the site in 1927 of the largest crowd ever to see a college football game, the 123,000 who watched USC lose to Notre Dame 7-6 [sigh…]. The venerable stadium hosted hundreds of high school football games including the Prep Bowl, the annual game between the champions of the public and Catholic schools of the city. It also hosted the annual College All-Star game each August, pitting the previous year's NFL champion against a college all-star team. Thousands of other events held there over the years included every imaginable outdoor activity, ranging from track meets and monster truck rallies, to political and religious rallies and visits of presidents and movie stars. In 1971, Soldier Field became the home of the Chicago Bears, who had previously played at Wrigley Field. In 2003 a historically- and architecturally-controversial renovation was completed, producing the state-of-the-art Bears home stadium of today. (Ford, 2009)

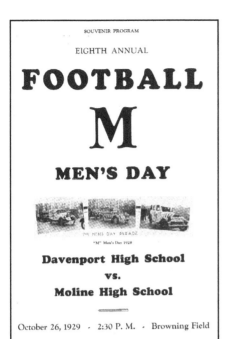

Courtesy of John Wetzel

M, 1930

"M Men's Day," which has been cele-brated annually at Browning Field since the early 1920s, honors football letter-winners from previous years. Shown here is cover of the program for the 1929 event, which included a parade.

Beginning in the fall of 1929, the Field House was always in the background for people viewing football from the south stands at Browning Field. This photograph shows high school action on the field in that year.

Lights on for the 1930s

Prior to 1930 most Moline football games, both home and away, were played on Saturday afternoons. Friday night games began after lights were first put in place at Browning in the summer of 1930 to permit night minor-league baseball games. In the first night football game, Moline beat East Moline, 18-0, before 4,000 fans on Friday, September 19th. The second night game, two weeks later, was a 39-6 victory over Dubuque in front of over 5,000 fans. Their star player was Jay Berwanger, who went on to play for the University of Chicago Maroons where he

was a two-time All American and became the first winner of the Heisman Trophy in 1935. In the losing cause against Moline he completed four consecutive forward passes but did not score.

Lights were also installed in 1930 at two Rock Island stadiums. The Rock Island High School football team started playing night games when they first used their new lighted Public Schools Stadium. Also in 1930, the Augustana College Vikings played their first night game at Ericsson Field on September 27 against Central College. At the same time the stadium's seating capacity

Lake County (IL) Discovery Museum, Curt Teich Postcard Archives

This 1940s postcard shows Rock Island Public Schools Stadium, which cost $80,000 and was opened in the fall of 1930. Rock Island won its first game in the new facility on October 9th under the lights, shutting out Kewanee, 21-0. The stadium's design has Art Deco touches and is one of the largest high school stadiums in the country, seating 15,000. The field was named after long-time coach "Shorty" Almquist in 1970. In the background of the photograph is the 1937 Rock Island High School building, which cost $1,250,000, including $480,000 in Federal Project Works Administration funds. (Rock Island Preservation Society, online). At the south (left) end of the main building is the gymnasium that hosted Rock Island basketball from 1937 until a new fieldhouse was opened in 1958. The fieldhouse is attached to the southwest corner of the school building.

Courtesy of Judy Belan

East Moline's Soule Bowl. Dr. E. A. Soule, president of the East Moline Park Board, proposed that a stadium be built in a natural "bowl" in Butterworth Park. Site preparation began in 1933 with funds from the state relief program. Like other Depression-era projects, this one was very labor-intensive, earth being moved around with wheelbarrows and shovels. Later work on the stadium was partially supported by grants from the Federal Works Progress Administration. Although not yet complete, Soule Bowl hosted its first game on October 17, 1936. Kewanee won, 7-6, over East Moline, then called the "Hilltoppers." The first home win came a week later, 39-0, over St. Joseph's of Rock Island, and the first game against Moline was on November 8th, which was won by the Maroons, 32-6. Lights were installed prior to the 1937 season, permitting night games. (A nice account of the creation and construction of Soule Bowl can be found in Judy Belan's 2004 book on East Moline.)

was expanded to about 6,000 by bringing bleachers, accommodating an additional 4,200 people, from Douglas Park (*Observer*, September 18).

By the late 1920s, local rivalries among Tri-City teams from Moline, Rock Island, and Davenport high schools had been well established. Then East Moline High School entered the scene. The "Hilltoppers" played their first game against the Moline varsity in 1928, losing to the Maroons 27-0 at Browning Field. In several previous seasons East Moline had fielded a team that played against the Moline "seconds." It was

This Big Nine football trophy is on display at Wharton Field House. It was retained in 1936 by Moline after the Maroons won the conference football championship three out of six years. The yearly winners shown on labels at the bottom are: 1930, Moline; 1931, Monmouth; 1932, East Moline; 1933, Galesburg; 1934, Rock Island; 1935, Moline; 1936, Moline.

C. Roseman, 2012

not until 1931 that Moline lost to the Hilltoppers, 6-0, in a game at Browning.

In a review of Moline football, 1900-1934, Eagle et al. (1935) reported that Moline had captured ten mythical state championships, won 199 games, lost 83, and tied 20, and completed three undefeated seasons. Their fourth undefeated season came in 1936, when the Maroons out-scored eight opponents 181-26. Moline completed that perfect season at Browning on Thanksgiving Day, November 26th, by beating the St. Louis champion, Beaumont High School, 14-6, even though Beaumont out-gained the Maroons, 526 yards to 238. The next day *Dispatch* sports editor Lynn Callaway chose to wax nostalgic on the outcome:

> Gridiron ghosts of long ago rode out of the past late yesterday afternoon, released by thirty years of grinding by the wheel of football fate, to cavort on the charmed turf of Browning Field to be licked and stormed through a chilling wind to a momentous climatic triumph . . . Even the cold, impersonal telegraphic key seemed to utter a note of the dramatic as it clicked out the story of a gallant comeback

waged by the men of the Maroon who charged back in a sensational second half to wreck the forces of Beaumont's St. Louis champions and finish off Moline's best football season in three decades . . . Approximately 5,000 persons . . . watched the protégés of coach George Senneff scoff at the very idea of defeat and give Moline its first perfect season since 1906, and their teacher his first clean slate since his arrival in the Plow City seventeen seasons ago.

M, 1943

George Senneff inspects a formation of Moline coaches on a chilly autumn afternoon in this photograph from the 1943 *M*. From left to right are Senneff, Harry Forber (player), Howard James, Roger Potter, Joe Vavrus, and Bill Bean.

M, 1943

There is little doubt that the Moline High School coach with the most distinguished overall record was George Senneff, pictured here. A graduate of Sterling High School and the University of Illinois, Senneff moved to Moline in 1920 after coaching three years at Taylorville. In that year he and Winnie Holmgren became the first Moline High School faculty members to be assigned coaching duties. Senneff coached the football team for 25 years, the basketball team for 21 years, and the track team for over twenty years. A number of his teams in these three sports were among the best in the state. His football coaching resulted in a record of 134 wins, seventy losses, and fifteen ties, and his 1936 team was undefeated. Senneff's basketball teams won fourth place in the state in 1934, 1935, and 1945, and third place in 1940. (*Dispatch*, December 24, 1954)

M, 1943

By the 1930s, and ever since, marching bands have been a major feature at Browning Field for high school football games. This view, from the 1943 *M*, shows the Moline High School band with Wharton Field House in the background. In that era, cars were allowed to park between the Field House and the football field, inside the corrugated metal fence that separated Browning from the Field House grounds.

Power Shift in the 1940s

George Senneff was a highly successful coach at Moline in the 1920s and 1930s. In those decades his teams lost to Rock Island only three times. During the six seasons from 1935 through 1940 the Maroons won a total of 43 games, losing

four and tying two, and outscored Rock Island
132-0. Then in 1941 a new coach appeared at
Rock Island, Shorty Almquist. In his first game
against Moline Almquist led the Rocks to a 27-0
win in front of 7,000 in Rock Island. The power
in that traditional rivalry had shifted. Rock
Island went on to defeat Moline five years
straight, and Almquist would lose to Moline only
three times during the 1940s and 1950s.

After some losing seasons in the World War II
years, a resurgence of Moline football came in
the late 1940s under coach Sam Drake. In 1948
the Maroons lost only to Davenport. That year
the game with Rock Island was eagerly anticipated (*Dispatch*, October 1): "All tickets for the
Moline – Rock Island clash were sold out early
this morning, assuring the Browning Field
contest of a new record attendance of 8,000
fans." At least that many fans showed up
and Moline won, 32-7. However the Rocks
got revenge in 1949 by prevailing 14-7,
Moline's only loss that year.

Then in 1950 the Maroons accomplished
their fifth undefeated season, the first
since 1936. They defeated their two closest
rivals, beating Rock Island 34-7 and Davenport 39-0, and their final victory was a
47-13 drubbing of Cedar Rapids Franklin
on November 11th at Browning. "Some
2,500 fans shivered through a first half in
which Moline rolled up a 33-0 lead and
then went home" (*Dispatch*, November
13). Austin Duke, who went on to play in
the Rose Bowl for the University of Illinois,
completed his season with a total of 1,004
rushing yards. In nine games that season
the Maroons racked up 260 points to opponents' 41. As spectacular as this sounds,
Russ Kiesele of the *Dispatch* (November 3)
put it in perspective by pointing out:

> Of Moline's five undefeated clubs,
> the 1904 club stands out as the
> most powerful with 304 points and
> the stingiest – no points were
> scored against it. The 1906 team
> gave up only five points – and those
> were to St. Ambrose College.

M, 1942

The headline above the photograph from the 1942 *M*, "One
Dead Davenporter," was probably not meant to be literal.
Alas, Davenport won the game, 20-0.

M, 1947

The 1946 Moline football team trotting from the Field House dressing room to the Browning football field through the gate in the fence
separating the two facilities. The team is led by Willie McAdams,
lower right, who earned All-State honors that year. Other players in
the front row are Al Stephens, Dick Larson, and Fred Samuelson,
and directly behind McAdams is Frank "Cork" Mahar. At the far left
are some younger lads and Coach Sam Drake, each showing admira-
tion for the high school team.

He went on to note that the 1950 Maroons "surpassed the famous Rock Island perfect teams of 1944 and 1949" by gaining more net yards from scrimmage. They totaled 3,017 yards (2,562 running and 455 passing), compared to the Rocks' 2,878 in 1949 and 2,809 in 1944.

The Second Half

In the last half of the twentieth century, after that 1950 perfect season, Moline's football fortunes at Browning were not as stellar as they were in the first half. Nonetheless several seasons stand out. Even though the Maroons won only two games in 1956, one of those victories was of special significance. On September 29th they defeated East St. Louis High on their home field, 13-12, breaking a 44-game winning streak for the Flyers dating back to 1951. In regular season games Moline beat them in 1948, 1949, and 1956, but lost to them in 1951 and 1957.

In 1967 Harley Rollinger arrived from Webster City, Iowa, to coach the Maroons to an undefeated season. They scored 227 points to 27 for their opponents and opened the season by breaking Davenport Central's thirty-game winning streak, beating the Blue Devils 19-0 in front of 6,000 spectators at Brady Street Stadium. The final game of the season, on November 10th, was at Browning against undefeated Cedar Rapids Washington. Two days before the game, the *Argus* reported that additional bleachers were being set up in anticipation of a large crowd. Five newspapers had asked for press box space and a Cedar Rapids TV station would film the game. Moline won 27-7 in front of about 8,000 fans, successfully completing their first undefeated season since 1950 and their first Mississippi

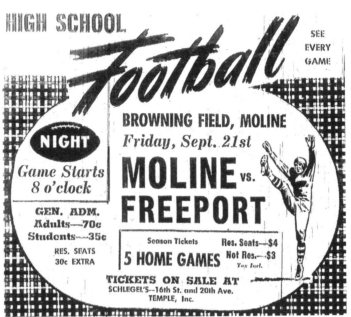

Dispatch, September 18, 1951

Promoting Moline High School football, on the field and on the radio.

Dispatch,
September 21, 1951

M, 1958

Bob Mason practicing his punting during the 1957 Moline High School football season.

Valley League championship. Rollinger went on to coach the Maroons in two one-loss seasons, in 1969 and 1970. These were the last of 29 seasons in which the Maroons were undefeated or lost only one game. Twenty-two of those 29 came before World War II. Of course, once state playoffs started in 1974 it was impossible to have an undefeated season without winning a state title.

Moline High School Football
One-Loss and Perfect Seasons

Year	Record	Lost to
1899	0-1	Rock Island 20-5
1900	9-0	
1901	5-1-2	Galesburg 18-10
1902	7-1-1	Davenport 35-0
1904	9-0	
1905	5-1-1	Rock Island 4-0
1906	10-0	
1907	8-1	Monmouth College 14-6
1913	9-1	Davenport 26-0
1916	7-1	Galesburg 25-7
1917	6-1-1	Davenport 41-6
1921	7-1	Davenport 6-0
1922	7-1	Champaign 28-0
1923	8-1	Scott (Toledo, OH) 34-0
1929	8-1-1	Waukegan 7-6
1932	8-1-1	East Moline 7-0
1935	8-1	New Trier 9-0
1936	8-0	
1937	8-1	DeVilbiss (Toledo) 14-6
1938	5-1-1	Davenport 7-0
1939	6-1-1	Evanston 7-0
1940	8-1	Davenport 7-0
1948	8-1	Davenport 14-6
1949	8-1	Rock Island 14-7
1950	9-0	
1954	5-1-3	Davenport 14-13
1967	9-0	
1969	8-1	Rock Island 20-14
1970	8-1	Rock Island 31-14

Source: Dye, 2012

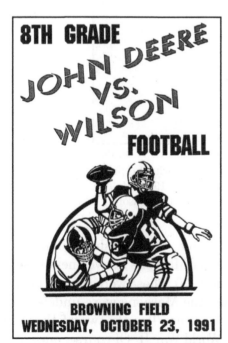

Courtesy of Jerry Wallaert

Over the years, Browning has been the site of hundreds of Junior High football games, like this one in 1991.

210

From the time the state playoffs started in 1974 through 2012, the Maroons qualified for state playoffs in sixteen seasons. Under coach Dan McGuire, the Maroons appeared in the playoffs six years in a row from 1995 through 2000, but in each case lost in the first round. They qualified four years in a row from 2004 through 2007 under coach Joel Ryser. Only three times have the Maroons reached the second round of playoffs, losing to Elgin Larkin in 1979 and to East St. Louis in 1991 and 2007.

Track and Field at Browning

According to Eagle et al. (1935), Moline track and field participation extends back to 1880 when the high school was a member of the Military Tract Association (essentially a predecessor to the Big Nine Conference). The Association sponsored all-day events that included not only athletics but also debate and literary competitions. By the 1890s, Moline was participating in several track meets including the Tri-City invitational, the Knox College invitational, the Western Illinois Track Association and Military Tract Association meets, and of course, a dual meet with Rock Island. Bicycle races were included in many meets until they were discontinued in 1902.

In the early years of track and field, the lads worked out at a small field just north of the high school building on 16th Street hill. The space and facilities were inadequate. This all changed in the spring of 1917 when Browning Field first welcomed the track team. The very first issue of the Moline High School newspaper, *The Line O' Type*, dated March 12, 1917, announced:

Mountain Range at Augustana? During the 1922 season, some Augustana College track practices and meets were held at Browning because of the poor condition of the Augustana track. The school newspaper, *Observer* (April 20) commiserated: "The deplorable condition of the cinder path which resembles a relief map of a western mountain range has hindered outdoor practice."

Eagle et al., 1935

This photograph, probably taken in 1905, shows Gilpin Stromberg at the track practice area immediately north of the high school on 16th Street, in a very small lot.

The school seems to have lost a great deal of interest in spring athletics. Possibly this is due to the fact that a suitable place to practice the outdoor work was not available. The Browning field has been fixed with a cinder track. This will make a good place for training, although it is rather far from the school.

For several decades thereafter the team had to trek a full ten blocks to reach their spring athletic facility at Browning – poor lads.

Over the years, Browning has been the site of numerous conference and other major multi-school track meets. Among those held in the 1920s, were a "Big Eight" meet in 1924 (including six schools from the Big Nine plus Davenport), the Big Nine meet in 1929, and the Black Hawk sectional meet on May 14, 1927. The latter attracted eighteen schools from four counties and 189 athletes.

Courtesy of Jerry Wallaert

C. Roseman, 2012

Moline won the district track championship in 1929 and earned this trophy, which is displayed at Wharton Field House.

The YMCA sponsored city-wide track meets at Browning in 1923 and other years.

211

MARSELL GOING UP

The photograph on the left, from the 1929 *M*, shows an athlete competing in the pole vault with the covered baseball grandstands at Browning Field in the background. On the right are Dick Larson (top) and Curt Trevor soaring above Browning Field in 1945, with Wharton Field House in the background

Big Nine Conference Meet, 1929. "The colors of nine Illinois high schools will wave over Browning field here today for the 19th annual track and field meet of the Big Nine conference. Picked as a favorite by dopesters [sports prognosticators] the Galesburg high school team will present a strong coterie that boasts, among other things, a relay team that flashed to a first place in the Kansas relays two weeks ago. Bam Barry, University of Iowa basketball coach who has just accepted a similar post at the University of Southern California, will officiate. Following are the high schools that will compete: Moline, East Moline, Rock Island, Geneseo, Canton, Monmouth, Galesburg, Princeton and Kewanee." (Sterling *Daily Gazette*, May 4)

Moline sent numerous athletes to the state track meet at Champaign in the early twentieth century. Nonetheless by 1935 only three had won individual state championships: Gilpin Stromberg in 1905 (low hurdles), Ross Santee in 1906 (broad jump), and Lee Osborn in 1924 (discus throw of 122 feet). Nonetheless, they fielded strong teams in several years, winning the Black Hawk meet five times between 1926 and 1935. (Eagle et al., 1935)

The Anders family provided several athletes who starred in track, football, and basketball at Moline High School. Flip Anders was the state champion in the 100-yard dash in 1937 and the champion in the 220-yard dash in both 1937 and 1938. His brother Jim, the first African American to play basketball at Moline, played at the state tournaments with the Maroons in both 1935 and 1936, his sophomore and junior years. However, he left school before his senior year to take a job to support his family. (Dye and Van-Vooren, 2008) Brothers Cal and Bob played on basketball teams placing second in the state in 1943 and 1951, respectively. Among the Anders in the next generation, John starred in football and won the state discus title on Moline's state-championship track team in 1960, while Curt played on Moline's last undefeated football team in 1967 and broke the state record in the discus throw. Also in that generation is Paul Carther, who was an All-State football lineman and state heavyweight wrestling champion in 1969. Carther went on to become a teacher and coach at Moline High School. Brad Baraks' 1982 book includes more on the Anders family, along with short biographies of numerous other local athletes, coaches, and journalists who have appeared at Wharton Field House and Browning Field.

M, 1937

Flip Anders running at Browning Field.

M, 1943

Cal Anders, front center, was one of the stars of the 1943 Moline High School Basketball team that placed second in the state tournament. In the photograph are: front row: Bill Hall, Harold Heiland, Anders, Al Van Landuyt, and Jim Grafton; center row: Porter Bennett, Eli Markovich, Jim Schell, LeRoy Skantz, Frank DeMeyer; back row: athletic director George Senneff, coach Roger Potter, and sophomore coach Joe Vavrus. Anders, DeMeyer, and Hall were named to the all-tournament team.

Curt Anders broad jumps to a new school record, 23′ 6¾″.

M, 1967

Curt Anders jumping a long distance at Browning Field in 1967.

M, 1961

John Anders, 1960 Illinois state discus throw champion.

213

The Shipley Era

Moline High School track coach from 1954 to 1985, Gene Shipley, presided over some excellent track athletes and teams that called Browning Field home. His 1960 team captured the state championship and his 1962 team finished second, both at Memorial Stadium in Champaign. The 1960 Moline title broke a string of four state championships by Chicago Heights Bloom, and 25 straight titles won by Chicago-area teams. The last downstate team to win had been Rockford High in 1935. (IHSA, online)

Courtesy of Jerry Wallaert

The championship team poses around their coach Gene Shipley (fifth from the left in the first row).

As a fitting celebration of the championship, the 1960 spring awards banquet included Olympic star Jesse Owens as guest speaker. The May 25th celebration, attended by 400 at the Moline High School auditorium, was held exactly 25 years after Owens made history as an Ohio State University athlete. At the Big 10 Conference track meet in Ann Arbor, Michigan, he "stunned the track world by setting three world records and tying a fourth in the greatest individual performance ever recorded in track" (Argus, May 26). Owens went on to win four gold medals at the 1936 Olympics in Berlin and later toured the United States as an inspirational speaker. Moline coach Shipley told Steve Batterson (2010) "Jesse had a lady friend in Geneseo, and he was around here quite often at that time. That's how the group that hosted our banquet was able to secure him as a speaker."

C. Roseman, 2013

The 1960 state track championship banner is hung in Wharton Field House.

Argus, May 26, 1960

Jesse Owens, front row center, posing with members of the Moline state championship track team in May 1960. Flanking Owens in the front are Dave Jackson and Duane Shrader. In the back are Coach Shipley, Ron Gunn, Dick Schluter, and Henry Richie.

Racing at the Stadium. Jesse Owens had appeared in the Quad Cities at least two previous times. In 1940 (June 30) and 1944 (August 28) he brought his travelling show to Municipal Stadium in Davenport. The show, held in conjunction with baseball games, included Owens demonstrating his speed in dashes and hurdles.

214

On a muddy day, the 1966 Moline track team worked out at Browning Field.

In 2005 the track at Browning Field was named for Coach Gene Shipley. The legendary coach is also honored with the Shipley Invitational, which annually attracts several teams to Browning. Shown here are girls running in the Invitational in 2013. Girls have competed in track at Moline High School since 1973.

Boys running at the Shipley Invitational meet on March 31, 2013.

Moline High School boys and girls track and cross country state champions are proudly displayed at Browning Field.

Moline Community College also used Browning Field. Here is a 1961 photograph of MCC student Doug Peterson throwing the discus.

Galaxy, 1961

This photograph from the 1940s or early 1950s shows the massive fence that separated Browning Field from the Field House at the time. In this scene, a smaller, temporary outfield fence was set up for baseball. The baseball diamond is off the photograph to the right and a group of lads are lounging inside the fence in center field.

215

High School Baseball and Soccer

While a student at Moline High School, Frank "Cork" Mahar prodded the school administration into establishing baseball. The team started in the spring of 1945 with Cliff Hyink as the first coach and Mahar as the catcher. In their first year, they played a total of eight games – four against Davenport—and lost them all. In subsequent years, their schedules expanded and records improved. In 1947 Archie Swanson took over as coach and the team won the Quad City Conference title. They continued to play home games at Browning through the spring of 1958. In August of that year, the baseball grandstand burned at Browning, after which home games were moved to a new baseball facility at the newly-opened high school.

M, 1948

The 1948 Moline High School baseball team emerges from the Browning Field dugout. This photograph from the *M* shows Coach Swanson, Perry Loding, Bill Mitton, Duane Sandler, Bob Stablein, Brian Baldwin, Ralph Masengarb, Jack Liljeberg, Dick Abrahamson, and Ronnie Hicks.

M, 1956

This photograph of Moline High School baseball players appeared in the 1956 *M*. The caption reads: "Larry Vanderheyden eyes one as it comes in toward the plate. The receiver is Jim Caldwell. Dave Hellyer, Mike Heitman and Clyde Storbeck await their turn at bat."

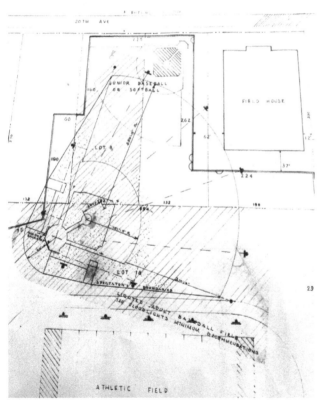

Moline Board of Education files

After the baseball grandstands burned down in August 1958, this plan was drawn for a possible new configuration of the baseball field at Browning. It would have minimized the overlap between the football field and the baseball diamond. Instead, a baseball field was created at the new high school location. In this era, a softball diamond was in use just west of the Field House, as shown in the upper part of the diagram.

Courtesy of Jerry Wallaert

Younger kids also played baseball at Browning. Here is Jerry Wallaert (first row, second from right) and his buddies from the Willard Grade School Dad's Club team ready to take the field in the summer of 1954.

216

Moline High School soccer teams, both boys and girls, played at Browning until 2010. The boys started in 1984 and the girls in 1992. In the fall of 2009, they played some games at Browning and some at their new "soccer bowl" near the high school. Then in 2010, after lights had been installed there, they made the new field their permanent home. Having a dedicated soccer field avoided scheduling conflicts with football at Browning, where Moline varsity and sophomore games were played along with some Alleman High School games. The move also allowed the use of a regulation-sized field which was not possible at Browning.

During their 26 years playing at Browning, the boys' team went to the district tournament eleven times, including four years in a row between 2003 and 2007. In 1989 they finished third in the state tournament. Since 1996, both the boys and girls have been coached by Rick Sanchez.

Squeezed at Browning Field? According to Moline soccer coach Rick Sanchez, Browning could not accommodate a regulation-size soccer field, which is 125 by 74 yards. Drainage holes bordering the 120 by 53-1/3 yard football field prevented the soccer field from being larger than about 115 by 60. In spite of the field's smaller size, a situation common to other high school football facilities, soccer games were played there within the rules.

Beyond High School Sports at Browning

Field and Sports Days: From 1890 to 1935, Adolf "Oppie" Oppenheimer was the supervisor of physical training for the Moline schools. He was a pioneer in organized physical education for school children and was an early advocate for physical activities for girls (Seusy et al., 2009). Over the years he organized public events in which school children would demonstrate various physical activities, including jumping, running, gymnastics, dance, and synchronized drills. His first, held in 1895 and called Calisthenics Day, involved over 1,000 boys and girls performing outdoors in front of a large crowd of parents, friends, and community members. Thirteen trolley cars were used to transport the students to a field near 27th Street and 3rd Avenue for the event.

Dispatch, May 29, 1913

As part of the 1913 Field Day, eighth graders participated in a Maypole dance directed by Miss Huldah Janssen, assistant supervisor of physical training for the Moline schools.

Beginning in 1913, the event was held annually at Browning Field and called the Moline Schools Field Day. The first, which featured activities by 3,590 school children, attracted a crowd of 10,000. That 1913 program started with 300 third and fourth grade children giving an exhibition in free movements, followed by fifth graders in a similar exercise. Then 300 sixth graders "took the field with a dumbbell exercise, so perfect in execution as to rival older and more experienced gymnasts. The entire 300 performers moved as one machine" (*Dispatch*, May 28).

Among other activities, 100 first and second graders raced onto the field dressed in Indian costumes, half of them braves who indulged in a wild "realistic war dance."

In its second year, 1914, again about 10,000 people watched 3,600 children perform. Thereafter the annual event, in some years called "Sports Day," continued to attract large crowds. The Dispatch (May 30), described the throng at the 1928 event:

> It was estimated that nearly 7,000 proud parents and friends were on hand to cheer the efforts of 4,000 boys and girls of the Moline public schools . . . Long before 1 o'clock the street cars leading to Browning field were filled with a throng of humanity, and for an hour before the first event on the program had begun, there was a constant stream of men, women and children pouring into the stands and onto the green turf of the field.

Oppenheimer continued to organize these and similar events until his death in 1935. For several years following his death, Oppie's daughter, Lillian Mengel, assisted in directing the Field Day activities at Browning. She was director of physical education for the Moline elementary

Adolph Oppenheimer

Calisthenics

Normal School of North America
Gymnastics – Indianapolis

Adolph Oppenheimer as pictured in the 1913 *M*. He is listed as a "Calisthenics" instructor who was educated at the Normal School of North American Gymnastics in Indianapolis, Indiana.

schools until her resignation in 1944, having worked for the schools since 1923. (*Dispatch*, July 12, 1944) Thereafter, the events continued at Browning for a few years. Again they typically involved over 3,000 students, and even more spectators. The 1947 Field Day "thrilled 8,300 persons, including 5,000 spectators who applauded enthusiastically and the 3,300 school boys and girls who danced, marched and sang with youthful gaiety" (*Dispatch*, July 21).

Dispatch, August 6, 1946

The 1946 Sports Day at Browning was held as part of a 98th anniversary celebration for the City of Moline. The sports activities were postponed one day because of rain. Pictured here are girls, aged nine to thirteen, participating in the jump rope event. Other activities included baton twirling for girls, and baseball throwing and bicycle trick riding for boys. "Most fun for the boys was the egg throwing contests, with participants ending up somewhat egg-splattered." (*Dispatch*, August 6)

Moline Exposition: In July 1924 the Moline Chamber of Commerce sponsored a six-day industrial exposition at Browning. It featured exhibits "of everything manufactured in Moline [and] designed to sell Moline and her products to the citizens of the city and surroundings" (*Dispatch*, July 4). The displays were set up in two tents on the baseball part of the field. In addition, the Brundage Shows brought in six rides and numerous amusement stands, set up on the west half of the football field. Vaudeville performances, including some outdoor aerial acts, were featured. To top off the entertainment, the 25-piece Moline Community Service Band played four concerts each day, and a large fireworks display was presented each evening. Total attendance was 27,000, including 7,000 who attended on the last day of the event, Saturday, July 12th.

1928 Railroad Tournament: The fifth annual tournament for Rock Island Lines employees came to the Tri-Cities on August 25, 1928. Hundreds of employees came to town by train to compete for prizes in a variety of athletic events. Roy W. Harter, a process supervisor at the railroad's Silvis shops who chaired the event, had been lobbying for three years to bring the tournament to the Tri-Cities. Harter assured *Rock Island Magazine* (March 1928) that:

> the business men of the Tri-Cities will do everything in their power to make the tournament a wonderful success. They will decorate the town from one end to the other. They will have cars at the hotels at the service of the athletes and visitors. The track facilities at Moline are but five minutes' ride from the hotels or yards where the Pullmans will be parked.

Fifteen track and field events, plus a tug-of-war and a competition among bands, were held at Browning Field. Other events included horse shoe pitching at Long View Park in Rock Island, tennis at Augustana College, golf at the Arsenal Golf Club, trap shooting at the Davenport Gun Club, and pistol shooting on the Arsenal. A little less strenuous event, checkers, was held in the lobby of the LeClaire Hotel, the tournament

headquarters. For the first time, Rock Island Railroad female employees were competing. They participated in tennis singles plus the 50-, 100-, and 220-yard dashes. Two events for children of employees were also added, the 50- and 100-yard dashes. Employees not only competed as individuals but also as representatives of nine railroad divisions (Chicago Terminal, Illinois-Silvis, Iowa, Cedar Rapids-Minnesota, Dakota, Nebraska-Colorado, and so forth). (The full program for the tournament can be found at RITS, online.)

Colorful Scene at Browning. Before the tournament, Rock Island Magazine writer T. J. O'Shaughnessy reported that members of each division were encouraged to display the color combination chosen by that division. For example, Chicago Terminal colors were Cardinal and Oxford, and Iowa colors were Burnt Orange and White. Interestingly, the Illinois-Silvis colors were Maroon and White – a Moliner must have had some influence in the choice! Clearly in promotional mode, O'Shaughnessy went on to anticipate the scene at the tournament: "Unbridle your fancy a moment. Picture, if you can, a beautiful green field, around which there is a splendid quarter mile oval track. See the green grass and white markers; see that motley array of athletes attired in scarlet and blue, in gold and white, in black and in green, and those other colors. Observe the commodious steel grandstand filled to overflowing with cheering waving crowds."

Rock Island Magazine, October 1928
Marching on the football field at the Rock Island Lines Tournament, August 1928. In the background is Wharton Field House under construction.

Rock Island Magazine, October 1928
About 5,000 people showed up for the afternoon events of the 1928 Rock Island Railroad Tournament at Browning Field. The south grandstand, shown here, was packed.

Preliminary track and field events were held at Browning in the morning while other events were taking place around the Tri-Cities. Then, at 1:30 p.m. about 5,000 spectators were on hand for the track and field finals and other events at Browning. At 5:45 in the afternoon, special trains left the Moline station for an evening victory banquet and awards ceremony at the Rock Island Arsenal cafeteria, which was attended by 700 people. In the team competition, Illinois-Silvis narrowly edged out Dakota for the Divisional title.

Midget Autos: During the 1930s, the quarter-mile cinder track at Browning was used for auto races. One such event, on the evening of July 4, 1935, was held for the benefit of the Moline Playground Fund under the auspices of the Moline American Legion. The cover of the printed program specifies that admission was 10 cents and warns "Pay No More."

At least 22 cars were entered, the most popular types being Eitos, Harleys, and Indians. Also entered were a Miller, a Johnson, a Wisconsin Special, a Saxon, an Austin, a Henderson, and a Dirzius. Time trials were held to determine starting positions in subsequent races. The fastest times in the single-lap trials were just over 23 seconds.

Motorcycles: Motor sports returned to Browning in the summer of 1947, when several professional Saturday-evening motorcycle race events were held, attracting several thousand fans in total. In anticipation of these events, the *Dispatch* (May 23) offered this analysis:

> Motorcycle racing is regarded as one of the most thrilling of all daring sports. It will be especially so on the short quarter-mile Moline cinder track which encircles the baseball field. There being no banked turns, a win depends upon a rider's ability to 'broad-side' around turns. He actually turns the corners on his left foot, the 'hot shoe.' This is where many crack-ups occur.

The first of the series, which was rained-out on May 24th, was held on June 14th. After another race was held in July, several improvements were made at Browning by the Park Board in preparation for the third race on August 2nd. The track was oiled and rolled to give riders more traction, a hazardous bump on the northwest turn was smoothed, and additional floodlights were added to the west turn. The *Dispatch* (August 2) cited one more improvement: "In addition the light standards near the track have been white-washed. This will eliminate a hazard for the 'hot shoe boys' as they will be able to see the poles more clearly."

Dispatch, July 3, 1935   *Dispatch*, September 4, 1947

Yes, motorized vehicles were raced on the un-banked cinder track at Browning Field. Here are advertisements for auto races in 1935 and motorcycle races in 1947.

The final race, on September 6th, featured two additional attractions: a parade of all types of two-wheeled motor-driven vehicles, including whizzer bikes, scooters, and midget cycles; and a race between two older motorcycles, a 1912 Harley-Davidson and a 1909 Super-X. Nearly 3,000 fans were there to see Bob Heath win the race on his Harley when the Super-X, with Charles Timmerman in the saddle, "coughed and conked out on the second lap." (*Dispatch*, September 8)

These races were sponsored by the Valley Cities Motorcycle Club and the Council of Associated Dad's Clubs of Moline in support of their boys baseball program. The following year, the school board declined to approve motorcycle racing at Browning. (*Dispatch*, April 7 and 20, 1948). Even though the Uptown merchants' organization wanted the races to continue, the board yielded to neighbors' complaints about the noise.

Dispatch, May 22, 1941

The "Battle of Thrills" featured daring acts involving animals and machines at Browning Field in May 1941. In this advertising image, world champion cowboy Candy Hammer introduces his horse Spot to automobile thrill driver Flash Williams.

Battle of Thrills: On May 23, 1941, the *Dispatch* headline blared "Automobiles to Be Smashed; Machine and Beast Mix at Browning Field." The newspaper promised:

> Champion cowboys and ace stuntmen who represent Candy Hammer's world championship rodeo and Flash

Williams' thrill drivers . . . will be gyrating out of the chutes upon the backs of maddened Brahma steers and 'killer' broncos, or behind the wheels of speeding automobiles that catapult from high ramps to crash back to the track with pile-driver force and roll and end in a series of demolishing acrobatics.

The Battle of Thrills, held four times on May 23-25, brought to town a herd of cowboys from the West led by Hammer, a former Texas Ranger. They dared to ride long-haired, shaggy Shetland bulls with "man-killing powers," along with Brahma steers from India, "as cunningly murderous as the leopards that stalk them through the jungles, tipping the scales at more than 1,500 pounds." The opening session on Friday evening was the first time this collection of stock had ever been in a public exhibition.

But wait, there's more. Not to be outdone by Hammer, Flash Williams' thrill drivers displayed various tricks while speeding down the track and creating spectacular crashes. Perhaps the highlight on the opening night was the "burning house crash" in which a car was hurtled about fifty feet through a blazing structure (*Dispatch*, May 24). After "several thousand thrill seekers screamed hysterical approval" at the Friday night opener, the *Dispatch* predicted that remaining performances "would shatter all previous attendance records in the local ball field." A city ambulance and a fire truck were on hand for each performance "to be constantly on the alert for the emergencies that are a five to one certainty."

Unscheduled Thrill. Some excitement was created on Friday evening "when two of the brahmas in a nasty mood after being ridden by the cowboys, leaped the fence of their pen and ran amok through a group of Flash Williams' thrill drivers. The stuntmen leaped to the roofs of stunt cars or raced across the field in a manner to indicate that they would take their danger behind the wheel of a speeding automobile." (*Dispatch*, May 24)

Horses Being Judged---
Scene from J. C.-Illowa Show in Moline

Dispatch, July 21, 1947

Horses on the football field for the Illowa Horsemen's Club horse show in July 1947.

Horse Show: In 1947 an enclosed ring and temporary bleachers were set up on the football field at Browning for a horse show held on July 19 and 20. It was the sixth annual Illowa Horsemen's Club horse show, sponsored by the Moline Junior Association of Commerce. Jim Dix commented on the event in the July 21st *Dispatch*:

> Some of the fanciest horses and ponies of the middlewest, slickly groomed and in their best bib and tucker, were exhibited in competition before crowds totaling approximately 2,500 persons at Browning field . . . About 135 finely bred show animals from stables in four states were shown in jumping, riding and harness classes last night, yesterday afternoon and Saturday evening . . . crowds filled the bleachers erected alongside the enclosed ring at each session.

Cash prizes totaling $3,100, along with 35 trophies, were presented to winning entries in ten divisions. Special features of the show included western stock horses galloping through an obstacle course and an exhibition by a group of female riders, The Cavalrettes, from the Utica Ridge Stables.

We're Loyal to You: The University of Illinois band performed at Wharton and/or Browning at least three times, 1982, 1989, and 1995. On Friday night, October 29, 1982, the Illini Marching Band performed at Browning while passing through on the way to Iowa City. The band, along with the Illini Flag Corps and Pompon Squad, performed before and at halftime of the high school football game between Moline and Alleman. The visit was arranged by Moline High band director Louis DiIulio, whose son Tony played trombone for the Illini band.

The Illini band was on its only road trip that season to perform at Iowa's Kinnick Stadium for the Iowa-Illinois football clash on Saturday. Band members stayed overnight with families of Moline band members and were fed a chicken dinner at the high school cafeteria before performing at Browning. To top off the evening, the Illini held a post-game pep rally at Wharton Field House.

Again stopping-over on the way to Iowa City, the band performed at Browning in 1995. On a chilly evening, November 3rd, the Illini appeared with high school bands from both Moline and Rock Island at the football game. Steve Schwaegler, Moline High band director said: "There's nothing like a Big 10 band live and in person. And, it's nice to bring this type of entertainment to the community" (Quad-Cities Online, October 31). The performances of all three bands were later shown on local cable television.

Browning Field Today

In recent decades, numerous improvements have been made to the field and structures at Browning. The cinder track was replaced with an all-weather track in 1972, and in 1973 new light arrays on ninety-foot-tall western red cedar poles were erected to replace the 1930 light poles. In 1995 a new all-metal south grandstand was built to replace the 1916 wooden structure. In 2004 a new brick entryway was added at the east end of the football field, connecting it with the large parking lot. In 2006, as part of a Browning Park improvement project, a new fence and gateway was added to the west side of the football field, opening-up the view of Browning (and Wharton) to the playground and 16th Street. The new structures at either end of the football field used red brick and were designed to blend with existing structures, including the Field House. In 2013, the 1973 lights and their poles were replaced.

Dispatch, September 14, 1989

This section of the bleachers on the north side of Browning Field was about to be repaired when this September 1989 photograph was taken. In that year the Moline Board of Education was considering building a new stadium near the high school, about a mile and a half east of Browning. After considerable discussion, along with public input, the decision was made to renovate Browning Field instead.

M, 1979

C. Roseman, 2013

In 1995 the original south wooden grandstand, erected in 1916, was replaced with a metal structure, and a new press box was added. These photographs compare old "see-through" stands as they appeared in 1979 (top) and the new ones in 2013 (bottom).

Moline Boosters Club. Numerous improvements at both Browning Field and Wharton Field House have been supported by the Moline Boosters Club. A non-profit organization, the club raises money through sales at concession stands and other activities.

C. Roseman, 2013

A new gateway and ticket booth was added to the east end of Browning Field in 2004.

C. Roseman, 2013

Improvements at Browning Park, just west of the football field, included a new fence and entrance to Browning Field, shown here in August 2013. The new fence replaced a row of trees that served as a visual barrier between the football field and the park. Now, both Wharton and Browning can be clearly seen from the park and from 16th Street.

Browning Field viewed from the northeast in the 1990s with the Wharton Field House chimney shown in the lower right of the photograph. At the top is the corner of 16th Street and 23rd Avenue (now Avenue of the Cities). Sometimes referred to as "Ice Cream Corner," the intersection hosts Whitey's and Country Style, two favorite places for fans to visit before and after football games and other events at Browning and Wharton. Whitey's and Country Style both serve ice cream, hard and soft, respectively.

The view from "Ice Cream Corner." This 2013 photograph shows two ice cream palaces, Country Style and Whitey's, with the lights of Browning Field and the roof of Wharton Field House in the background.

Chapter 9

Professional Sports at Browning

"prettiest park in the Valley league" – Moline *Dispatch*

Professional Football

Professional football in Moline dates back to at least 1907, and probably earlier. A number of early twentieth-century Moline teams were organized and played for a season or two – in some cases only a game or two. Among them were the West Ends, the East Ends, and the Illini. These and teams in other communities played limited schedules in October and November and were primarily made up of local players, many with high school football experience, who played for little or no pay. Often referred to as semi-professional teams, they were local clubs composed of men who simply liked to play football.

[Semi-] Professional Football Teams in Moline, 1907-1930

East Ends: 1907-10	Dodgers: 1917
West Ends: 1907-12	Federals: 1917
Olympics: 1912-14	Clubhouse: 1919
Illini: 1910-13	Fans Association: 1919
Indians/Red Men: 1914-17; 1919-30	Tractors/Athletics: 1920
	Wild Cats: 1930
Crescents: 1915-17; 1919	

Sources: Professional Football Archives, online; Rock Island Independents, online

The West Ends and the Illini were the most successful early teams. The West Ends claimed the Illinois state professional championship in 1909 and the Illini were undefeated in nine games in 1910 and 1911. In those two years the Illini played teams from Moline, Peoria, and Spring Valley at Athletic Park before moving to Browning Field in 1912. Athletic Park was located east of Riverside Cemetery on the north side of 4th Avenue between 36th and 37th Streets and was at times also called Three-I League Park, Moline Baseball Park, and Red Men Park.

The Illini played in the first professional game at Browning Field on Sunday, October 6, 1912, the day after the first Moline High School game at Browning. They faced the Olympics, which was playing in its first year. The result was a 0-0 tie over four ten-minute quarters in front of about 1,000 fans. The *Dispatch* (October 7) described the action:

> The forward pass was tried several times, chiefly by the Olympics, but gains in this manner were not large. At least twice opponents intercepted the pass, and three times the man elected failed to catch the ball.

In the second professional game at Browning, the Rock Island Independents defeated the Illini, 6-0, with about 2,000 fans in attendance. The Independents, a team that would claim fame a few years later as one of the original members of the National Football League, began play in Rock Island in 1907.

The Independents in 1912. "The Rock Island Independents were organized . . . around the talents of Arthur W. Salzmann and Frank "Fat" Smith, the stars of the 1911 Rock Island High School team that defeated Moline High School and caused a riot between the fans of the two schools. In their first [game] on October 13, 1912, the Rock Island Independents beat the Moline Illini 6 to 0, a significant feat because the Moline Illini, along with the Evanston North Ends, had claimed the 1911 Illinois state independent football championship." (McClellan, 1998)

Another game with the Independents, which had been scheduled for November 17, was cancelled. The following year, 1913, the Illini beat the Independents 13-0, in a season that included five home games at Browning and one game in Peoria. That was a very active year at Browning Field; the Illini and Olympics played a total of nine games there against other opponents and three against each other. In total, about sixty professional games were played at Browning Field between 1912 and 1930.

The most successful and lasting Moline team was the Indians who played from 1914 to 1930, except for the war year of 1918. They were also called the Red Men because they were sponsored by the local lodge of the Improved Order of Red Men, a fraternal organization. In their first year, they played six games at Browning Field, mostly against local teams, then for the next three seasons played home games at Athletic Park. In total the Indians played about 25 games at Browning. With shorter life spans, the Olympics played there at least fifteen times and the Illini at least ten.

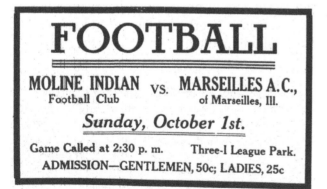

FOOTBALL

MOLINE INDIAN vs. MARSEILLES A.C.,
Football Club of Marseilles, Ill.

Sunday, October 1st.

Game Called at 2:30 p. m.   Three-I League Park.
ADMISSION—GENTLEMEN, 50c; LADIES, 25c

Dispatch, September 30, 1916

In 1916 Athletic Park was also known as "Three-I League Park" because the field was also home to the Moline professional baseball team, the Plow Boys, members of the Three-I League.

Beginning in 1919 the Indians/Red Men made Browning their home field for the remainder of their history. Generally, they played other locals, plus teams scattered across Illinois and Iowa. Among those visiting Browning to play the Indians were: the Rock Island Rialtos (1919); Chicago Boosters (1921); Waterloo A. C. (1922); Rockford Olympics (1922); and Des Moines Henry Ford (1923). Their season won-loss records ranged from poor to fair, and included one or two ties in most years.

The Indians played four games against the Rock Island Independents, a member of the NFL at the time. In 1923 and 1924, the games were close, 9-6 and 7-0. The Independents, however, were not as kind in other years, winning 26-0 in 1922 and 13-0 in 1927. All four games were played at Douglas Park in Rock Island.

None of the Moline teams reached the highest level of pro football at the time, the American Professional Football Association (AFPA), which was formed in 1920 and morphed into the National Football League (NFL) in 1922. The first game in the AFPA, which today is considered to be the first NFL game, was played at Douglas Park, where the Rock Island Independents beat the St. Paul Ideals, 48-0. The Independents continued playing in those leagues through the 1925 season, hosting at Douglas Park some teams familiar to twenty-first century football fans, including the Bears, Chicago Cardinals, Green Bay Packers, and Canton

Dispatch, October 9, 1953

C. Roseman, 2012

On the left, the 1923 Moline Indians team is posing at the east end of Browning Field. That year they had their best record, with seven wins and two ties, losing only to the Independents at Douglas Park in Rock Island. The Indians played only two games at Browning that year, defeating the Des Moines Henry Ford, 25-7, and the Rockford Gophers, 7-2. The 2012 photograph on the right is provided for skeptical readers who wonder if the Indians, seen on the left, were really photographed at Browning. Taken from about the same location, both show the same house in the background.

A Color Barrier Broken then Restored. When Duke Slater suited up for an Independents' game on October 1, 1922, at Douglas Park, he became the first African American lineman to play in the National Football League. On that day he led the Rock Island team to a 19-14 victory over the Green Bay Packers and their quarterback Curly Lambeau. Slater had starred at Clinton, Iowa, High School, then at the   University of Iowa where he was an All-American on some of Iowa's greatest teams of all time. While he was on the team, the Hawkeyes posted a 23-6-1 record. In 1951 he was named to the first class of the College Football Hall of Fame. Slater played five seasons with the Independents and was named All-Pro in three of those seasons; then he played five more for the Chicago Cardinals. He missed only one game as a pro, when the Independents visited the Kansas City Blues in 1924. Slater was not allowed to play because of a "gentlemen's agreement" that African Americans would not play in the state of Missouri. After his football career, Slater became a distinguished lawyer and judge. (Slater Bio, online)

Neal Rozendaal, who wrote a 2012 biography of Duke Slater, summarized the momentous importance of Slater's impact on the NFL. "He single-handedly kept the door open for African-Americans in pro football and delayed a 'color ban' from taking effect in the NFL for seven years. The league wanted to impose a ban in 1927, but Slater's consistently outstanding play wouldn't let them. It wasn't until two years after Slater retired from the NFL that the league finally pushed through a ban on African-Americans that lasted for twelve years until 1946."

Rock Island County Historical Society

This undated photograph shows a baseball game at Douglas Park in Rock Island. Visible are lines for the football field. Both the football Independents and their minor league baseball counterparts, the Islanders, played there for many years. Before being named Douglas Park in 1917, it was known as Island City Park.

(Ohio) Bulldogs. They also played away games at both Wrigley Field and Comiskey Park in Chicago.

After leaving the NFL, the Independents played the 1926 season in the American Football League, the only year of its existence. The AFL included teams from Chicago, New York, Boston, Cleveland, Newark, Philadelphia, Brooklyn, and a travelling team that claimed a home base in Los Angeles but never played in the City of Angels. In that year the Independents played all three of their home games at Browning Field because it had a larger seating capacity than Douglas Park, totaling about 8000 with the new bleachers they set up on the north side of the field. Two of their home games were victories over the Chicago Bulls and the Pacific Coast Golden Bears.

The highlight, however, was on October 3rd when they hosted the New York Yankees [football team] in front of about 5,000 fans. The game brought to Browning two of the greatest stars to ever play football. The Independents' star was Duke Slater, the brilliant lineman from Iowa, and the Yankee star was "Red" Grange, a football legend from the University of Illinois. The game was essentially decided by the middle of the third quarter when the Yankees led 20-0. In his biography of Slater, Rozendall (2012) noted: "Fans flocked for home with the Yankees comfortably ahead, Grange on the bench for the entire fourth quarter, and a pouring rain dampening everyone's interest." Later in the season, the Independents lost again to New York, 35-0, in front of 35,000 at Yankee Stadium.

After the AFL folded at the end of the 1926 season, a diminished version of the Independents

Dispatch, November 9, 1929

According to this *Dispatch* advertisement, the Indians were supposed to play the Muskies on November 10, 1929. However, manager Eddie Weime cancelled the game because of bad weather, for fear that he would not be able to cover the $250 he had guaranteed the Muscatine team. The game was subsequently rescheduled for November 24th, when the two teams battled to a 0-0 tie.

returned to Douglas Park for the 1927 and 1928 seasons. It was a far cry from the NFL. They played mostly nearby teams and won only three games at home – against the Clinton Legions, Chicago Karpen Indians, and the Moline Indians – all in front of smaller crowds than they had been accustomed to previously.

Giants: On October 12, 1930, the Indians faced the Illinois Giants from Peoria, known also as the "Colored Giants" because of the predominance of African American players on the team. Giants players included brothers Ernie and "Ink" Page, who had starred in high school at Peoria Central.

The Moline Indians continued to play through 1930, a season in which they lost two away games and posted a 3-2 record at Browning. In their very last game, on November 2, they prevailed 6-0 over the Moline Wild Cats, a team whose members were mostly former Moline High School players. Among their stars were ball-carriers Leroy Esterdahl and Joe Choate.

The Galloping Ghost. An advertisement for the Independents-Yankees game at Browning Field in the *Dispatch* (October 1, 1926) introduced Grange as "the greatest of all football stars; one famous from coast to coast; a product of Illinois [Wheaton]; one who really needs no introduction to the people in this section as America's greatest football warrior."

The Bears at Browning

The Rock Island Independents re-emerged in 1936 as a member of the Northwest Professional Football League, which included teams from Iowa, Minnesota, Wisconsin, and Michigan. The league lasted for only three years and the Independents were in it for only one. On a Tuesday evening, September 22nd – five days before their regular season began – the Independents hosted the NFL Chicago Bears in perfect weather at Browning Field. The game was sponsored by the Moline Junior Association of Commerce, whose members worked hard to sell advanced tickets hoping for a large crowd to cover the costs required to attract the Bears. In addition:

> Practically the entire membership of the organization will be working in one capacity or another at the field. A special detail of police has been secured to handle traffic and to police the grounds. The gridiron itself is in excellent condition and the lighting plant has been completely reconditioned for the fall prep season, assuring the pro teams of probably the best lighting they will enjoy at any time. (*Argus*, September 22)

This was the only game the Bears ever played in Moline and they were heavily favored to beat the Independents. Since the origins of the NFL in the early 1920s, the Bears had experienced only one losing season. They were very strong in the early 1930s – since 1931 they had won 36 regular season games and lost seven. The game at Browning Field attracted about 4,000 fans and was considered a success from an attendance standpoint. Some considered it a success from a football standpoint as well, since the Independents managed to score on the mighty Bears! The day after the Independents lost 34-6, Lynn Callaway of the *Dispatch* attempted to comfort local fans in their loss:

> The Rock Island eleven, obviously outweighed and just as certainly outnumbered and surpassed in football skill, put up a remarkable battle against their

famous rivals. After failing to cash in on a golden opportunity to score in the opening minutes of play and after being beaten down by a human steamroller which had ten blockers for the ball carrier on almost every play, the plucky Indees, coached by Joe Kurth of Notre Dame, fought to the finish and were finally rewarded with a touchdown on a beautiful play.

The previous demise of the Moline Indians in 1930, and this last attempt to revive the Rock Island Independents in 1936, represented the end of a golden era of professional football in the Quad Cities, which had peaked in the mid-1920s. In later decades, a number of local semi-professional football teams were formed. They lasted for varying lengths of time and played teams in nearby towns and across the Midwest. Some teams played periodically at Browning Field, including the Quad City Mohawks in the 1950s and 1970s, but no team claimed Browning as a home field for a sustained period of time.

C. Roseman, 2013

Legendary Chicago Bears player Bronko Nagurski scored a touchdown at Browning Field in the 1936 Bears victory over the Independents. In 2013, 77 years later, a nostalgic urge brought him back to inspect the field.

Plow Boys Baseball

Moline's longest-lasting minor league baseball team, the Plow Boys (called simply "The Plows" by some), played in two different leagues during its history from 1914 to 1941. They were part of the Three-I [Iowa, Illinois, Indiana] League from 1914 through 1923, then again from 1937 through 1941. In between, from 1924 through 1932, they played in the Mississippi Valley League. The team did not play during times of national strife: 1918 during World War I, the Great Depression years of the early 1930s, and World War II years in the early 1940s. In an attempt to bring back minor league baseball after the war, a new team, the Moline A's, was formed in 1947 as a farm team of the Philadelphia Athletics. Playing in the Central Association, they suffered from poor attendance and lasted only a season-and-a-half. In mid-season 1948 they moved down the road to become the Kewanee A's. (Records and other information on the Moline minor league baseball teams can be found at Baseball Reference, online.)

The Three-I League began play in 1901 with eight teams including those from Rock Island and Davenport. The Moline Plow Boys began play in league in 1914, their first season as an official minor league baseball team. The team from

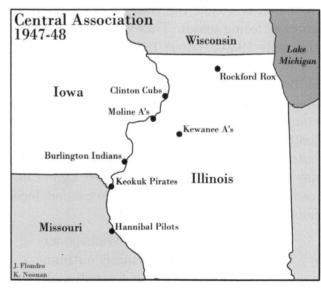

Minor league baseball teams that played in the same leagues as the Plow Boys and Moline A's, beginning in 1920 when the Plows first played at Browning Field.

232

Athletic Park, or Three-I League Park, as pictured in the Moline High School annual, *M*, in 1916. The high school played football games there in 1915 and 1916. Professional baseball and football teams played there early in the twentieth century before moving to Browning Field.

Danville, the Speakers, had moved to Moline on July 14th of that year to become the Plow Boys. Through the 1919 season they played at Three-I Park.

In their second season, 1915, the Plow Boys earned the league championship for the second half of the season by beating the Davenport Blue Sox in a best-of-seven playoff, winning four games to Davenport's one. The *Dispatch* (July 31, 1928) boasted on the season: "In winning its first flag, Moline, one of the smallest cities in the Three-I circuit, put such burgs as Peoria, Rockford and Davenport to shame by playing to a total season attendance of 42,954." Also, for at least five years beginning in 1915, the Plow Boys hosted the Chicago White Sox for pre-season games. The Sox would typically play games in the Southwest, Texas, Oklahoma, and Kansas, before visiting the Tri-Cities on their way home to Chicago. On April 13, 1915, the Plow Boys beat the major league team 5-4 in front of a crowd of 1505 at Three-I Field.

Plow Boys' Three-I League Records, 1914-23

Season	Record	Place	League Champion
1914 (Danville)	26-53		
1914 (Moline)	20-33	8th	Davenport
1915 (1st half)	35-32	4th	Davenport
1915 (2nd half)	40-19	1st	Moline
1916	59-76	5th	Peoria
1917	27-38	6th	Peoria
1919	40-81	6th (last)	Bloomington
1920	69-70	4th	Bloomington
1921	78-55	1st	Moline
1922	49-89	8th (last)	Terre Haute
1923	45-91	8th (last)	Decatur

Source: Three-I League, online

In 1919, Warren Giles became president of the Moline Fans Association, which operated the Plow Boys. Giles was born in Tiskilwa, Illinois, and grew up in Moline. Even though he had no previous baseball experience, his leadership of the Plow Boys increased interest in the team and its performance on the field, which culminated in a Three-I League championship in 1921. Giles went on to become the general manager of the major league Cincinnati Reds, 1937 to 1951, and then was president of the National League, a position he held for eighteen years. He was elected to the Baseball Hall of Fame in 1979.

Giles—coach; Bergsten, Ryberg,
Crampton, Swanson,
Conrey, Johnson.

M, 1916

For a good part of the first half of the twentieth century, both boys and girls in each of the four classes at Moline High School, freshman through senior, organized basketball teams. They would play each other for the school championship. During at least two seasons, 1917 and 1918, Warren Giles coached class teams. In 1916 he coached both the juniors, which won the tournament, and the sophomores, which lost to the juniors in the championship. Here is Giles pictured with his sophomore class team.

The 1919 Plow Boys' season – the last they would play at Three-I Park – began with another exhibition game against the Chicago White Sox. It was played on April 21st, the day before the Sox opened the regular season in Chicago. After the Chicagoans arrived in Rock Island at 3:30 a.m. on a special train, their car was brought to Moline for a 7:30 breakfast. The Sox spent all day in Moline, leaving at midnight.

The game was scheduled to begin at 4 p.m. to accommodate first-shift factory workers, who would get off work at 3 or 3:30. The work train, which carried employees of the Silvis shops to their homes in Moline, Rock Island, and Davenport, stopped at 37th Street to allow workers to attend the game. Some merchants closed early so their clerks could attend. The outcome of the

game was summarized by Johnny Walker in the *Dispatch* (April 22):

> Bombarding the outer gardens with base knocks, the Chicago Hose trampled over the Plow Boys and 1,700 supporting fans yesterday to the tune of 13 to 0 in a game featured principally by the nine misplays committed by the inner and outer defenses of the Hughesmen [a reference to Plows' manager George Hughes]. Of the thirteen runs scored by the Hosiery, only four were earned, the kicks accounting for nine of the tallies.

In preparation for the game, concessionaire "Curly" Anderson redecorated the concession stand under the grandstand and stocked supplies. No doubt to the delight of many fans, "A special order for peanuts of the hump-back, double jointed variety has been wired to California, or wherever they grow." (*Dispatch,* April 18)

To Browning

With Warren Giles in charge, the team moved to Browning Field for the 1920 season. In the spring of that year, a new baseball diamond was laid out with the following distances, in feet, from home plate to the fences: 550 (left field), 440 (center), and 377 (right). A new crescent-shaped baseball grandstand was built behind home plate, at the east end of the football field. A large canopy covered the curved stands and in 1925 a similar covering was added above the third base stands. First-base stands were added but never covered. The *Dispatch* (April 1) described the new facility:

> Browning field, after Fred Brandt, superintendent of parks in Moline, gets through with it, will be one of the most beautiful minor league athletic fields in the country. The fence, which will be of heavy wire mesh, will be hidden from view on the inside by a solid mass of green shrubbery and vines, not only presenting a beautiful background for the ball game, but also compelling

spectators to visit the box office in order to see the game. The grandstand, players' benches, and press stand will be painted a battleship gray and the huge bleachers along the south side of the field and along the first base line will be cleaned and painted. The clubhouse in the rear of the stand is also to be painted in gray and the playing field will be modeled after the best of the major league diamonds.

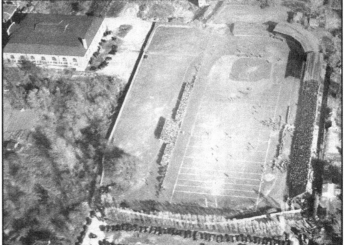

M, 1940

A view of the baseball grandstands at Browning Field. In the background are the crescent-shaped stands and canopy behind home plate, constructed in 1920. The other canopy, over the left field stands, was added in 1925.

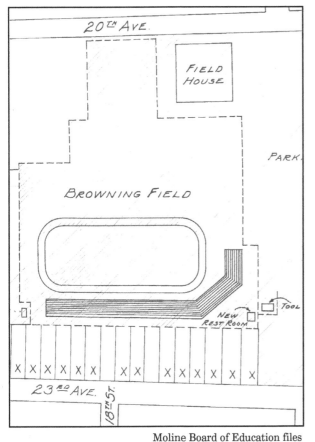

Moline Board of Education files

M, 1930

The 1952 map and the 1929 aerial photograph, taken from the west, together show the baseball diamond and grandstands at Browning Field, and their locations relative to Wharton Field House.

The first game at the new Browning baseball diamond was on April 12, 1920, before the regular season started and before the new facility was dedicated. For fifth time, the Chicago White Sox came to town to play the Plow Boys. The Sox were a strong team, which in 1920 came close to repeating their American League championship. They failed to do so when several players were suspended near the end of the season as a result of the Black Sox scandal from the 1919 World Series.

The exhibition game was scheduled for 2:30 p.m., so the Sox could catch an early train to Chicago. But the Sox brought to town only part of their team – apparently not the strongest part – and lost to the Plows 7-1. Newspaper reports noted that they were not only incompetent but also in a hurry to finish the game to catch the train. Pressure had been put on Giles to cancel the game because of very cold weather. He refused and only 500 fans showed up. However, they all probably heard Giles: "That loud persistent noise in the grandstand was President Giles training for the regular Three-I season." (*Dispatch*, April 13)

The new facility was officially dedicated three weeks later, on Wednesday afternoon, May 5th, in conjunction with a game against Terre Haute. Stores and some factories closed to allow employees to attend the event, which began with a parade through downtown Moline. Fifty cars carried players from both teams and dignitaries

in the parade. The 2,600 attending the dedication saw Mayor Charles Skinner throw out the first pitch and the Plows win 4-1. The Terre Haute team was managed by a Hall of Fame pitcher, "Three Finger" Mordecai Brown.

Rock Island County Historical Society

This undated photograph shows some of the Plow Boys near the dugout at Browning Field, probably wearing home and away uniforms.

In their second season at their new home, 1921, Giles arranged for Connie Mack, head of the major league Philadelphia A's, to send some players to Moline along with his son, Earle Mack, who would manage the team. "Earle, who played a snappy first base and who could score more runs on fewer hits than any pilot Moline fans ever had seen, was a 'wow' from the start." (*Dispatch*, July 31, 1928)

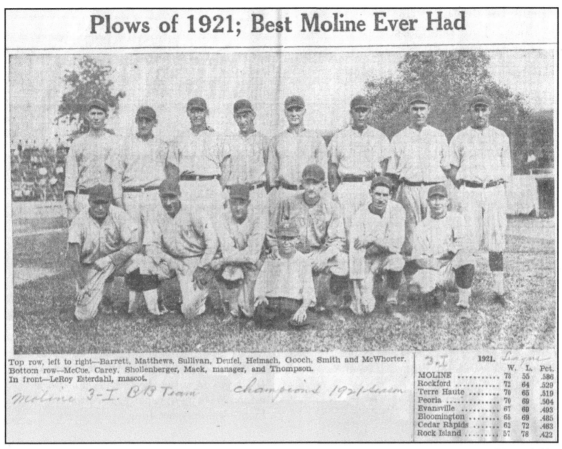

Plows of 1921; Best Moline Ever Had

Top row, left to right—Barrett, Matthews, Sullivan, Deufel, Heimach, Gooch, Smith and McWhorter. Bottom row—McCue, Carey, Shollenberger, Mack, manager, and Thompson. In front—LeRoy Esterdahl, mascot.

3-I	1921.		
	W.	L.	Pct.
MOLINE	78	55	.586
Rockford	72	64	.529
Terre Haute	70	65	.519
Peoria	70	69	.504
Evansville	67	69	.493
Bloomington	65	69	.485
Cedar Rapids	62	72	.463
Rock Island	57	78	.422

Dispatch files

The Moline Plow Boys were Three-I League champions in 1921.

That year the Plows won their second Three-I League championship, finishing with 78 wins and 55 losses, 7½ games ahead of Rockford.

After a couple of poor seasons, in terms of both wins and attendance, the Plows moved to the Mississippi Valley League in 1924, the first of their nine seasons in that circuit. The *Dispatch* (July 31, 1928) claimed that visiting teams in this league called Browning the 'prettiest park in the Valley league.' The team was moderately successful during this eight year stretch, placing second three times. Except for the informal arrangement with the Philadelphia A's in the early 1920s, the Plow Boys did not have a farm-team affiliation until 1932, their last year in the Mississippi Valley League. The Detroit Tigers took them on that year and hired Dutch Lorbeer to manage the team and play catcher, the result being a sixth place finish. The league lasted one more year before closing down after the 1933

Rock Island County Historical Society

Opening day poster of the 1922 Three-I League in Moline. General Admission tickets cost 50 cents and Grandstand tickets went for 25 cents.

237

season, during the depths of the Great Depression. The Rock Island Islanders were the only team to play through all Mississippi Valley League years, 1922-1933.

Plow Boys' Mississippi Valley League Records, 1924-32

Season	Record	Place	League Champion
1924	59-65	5th	Waterloo
1925	73-52	2nd	Cedar Rapids
1926	71-50	2nd	Ottumwa
1927	63-55	5th	Dubuque
1928	69-54	2nd	Waterloo
1929	63-63	4th	Cedar Rapids
1930	63-62	4th	Cedar Rapids
1931	68-58	3rd	Keokuk
1932	55-66	6th	Davenport

Source: Baseball Reference, online

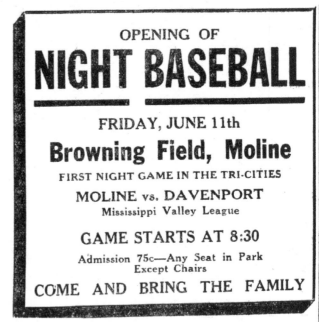

Argus, July 9, 1930

The "first night [baseball] game in the Tri-Cities" was held at Browning Field on July 11, 1930. This advertisement in the *Argus* from two days earlier announces the big event, although the newspaper copy editor missed the typo: the month was July, not June.

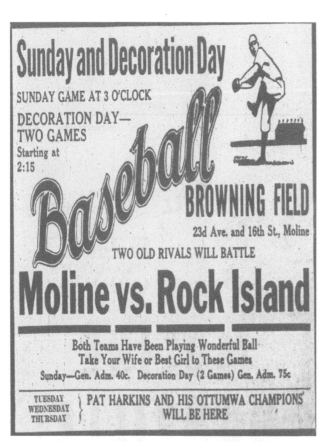

Dispatch, May 28, 1927

Athletic rivalries between Moline and Rock Island were not limited to high schools. In this 1927 Mississippi Valley League game the Plow Boys hosted the Islanders.

Courtesy of Jerry Wallaert

Annual passes to Plow Boys games from 1923 when they played in the Three-I League and 1928 when they played in the Mississippi Valley League.

Lights Go Up, Lights Come Down

In the summer of 1930, eight wooden poles supporting lights were installed for the football and baseball fields at Browning Field. On the evening of July 11th, 3,611 fans saw the Plow Boys host the Davenport Blue Sox in a game that began at 8:30. It was the first night baseball game in the Tri-Cities and the first athletic contest under the lights at Browning. The *Dispatch* (July 12) set the scene:

> While the beauty of the scene held the watchers in their seats until 11 p.m., the Moline section found another very sound reason for enjoying the program to the utmost. This was furnished by the scoreboard, which read 8 to 5 in the Plows' favor at the finish.

Beginning that year three of the light poles had to be removed each season from right and center field to accommodate baseball, and then reinstalled for the football season. This practice ended in 1948 when the poles were rearranged to accommodate both sports without moving them twice a year (*Dispatch*, April 20). Perhaps

Night Baseball Scene at Browning Field

Argus, July 12, 1930

The first night baseball game in Moline and the Tri-Cities drew 3,611 fans to Browning Field. This *Argus* photograph, which focuses on the left field covered bleachers, was probably taken from atop the crescent-shaped canopy behind home plate.

as the result of having been uprooted and re-rooted each year, one of them came crashing down in 1969. It fell onto some bleachers on the north side of the football field, having rotted at the bottom. In 1973, the 1930 wooden light poles were removed and replaced by new light arrays on four new wooden poles.

Dispatch files

Dispatch files

During a windstorm on October 9, 1969, this light pole fell onto the north football bleachers, having rotted at the bottom. The crash occurred shortly after the completion of an afternoon sophomore game in which Moline defeated Alleman 24-21. No one was injured. The original 1930 poles were replaced in 1973.

New light arrays and poles being installed, August 2013. The original Browning Field light poles lasted 43 years, from 1930 to 1973. The next set was composed of four magnificent masts of western red cedar, ninety feet tall. After forty years, in 2013, they were replaced with four metal poles. The newer ones are about the same height and made of galvanized steel.

Night Baseball Comes to the Minor Leagues The lighting of Browning Field in July 1930 came during the first season of night baseball in the minor leagues. The first professional baseball game under the lights was at Western League Park in Des Moines, Iowa, on May 2nd of that year. Almost 12,000 fans were on hand to see the home team Demons defeat the Wichita Aviators, 13-6. The idea of night baseball had drawn so much interest nationally that the NBC radio network agreed to broadcast the game. The start of the game was delayed because, owing to scheduling conflicts, the network could not start coverage until 10:30 p.m. eastern time. (Iowa Cubs, online)

During the 1930 season, the Mississippi Valley League was quick to adopt night baseball. The night before lights were introduced at Browning on July 11th, the first night game was played at Burlington between the Bees and the visiting Rock Island Islanders. An advertisement for the game, placed in the *Argus* on July 8th, urged Islander fans to drive to Burlington for the game where they would find "ample parking space inside the grounds." By mid-July, at least six teams in the league were playing under home-field lights: Burlington, Moline, Rock Island, Cedar Rapids, Dubuque, and Waterloo. However another five years would pass before the first night game in the major leagues, which was held in Cincinnati on May 24, 1935.

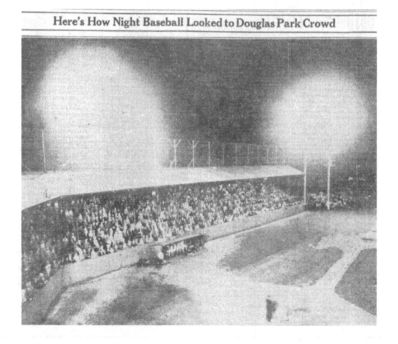

Here's How Night Baseball Looked to Douglas Park Crowd

On July 14, 1930, three days after night baseball was introduced at Browning Field, Douglas Park in Rock Island held its first night game. Maurice Corken of the Argus observed: "Baseball under artificial lights was a revelation to the crowd which packed the grandstand, the regular bleachers and the two auxiliary stands in right and left fields." That evening the Islanders defeated the Keokuk Indians 3-1.

The 1938 Plow Boys team lined up on the Browning infield with Wharton Field House in the background.

Back to the Three-I League With the Cubs

The Plow Boys re-emerged in the Three-I League in 1937, starting a four-year stint as a farm club for the Chicago Cubs. They secured the league championship in the second half of that season by winning a playoff series against the Clinton Owls, four games to two. The glory of their title, however, was somewhat diminished by the fact that two of the six teams – the Bloomington Bengals and the Terre Haute Tots – had dropped out of the league at the conclusion of the first half of the season on July 3. This left only three teams for the Plows to play in the second half, Clinton, the Decatur Commodores, and the Peoria Reds. Season attendance at Browning in 1937 was about 40,000, an average of approximately 850 per game.

Plow Boys' Three-I League Records, 1937-41

Season	Record	Place	League Champion
1937 (1st half)	33-25	2nd	Clinton
1937 (2nd half)	41-16	1st	Moline
1938	67-59	3rd	Evansville
1939	49-73	7th	Cedar Rapids
1940	46-78	7th	Cedar Rapids
1941	43-82	8th (last)	Evansville

Source: Three-I League, online

In their second season as the parent club of the Plow Boys, the Chicago Cubs came to town for their final stop on a spring pre-season tour. On April 14, 1938, they faced the Plows in a Thursday afternoon exhibition game. Local merchants took advantage of the event by promoting special "Cubs Day" sales through advertisements in the *Dispatch* on April 13th. Two major downtown stores, Sears and Montgomery Wards, devoted full-page ads to Cubs Day.

The visiting team arrived early by train and spent part of the morning signing autographs in the lobby of the LeClaire Hotel. The 3,800 fans who appeared for the 1:30 game were treated to an early Plow Boys' lead, 3-0. Cubs manager Charlie Grimm had promised to play his regulars for at least half of the game. He kept his promise, and by the 6th inning the regulars were in and the rout was on. In the end the Cubs prevailed 18-4. (*Dispatch*, April 15)

Dispatch, April 11, 1938

Tuck Stainback, a reserve outfielder for the Cubs, signs autographs before the Cubs-Plow Boys game in 1938. The *Dispatch* claimed the crowd of 3,800 "was one of the largest ever to see a game at Browning field."

Hack Hits Triple in Moline

Cubs' player Stan Hack at the plate, batting against the Plow Boys, with the scoreboard and the Field House in the background. The Plow Boys' catcher is Jim Steiner and the umpire is Eddie Borski.

Cubs' Curse?

It was almost as if the Cubs, on that April day, had spread to the Plows their unique and long-term practice of mediocrity. In the season of the first Cubs visit, 1938, the Plows dropped to third place in the standings, and thereafter their fortunes declined precipitously, both on the diamond and in the stands. In their last two years as a Cubs' farm team, 1939 and 1940, they had sunk to seventh place. And in both of those years, the Cubs again visited Browning Field.

The 1939 and 1940 the Cubs' visits were at mid-season. On July 31, 1939, 3,557 fans saw the Cubs win 7-4, although apparently their manager, Gabby Hartnett, made adjustments in the lineup to keep the game close. Lynn Callaway of the *Dispatch* noted that the game was not exciting but that star player "Dizzy Dean stole the show and made the expenditure of a dollar or more which each adult fan had to shell out worthwhile." Calloway went on:

> The climax came, however, after the ball game was all over and almost everyone else had gone home. Dizzy missed the train which had been held up forty-five minutes in Moline to accommodate the Chicago Team. 'I was takin' a bath up in my room,' was his explanation. An automobile was commandeered and the

big pitcher was raced to East Moline where the Rock Island Lines obligingly held up the long over-due train another ten minutes. Diz was stowed safely away aboard the diner before the train resumed its eastward journey.

Billy Herman batting for the Cubs at Browning Field in 1939 in front of 3,557 fans. Visible in the background are the right field stands at the east end of Browning Field.

The Cubs came back to Moline on July 8, 1940. The *Chicago Tribune* (July 9) mused: "The Chicago Cubs, enjoying a holiday from major league competition, defeated the Moline plows of the Three-Eye league, 8 to 7, in a loosely played game today. Nearly 1,200 [actually 1,122] fans enjoyed the clowning of Gabby Hartnett, who was behind the plate for the final four innings." Callaway of the *Dispatch* added: "Hartnett and his carefree charges apparently did not want to make it look too bad, so they clowned the last few innings." Only about one-third as many fans showed up to see the Cubs in 1940 compared to 1939. It was the last visit of the Cubs to Browning Field.

Argus, July 9, 1940

Managers Gabby Hartnett of the Cubs and Mike Gazella of the Plow Boys met before the July 1940 game at Browning.

In 1940 the Plow Boys attracted only about 16,000 fans. To raise additional revenue for the team the Moline Fans Association sponsored special events that year as they had done in the past. In addition to the date with the Cubs in July, these included a special appearance of Babe Ruth in June and an August 8th boxing show attended by 1,500. Nonetheless, their final year with the Three-I, 1941, was equally disappointing – they earned last place, again in front of a total of 16,000 home fans.

The Bambino to the Rescue?

On June 26, 1940, Babe Ruth came to Browning to exhibit his hitting prowess before a game between the Plows Boys and the Springfield Brownies. A local urban legend has it that "the Bambino" hit balls from home plate in Browning Field onto the roof of Wharton Field House. Not so, according to the *Dispatch* (June 27), which reported that Ruth hit 24 of 33 pitches gently delivered to him by Plows' manager Mike Gazella, a former teammate of Ruth. Only one of the Bronx Bomber's blasts went over the fence, a 340 footer that landed near the Field House, but not on its roof. Total attendance was 1,752, the largest of the season. It included 1,058 men's and 266 ladies' paid admissions, plus the knot-hole gang and some children who were admitted free through park programs. The Plows beat the Brownies 9-8 on a bases-loaded walk in the ninth inning.

Left hook? According to Jack Dye, Babe Ruth played golf at Short Hills Country Club with Herman Nelson, Ax Adolphson, and others during his visit to the Quad Cities. Apparently Ruth had a left hook, at least in his golf drives.

Ruth was in town to lead a baseball clinic at Davenport's Municipal Stadium (now Modern Woodman Park). The retired home-run king was accompanied by his wife, daughter, and some big-name baseball players. The Davenport *Democrat and Leader* (June 23) noted: "Saturday afternoon the Babe's 10-day baseball school, under the auspices of Kaaba Shrine, opened in earnest with approximately 60 youngsters being put thru their paces on the levee front before the watchful eyes of the star-studded staff." The stars included former major-leaguers Rabbit Maranville, Hippo Vaughn, Bob O'Farrell, and Jack Sheehan. Rogers Hornsby, who two years later would be elected to the baseball Hall of Fame, was scheduled to appear but had to pull out at the last minute when he was named manager of the minor league team in Oklahoma City.

The Show Goes On During the week of Babe Ruth's visit several crowd-pleasing activities were planned (*Democrat and Leader*, June 24, 25, and 28, 1940). One was to attempt "one of the greatest tricks in baseball – catch a ball from an airplane." A plane was to fly over Municipal Stadium on Thursday, June 27th, and drop baseballs to waiting players below. Apparently the authorities took a dim view of the idea, and would not allow the plane to fly so low over the field.

The cancellation did not spoil the event, as another gimmick was successfully staged that evening. It was a contest to determine if anyone could throw a baseball from the street to the top of the Union Bank building in downtown Davenport, a height of 115 feet. Strict rules were specified for the contest. Among them: "Anyone breaking a window and attempting to run from the scene may be collared by the law," and "No substitutes will be allowed, since it has been claimed already that lemons and one potato have been found on the roof." When told about the contest, Ruth said it could not be done and he, himself, could not throw a baseball that high. He went on to say: "There's a difference between throwing a lemon and a baseball that high. A lemon will travel better in the air." The Babe was wrong – six of 27 entrants accomplished the feat (throwing baseballs, we assume).

Rock Island County Historical Society

These pro players are unidentified and the photograph undated, but the pose is precious with Wharton Field House in the background.

Philadelphia, Moline, Kewanee

After World War II, professional baseball returned to Browning Field, but for only a season-and-a-half. In 1947 the major league Philadelphia Athletics established a farm team in Moline, the A's. They played in the Central Association, which had teams affiliated with the Cubs, St. Louis Browns, Cincinnati, Cleveland, and Pittsburgh. The Moline A's proceeded to finish last in the league in 1947, losing $33,000 for the parent club in the process.

Moline A's Central Association Records, 1947-48

Season	Record	Place	League Champion
1947	51-74	6th (last)	Clinton
1948	53-74*	6th (last)	Clinton
	*17-25 in Moline		

(Source: Sumner, 2000)

In early June 1948, Harry O'Donnell, chief scout for the Philadelphia Athletics, visited Moline and lamented that the A's had "drawn a little over 3,000 adult paid admissions in 16 home games in Browning field. That's less than 200 per game. You can't even begin to come near breaking even with that kind of attendance." Most teams in the Central Association were averaging over 1000 per game, including the last place club, Burlington. (*Dispatch*, June 11)

The A's organization fretted not only about the poor attendance, but also about their loss of money ($10,000 so far in 1948). However, yet another problem soon arose. The right field fence had been moved in to a distance of 216 feet from home plate to accommodate tents to be used in the upcoming Moline centennial celebration. (*Dispatch*, June 11) This may have been the final straw and by mid-June the organization had decided to move the team to Kewanee.

The last Moline A's game was to have been played on Friday, June 18, 1948, but the field was in no condition to accommodate baseball. Because the outfield was full of ruts created by trucks and tractors preparing for the centennial, the game was cancelled. Thus ended over three decades of regular professional baseball at Browning Field. The Kewanee A's finished the 1948 season with a losing record, but won 68 and lost 60 in the following year. Then, after the 1949 season, both the A's and the Central Association folded.

Enter the Tigers

Professional baseball returned to Browning Field for a brief period in the spring of 1951 thanks to the spring rise in the Mississippi River. The stadium in Davenport was flooded, so the Quad City Tigers of the Three-I League played six games at Browning, the first against Evansville on April 29th. The *Dispatch* (April 28) described the preparations for the opening day:

> The field has been undergoing a 'face lifting' the past three days; the lights have been moved from the football field to the baseball field, and the grandstand and bleachers have been given a thorough cleaning . . . The usual opening day ceremonies will be held, and the first ball will be pitched by Alderman Jesse McCandless, representing Mayor Hjalmar Oakleaf, who is out of the city. Mayors of the other Quad-Cities will also take part.

Dispatch, April 28, 1951

The Quad City Tigers played six games at Browning Field in the spring of 1951 when the Mississippi River flooded Municipal Stadium in Davenport. The opening game against Evansville drew 1878 fans.

Chapter 10

Celebrations at Wharton Field House and Browning Field

"the greatest day in the history of the world" – Rock Island *Argus*

Courtesy of Chris Carmack

This aerial photograph of Browning Field and Wharton Field House was taken by Chris Carmack on April 9, 2008. The view from the southeast also shows the large parking lot on the right, east of the Field House, and Browning Park on the left, west of the football field.

Throughout the twentieth century, and into the twenty-first, Wharton Field House and Browning Field have played significant roles as gathering places for a variety of community events. None were more significant than the gatherings that celebrated milestones in local and national affairs, including cessation of war, graduations, and anniversaries. This chapter recalls some of these celebrations.

Armistice Day, 1918

On Monday, November 11, 1918, the *Argus* urged people to come together for a grand parade to be held that evening in Moline as a climax to the World War I victory celebration. "Every man, woman and child is urged to participate in the celebration in honor of the greatest day in the history of the world." Attended by 15,000, the parade started at 6 p.m. in downtown Moline, wended its way through the business district and residential areas, and ended at Browning Field. A huge bonfire was built at Browning in which an effigy of the Kaiser was "cremated." At the celebration "15,000 voices united in singing America." (*Argus*, November 12) Later in the evening a community dance attended by 2,000 was held at the ballroom of the Manufacturers Hotel in downtown Moline. (The Manufacturers was the largest hotel in Moline at the time, but would be upstaged four years later by the opening of the LeClaire Hotel.)

Graduation Ceremonies

Since 1934, Moline High School has used the Field House for its graduation ceremonies in the late spring of each year. Prior to 1952, January ceremonies for mid-year graduates were also held at the big arena.

When Ben McAdams was superintendent of schools in the 1990s, a proposal was put forth to move the ceremonies to The Mark of The Quad Cities, which was opened in 1993. Located in downtown Moline, The Mark (now the iWireless Center) is much larger and, more importantly given the time of the year for these ceremonies, it is air conditioned. However, tradition-minded Moliners insisted that the annual event continue at Wharton. Sweaty high school graduation ceremonies will continue for the foreseeable future.

Other graduation exercises have been held at the Field House including some for Black Hawk College in the 1970s. One of the more unusual served much younger graduates. On June 1, 1949, 283 eighth graders from 56 village and rural schools participated in graduation ceremonies at Wharton. Rock Island County superintendent of schools, Floyd Shetter, delivered the keynote address, "People Are Good," and expressed his appreciation to the Moline schools for use of the Field House. Moline superintendent, Alex Jardine, welcomed the graduates to the Rock Island County high schools.

M, 1961

A central feature of Moline High School graduation ceremonies at the Field House is the big M near the north end of the floor through which faculty and graduates process. This photograph is from the 1960 ceremony.

Dispatch, May 26, 1984

1984 Moline High School graduation ceremony.

In the twenty-first century a packed house is rare at the Field House. The annual high school graduation ceremonies are exceptions. The 2013 event, shown here, filled the arena to the rafters.

C. Roseman, 2013

John Deere Centennial

One of the more spectacular events at Wharton Field House was Deere & Company's six-day 100th anniversary celebration in 1937. Writing in the *Dispatch* on April 13th, Russell Gingles summarized the opening night of the event:

> Transformed into a huge theater and decorated with hundreds of flags and banners, Moline field house last night was jammed with an estimated crowd close to 5,000 persons who alternately thrilled and applauded while on stage

and screen programs were presented in commemoration of the 100th anniversary of the invention of the steel plow by John Deere.

The seven programs, six held Monday through Saturday evenings and one on Saturday afternoon, were produced for the benefit of John Deere employees, family members, and guests; not the general public. Workers at the various Deere facilities in the Quad Cities were parsed among the performances as follows:

Deere & Company archives

On the first night of the company's centennial celebration, Deere employees and their families filled the arena.

Deere & Company archives

Each of the seven sessions drew about 5,000 people.

Monday and Tuesday evenings:
Plow Works; Deere and Mansur Works

Wednesday, Friday, and Saturday evenings and Saturday afternoon:
Spreader Works; Union Malleable Iron company; Wagon Works; Plow Works; and general offices

Friday and Saturday evenings:
Harvester Works

Blue Blacksmith. The highlight of each session was a showing of the movie "The Blacksmith's Gift" starring Monte Blue, which was produced for Deere & Company. It tells the story of John Deere's development of the steel plow in Grand Detour, Illinois. Blue appeared on stage before each showing "dressed in a crimson shirt and wearing the leather apron and boots of the blacksmith he characterizes" (*Dispatch*, April 13). Monte Blue, born Gerard Montgomery Bluefeather, was fifty years old at the time. He performed in silent films, the talkies, and even television in his later career.

Deere & Company archives

For the Deere centennial and numerous other events at Wharton, a large stage at the south end of the arena was used for performances and presentations.

1837 — 1937

John Deere
CENTENNIAL PROGRAM

MOLINE FIELD HOUSE
MOLINE, ILLINOIS
April 12th to 17th Inclusive

PROGRAM

PROLOGUE · · MONTE BLUE

"THE BLACKSMITH'S GIFT"
(On the Screen)

HERBIE KAY AND HIS ORCHESTRA

DOROTHY BYTON'S 12 DEBUTANTES

FIVE TIP-TOP GIRLS

JESS LIBONATI TRIO

WALTER NILSSON

ALLEN & KENT

DOROTHY BYTON'S 12 DEBUTANTES

KARRE LE BARRON TRIO

ADA BROWN

3 SAMUELS & HARRIET HAYES

SIX LUCKY BOYS

YOST'S 12 SINGING ENSIGNS

DOROTHY BYTON'S 12 DEBUTANTES

FINALE

The cover of the printed program for the Deere centennial features the man himself. The inside of the program details the diversity of entertainment. Like numerous festivals at Wharton, this was a real variety show. Following the movie, numerous vaudeville acts were presented. The *Dispatch* of April 13th proclaimed that Deere spared no expense "to assemble the best in the entertainment world." Included in the assemblage was Herbie Kay "and his popular radio and dance band. Better known perhaps than any other orchestra on the airwaves." Among the individual acts were Walter Nilsson, "as clever a comedy cyclist as vaudeville has ever produced"; and the Six Lucky Boys, "acrobats who greatly overshadow the usual stage and state fair variety."

Monte Blue, right, leading a performance by the orchestra, singers, and dancers.

Monte Blue on stage performing his black-smithing duties.

251

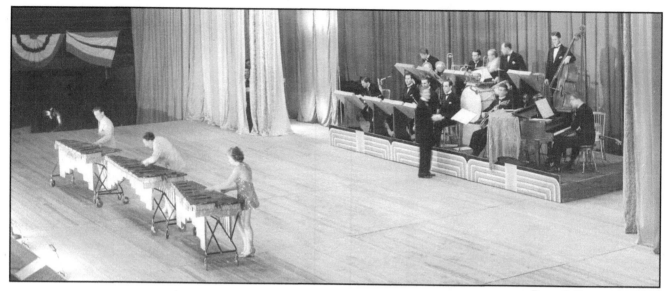

Deere & Company archives

Xylophones and the orchestra on stage.

The seven programs at the Field House attracted some 35,000 people. The following week the whole troupe, including Monte Blue and the vaudeville acts, made five evening appearances in Waterloo, Iowa. The *Dispatch* (April 17) speculated that 25,000 to 30,000 would attend the shows there, a reasonable possibility given the large number of Deere employees in Waterloo and the large seating capacity of the Hippodrome, site of the show.

postcard image

The original Waterloo Hippodrome, which dated back to 1919, was replaced in 1936 by a much larger arena shown here. It is on the site of the National Cattle Congress, which has been held annually for over a century. The size of the new Hippodrome impressed the Nashua (Iowa) *Reporter*: "Madame Holstein, Ayrshire, Brown Swiss, Guernsey and Jersey and Big Boy Belgian may not appreciate the beauty and utility of the new hippodrome, but a lot of human bipeds will, for the past several years lack of room made it necessary to turn thousands away" (September 2, 1936). The professional basketball Tri-Cities Blackhawks played at the Hippodrome against the Waterloo Hawks between 1948 and 1950. Crowds exceeding 7,000 attended some of the Hawks games there. Now called McElroy Auditorium, the large arena has hosted a great variety of sporting, entertainment, and other events over the years, much like Wharton Field House in Moline.

V-E Day

Beginning in the early 1940s, the Tri-City Symphony Orchestra held annual spring youth concerts at Wharton Field House. Children were excused from school – usually on a Monday morning – to hear the orchestra at Wharton. Memorable as some of these might have been, it would be difficult to imagine a more memorable experience than the concert of 1945.

The Monday evening *Dispatch* of May 7, 1945, carried this headline: "2,500 Children Listen Attentively to Symphony as 'V-E Day' Whistles Blow." The Orchestra planned children's concerts in both Moline and Rock Island on this date. To prepare for the concert at Wharton, the Symphony board had made improvements in the acoustics. Little did they know that a celebration would break out that morning because of the announced cessation of World War II fighting in Europe. As the children were assembling at the Field House for the 9:15 a.m. concert, factory whistles were already blowing. The *Dispatch* described the scene:

> the news was new enough to leave everything up in the air as to what was really happening. As a result, the 2,500 boys and girls went into the field house in an orderly manner and sat enrapt through a beautiful concert for an hour and fifteen minutes, and then with a wild whoop swept from the building when the announcement was made that V-E Day had arrived, and 'you do not have to go back to school until –' No one heard the last of the sentence as the celebration had begun."

Because of the V-E Day celebration, the 11 a.m. concert at the Rock Island High School auditorium drew a crowd only half the expected size.

Moline's 98th and 100th Anniversaries

During the week of August 5, 1946, the City of Moline celebrated the 98th anniversary of its incorporation as a town in 1848. The celebration opened with a sports day, which had to be moved from Monday to Tuesday because of inclement weather. Events at Browning Field included a girls' baton twirling contest, a baseball game between teams from Coolidge and John Deere schools, and an amateur boxing show (described in Chapter 5). Elsewhere in town a swimming and tennis competition was held at Riverside Park, softball games at Stephens Park, and a "skish meet" at the Prospect Park lagoon. Also, a downtown children's parade attracted an estimated 15,000 spectators.

> **Skish?** According to the *Dispatch* (August 3, 1946) the skish meet was a fly and bait casting competition. "Under the supervision of John Jarpa and Art Bivans of the Moline Conservation Club, entries will cast at target rings in the lagoon for points."

Two years later, in June 1948, a nine-day celebration commemorated the 100th anniversary of Moline's incorporation as a town. It was an incredibly busy event filled with a variety of activities. Although events were held all over the city, both Browning and Wharton played central roles. Among the activities around town were the opening ceremony and several band concerts at Stephens Square; an all-star softball game at Stephens Park; a tennis tournament, children's fair, and horsemanship demonstration at Riverside Park; an air show at the airport; outboard hydroplane races on the Mississippi River; and historical window displays, a street dance, and a parade in the downtown area. On Tuesday, June 22nd, Hollywood stars showed up for the world premiere of the movie "Mickey" at the LeClaire Theatre.

> **"Mickey,"** starring Lois Butler, is about the experiences of a young small-town girl who has difficulty balancing her musical talent with her desire to play baseball. The film was based on the novel, *Clementine*, by Peggy Goodin. A summary of the film can be found at TCM, online.

Browning Field Ready for Centennial

Dispatch, June 18, 1948

A stage being set up at Browning Field with tents and Wharton Field House in the background. The "Moline Milestones" pageant was presented over five evenings on the stage, and the tents housed industrial and other exhibits.

Pioneers Scene from Moline Milestones

Dispatch files

Covered wagons and pioneers on stage at Browning Field as part of the "Moline Milestones" pageant. The first night performance attracted 5,000.

Dispatch, June 22, 1948

The "Moline Milestones" pageant included a routine in which the Native American warrior Black Hawk surrenders to American soldiers to end the Black Hawk War.

Browning Field was the site of industrial exhibits, a P-51 aircraft training exhibit, and several outdoor performances of a colossal production called "Moline Milestones" written especially for this event. Wharton housed merchants' booths throughout the week. Other events at Wharton and Browning, as listed in the centennial program, included the following:

Saturday, June 19: Opening of industrial exhibits and P-51 aircraft training exhibit at Browning and merchants' booths at Wharton

Sunday, June 20: Swedish religious service and performance of the Army Ground Forces Band at Wharton

Monday, June 21: First performance of "Moline Milestones" and coronation of Charlotte Nutt as centennial queen at Browning; appearance of Sweden's Prince Bertil at Wharton

Wednesday, June 23: Turners' gymnastic and trampoline exhibit at Browning

Thursday, June 24: rural group activities at Browning; downtown Moline parade; Queen's Reception Ball and appearance of Tommy Dorsey at Wharton

Friday, June 25: "Century of Fashion" show at Wharton

Saturday, June 26: presentation of sports trophies at Browning; nationwide broadcast of the "Chicago Theatre of the Air" at Wharton

Sunday, June 27: Vacation Bible School demonstration day at Wharton; seventh and final performance of "Moline Milestones" and official closing ceremonies at Browning

Some truly special events were held at Wharton Field House for the celebration. On Monday, June 21st, Prince Bertil of Sweden, grandson of King Gustaf V, appeared. The prince, who was touring the Midwest with other Swedish dignitaries as part of a Swedish pioneer celebration, was introduced by Augustana College President Conrad Bergendoff. In his comments, the prince made the connection between his people and Moline's centennial: "We, of Sweden, should note with satisfaction that our sons and daughters have made their contribution to the building of this wonderful city of yours." (*Argus*, June 22)

On Thursday Tommy Dorsey and his orchestra performed for the Queen's Ball at Wharton. Dorsey brought along a group of

Deere & Company archives

The tent housing the Deere & Company exhibit at the 1948 Moline centennial featured not only farm equipment, but also a model of a sleek-styled "filling station."

entertainers, including Moline native Louie Bellson. At 10 p.m. the orchestra played for a thirty-minute radio broadcast initiated by Moline radio station WQUA and sent to over 400 stations nationwide on the Mutual Broadcasting Network. Tickets for the ball were not only sold at local businesses, but also by the candidates for Queen of the Centennial.

FOLLOW THE AIRSHIP
TO BROWNING FIELD
MOLINE
and

Moline Centennial
1848-1948

"MOLINE MILESTONES"

Huge Stage Spectacle, Cast of 1,000
Every Night Except Thursday and Friday at 8:30 p. m.
*Come early. Visit the Industrial and
P-51 Aircraft Exhibits (close at 8:30 p. m.)*

RURAL DAY—JUNE 24

★ Rural Group Activities—Browning Field, 10:30 and 2 p. m.
★ Civic and Patriotic Parade—Downtown, 6:30 p. m.
★ Queen's Reception Ball—Wharton Field House, Tommy Dorsey's Band, 9 p. m.

Other Events to Come:

Style Shows, Wharton Field House—Friday at 2 and 8 o'clock p. m.; Sports Events every day; Outboard Hydroplane Races, Mississippi River Front between 23rd and 35th Street—Saturday at 2 p. m.

Final Performance "Moline Milestones" Sunday, 8:30 p. m.

Argus, June 22, 1948

This advertisement, appearing in the *Argus* on June 22nd, highlights some of the attractions of the 1948 centennial. It claims that "Moline Milestones" was a "huge stage spectacle" with a cast of 1,000!

> **Popular Parade.** A memorable parade led up to Thursday evening's Queen's Ball. The *Argus* (June 25) described it: "With the weather continuing to cooperate, the Moline centennial celebration yesterday drew probably the largest crowd that will see any event of the 100-year fete. A throng estimated at 30,000 persons jammed downtown Moline last evening to watch the large civic, fraternal, and patriotic parade pass in review for almost an hour. Later last night, more than three thousand dance enthusiasts packed Wharton fieldhouse featuring Tommy Dorsey and his band."

Another highlight of the celebration at Wharton was the nationwide radio broadcast of the Chicago Theater of the Air on Saturday night, June 26th. At 8 p.m. the "Moline Milestones" production was brought indoors to the Field House and transmitted live nationally on the Mutual Radio Network. At 9 p.m. a transcription was broadcast locally on WQUA.

Earlier that day at Browning Field, Moline native Warren Giles, then president of the Cincinnati Reds major league baseball team, presented awards and trophies to winners of the sports competition. His visit came just days after the last game was played at Browning by the A's, Moline's last minor league baseball team. It seems ironic that Giles would appear in Moline at the end of minor league ball here, because he had played such an important role in developing the Plow Boys when they first played at Browning in the early 1920s.

Courtesy of Jerry Wallaert

Cardboard glasses were used to promote the 1948 centennial celebration.

Dispatch, June 17, 1948

This cachet was created for the centennial by the Quad City Stamp Club. Mail orders were being accepted by the club for the cachet "over which the Moline post office will use a special magenta cancellation, a reproduction of that used here 100 years ago." (*Dispatch,* June 17, 1948)

The final event of the celebration was to have been held at Browning Field on Sunday, June 27th, but was postponed until Monday because of rain. A crowd of 1,800 attended the final performance of "Moline Milestones" and the closing ceremony hosted by Alex Jardine, Moline schools superintendent. The *Argus* (June 29), described the finale:

> In the closing ceremony, Miss Charlotte Nutt, queen of the centennial, was given the flaming torch of progress, after it had been handed down from one generation to the next. She held it aloft in entering into the next century, as the entire ensemble sang 'My Country 'Tis of Thee.'

After the centennial celebration, the school board decided to re-sod Browning Field. In previous years a hard surface had developed in the middle of the field when cold weather appeared during the football season. "Members of last year's Maroons and opponents complained about the bruises and skin burns they incurred on the field." Because this problem was further exacerbated by the centennial activities on the field, the Centennial Committee contributed $2,000 to cover the majority of the cost. (*Dispatch,* July 8).

Another Moline Centennial, 1972

Moline was first platted in 1843, and then was incorporated with the State of Illinois as a town in 1848. The 1948 centennial event celebrated that milestone. In 1872 Moline was re-incorporated as a city and adopted the mayor/council form of government. This called for another centennial celebration.

The 1972 celebration was much more modest than the 1948 version. It was a one-day affair on Saturday, September 2nd, held during the daytime at Wharton Field House and in the evening at Browning Field. For the 10 a.m. opening, booths were set up at Wharton, displaying costumes, food, and handicrafts for various ethnic groups, including people of Swedish, Belgian, Mexican, Greek, German, and African American heritage. Other displays featured antique farm implements and automobiles, including some made in Moline. In the afternoon a local band, the Dukes of Rhythm, played. "Reflections '72," a pageant highlighting the history of Moline written by David Collins, also was presented. The evening concluded with a fireworks display at Browning Field. About 6,000 people attended the celebration at Wharton, and about 3,500 at Browning on a "cold and threatening night." (*Dispatch*, August 4) In spite of the weather, the *Dispatch* noted only one flaw in the program at Browning: the antique car parade was cancelled because "the field was soggy from the early morning rain and officials felt the narrow wheels of the cars would cut up the turf."

Bicentennial Celebration, 1976

In 1976, a Sunday "Fourth of July Spectacular" celebrated the nation's bicentennial. Evening events at Browning included a track meet involving the summer track clubs from Moline, East Moline, and Galesburg along with performances by the American Legion Color Guard, the Coolidge Junior High fife and drum corps, and the Moline High School summer band. A highlight of the evening was the performance of "The Impossible Dream," an original pageant by David Collins with 150 performers. A fireworks display ended the program.

A week earlier, on Saturday, June 26th, a week-long bicentennial celebration opened with the American Midsummer Festival at Wharton. The event, organized by a committee headed by H. E. Doyle and John Wetzel, was open from noon until 10:30 p.m. with variety shows at 2

Fireworks Fizzle. The Sunday evening fireworks at Browning created some excitement, at least for firefighters. Two rockets exploded too close to the ground and dropped ashes onto a fire truck, burning some small holes in a tarpaulin on the truck. No injuries resulted, but the night before five people were injured by fireworks at Soule Bowl in East Moline. One aerial display showered several spectators when it exploded near the ground. Another exploded on the ground, injuring an employee of the firm that set up the fireworks. (*Dispatch*, July 6, 1976)

Greatest Parade, 1922 Fifty years earlier, Moline celebrated its 50th anniversary as a city with a downtown parade in the morning, games and a band concert at Riverside Park in the afternoon, and a street dance at 17th Street and 6th Avenue in the evening. Some 10,000 people were at Riverside, 5,000 at the dance, and 5,000 at the parade. The local newspapers battled for headline superlative supremacy in their October 2nd afternoon editions: *Dispatch*, PARADE GREATEST IN CITY HISTORY; *Argus*, BIGGEST EVENT IN THE HISTORY OF THE PLOW CITY. The *Dispatch* went on to engage in a bit of prognostication: "In 1972 the pioneers of 1922 will still be talking about the mammoth procession which was the main feature of Moline's golden anniversary."

and 7:30 p.m. Music and dancing was presented by members of several ethnic groups along with a nineteen-piece orchestra, "The Bicentennials," led by Bob Lofgren. Drummer Louie Bellson, who grew up in Moline, was a featured performer. Bellson had performed several times in the past at Wharton Field House, including while he was in high school and at the 1948 Moline centennial celebration, and in later years he performed at a number of other locations in the Quad Cities.

Argus, February 5, 1966

While he was a student at Moline High School, Louie Bellson won national solo drum competitions in 1939, 1940, and 1941. In this photograph he is receiving congratulations from Gene Krupa (left) for winning the 1941 Gene Krupa/Slingerland National Amateur Swing Drummers Contest at the Wurlitzer Auditorium in New York City. About 15,000 had entered the contest. This event brought initial fame to the young Bellson, who would go on to be regarded as one of the greatest drummers ever.

257

M, 1942

Louie Bellson is posing here with the Moline High School orchestra in 1942. Bellson is in the second row with the light-colored coat, standing – appropriately – next to a drum. After his graduation in 1942, Bellson immediately went to Hollywood to join the Ted Fio Rito Orchestra, where he became friends with budding movie star June Haver from Rock Island. Three months later he joined the Benny Goodman band. After serving in World War II, Bellson played with Tommy Dorsey, Harry James, Duke Ellington, and other "big band" era orchestras and performers. In 1952 he married singer Pearl Bailey. Through a distinguished career, Bellson composed and recorded music, led orchestras, and appeared on television before passing away in 2009. (Sanders, 1966)

Representatives from various ethnic groups were invited to set up booths displaying foods, craft items, costumes and symbols of their cultural heritage. Below are some of the items and themes each group used for their heritage displays, as listed in the festival program:

African American – Slides and prints of Black art works
Belgian - Lace; Rolle Bolle; pigeons; wooden shoes
German – Turner and Singing Society photographs
Greek – Byzantine and classical Greet art
Italian – History of Italian American heritage
Jewish – Tallit; tefillin
Mexican – Pottery; linen; silver; embroideries
Swedish – Items brought to the U. S. by immigrants

Wharton Field House Celebrates 30, 50, 60, 75, and 85 Years

Thirty Years: The 30th anniversary celebration, sponsored by the Letterman's Club, was held on December 26, 1958, at a basketball game between Moline and Cedar Rapids Washington, which was won by the Maroons 72-56. The printed program features articles on the history of the arena along with short biographies of Winnie Holmgren, who had managed the Field House for its entire thirty-year history, and T. F. Wharton, after whom the arena was named in 1940.

Fifty Years: This celebration, on December 16, 1978, started with an afternoon gathering at the Elks Club. It brought together 150 past coaches and players of Moline High School boys basketball, including eight members of the 1928 team that played in the game at the Field House dedication, plus a few guests. Perhaps the oldest attendee was Clyde Burgston, who was a member of the 1910 Moline team.

Grandsons of T. F. Wharton, Richard and Russell Wharton, presented a plaque to Moline High School on behalf of the Wharton family. Richard Wharton said: "This is a symbol of tradition and spirit here, and may you never lose that in Moline. May Wharton Field House last

Dispatch, December 17, 1978

Russell and Richard Wharton, grandsons of T. F. Wharton, at the Wharton Field House 50th anniversary celebration in 1978.

another 50 years" (*Dispatch*, December 17). The Wharton brothers also returned to Moline the loving cup that was presented to their grandfather at the 1928 dedication of the Field House.

The celebration continued with boys basketball in the evening at the Field House, which according to the *Dispatch* was only "half-full." One of the nice touches of this celebration was the invitation to the Kewanee basketball team to play the Maroons fifty years after the two teams had played in the first Field House game in 1928, which Moline won 22-15. However, the plan did not work out quite as well this time: Kewanee won 66-63. The Boilermakers scored as many points in the third quarter (22) as the Maroons had in the entire 1928 game!

The elaborate printed program, which was prepared for the event, mimics the design of the program for the arena dedication fifty years earlier. It incorporates a number of pages from the original 1928 program, including a list of bond purchasers; diagrams, photographs, and details of the original Field House; along with features on the two college teams that played at the 1928 dedication, Iowa and Marquette. To those pages it adds profiles of Field House managers C. W. Holmgren and Ed Lemon and

year-by-year regular season and state tournament boys basketball statistics.

Sixty Years: Ten years later the anniversary event broke new ground. Previous ones had celebrated the history of the arena almost exclusively through boys high school basketball. This time girls basketball was included. Again Kewanee was invited to be Moline's opponent. The girls' sophomore and varsity teams played Kewanee to start the evening. Then an anniversary ceremony was held, followed by the varsity boys' game. The Moline varsity girls trounced the Boilermakers 81-55 to bring their season record to 11-0. The Maroon boys came away with a 53-36 win for only their second victory of the season. The *Dispatch* (December 21) described the crowd as "sparse."

The ceremony honored former boys basketball coaches Jack Foley, Herb Thompson, and Whitey Verstraete, members of the Illinois Basketball Hall of Fame, and long-time Field House manager Ed Lemon. In attendance was Jim Rosborough, who told Tom Johnston of the *Dispatch* (December 18) that he and Mervin Horton were the only members still alive from that 1928 team.

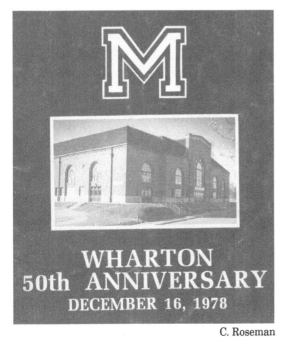

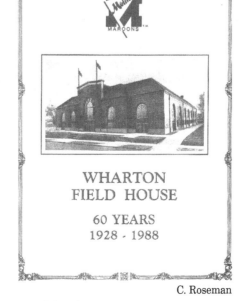

C. Roseman   C. Roseman

Covers for the 50th and 60th anniversary celebration programs.

75 Years: The highlight of the 75th anniversary was an M-Men's Club luncheon on the basketball floor at Wharton on Saturday, December 19, 2003. Attended by 400, it brought together former boys basketball players, coaches, and guests, including the two oldest M-Men, Don Bohman, age 87, and Bob Crippen, 86. That evening, the celebration was capped by a Maroon victory over Rich South, 57-48.

> **Dr. Lee Scores Big.** Moline superintendent of schools, Dr. Cal Lee, presented a brief welcome to those assembled for the 75th anniversary. Befitting of the occasion he told the story of acclaim he received for his performance in a high school basketball game. At the time Lee was a junior and sixth man on the team. In one game the star of the team, Jeff Wheat, scored 47 points while Lee scored only one basket near the end of the game. Lee's buddy, a sports reporter for the school newspaper, wrote and published a headline for the game story: "Wheat and Lee Combine for 49 Points!"

The featured speaker at the luncheon was Scott Thompson, an All-State basketball player at Moline and former college player and coach who at the time was working in the Department of Development at Cornell University in New York. Steve Kuberski, a former Moline All-Stater who played nine seasons in the National Basketball Association, was also in attendance. He told the *Dispatch* (December 19):

> I try to tell people back East, but they just don't understand. They can't believe we'd get 5,000 to 6,000 (fans) for a high school game. They're amazed that when I played, we used to have 5,000 season ticket-holders. When I show them pictures of Wharton, they think it's a big-time college arena. They can't understand our rivalries—the great games we had, and still have, with Rock Island and East Moline and Alleman. I tell them to think of the movie, 'Hoosiers,' only on a larger scale. We're not a bunch of small, farming communities. These are industrial towns.

Browning Field, 100th Anniversary

On October 5, 2012, the Moline High School football team faced Alleman at Browning. It was 100 years, to the day, after the first high school football game was played at the field. A display of historical Browning Field photographs and memorabilia was set up by Jerry Wallaert in Wharton Field House before the game. A pre-game ceremony on the field, recognizing the 100-year history, was culminated with the release of 100 maroon and white balloons. The morning of the event (October 5) the *Dispatch* and *Argus* published a special section that included a history of Browning Field written by Jack Dye, a former Moline teacher and coach. Dye also had compiled a list of the scores of all Moline High School football games, from 1899 to 2012, which was distributed at the celebration.

> **Rosborough Roots.** At the time of the 75th anniversary the former Maroon star with perhaps the deepest roots in the Field House was Jim Rosborough, whose father made the first basket at the first game 75 years earlier and whose grandfather was president of the school board at that time. Unfortunately, Rosborough was not able to attend the celebration because of his obligations as assistant basketball coach at the University of Arizona. However, his son, Jon, had visited the Field House the previous year, playing for the Canyon del Oro High School in Arizona. The Maroons won that game, 77-67, while Jon represented the fourth generation Rosborough to be closely associated with the Field House. (Van Vooren and Dye, 2008)

Carlson Trophy Revived. First awarded on November 4, 1977, the Paul Carlson Trophy was meant to be passed each year to the winner of the Alleman vs. Moline football game. It was initiated "on Paul Carlson Appreciation Day, marking the 25 years of service the *Daily Dispatch* sports editor has contributed to prep athletics in the Quad City area" (*Dispatch*, November 5). Moline won it that year for its 34-7 victory over Alleman. However, the Carlson Trophy had not travelled for several years before 2012, having been kept at Alleman High School. The trophy was recovered and re-dedicated by Carlson's widow, Janet Meyer, at the Browning Field centennial celebration on October 5, 2012. After the game it travelled back to Alleman, the Pioneers having beaten the Maroons, 20-0.

C. Roseman, 2013

For the 85th anniversary of the Field House in December 2013, public address announcer John Bradley (right) reminded the crowd of the amazing variety of events held at Wharton over the years. Joining him at the big M at center court are (left to right) Todd Rosenthal, Moline High School athletic director; Dr. David Moyer, Moline schools superintendent (holding the Wharton loving cup); Jerry Patrick, president of the Boosters Club; and Dan McGuire, MHS principal.

Wharton Field House, 85th Anniversary

On Friday evening, December 20, 2013, Wharton's 85th anniversary was celebrated with a short ceremony at a high school basketball game between Moline and Alleman, which the Maroons won 65-47. A few weeks later, this book appeared, providing a permanent memory of the rich 85-year history of Wharton Field House, along with its companion, the 100-plus- year-old Browning Field.

Appendix A
Visit to Indiana

During the winter of 1926-27, when plans for the Moline Field House were in their infancy, a committee including athletic manager C. W. Holmgren, coach George Senneff, and architect William Schulzke took a field trip. Their purpose was to examine other large arenas and gather information about their financing, construction, and operation. Because no large high school arenas had been built in Illinois, they went to Indiana where basketball was thriving, especially in small towns and medium-sized cities. Some of their ideas for the Moline arena were hatched in the Hoosier State. Among the Indiana places they visited were Logansport and Marion.

No doubt the Logansport connection was established by Reverend W. A. Steinkraus of Moline's First Baptist Church. Before moving to Moline he had lived in Logansport and helped that community plan and fund a new 5,000-seat high school gym, which opened in January 1927. In early 1928, Moline's campaign for their new arena was buoyed by a letter sent to Steinkraus from a friend in Indiana, which stated that the Logansport facility was often filled for sporting events and "was such a success that they were already paying off the stock or bonds." (Klann, 1928)

The new gym was called the "Berry Bowl" after the nickname of the Logansport High School teams, the Berries (as in "Loganberries"). Like Moline's, their project was the result of a community effort. The $105,000 cost of the Berry Bowl was financed by bonds purchased by 208 members of a gymnasium association. On the day of the first game there, January 15, 1927, the Logansport *Press* bragged:

There is none finer in Indiana for the purpose. It was built with basketball as the sole thought in mind and the result is what the people will find tonight – an indoor athletic arena without a post to obstruct the view from any angle. Hundreds of people tonight will see the Logansport net teams play for the first

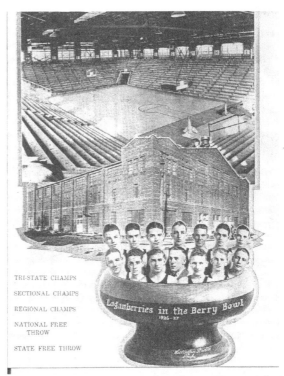

TRI-STATE CHAMPS

SECTIONAL CHAMPS

REGIONAL CHAMPS

NATIONAL FREE THROW

STATE FREE THROW

Loganberries in the Berry Bowl
1926-27

Cass County Historical Society

Berry Bowl, Logansport, Indiana, 1927. Like the Moline Field House, the Berry Bowl had a brick exterior. Inside, however, the two arenas were designed differently. The Berry Bowl was built primarily for basketball, was more compact, and had permanent stands on all four sides extending down to the floor. Above entryways in each of the four corners were clusters of seats called "crows nests." The Moline Field House, in contrast, is an all-purpose arena with permanent seats in balconies on three sides. The Berry Bowl was razed in 1975.

time this season. Hundreds more will see a basketball game for the first time in their lives. People who hesitated to attempt entrance to the old gym and take a chance on getting seated will have no more reason to hesitate.

The Logansport Berries defeated the Rochester Zebras in that first game in front of about 4,500 spectators in the new arena. Perhaps Logansport (population of about 18,500) chose a school from a town about one-fifth its size to insure victory in that initial game. (Of course, Moline followed the same strategy, although not to the same extreme: Moline's population of 32,000 was only about twice the size of Kewanee's.) The Berries ended the season with a 25-2 record and went to the state tournament. There they lost 27-14 to Martinsville whose star player, John Wooden, would go on to become the legendary UCLA coach known as the "Wizard of Westwood."

The Marion Memorial Coliseum opened about a year after the Berry Bowl, on January 10, 1928. Its initial seating capacity of 5,500 was slightly larger than either the Berry Bowl or the original Moline Field House. The Coliseum was financed by a private holding company, which leased it to the schools. In the initial game, the Anderson High School team beat Marion 35-24 in front of a full house. (Perhaps Marion, population 24,000, should not have invited a team from a town with 40,000 people!) In 1970, Marion High School basketball was moved to the new Bill Green Athletic Arena, which seats over 7,000.

The two new Indiana basketball palaces drew a lot of attention, especially from nearby towns. Just a week after the Berry Bowl opened, the Kokomo Wildcats lost the game there to Logansport, 44-33, perhaps star-struck by the visit to the large, imposing arena. A writer at the *Kokomo Tribune* (January 22, 1927) may also have been star-struck:

> the mass of some 5,000 spectators rocked and weaved in delirium. Logansport's new gym is all that it is cracked up to be – a marvelous place to play basketball. In the few minutes before the game and between halves, fans relaxed from the high tension of excitement and gazed in wonder at the marvels of the building. In the first place there were 5,000 spectators comfortably seated without even a wire to obstruct view. Of this number, between 800 and 900 were loyal Kokomo fans.

About a year later, on Saturday, January 21, the same Kokomo team visited Marion's new Coliseum just eleven days after it had opened. The *Tribune* (January 17, 1928) again offered superlatives:

MEMORIAL COLISEUM, MARION, IND.

Postcard image

The 1928 Marion Memorial Coliseum is a brick structure that cost $125,000 to construct. With outside dimensions of 209 by 162 feet, it is slightly larger than the Moline Field House. Like the original Moline facility it was built as a multi-purpose arena and had a running track surrounding the basketball floor. It opened with permanent bench seats on a U-shaped "upper concourse" but, unlike Moline's arena, its roof was supported by vertical posts that blocked the view from some of the permanent seats. On the open end were an elevated stage and the Charles G. Barley Memorial Organ, which was dedicated in November 1928. Today the facility, owned and operated by the STAR Financial YMCA, continues to host a variety of activities and events. Perhaps the most notable is the annual Marion Easter Pageant, which was started in 1937. (Fricke, online)

The game at Marion will be played in Marion's new Memorial Coliseum and field house, a magnificent building – undoubtedly the best and biggest athletic plant owned by a high school in Indiana. It would be well worth the time and expense of Kokomo fans traveling to Marion to see that building. A great number of fans are planning on making the trip.

Appendix B
Browning Field Timeline

1910, June 14: John T. Browning willed the land for Browning Field to the City of Moline

1912: Field prepared and first bleachers erected

1912, September 28: First Moline High School football game – lost to alumni 6-0

1912, October 5: First MHS regular season football game – beat Maquoketa 34-0

1912, October 6: First professional football game – Moline Illini tied the Moline Olympics, 0-0

1916: Large wooden football bleachers on the south side of the field constructed

1916: Quarter-mile cinder track installed

1919: Moline Indians (Red Men) professional football team started play at Browning

1920, April 12: First professional baseball game – Moline Plow Boys beat the Chicago White Sox, 7-1

1920, May 5: New, crescent-shaped baseball covered grandstand dedicated

1921: With Warren Giles as club president, Plow Boys won the Three-I League championship

1925: Plow Boys spent $2,800 to erect a canopy over the left field baseball stands

1925, November 14: MHS football team loses 10-0 to Male High of Louisville, Kentucky

1926: Rock Island Independents football team played home games at Browning

1926, October 3: Independents lost to New York [football] Yankees and Red Grange, 26-0

1928, August 25: Rock Island Railroad games

1929: Rock Island Public Schools Stadium opened

1930, July 11: First night baseball game in the Tri-Cities, illuminated by lights on eight poles

1930, September 19: First night high school football game – Moline 18, East Moline 0

1936, October 17: First game at new East Moline stadium, Soule Bowl

1936, 1950, and 1967: Undefeated seasons for Moline High School football

1936, September 22: Rock Island Independents lost to the Chicago Bears at Browning

1938, April 14; July 31, 1939; and July 8, 1940: Chicago Cubs played the Plow Boys at Browning

1940: Babe Ruth put on a batting exhibition and hit only one ball over the fence

1945: Moline High School baseball started, and played at Browning through the spring of 1958

1947, September 29: Browning Field property transferred from the City of Moline to the school district

1948, June: Moline A's played their last professional baseball games at Browning

1948, June: Moline centennial celebration at Browning Field and Wharton Field House

1948: New toilet facilities and outfield fence erected; light poles rearranged

1957: Final Northwest Conference athletic event, the conference track meet

1958, August 25: Browning baseball grandstands burn down

1959, 1986, and 1989: repairs made to south football bleachers

1960: Moline High School track team won the Illinois state title

1969, October 9: Wind storm toppled one of eight wooden light poles

1972: School board decided not to build a new stadium west of the new high school

1972: New all-weather track installed

1973: 1930 light poles removed; replaced by new light arrays on four new wooden poles

1973: Moline High School Girls track competition started

1982, October 29: Illini band visited

1984: High School soccer started play at Browning

1986: Moline Boosters Club created – funded repair of concession stands and restrooms

1993 and 1999: All-weather track resurfaced

1995: New all-metal football south bleachers built to replace the 1916 wooden structure

2004: New brick entryway built at east end of the football field

2005: Track named after long-time coach Gene Shipley

2009: New fence and gate at the west end of the football field, facing Browning Park

2012, October 5: 100th anniversary celebration

2013, August: New light arrays and four new light poles replace the 1973 poles and lights

2014: Heritage Documentaries, Inc. published a book on the history of Wharton Field House and Browning Field

Appendix C
Wharton Field House Timeline

1927: Moline school representatives traveled to Indiana looking for ideas for a new field house

1927, December: Architect William Schulzke released a sketch for a field house to be located west of Browning Field

1928, February: Schulzke released a new field house design for a location north of Browning

1928, February: Maroon and White Association organized to raise money for construction

1928, April: Fundraising campaign led by Theodore Finley Wharton completed; over 1200 people purchased bonds

1928, June: Ground broken for the new arena

1928, December 21: Moline Field House dedicated

1929, April 22: First major non-sporting event – the week-long Quad Cities Pageant of Progress

1930, February 21: First full house for a high school basketball game; 5,500 attended the Moline-Monmouth contest on "Ten-cent" night

1930: 6500 witnessed the wedding of Beulah Veeder and Clarence Peterson at the Pageant of Progress

1931: Exhibition matches with champion professional boxers Max Schmeling and Jack Dempsey

1933: In college basketball St. Ambrose played Iowa and Augustana played Illinois

1934: First Moline High School graduation ceremonies

1936, February 10: First "big band" appeared, Jan Garber Orchestra (dancing until 2 a.m.!)

1937, April 12-17: Week-long John Deere centennial celebration

1939, December 27: In college basketball Augustana played reigning national champion Oregon

1940: Field House debt refinanced and the building turned over to the Moline schools from the Maroon and White Association

1940, November 2: Wendell Willkie appeared three days before losing the presidential election

1941, July 1: Field House renamed to honor Theodore Finley Wharton

1941: Katherine Butterworth donated a plot of land east of the building, now a parking lot

1943, April 28: Lawrence Welk Orchestra appeared with "Champagne Lady" Jane Walton

1943, October 13: T. F. Wharton died at the age of 73

1943, June 30: Exhibit of war equipment manufactured by Deere & Company

1945, May 7: 2,500 school children at symphony concert learned the war in Europe had ended

1945: First broadcasting booth built at the top of the west balcony

1947, January 3: Professional basketball Tri-Cities Blackhawks played their first game

1948, June: Moline centennial celebration included two nationwide radio broadcasts from

Wharton – the Tommy Dorsey Orchestra and the Chicago Theatre of the Air

1948 and 1949, August: Rock Island County Fair held on Wharton grounds

1949, June 18: First Miss Moline Pageant

1949, January 18: Heavyweight boxing champion Joe Lewis in exhibition match

1949: Cubical scoreboard purchased and hung above the center of the basketball floor

1950, January 20: Gorgeous George wrestled George Temple, brother of Shirley Temple

1950, May 20: Jack Benny show brought in $27,000, the largest gross up to that time

1951: Tri-Cities Blackhawks moved to Milwaukee and changed their name to the Hawks

1954, May 17: Dean Martin and Jerry Lewis show

1954, June 11-16: World's largest portable pool set up over basketball floor for the Water Follies

1956, March 8: Bill Haley and the Comets appeared

1956, November 8: Last of 31 annual Kiwanis Farm Parties

1957, February 8: Moline basketball player Vern Johnson shattered a glass backboard

1959, April 18: Captain Kangaroo appeared with the Tri-City Symphony Orchestra

1959, May 29 and 30: Miss Illinois Pageant

1961, February 19: USSR men's and women's gymnastics teams performed

1961: Ed Lemon replaced "Winnie" Holmgren who had managed the Field House since 1928

1963, March 18: Record high school basketball crowd, 6538, watched "Super-sectional" state tournament game between Aledo and Rockford Auburn

1963, April 19: Johnny Cash performed with Skeeter Davis and June Carter

1966, October 27: Harry Belafonte appeared and complained about the acoustics

1968, February 16: Moline-Galesburg high school basketball game televised in color by WQAD

1968, October 9: Visit of Richard Nixon drew 6500 into the arena; 4000 others turned away

1968, October 21: Presidential candidate George Wallace drawed protesters

1971, March 6: More than 3000 turned away as Globetrotters played to a packed house

1972, April 3: A rock band, The Byrds, appeared

1973: Last of the Easter Sunrise Services, which had been held annually since 1948

1974-75: First season of Moline girls high school basketball

1978, December 16: Fiftieth anniversary of Wharton celebrated

1987, November 20: 6047 watched Continental Basketball Association Thunder play first game

1988: The 1949 cubical scoreboard replaced with two flat scoreboards

1990, January 21: CBA All-Star Game televised by ESPN

1990, March 13: DJ Jazzy Jeff and the Fresh Prince performed

1993, March 26: A record crowd of 6288 watched the Thunder's last game at Wharton before the team moved to The Mark of the Quad Cities

1997: Moline High School girls volleyball team began playing games at Wharton

1997, December 12: A new floor, replacing the original raised basketball floor, was dedicated

2000, July 12: Moline Board of Education refused to allow designation of Wharton Field House as a Historic Landmark

2003, 2004, and 2008: Wharton hosted state high school wrestling meets

2003, December 20: Seventy-fifth anniversary of Wharton celebrated

2014: Heritage Documentaries, Inc. published a book on the history of Wharton Field House and Browning Field

Bibliography

Books and Pamphlets:

Abdul-Jabbar, Kareem, 2007. *On the Shoulders of Giants: My Journey Through the Harlem Renaissance.* New York: Simon & Schuster.

Allee, Bill, Ed., 2005. *The Home Team: Sports Memories of the Quad Cities, 1920s-1960s.* Moline, IL: Moline Publishing.

Baraks, Brad, 1982. *Quad-City Sports Greats.* Rock Island, IL: Quest.

Belan, Judy, 2004. East Moline: *A Centennial History.* East Moline, IL: Centennial Committee.

Bell, Taylor H. A., 2004. *Sweet Charlie, Dike, Cazzie, and Bobby Joe: High School Basketball in Illinois.* Urbana: University of Illinois Press.

Campbell, Nelson, (ed.), 1990. *Illinky: High School Basketball in Illinois, Indiana, and Kentucky.* New York: Penguin.

Coopman, Dave, 2007. *WQUA Radio 1230: Moline's Hometown Station.* Moline, IL: Heritage Documentaries.

Coopman, David T., 2010. *Davenport's WOC AM-FM-TV.* Charleston, SC: Arcadia.

Delany, Tim and Tim Madigan, 2009. *Sociology of Sports: An Introduction.* Jefferson, NC: McFarland.

Eagle, Edward, et al., 1935. *The History of Moline Senior High School.* Moline, IL: Moline Senior High School, Social Science Department. (reprinted in five installments in the *Dispatch* in 1935; the fourth, on sports, is in the June 22 issue).

Ford, Liam T. A., 2009. *Soldier Field: A Stadium and its City.* Chicago: University of Chicago Press.

Abul-Jabbar, Kareem, 2007. *On the Shoulders of Giants: My Journey Through the Harlem Renaissance.* New York: Simon & Schuster.

Goodin, Peggy, 1946. *Clementine.* New York: E. P. Dutton.

Gould, Todd, 1998. *Pioneers of the Hardwood: Indiana and the Birth of Professional Basketball.* Bloomington: Indiana University Press.

Grasso, John, 2011. *Historical Dictionary of Basketball.* Lanham, MD: Scarecrow Press.

Hamilton, Donald E., 1993. *Hoosier Temples: A Pictorial History of Indiana's High School Basketball Gyms.* St. Louis: G. Bradley.

Horn, Maurice (ed.), 1999. *The World Encyclopedia of Comics.* Philadelphia: Chelsea House.

Knapp, D. John 1983. *A History of Moline High School Basketball.* Bauden.

Lenzi, Diana Eddleman, 1997. *Dike Eddleman: Illinois' Greatest Athlete.* Champaign, IL: Sports Publishing.

McClellan, Keith, 1998. *The Sunday Game: At the Dawn of Professional Football.* Akron, OH: University of Akron Press.

Munn, Dagmar Nissen, 2012. *My Father's Dream of an Olympic Trampoline: Life Story of George Nissen, Inventor of the Trampoline.* Tucson, AZ: Wheatmark.

National Pro Basketball League Magazine, 1949 edition. J. Andrew Bolinger, Publisher and Editor. West Liberty, Iowa: Liberty.

Nelson, Murry R., 2009. *The National Basketball League: A History.* Jefferson, NC: McFarland.

Nelson, Roger, 1995. *The Zollner Piston Story.* Fort Wayne, IN: Allen County Public Library Foundation.

Peterson, Robert W., 1990. *Cages to Jump Shots: Pro Basketball's Early Years*. New York: Oxford University Press.

Perlstein, Rick, 2001. *Before the Storm: Barry Goldwater and the Unmaking of the American Consensus*. New York: Hill and Wang.

Rozendaal, Neal, 2012. *Duke Slater: Pioneering NFL Player and Judge*. Jefferson, NC: McFarland.

Schumacher, Michael, 2008. *Mr. Basketball: George Mikan, the Minneapolis Lakers, and the Birth of the NBA*. Minneapolis: University of Minnesota Press.

Seusy, Kathleen, Diann Moore, Curtis C. Roseman, and Regena Schantz, 2009. *Echoes from Riverside Cemetery: Moline, Illinois*. Moline: Heritage Documentaries.

Sumner, Benjamin Barrett, 2000. *Minor League Baseball Standings: All North American Leagues, Through 1999*. Jefferson, NC: McFarland.

Svendsen, Marlys, n.d. *Davenport, a Pictorial History, 1836-1986*. G. Bradley.

Thomas, Ron, 2002. *They Cleared the Lane: The NBA's Black Pioneers*. Lincoln: University of Nebraska Press.

Van Vooren, George and Jack Dye, 2008. *A Century of Moline Boys' Basketball: 1904-2007*. Moline, IL: Moline Boosters Club and Moline M-Men.

Articles:

Allee, Bill, 1977. "Ashe, Okker, Stove, Cuypers visit Q-C area," *Dispatch*, October 13.

Allee, Bill, 1998. "Wharton Field House," Quad-Cities Online, January 25.

Batterson, Steve, 2010. "Gene Shipley's 'boys' are coming home Saturday," Quad-City *Times* (online), March 31.

Bergstrand, Tom, 1971. "E. M. Boxers Dominate Ring Show," *Dispatch*, February 8.

Buresh, Dorothy, 1961. "Aim to Satisfy, Impresario Says," *Dispatch*, March 8.

Buresh, Dorothy, 1971. "The Flair Of Mr. Flambo," *Dispatch,* August 21.

Callaway, Lynn, 1936a. "More than 4000 Watch Bears Conquer Rock Island, 34-6," Dispatch, September 23.

Callaway, Lynn, 1936b. "Maroons Refuse to Quit in 14-6 Triumph over St. Louis Team," *Dispatch*, November 27.

Callaway, Lynn, 1939. "Crowd of 3557 Gets Thrills and Laughs Out of Big Leaguers," *Dispatch*, August 1.

Callaway, Lynn, 1940a. "Cubs Barely Defeat Moline...," *Dispatch*, July 9.

Callaway, Lynn, 1940b. "Big Crowd Expected For Boxing Show at Moline's Ball Park," *Dispatch*, August 7.

Carlson, Paul, 1957. "Islander Broadsides Finally Level Maroons," *Dispatch*, February 9.

Carlson, Paul, 1978. "Wharton Field House: 50 Years of Memories," *Dispatch*, December 19.

Corken, Maurice, 1930. "Packed Stands Greet First Night Baseball Game...," *Argus*, July 15.

DeVrieze, Craig, 1986. "Quad-Cities in running for CBA franchise," *Dispatch*, December 28.

DeVrieze, Craig, 1987. "Basketball franchise is official," *Dispatch*, February 25.

DeVrieze, Craig, 1988. "Plane-ly speaking, Thunder grounded," *Dispatch*, January 19.

DeVrieze, Craig, 1988. "Thunder looks for a home" and "Thunder draws record crowds," *Dispatch* and *Argus*, February 14.

DeVrieze, Craig, 1989. "Thunder to host 1990 CBA All-Star game at Wharton," *Argus*, February 4.

DeVrieze, Craig, 1993. "Storied Halas & Co. history forgets first Bear foe," *Dispatch*, October 3.

Dix, Jim, 1947. "To Allow Sunday Sports At Wharton Field House," *Dispatch*, August 19.

Dix, Jim, 1947. "About 2,500 Look On as Show Horses Are Exhibited Here in Weekend Event," *Dispatch*, July 21.

Doxie, Don, 1996. "Tri-Cities Blackhawks Were in the Right Place," Quad-City *Times*, February 4.

Doxie, Don, 2006. "Auerbach enjoyed Tri-Cities," Quad-City *Times*, October 30.

Dye, Jack, 2012. "100 Years of Browning Field, Moline, Illinois." *Dispatch* and *Argus*, October 5.

Easterlund, Dawn, 1972. "Rock Group Scores in Field House Show," *Dispatch*, November 2.

Gingles, Russell, 1937. "Deere Centennial Show Thrills Crowd of 5,000," *Dispatch*, April 13.

Hoffman, Harvey, 1954. "In Moline," Davenport *Daily Times*, May 18.

Johnson, Gil, 1946. "From the Press Box," *Dispatch*, February 1.

Kiesele, Russ, 1946. "Syracuse Pros Defeat Chicago Gears, 57-55," *Dispatch*, December 7.

Kiesele, Russ, 1949. "From the Pressbox," *Dispatch*, December 19.

Kiesele, Russ, 1951. "Fans Enjoy Big Night," *Dispatch*, February 15.

Kinney, Bill, 1949. "Hawks Rally Shy Before 6,270 – Lakers Triumph, 78-76," *Argus*, December 27.

Kinney, Bill, 1951. "Quad-Cities Facing Possible Loss of Hawks," *Argus*, January 20.

Kinney, Bill, 1951. "Hawks Dissolve – Sell for $27,000; League offer is Approved by Stock Owners," *Argus*, September 11.

Klann, F. A., 1928. "Plan for Field House Endorsed by Association," *Dispatch*, February 10.

Klann, Fred, 1949. "Off the Beaten Path," *Dispatch*, October 24.

Lawrence, Mike, 1966. "Ted Kennedy Calls Douglas A Patriot," Davenport *Times-Democrat*, October 29.

Lewis, Suzy, 1990. "RAP music's hotbed acts here Tuesday," *Dispatch* and Rock Island *Argus*, March 8.

McElwain, Bill, 1965. "Showbiz is Risky Biz," *Dispatch*, November 18.

Marose, Paul, 1980. "pro fists fill night," *Dispatch*, November 20.

Marose, Paul, 1981. "Friday night at the fights," *Dispatch*, April 23.

Marose, Paul, 1981. "Bester brought down by 'Elvis Express,'" *Dispatch*, April 25.

Marx, John, 1993. "Thunder about to leave home," *Dispatch*, March 25.

Meenan, Jim, 1986. "Tri-City Blackhawks played in infant NBA," *Argus*, November 9.

Meenan, Jim, 2002. "Anne Potter-DeLong's boost to Q-Cs should never be forgotten," Quad-Cities Online, April 8.

Moorhusen, Don, 1931. "Tell History of Browning Field." *Dispatch*, March 26.

O'Shaughnessy, T. J., 1928. "Plans for 1928 Tournament Well Under Way," *Rock Island Magazine*, July.

Patten, Pat, 1930. "Isoz and Burner Fight Draw in Moline's First Legal Ring Show," *Dispatch*, October 11.

Pearson, Rita, 1987. "Pact lets Thunder roll into Wharton," *Dispatch*, July 15.

Pearson, Rita, 1988. "Board: In Wharton, there is no beer," *Dispatch*, May 11.

Rexroat, Dee Ann, 1993. "New Moline Arena Mark Heats up Concert Scene," Cedar Rapids *Gazette*, May 28.

Sanders, Charles H., 1963. "Folk Music by Kingstons 'Sends' 5,000," *Dispatch*, March 11.

Sanders, Charles H., 1966. "Louis Bellson Decided on Career As Jazz Drummer at Age of 5," *Argus*, February 5.

Sands, Bob, 1948. "Milestones Is Rated Big Hit," *Dispatch*, June 22.

Shane, Mary, 1982. "Moline bouts lack punch," *Dispatch*, February 7.

Shinske, Art, 1946. "Thousands Jammed Moline's Business Section...," *Dispatch*, August 9.

Swanson, Beth, 1983. "The Man at field house," *Dispatch*, August 9.

Walker, Johnny, 1919. "Hose Bombard Gardens with Base Hits, 13-0," *Dispatch*, April 22.

Watt, Anthony, 2006. "The heat is on: Schools benefit from fiery fundraiser," Quad-Cities Online, October 13.

Wendland, Jeff, 2001. "Rock-bottom attendance," *Dispatch* and *Argus*, January 30.

Willard, John, 2003. "Wharton: House of History," Quad-City *Times*, December 14.

Unpublished pamphlets, documents, etc:

Browning Agreement, between the City of Moline and the Board of Education of School District No. 40, October 7, 1947.

Dedication Program, Moline Field House, December 21, 1928.

Dye, Jack, 2004. *Browning Field 1910 – 2004.* mimeo.

Dye, Jack, 2012. *Moline High School Football Scores, 1899-2011.* mimeo.

The Maroon and White Handbook, 1943. Moline Public Schools, pamphlet.

M-Men's Day program, 1937. Sixteenth annual M-Men's Day, November 13.

Program for the Dedication of the Field House by the Children of the Moline Public Schools, January 17, 1929.

Swanson, Leslie, 1978. Interview text provided by his daughter, Vickie Wassenhove.

Websites (all accessed January 2014):

Baseball Reference: http://www.baseball-reference.com

Basketball Historian: http://www.basketballhistorian.com

Basketball Reference: http://www.basketball-reference.com

Basketball Research (Association for Professional Basketball Research): http://www.apbr.org

BoxRec (Boxing records): http://boxrec.com

Braunwart, Bob and Bob Carroll, 1983. "The Rock Island Independents." http://www.profootballresearchers.org/Coffin_Corner/05-03-131.pdf

Butler Sports: http://www.butlersports.com/information/facilities/hinkle_fieldhouse

CBA History: http://www.apbr.org/cba7801.html

Classic Rock Concerts: http://www.classic-rock-concerts.com/cities/782

Clauser Bio: http://digital.library.okstate.edu/encyclopedia/entries/C/CL007.html

Col Ballroom: http://www.thecolballroom.com

College Football Hall of Fame: http://www.collegefootball.org/Programs/CollegeFootballHallofFame.aspx

Eddleman Obituary: http://www.fightingillini.com/genrel/080101aaa.html

Fricke, A. J. Memorial Coliseum: http://www.marion.lib.in.us/commhist/thisoldhouse/coliseum/building.html

Gopher Sports: http://www.gophersports.com/facilities/williams-arena.html

Hinkle Fieldhouse: http://www.butlersports.com/information/facilities/hinkle_fieldhouse

Hoopedia: http://hoopedia.nba.com

Huff Gym: http://www.fightingillini.com/facilities/huffhall.html

IHSA (Illinois High School Association): http://www.ihsa.org

Iowa Cubs: http://www.milb.com

Kiwanis Moline: http://www.molinekiwanis.org

NBA (National Basketball Association) History: http://www.nba.com/history/records

NBA Hoops: http://nbahoopsonline.com/History/Leagues/NBL/alltimescoring.html

NBA Universe: http://www.nbauniverse.com

NBL (National Basketball League): http://www.apbr.org/nblstand.html

Oldefest Obituary: http://www.meaningfulfunerals.net/fh/obituaries/obituary.cfm?o_id=1837507&fh_id=10762

Pro Wrestling America: http://www.pro-wrestling-america.com/

Professional Basketball: http://www.jimwegryn.com/Names/BasketballTeams.htm

Professional Football Archives: profootballarchives.com

QCThunder: http://www.qcthunder.com

Quad-Cities Online: http://www.qconline.com

RITS (Rock Island Technical Society): http://www.rits.org/www/histories/smithsports/smithsports.html

Rock Island Independents: http://www.rockislandindependents.com

Rock Island Preservation Society: http://www.rockislandpreservation.org

Sabres Alumni: http://www.sabresalumni.com/page.cshtml/4

Slater Bio: http://nealrozendaal.com/dukeslater/about-duke-slater/

TCM (Turner Classic Movies): http://www.tcm.com/tcmdb/title/83398/Mickey/

Three-I League: http://www.three-eye.com

Tri-Cities Blackhawks: http://www.sportsecyclopedia.com/nba/tri/tricities.html

U. S. Cellular Arena: http://uscellulararena.org/media/mediafile_attachments/01/131-facilities timeline070113.pdf

Wrestling Data: http://www.wrestlingdata.com

Index

Moline: City of, 1, 196; 50th Anniversary, 257; 98th Anniversary, 112, 218, 253; 100th Anniversary, 253; 1972 Re-incorporated Centennial, 256; Centennial Celebration, 133, 244; Centennial Committee, 256; Hospital, 195; Library Board, 195; Park Board, 220; Public Library, 158, 195; Wellness Fairs, 43

Moline High School: Alumni, 198, 200; Boosters Club, 41-42, 224, 261; Graduation, 248; Letterman's Club, 35, 258; Moline Lights (football B team), 20

Moline Playground Fund, 220

Moline School District # 40, 21, 25, 29, 159; Board of Education (school board), 29-30, 32-33, 215, 41-42, 101, 112, 117, 180, 221, 223, 235; Commencement, 33, 44; Field Days (Calisthenics Days), 76, 217-218; Sports Day, 112, 218; Superintendent, 165, 256, 260, 261

Montana, 192: Centennial Train, 192

Montz, Mel, 187

Moore: Diann, 42; Bob, 66; Glenn, 189

Moorhusen, Harley, 180

Mooseheart, 190

Motor Vehicles: Buick, 157; Chevrolet, 157; Chrysler, 157; Desoto, 157; Dodge, 157; Durant, 157; Erskine, 157; Essex, 157; Ford, 157; Graham, 157; Hudson, 157; Hupmobile, 157; Lincoln, 157; Marmon, 157; Marquette, 157; Nash, 157; Oakland, 157; Olds, 157; Pontiac, 157; Roosevelt, 157; Studebaker, 157; Viking, 157; Whippet, 157; Willys, 157

Motor Vehicle Brands, Midget: Austin, 220; Dirzius, 220; Eitos, 220; Harleys, 220; Henderson, 220; Indians, 220; Johnson, 220; Miller, 220; Saxon, 220; Wisconsin Special, 220

Motorcycles: Harley Davidson, 221; Races, 220; Super-X, 221; Valley Cities Motorcycle Club, 221

Movies: *The Blacksmith's Gift*, 250; *Case of the the Tremendous Trifle*, 170; *Earth Movers*, 170; *Film Communiqué No. 8*, I, 170; *Hitler's Madness*, 65; *Hoosiers*, 27, 260; *I Surrender*, 65; *Mickey*, 253; *Previous Freedom*, 65; *Private Buckaroo*, 136; *Rootin Tootin Rhythm*, 166

Moyer, David, 261

Mullen, Jean, 65

Murray, Rochelle, 193

Murtey, Ivan, 158

Naismith, James, 26

Nancolleth Beryl, 157

Neary, Jack 135

Nebraska: Boys Town, 139; Omaha, 128, 151

Nelson: Don (announcer), 150; Don (basketball), 98; Elmer (Mrs.), 163; Herman, 243

Nero, 114

New Jersey: Atlantic City, 172; Madison, 157; Newark, 230

New York: Brooklyn, 230; Buffalo, 78-79; New York City, 69, 81-82, 95, 97, 113, 116-117, 158, 173, 189, 192, 230, 257; Rochester, 97, 195; Syracuse, 92, 97

Nissen, George, 76

Nixon, Richard, 45, 181

Nordine, Louis, 23

North Dakota, Fargo, 128

Nutt, Charlotte, 254, 256

Nutting, E. P., 5-6, 17

Oakleaf, Hjalmar, 245

O'Donnell, Harry, 244; John, 17, 88

Ohio, 30, 81: Akron, 77; Cincinnati, 97, 115, 203; Cleveland, 114, 118, 230; Fostoria, 163; Toledo, 52, 78, 200; Youngstown, 78

Oklahoma, 233; Oklahoma City, 243; Tulsa, 110, 166

Olson, Elinor E. Johnson, 8, 17

Olympic Games, 142, 189; Berlin, 214; London, 89; Los Angeles, 141; Melbourne, 189

Ontiveros, John, 71

Oppenheimer, Adolph "Oppie", 21, 76, 217-218

Orathwell, Samuel, 170

Organizations: 4-H Club, 158, 164, 190; AFL, 166; American Independent Party, 184; Boy Scouts, 158, 190-191; Cancer Society (Relay for Life), 43; Cerebral Palsy, 151; Chicago Tribune Charities, Inc. 119; CIO, 166; Clinton Turner Society, 189; Community Volunteer Fire Department (Colona, IL), 149; Crocodile Club (Croc Hops), 150; Davenport Gun Club, 219; Elks Lodge (Moline), 24, 113; Fraternal Order of Eagles, 131; Girl Scouts, 191; Handel Oratorio Society, 50; Illinois Farm and Home Bureau, 163; Illinois State Fair, 172; Improved Order of Red Men, 228; Iowa Rock and Roll Music Association Hall of Fame in 1999, 137; Junior Board of the Tri-City Symphony Orchestra Association, 151; Kaaba Shrine,

243; Kings's Daughters (Emma J. Kough Circle); 157; Kiwanis, 33, 161-163; Knights of Columbus of East Moline and Moline (Leo Council), 139; Lions Club (Moline), 142; Moline American Legion, 21, 150, 158, 180, 187, 220, 257; Moline Associated Council of Dad's Clubs, 170, 176, 221; Moline Association of Commerce, 36, 163, 165, 170; Moline Conservation Club; 184, 253; Moline Junior Chamber of Commerce (Jaycee's), 69, 138, 144, 166, 170-1, 187-188, 222, 231; Moline Masonic Lodge, 132; Moline Public Hospital Auxiliary, 188; Moline Public Schools Foundation, 43, 193; Moline Safety Council, 166; Moose Lodge, 139, 180, 190-191; Moose Lodge Drill Team, 180; Muscular Dystrophy, 120; Museum of Chiropractic History, 153; National Cattle Congress, 252; National Foundation for Infantile Paralysis; 138; Order of the Eastern Star (Youth Guidance Committee), 191; Optimist (Moline), 115, 138; Progressive Party, 180; Project Works Administration, 205; Quad Cities Mexican American Organization, 137; Red Cross, 43, 190; Relatives and Friends of Polio Victims, 139; Rock Island County Board of Realtors, 193; Rock Island County March of Dimes, 191; Salvation Army (Moline), 195; Seabees, 170; Shrine Club (Black Hawk), 140-141; STAR Financial YMCA, 264; Turner Society (Davenport), 189; Turner Society (Moline), 76, 189, 254; Uptown Merchants', 221; Willard Grade School Dad's Club, 216; Willard L. Velie Jr. Post No. 5123 Veterans of Foreign Wars, 138, 180; USO, 171, 187; Works Progress Administration, 206; World Wildlife Fund (WWF), 130; YMCA (Moline), 81, 158, 198, 211; YWCA, 158; Youth For Christ, 173; Zal Grotto, 131-132, 139, 170

Organizations, Sports: AAU (Amateur Athletic Union), 78, 118-119, 186; Blackhawks Sports, Inc., 33, 92; College Football Hall of Fame, 229; Illinois Basketball Hall of Fame, 259; Illinois High School Association (IHSA), 47, 57; Illinois State Athletic Commission, 113,128; Illinois Wrestling Coaches and Officials Association Hall of Fame, 71; Logansport High School Gymnasium Association, 7; Maroon and White Association, 1, 6-8, 10, 18-19, 23-25,

29, 44, 113; Moline City Tennis Committee, 187; Moline Fans Association, 227, 233, 243; Moline High School Athletic Association, 187, 199; National Collegiate Athletic Association (NCAA), 26, 69, 74, 89, 129; Quad Cities Basketball Club, Inc., 100; Quint Cities Tennis Foundation, 188

Osborn, Lee, 212

O'Shaughnessy, T. J., 219

Ostrand, Margaret Lievens, 9

Owens: Jesse , 214; Mike, 42

Pack, Stewart, 192

Paige, Satchel, 100

Pageants/Festivals: All-City Band Festival, 178; American Midsummer Festival, 257; Chicagoland Music Festival, 177; Children's Literature Festival, 193; Marion Easter Pageant, 264; Miss America Pageant, 172; Miss Illinois Pageant, 2, 171-172; Miss Moline Pageant, 32, 163, 171-172; Miss Rock Island, 163; Mississippi Valley Music Festival, 33; Moline Milestones Pageant, 254-255; Moline Youth Music Festival, 170, 176; Orchestra-Chorus Festival, 176; Quad Cities Pageant of Progress, 21-22, 154, 157-159, 161; Sixth Grade Music Festival, 177; Wisconsin Spectacle of Music, 177

Panaggio: Don, 102; Mauro, 102-103

Parker, Tom, 139-141

Parks/Preserves: Athletic (Moline), 2, 110, 199-200, 227-228, 233; Blackhawk Forest Preserve, 163; Browning, 8, 12, 196, 222; Butterworth, 206; Douglas (Rock Island), 163, 206, 228-230, 240; Indian Bluff Forest, 163; Illiniwek Forest, 164; Island City (Rock Island), 229; Long View, 219; Moline Baseball, 227; Prospect, 195, 253; Red Men, 227; Riverside, 2, 110, 196-197, 200, 253, 257; Stephens, 253; Stephens Square, 253; Three-I League, 227-228, 233-134

Patrick, Jerry, 261

Patten, Pat, 23, 113, 204

Payden, Betty, 66

Pearson, Rita, 105

Pennsylvania: Philadelphia, 95, 97, 230; Pittsburgh, 37

Percy, Charles, 181

Perry, John S., 163

Wiman, Charles Deere, 20

Wisconsin, 140, 231: Ashland, 30; Green Bay, 92, 151, Milwaukee, 19, 96-98, 118, 127, 177; Oshkosh, 78; Platteville, 122; Sheboygan, 78

Wise, Walter, 192

Wood: A. W., 172; Beder, 7, 19; Scott, 177

Wooden, John (Wizard of Westwood), 264

Wrestlers, Professional: Andre the Giant, 130; Little Beaver, 125; Arthur L. Beauchene, Larry "Leaping Larry" Cheney, (Detroit Speedster), 32, 129; Big Boss Man, 130; "Battling" Burner, 113; Brutus Beefcake, 130; Moose Cholak, 125; Don Curtis, 128; Dino Bravo, 130; Dr. X, 125; Earthquake, 130; Verne Gagne, 125, 128-130; Benito Gardini, 125; "Gorgeous George" George Wagner, 2, 122-124; Rene Goulet, 125; Larry "the Ax" Henning, 125; Hercules, 130; Hulk Hogan, 130; Jimmy "Pee Wee" James, 125, 138; Don Leo Jonathan, 126; Don Koch, 122; Killer Kowalski, 125; Mark Lewin, 128; Ed "Strangler" Lewis, 126; Reggie "Crusher" Lisowski, 125-126; Lord Clayton Littlebrook, 125; Sky Low Low, 125; Roy McClarity, 126; The Mighty Atlas, 125, 128; Mr. Moto, 125-126; Art Neilson, 125-127; Leo "the Lion" Nomellini, 125-126; Pat O'Connor, 125-126; Bob Orton, 126; Angelo Poffo, 129; Rick Rude, 130; Sapphire, 130; Terrible Hans Schmidt, 125-126; Belle Star, 125; George Temple, 123-124; Lou Thesz, 125-127-128; Maurice "French Angel" Tillet, 122; Tugboat, 130; Ultimate Warrior, 130; Mad Dog Vachon, 125, 127-128; Boris Volkoff, 128; Nicoli Volkoff, 128; Yukon Eric, 125, 126

Wrestling, Professional Organizations: American Wrestling Association (AWA), 128; National Wrestling Alliance, 126; World Wrestling 5Entertainment (WWE), 130; World Wrestling Federation (WWF), 139

Wyoming, 101

Yeager, 30-31, 203

Youngdahl, Earl, 173, 176-177

Youngquist, Carol, 67

Zollner, Fred, 97